RIVERS

OF **INK**

SELECTED ESSAYS

RIVERS
OF INK

SELECTED ESSAYS

CLAIRE CHAMBERS

OXFORD
UNIVERSITY PRESS

OXFORD
UNIVERSITY PRESS

Oxford University Press is a department of the University of Oxford.
It furthers the University's objective of excellence in research, scholarship,
and education by publishing worldwide. Oxford is a registered trade mark of
Oxford University Press in the UK and in certain other countries

Published in Pakistan by
Ameena Saiyid, Oxford University Press
No.38, Sector 15, Korangi Industrial Area,
PO Box 8214, Karachi-74900, Pakistan

ISBN 978-0-19-940662-3

Typeset in Adobe Caslon Pro
Printed on 80gsm Local Offset Paper

Printed by The Times Press Pvt. Ltd., Karachi

Acknowledgements
Photography Credits: Claire Chambers figures 1–2 and 4;
Monira Ahmed Chowdhury and Hasan Ahmed figure 3

To my mother and father,
Susan Derry and Richard Gavin Chambers,
with much love.

Contents

Acknowledgements   xi

Introduction   xv

I: Play on Words

1. Writing Beyond Borders   3
2. Postcolonial Lives   8
3. 'To Love the Moor': Postcolonial Artists Write   13
   Back to Shakespeare's *Othello*
4. The Princess and the Priest: Richard Dawkins'   33
   Attack on Fairy Tales
5. Journalists in Fiction and Reality   36

II: Pakistan's Cities and Regions

6. The Baloch Who Is Missing: Representations of   43
   Balochistan in Anglophone Prose
7. Holy Women, *Waderas*, and 'Weapons of the Weak':   58
   Sindh in Contemporary Women's Writing
8. '*Lahore Lahore Hai*': Bapsi Sidhwa and Mohsin   63
   Hamid's Urban Fiction
9. Literary Peshawar: From Kipling to the   87
   Present Day
10. On a Hair Trigger: Images of Kashmir   92
    in Literature
11. Isloo and Pindi on Page and Screen   98

III: Human Rights and Inhuman Wrongs

12. Torturing the 'Other': Who is the Barbarian? — 119
13. Culture and the Arab Spring — 128
14. Advocacy Without Footnotes: Pakistani Cultural Production and Human Rights — 141
15. The Ugly Face of Attacks: Facing Up to Acid Violence in South Asian Writing — 152
16. 'The Reality and the Record': Muslim Refugee Stories — 159

IV: Muslims, Islamophobia, and Racism in Britain

17. We Are Here Because You Were There — 179
18. Early Twentieth-Century Muslim Women's Travel Accounts of Britain — 184
19. Disorientation as Loss of the East: Muhammad Marmaduke Pickthall's Fiction — 189
20. From 'England-Returned' to 'Myth of Return' to the Point of No Return — 194
21. Islamophobia: Orwellian 'Newspeak' or Racially Inflected Hatred? — 198
22. 'Colour-Blind' Nigel Farage Lives in a White-Washed World — 203
23. Freedom as Floating or Falling — 206
24. Writing Muslim Lives — 214
25. Who Do YA Think You're Representing? Diversity in Young Adult Fiction — 219
26. Laughing At Ourselves — 227
27. Banglaphone Fiction: British Sylhetis in Writing by *Londoni* Authors — 232
28. In Praise of the Chapaterati — 256
29. Boris Johnson Lights Out for Virgin Territory — 264
30. Fight the Bannonality of Evil — 270

V: Education, Theory, and the Creative Industries

    31. A Fanonian Summer   283

    32. Edward Said's *Orientalism*: Its Influence   289
        and Legacy

    33. The Barbarians Are at the Gate: On   292
        Self-Construction and the 'Other'

    34. Who's Saving Whom?: Postcolonialism   297
        and Feminism

    35. Festal or Fecal?: The Global Literary Festival   307

    36. The State We're In: Global Higher Education   312

Bibliography   323
Index   373

Acknowledgements

I AM INDEBTED TO Ameena Saiyid, Nadia Ghani, Afifa Ali, and everyone else at Oxford University Press who helped to pull this essay collection together. The book could not have been written without the help of editor extraordinaire, Elizabeth Welsh. Elizabeth's astuteness, gimlet eye, discerning taste, and encyclopedic knowledge of grammar and style made everything possible—to such an extent that I can hardly imagine writing another book without her support. That said, although it would be a relief to outsource the responsibility for any mistakes, this manuscript's errors, infelicities, and misfirings are all my own.

To the team at the eminent Pakistani newspaper *Dawn*, as well as to the organization for permission to reprint my material, my thanks. I am grateful to have been allowed to reprint material from the following publications: *Crossings: A Journal of English Studies* (Dhaka) and the *Journal of Commonwealth Literature* (SAGE, London). At these publications, Shamsad Mortuza, Kaiser Haq, and Livia Melandri were extremely constructive and convivial. Expressions of gratitude are also due to *Postcolonial Interventions*, *The Conversation* (UK), and the *Postcolonial Studies Association Newsletter*, where I am the copyright holder, but from which I gained significantly from their rigorous and sympathetic editing processes (grateful mentions go to Abin Chakraborty and Lucinda Newns). Professor Shirley Chew kindly allowed me to revise and update '"The Reality and the Record": Muslim Asylum Accounts' from the journal she founded and continues to edit, *Moving Worlds* (12.2 (2012): 143–54). Heartfelt thanks to Shirley, too, for giving me a very sound academic base back in the days of my PhD and beyond. Chapter 8, "*Lahore Lahore Hai*": Bapsi Sidhwa and Mohsin Hamid's Urban Fiction', is derived in part from an article published in *South Asian Diaspora* on 6 May 2014, available online: http://www.tandfonline.com/doi/full/10.1080/19438192.2014.91246. This essay was revised and republished in the edited collection *Postcolonial Urban Outcasts: City Margins in South Asian Literature* (Routledge, 2017), whose editors Madhurima Chakraborty and Umme al-Wazedi deserve thanks for their painstaking work and friendly camaraderie. Routledge and Taylor & Francis granted generous permission to reprint this essay.

I am grateful to *3 Quarks Daily*'s Abbas Raza, not only for his astute editorship and patient toleration of flagrant deadline flouting, but for also the recipes from his book *Pakistani and North Indian Cooking*, which helped to make the writing process more delicious. I would like to pay tribute to Muneeza Shamsie, the pre-eminent literary critic, for her inexhaustible mental speed dial of Pakistani writing in English, and for her munificence in suggesting further books to read—particularly when I was writing the chapters dealing with Sindh and Rawalpindi. I really appreciated the help and enthusiasm of Jaya Bhattacharji Rose in relation to the Sindh chapter and more broadly.

There are too many writers to thank for me to name them individually. I hope that those authors who spoke at events with me, sent me books, articles, and poems, interacted with me in person or on social media, and even on occasion helped me with my editing of my work know how obliged I am. Moreover, I am thankful to the many writers whose acquaintance I have not yet made for making me feel as though I know them through their fine work explored in this volume.

I'm grateful to Alice Hall for introducing me to Toni Morrison's *Desdemona* on the Global Literature module that we co-taught at the University of York. Another colleague at York, David Attwell, never failed to lift my spirits with words of encouragement, and to feed my intellect with conversations about J. M. Coetzee, post-coloniality, and the state of global higher education. I am profoundly beholden to Sue Chaplin from Leeds Beckett University for working with me on Sarwat Chadda's vampire fiction. In between bestowing humour and a little Bollywood glamour on Lucknow, Florian Stadtler found the time to read Chapter 30 and offer his valuable perspective as an expert on (among other things) Noor Inayat Khan. Huge thanks too to Stewart Mottram for last-minute *Othello* checks. Rachael Gilmour's insights during snatched conversations near King's Cross were invaluable and inspiring, and I hope for many more of these intellectually stimulating discussions. Finally, four overseas colleagues provided invaluable perspectives: Aroosa Kanwal and Mushtaq Bilal from Pakistan and Yeliz Biber and Pürnur Altay with their Turkish standpoints.

Our children, Joash and Derry, as ever, acted as the emojis to my staid prose, giving me a smiley face even when the writing got tough. In his role as my tech support, Joash worked magic on a photograph of Noor Inayat Khan's statue, while Derry invented a wonderfully surreal alternative title for this book: *Waterfalls of Octopi*. With his characteristic kindness, my husband Rob made nutritious porridge in winter and bircher muesli in summer, both of which gave the necessary power to my elbow. Finally, this book goes out to my parents for all those Sunday lunches cooked, childcare emergencies resolved, and table tennis trips organized. Since becoming a parent myself thirteen years ago, I marvel even more at everything you have done for my brother Stephen and me, and now for our own children.

Introduction

M Y INTEREST IN SOUTH ASIAN LITERATURE was ignited during my year just prior to university, 1993 to 1994. I spent this gap year teaching English to school children in Mardan and Peshawar, cities in the northwestern Pakistani region of Khyber Pakhtunkhwa (formerly known as the North-West Frontier Province or NWFP). An obsessive reader, I immediately joined Peshawar's old-fashioned public library, and found myself endlessly borrowing the same Thomas Hardy, George Eliot, Georgette Heyer, and Agatha Christie books from its limited collection.

One day I found a copy of Salman Rushdie's *Midnight's Children*, which I gulped down during a single weekend at the family home I lived in and in the women's areas of cafes and parks. Upon noticing that I was engrossed in *Midnight's Children*, several English-speaking Pakistanis felt compelled to comment (in a variety of ways, but always with the same sentiment): 'That book is all right, but his other book is very bad.' When I read *The Satanic Verses* several years later, I could understand the offence caused by Rushdie's often Orientalist portrayal of religious Muslims and the Prophet Muhammad (PBUH). Reading *Midnight's Children* though was revelatory; this was the first time I'd encountered descriptions of a life much like the one I was living in Peshawar: people at prayer; gaudy advertising hoardings; Bollywood movies; and idiomatic, inventive speech patterns—even if the book was marketed, patronizingly and incorrectly, as 'a continent finding its voice' (Blaise up).

At university I read English literature, but what really energized me were my further encounters with Indian writers, then enjoying great success as part of the 'Indo-chic' of the 1990s. Sometimes dubbed 'Rushdie's children', a (slightly) younger generation of South Asian writers who began their careers in the 1980s and 1990s wrote a glut of forgettable novels in the magic realist style, replete with separated twins, talking animals, filmi references, and miraculous talents. Yet the best of this generation—Vikram Seth, Amitav Ghosh, Vikram Chandra, Arundhati Roy, and Rohinton Mistry—either avoided magic realism altogether, or worked with it before moving on to experiment with other forms.

At the same time, Sri Lankan writers such as Michael Ondaatje, Shyam Selvadurai, Carl Muller, and Romesh Gunesekera were also making an important contribution to the international literary scene. For example, Selvadurai's *Funny Boy* is a Bildungsroman about the increasing tensions between Tamils and Sinhalese in the late 1970s and early 1980s, culminating in the riots and unrest of 1983 onwards. It is also about the loss of an idyllic childhood world, and the realization that growing up, for Arjie, involves learning about his ethnic and sexual identities—often a painful process. In *Anil's Ghost*, by contrast, Ondaatje deliberately refuses to discuss the various political arguments of the three warring factions in Sri Lanka, because to present their claims might give them credence. Instead, Ondaatje presents the war as a Orwellian exercise in violence and weasel words, which is expressed through Gamini, the traumatized, amphetamine-fuelled doctor who works with the war's victims and 'turned away from every person who stood up for a war' (119).

In the 1990s emerged the irreverent, often humorous fictions of South Asian writers in Britain, which were nonetheless attentive to racism and social exclusion. This new wave of diasporic writing arguably began with Hanif Kureishi's *The Buddha of Suburbia*, and continued with novels by Meera Syal and M. Y. Alam, and more recently, Monica Ali, Gautam Malkani, and Ayisha Malik. Central to these texts is discussion of mixed, 'hybrid' identities; pop music and popular culture; language and slang; intergenerational tensions; and multiculturalism, racism, religion, and belonging.

In the 2000s, as has been widely documented, there was a flowering of Pakistani writing in English, its authors now featuring prominently in the international literary scene as award winners or nominees, bestselling authors, festival speakers, and, increasingly, topics for research students and critics. To discuss only the fiction: the success of such novels as Nadeem Aslam's *Maps for Lost Lovers* (longlisted for the 2004 Man Booker Prize), Mohsin Hamid's *The Reluctant Fundamentalist* (2007 Booker Prize nominee), Mohammed Hanif's *A Case of Exploding Mangoes* (longlisted for the 2008 Booker), and Kamila Shamsie's *Burnt Shadows* (2009 Orange Prize shortlist) has led to justifiably large fanfares for American-educated Pakistani writers such as Ali Sethi and Daniyal Mueenuddin. However, this attention paid to the (undeniably excellent) 'Big Five' of Hamid, Hanif, Shamsie, Mueenuddin, and Aslam can lead to neglect of other less well-known but equally powerful writers from Pakistan, such as Sara Suleri Goodyear, Aamer Hussein, and Uzma Aslam Khan.

Amid all the excitement about the 'New Pakistani Writing', Indian writers have not been forgotten, and Kiran Desai's and Aravind Adiga's Booker prizes during the 2000s testify that Indian writing is far from being a spent force. Emerging themes in Indian writing include scrutiny of the BJP's 2004 campaign slogan, 'India Shining', which was intended to indicate that the wealth generated by the country's brave new free market economy would trickle down, benefitting all. Texts such as Vikram Chandra's *Sacred Games* and Siddhartha Deb's *The Beautiful and the Damned* make it clear that corruption and gangsterism have stemmed any potential trickle, and that India's poor have gained nothing from the rise of the 'beautiful' super-rich.

South Asian writing more broadly shows a related interest in domestic servants. From Bapsi Sidhwa's Ayah to Arundhati Roy's Velutha, or Rana in Moni Mohsin's *The End of Innocence*, servants and their families are far more prominent in subcontinental fiction than they have been in the West since the demise of Jeeves and Wooster. As Alison Light writes about the relationship between Virginia Woolf and her maid Nellie: 'This was a story about mutual—and unequal—dependence but it was also about social differences, about class feelings and attitudes' (xiv). Add religion and caste into the mix, and you have the story of servants in South Asia today, as Maryam Mirza shows in her searching monograph *Intimate Class Acts*. In contrast, authors based in the West (with such notable exceptions as Kathryn Stockett and Hanif Kureishi) tend to ignore the existence of an often racialized underclass who clean, look after children, and provide sexual services.

Bangladesh, too, is developing a dynamic body of English-language fiction, with writers including Adib Khan and Tahmima Anam. Here, the 1971 War is a significant concern—one which has also provoked Pakistani English-language responses from authors such as Kamila Shamsie (*Kartography*), Moni Mohsin (*The End of Innocence*), and Sorayya Khan (*Noor*). As I discuss in Chapter 27, 'Banglaphone Fiction', in her second novel, *The Good Muslim*, Tahmima Anam moves on to consider the 1971 War from a 1980s vantage point, and also the turn taken by the young Bangladeshi state under the dictatorship of Hussain Muhammad Ershad and the growing influence of the Islamic Right.

Perhaps the most interesting development is to be found in

the realm of genre. As well as the move away from magic realism, South Asia is currently experiencing an explosion of popular Anglophone forms. This is particularly evident in India, given the stratospheric rise of Chetan Bhagat, author of numerous commercial hits, including *One Night @ the Call Centre*. However, this trend is also apparent on a smaller scale in Pakistan, with erotic fiction like Sabiha Bano's *Challawa* reissued in English and chick lit by Moni Mohsin (*Duty Free*), Maha Khan Phillips, and Saba Imtiaz released to international fanfare. In diasporic Britain, the success of children's fiction and popular autobiographies by such writers as Sarwat Chadda and Shelina Zahra Janmohamed proves that authors of South Asian background are being recognized by mainstream commercial publishers and finding readers outside the traditional literary fiction market. There remains much to be done, but a diversification of genres, publishers, and writers jostling for space in the growing print and e-book markets of South Asia and its diaspora is surely grounds for cautious optimism about the future of English-language writing.

THE FIRST SECTION OF THIS VOLUME is a kind of throat-clearing exercise or limbering up, comprising four essays on various aspects of contemporary writing. Starting with discussion of the limits or boundaries of literature, I go on to explore the lives and life writing of postcolonial authors. Next comes consideration of the postcolonial notion of 'writing back' as it applies to creative reworkings—by artists from the African diaspora and India—of that canonical play par excellence, William Shakespeare's *Othello*. Moving on to the importance of stories and storytelling, I challenge New Atheist thinker Richard Dawkins' dismissal of fairy tales due to their capacity to 'teach' children about irrationality. In a world where lies are believed as 'alternative facts' and truths rejected as 'fake news', I close Part I by writing in praise of journalism, examining how authors have represented Pakistan's reporters who put their lives on the line in the uncovering of truth.

Part II benefits from my exploration of Pakistan during my formative pre-university year teaching English in Khyber Pakhtunkhwa, which travels provided insight into the country's diversity. The first chapter in 'Pakistan's Cities and Regions' analyses literature dealing with the nation's most troubled province, Balochistan. From there we travel west to rural Sindh, as depicted in the work of four women writers. Following that, I examine historic, cultural Lahore and two of the city's most celebrated authors, before my residency in the city comes into play, lending detailed experience to the discussion of literary Peshawar. War-torn Kashmir, bureaucratic Islamabad, and military Rawalpindi are scrutinized in the final two chapters of this section. It should be noted that Part II makes no claim to comprehensiveness, but rather offers snapshots of Pakistan's literary geography in this, the seventieth year of the nation's birth. I hope to supplement this in future writing on Karachi, the Pakistani village, and the Northern Areas, among other topics.

The book then takes a darker turn with five pieces about human rights abuses and crimes against humanity. Beginning with a chapter on the issue of torture, the next chapter deals with the cultural outpouring that brimmed over from the Arab Spring and with the brutal suppression of this 'creative insurgency' in what became an Arab Winter. After that, I consider the 'universality' of human rights from a philosophical perspective, as well as scrutinizing the literary form of the human rights report and interrogating how civil liberties have been explored in Pakistani cultural production. What follows is a drilling down into one particular manifestation of human rights abuses, in the form of acid violence and its portrayal in South Asian fiction and film. Part III closes with an evaluation of the stories arising from one of the greatest human rights catastrophes in living memory: the global refugee crisis.

Part IV is extensive in scope and breadth, bringing together research into Muslims, Islamophobia, and racism in Britain and beyond that I have been conducting for the last twelve years. From the travel writing of women authors who visited Britain in the Edwardian period, via the history of the British curry industry, to Boris Johnson's, Steve Bannon's, and Donald Trump's latest iniquities, this part of the book deals primarily with the view from outside Pakistan. The diasporic outlook matters because migration is perhaps the defining condition of the twenty-first century, despite it regularly being misunderstood and dehumanized. As such, the longer history and colonial roots of travel and immigration demand urgent excavation.

Casting a spotlight onto academia and the culture industry, the final part encompasses chapters on the literary theorists and activists, Frantz Fanon and Edward W. Said, on the theoretical concepts of postcolonial feminism and 'Self' versus 'Other', and on literature festivals and higher education from a global perspective.

Rivers of Ink was eventually chosen as a title when I realized how many words I'd written in my impassioned journalistic outpourings for *Dawn*, *3 Quarks Daily*, and other outlets over the course of five years. The phrase comes from the Spanish idiom *verter ríos de tinta* meaning 'to pour rivers of ink', corresponding to the English saying, 'much ink has been spilt'. If even a fraction of the ink cartridges I drained over the last half-decade were in service of equality, anti-racism, and internationalism, or (re) introduced readers to a confident and diverse body of texts, I will be happy. Coincidentally, *Rivers of Ink* recalls the titles of two influential subcontinental novels: Qurratulain Hyder's *Aag Ka Darya* (River of Fire), which deals, amongst other subjects, with Partition and the post-Second World War South Asian diaspora;

and *River of Smoke*, in which the nineteenth-century Opium Wars enable Amitav Ghosh to impart wisdom on present-day globalization and the political grounds of free trade arguments. Through my image of a fast-moving body of dark, blackened water—a liquid usually associated with purity, vitality, and the capacity for cleansing—I was also extending a brief but heartfelt nod to two feminist texts. Turkish novelist Elif Shafak's memoir of her postnatal breakdown and her writing life, *Black Milk*, has meant a great deal to me as a scribbling mother. And, as if in photographic negative, the title of French feminist Hélène Cixous's collection *White Ink* also calls to mind breast milk, suggesting the distinctiveness of women's writing, or what Cixous terms *écriture féminine*. Especially to British readers, the idiom also has troubling, violent connotations in light of Enoch Powell's racist 1968 'Rivers of Blood' speech. Since a crucial section of my book is about the British multicultural context in which racism is sadly still rife forty years after Powell's speech, this title seemed apt. Although these times of Brexit, the Trump presidency, Vladimir Putin's pugilism, and Narendra Modi's seeming consolidation of power are frightening, I dare to hope that less ink will need spilling in the coming years over basic issues of human rights and social justice.

I
PLAY ON WORDS

1

Writing Beyond Borders

IN HIS POEM 'THE SCHOONER *FLIGHT*', Derek Walcott, with his multivalent Caribbean heritage, declares, 'either I'm nobody, or I'm a nation' (346). For someone of mixed background or a writer, there is no contradiction to be found in this simultaneously optimistic and precarious identification. In an interview I conducted with British–Pakistani author Nadeem Aslam, he made a similar assertion: 'As a writer, an artist, and a thinker, the only nationality I have is my desk: this is my passport' (qtd. in Chambers *British*: 157).

As laudable as these ideals are, can literature exist without certain borders, classifications, and systems of ordering? As an example, think of the bookshop. The moment I walk into Liberty or Oxford University Press bookstores in Pakistan, and similarly Waterstones or Blackwell's in Britain, I am immediately confronted with divisions and decisions that have been made on my behalf. Do I want a children's story for my two boys? Head downstairs to the kids' section. A cookery book? Certainly, madam, it's over there in 'lifestyle'. Something by J. K. Rowling? A tricky one to classify, our Joanne. Her 2013 novel *The Cuckoo's Calling* was confined to the crime fiction ghetto when it was thought to have been written by an obscure Scottish writer, Robert Galbraith. Now everyone knows it is authored by Britain's most recognizable literary brand name, the book features prominently in the adult fiction section. And as for the *Harry Potter* series, taxonomies break down: one can find the books and associated merchandise in the adult, children, and fantasy sections, as well as in the DVD and games sections.

Perhaps it's unsurprising that one of the most successful international booksellers of the late 1990s and early 2000s was called Borders. Yet with the rise of the Internet and accompanying rise in online shopping, this retailer collapsed. Is it reading too much into a name to suggest that borderless cyberspace is leading to the demise of literary classifications?

The leading online bookstore Amazon is jittery about the prospect of entry into the market in Pakistan (The Most Dangerous Country in the World™), but is doing a roaring trade in apparently shining India next door. If, as seems likely, Amazon eventually enters the Pakistani book market, it is worth knowing that each customer's unique digital identity means that the online storefront is tailored to their personal tastes. When I log on to Amazon, based on my purchasing and browsing history, algorithms suggest a shortlist of further, similar titles—for example, Jack Shaheen's *Reel Bad Arabs: How Hollywood Vilifies a People* and Peter Morey's and Amina Yaqin's *Framing Muslims*. (In the light of Edward Snowden's revelations, I dread to think what British intelligence and security make of my digital fingerprint!) So, granted, there is some breakdown of conventional classifications on my individual page; however, the 'browse books' search function tool is divided in the same manner as a physical bookshop is, with alphabetized categories including, for example, art, architecture and photography, biography, and crime, thrillers, and mystery.

Thus, borders can function as a helpful springboard into the discovery of a constellation of new, exciting texts. There simply isn't enough time to read every book, especially now that web-based self-publishing platforms and e-commerce are giving everyone the chance to produce and distribute the novel that (so we're told) is in each of us. Generic and other classifications can serve as a map through which we navigate the thick undergrowth of the contemporary publishing scene.

But there are borders other than those belonging to genre. National, ethnic, religious, linguistic, and gender boundaries can work to constrict and constrain writers, as well as acting as enabling springboards propelling readers towards texts. As Edward W. Said delineated in the seminal work *The World, The Text, and the Critic*: 'The large cultural-national designation of European culture as the privileged norm carried with it a formidable battery of other distinctions between ours and theirs, between proper and improper, European and non-European, higher and lower' (14). Here Said reminds us, as he did throughout his career, that colonialism and its more recent incarnations dictated that other cultures are defined by everything that Europe, allegedly, is not. Thus, if European culture defines itself as high culture and proper, then non-European culture is stereotyped as low culture and improper. Such unequal binary oppositions always posit the non-European as the weak partner.

Bearing Said's salient warning in mind, are labels such as 'Pakistani writing in English', 'South Asian literature', 'women's writing', and 'British Muslim fictions' ever useful? I coined the last phrase—'British Muslim fictions'—so, given this, it is apparent that I hold that they have a function, as long as they are used judiciously and are accorded sufficient elasticity. We must aim for an accommodating, fluid world (of) literature. In this ideal world, distinctions are constantly challenged, mutating, and overlapping. The intelligentsia should never restrict or marshal the writer using metaphorical identity cards, checkpoints, or border police. Borders are beneficial only if they allow space for the author, the scholar, and the reader to write or think beyond them. Let us take just one example from Pakistan and its diaspora. In the West, Pakistani authors tend to be analysed alongside their peers in India, Bangladesh, and Sri Lanka, as part of broader South Asian trends.

There is, of course, some logic to this, but Pakistan differs from those other nations in that it has concerns and links to the Middle East, Central Asia, East Africa, and beyond, which derive from its western position within the subcontinent and its Muslim identity.

I am no cheerleader for a unified global Muslim community or ummah and know that exaggeration of the ummah ideal can lead to the very real tensions between different Muslim groups being underestimated. However, the approach I took in *British Muslim Fictions* (2011) had the advantage of bringing together writers with connections to the Arab world, Africa, and South Asia to shed light on each other. As a political move, I situated the thirteen writers I interviewed and discussed in *British Muslim Fictions* within the boundary of 'Britishness', whether or not they had been born in Britain and irrespective of how long they had lived there. One of the most intriguing discoveries in the course of my research was that the writers fell roughly into three categories: the first being a British-born group (Hanif Kureishi, Zahid Hussain, and Robin Yassin-Kassab); the second and largest group comprising writers who had arrived in Britain at an impressionable age, either in their teens or early twenties (Fadia Faqir, Ahdaf Soueif, Nadeem Aslam, Abdulrazak Gurnah, Tariq Ali, and Aamer Hussein); and the third group occupying a state of exile, using Britain as a base from which to write their fiction, which often explores other nations in more detail than the UK (Kamila Shamsie, Leila Aboulela, Mohsin Hamid, and Tahmima Anam). Perhaps this should not surprise us, for writers are often adept at literal, as well as figurative, border crossing, tending to be widely travelled with multiple, well-stamped passports.

However, categorization is not as clear-cut as these three demarcations suggest. At least two of the British-born writers, Yassin-Kassab and Hussain, have spent long periods of time overseas and are multilingual. Similarly, apparent exiles like Anam and Shamsie are rightly included in discussions of the UK's literary scene, such as Granta's 'Best of Young British Novelists' collection (Freeman). The majority of these writers, therefore, do not have hyphenated identities, nor can they be considered émigrés, but instead they write from in-between positions connecting East and West. Nadeem Aslam is right, then, to suggest that writers' nationalities are best described in terms of their desks.

2

Postcolonial Lives

T HE POSTCOLONIAL LITERARY WORLD lost two giants in 2013: Nigeria's Chinua Achebe, and Doris Lessing, who was born in Persia, raised in Southern Rhodesia, and resident in England for most of her life. It lost a third if we view Seamus Heaney as a postcolonial poet, but let's not become mired in the debate as to whether Irish writers should be considered postcolonial, nor in the tortuous argument about what constitutes postcoloniality. Achebe's death led many admirers from the African continent and beyond to demand he be posthumously awarded the Nobel Prize for Literature. This petition was labelled 'obscene' by his countryman, Nobel laureate Wole Soyinka, who satirized the mournful perspective on Achebe's reputation shadowed by 'an unlit lamp labelled "Nobel"' (qtd. in Flood 'Achebe': np.). Obituaries for Lessing, by contrast, repeated the anecdote that when she was apprehended on her doorstep in 2007 by a journalist intent on conveying the news of her Nobel Prize win, she barked: 'Oh, Christ' (see, for example, Schwartz np.). In the meantime, 2013's Nobel went to another author with postcolonial credentials— Canada's previously underrated short story writer, Alice Munro. This litany of obituaries and varied responses to literary prizes (or lack thereof) prompted me to think about the lives of our major world writers, and how these lives are publicly staged and commemorated. In particular, I was intrigued to discover what part is played by biographies and memoirs, literary awards, book festivals, and archives (or their ephemeral electronic equivalent, Twitter feeds) in the management of the writer's image and the creation of literary celebrities.

Some answers are hazarded by Hanif Kureishi in his novel *The Last Word*, which centres on Mamoon Azam—an Indian author, who in his youth was an *enfant terrible* and is now viewed as an *éminence grise* of the literary world. To Mamoon's claustrophobic, crumbling country house comes a young, upper-class biographer named Harry Johnson. Harry is eager to write Mamoon's life story; he believes this book will be career-defining, because, for him and many others, 'writers were gods, heroes, rock stars' (2). Even more exciting than the prospect of his literary biography's success is the opportunity to seduce the insipid, subservient, or termagant women who populate Kureishi's countryside locale. Critics such as David Sexton have been quick to identify the parallels between the Mamoon–Harry pairing and the relationship of yet another Nobel laureate—the Indo-Caribbean writer V. S. Naipaul—with his authorized biographer Patrick French. In 2008, the younger man, French, published his peerless biography, *The World Is What It Is*, after years spent poking around Naipaul's Tulsa archive and interviewing him on numerous occasions at his Wiltshire home. Despite his lack of acknowledgement as to this uncanny parallel, it is clear that Kureishi is fictionalizing the Naipaul–French encounter, transplanting the Wiltshire setting to Somerset, and retaining what French calls Naipaul's 'outrageous, funny, impossible' (xv) personality and his insecure, even hate-filled attitudes to women and practising Muslims. Kureishi also only faintly disguises the great writer's three successive, but overlapping, life partners: English intellectual Pat is renamed Peggy in *The Last Word*; sexually adventurous, yet put-upon Argentinian mistress Margaret becomes Colombian Marion; while Pakistani Nadira Naipaul is thinly disguised as a theatrical, curry-cooking Italian, Liana Luccioni.

However, Patrick French is barely recognizable in the novel's blond fool Harry, and Kureishi plausibly (and unwisely) claims not to have read the former's biography. An additional layer of resemblance is found in the probably coincidental fact that French's occasional op-ed column for Indian news magazine *The Week* has the similar title 'Last Word' (see, for instance, French 'Arab').

Naipaul's longstanding, much-disputed insistence on the importance of conveying the 'truth' about the world begs the question as to whether it is possible to write a truthful biography of a living author. In an obituary for John Steinbeck in 1970, Naipaul wrote: 'A writer is in the end not his books, but his myth. And that myth is in the keeping of others' (qtd. in French *World*: 283). There is a symbiotic relationship between the author writing himself into his fiction and the biographers, academics, friends, lovers, and critics who act as custodians of his literary work and act to perpetuate the myth of the author, both during their lifetime, as well as (and often most importantly) after death. Most of the living or recently deceased authors discussed in this chapter have published memoirs or autobiographical fiction, thus pre-empting potential biographers. The South African Nobel laureate, J. M. Coetzee, observes that 'all autobiography is story-telling, all writing is autobiography' (Coetzee and Attwell 391). We see this slippage between (auto)biography and fiction in Kureishi's *Intimacy* and *My Ear at His Heart*, Naipaul's *A House for Mr Biswas* and *The Enigma of Arrival*, Coetzee's *Diary of a Bad Year* and *Slow Man*, Lessing's *Under My Skin* and *Alfred and Emily*, Munro's *The View From Castle Rock*, Achebe's *There Was a Country*, and Soyinka's *You Must Set Forth at Dawn*, among other works. Indeed, the urge for self-reflection and desire to intermingle truth with fiction seems to become stronger as the writer ages.

Also noticeable is a reawakened interest in the author's parents, as demonstrated by several of the authors under discussion. A dream inherited from the father to become a writer is often fulfilled by the son (for example, Naipaul, Kureishi, Orhan Pamuk, Nadeem Aslam, and others have all achieved writerly success where their fathers failed), or the woman writer compares her mother's limited opportunities with her own wider horizons (examples include Lessing's *Alfred and Emily* and Lorna Goodison's *From Harvey River*). It is ironic, then, that Rushdie wrote in his nonplussed review of Naipaul's *The Enigma of Arrival* in 1987: '[W]hen the strength for fiction fails the writer, what remains is autobiography' (*Imaginary*: 150; NB: Rushdie's sprawling, score-settling memoir, *Joseph Anton*, came out in 2012).

A few years ago, I attended a lecture at the University of York given by David Attwell, author of a literary biography of Coetzee. Attwell traced Coetzee's view that writers commonly experience an attenuation in their writing as they grow older; their prose becomes progressively cooler, more schematic, and increasingly interested in the writing process itself. While from an outside perspective this could seem like a deterioration in ability, Attwell movingly suggested that it is experienced as a purging that enables the writer to refocus on pressing issues, as they come to terms with their own mortality. The following remark from Coetzee is employed as an epigraph, as well as prefacing a chapter in Attwell's masterful *J. M. Coetzee and the Life of Writing*:

> One can think of a life in art, schematically, in two or perhaps three stages. In the first you find, or pose for yourself, a great question. In the second you labor away at answering it. And then, if you live long enough, you come to the third stage, when the aforesaid great question begins to bore you, and you need to look elsewhere (qtd. in Attwell *Life*: 233; emphasis in original).

Kureishi expresses this slightly differently when he says: 'I'm not sure you become more fluent as you get older, but you become less fearful of imagined consequences' (*Collected*: 293). Even if *The Last Word* is uneven in its execution, Kureishi, as always, hits the literary zeitgeist with his choice of subject. The novel touches on some of world literature's decidedly contemporary issues: migration, racism, scandals, spats, the publishing industry, the process of canonization, what Graham Huggan calls the 'postcolonial exotic', the literary marketplace, and the role of the public intellectual. Whether we like it or not, the creation of literary celebrities and the management of the author's image are important factors in the global literary marketplace today.

3

'To Love the Moor' (I.i.40):
Postcolonial Artists Write Back
to Shakespeare's *Othello*

IN LATE SUMMER OF 1600, Moroccan ambassador Abd al-Wahid bin Masoud bin Muhammad al-Annuri came to London. Along with his entourage of more than a dozen delegates, he resided in England's capital city for six months. Some believe that he provided inspiration for William Shakespeare's *Othello*, first performed soon afterwards in 1604 (B. Harris 23–30), although this is contested by other scholars such as Gustav Ungerer (102). Al-Annuri's presence in England arose from Elizabeth I's dream of creating a durable and mutually beneficial alliance with the unfamiliar Muslim world. In 1570, Elizabeth had been excommunicated by Pope Pius V for her Protestant beliefs and for reinstating the reformed church established by her father, Henry VIII. Following this ostracism from Catholic Europe, the Queen began encouraging trade with Turkey, Persia, and Morocco. English Protestants saw their antipathy towards idol worship and veneration of a holy book reflected in Sunni Muslim religious practice. In his monograph *This Orient Isle*, Jerry Brotton rightly highlights the financial shrewdness that lay behind some Elizabethan Englanders' belief in a mirroring between their Protestantism and the Muslim religion. Brotton remarks that Islam was viewed as 'a faith with which [England] could do business' (13). Yet Elizabethans on the whole misunderstood Islam and refused to accept the religion on its own terms. The English imposed on Muslims anything other than their correct name; they were 'Mahomedans', 'Turks', 'Ottomites', 'Moriscos', 'barbarians', or 'Saracens'.

Such lexical deviation chimes with the inconsistent treatment the Moroccan delegation received in England. At first, Elizabeth fêted the 42-year-old al-Annuri and his team with pageantry, jousting, and lavish meals. She had already become addicted to Moroccan sugar, the cause of her famously ruined teeth. The Queen gave sweeteners in return to the North Africans with the aim of fostering trade, political ties, and a military alliance against Catholic Spain. In contrast to the official response, the English masses increasingly expressed hostility towards the Moroccan visitors. Following frequent food shortages in the 1590s and a failed coup led by Robert Devereux, Second Earl of Essex in 1601 (Younger 591), the jittery London public turned against the strangers—the first Muslims that most of them had ever seen. Rumours abounded that the delegation comprised spies rather than envoys, and a moral panic developed over stories that the visitors had poisoned members of their own party (Brotton 271). In response, Elizabeth made a declaration of protection for her 'natural subjects', whom she described as being 'greatly distressed' in these times of scarcity. She disingenuously expressed alarm at 'the great number of Negars and Blackamoors which (as she is informed) are crept into this realm since the troubles between Her Highness and the King of Spain' (Elizabeth I np.). Echoing the 'great annoyance' of her subjects concerning the lavish honouring of her visitors, the queen went further, criticizing them as 'infidels, having no understanding of Christ or his Gospel' (Elizabeth I np.). Recommending their immediate isolation and swift deportation, she resorted to the device still popular today of gaining political capital from attacking immigrants. Wisely deciding that the time had come to leave England, al-Annuri and his followers retreated to Morocco in February 1601.

William Shakespeare's *The Merchant of Venice* was first performed in 1605. It featured a richly dressed man, the Prince of Morocco, who tries to woo the beautiful and witty heroine, Portia. He is the first of the playwright's 'Moors', since *The Merchant of Venice* is thought to have been written in the late 1590s. In the play, the Prince of Morocco is eloquent and handsome; he is described as '*a tawny Moor all in white*' who cuts a conspicuous figure (II.i:1; stage direction; emphasis in original). Just as his outward appearance is designed to impress, so, too, is the Prince of Morocco seduced by opulent surfaces. He fails the test set out in Portia's late father's will, whereby her potential husbands have to choose correctly from three caskets of gold, silver, and lead. Naturally, the Prince selects the gold casket, concluding that 'so rich a gem' as Portia could not possibly be 'set in worse than gold' (II.vii.55). He thus loses Portia's hand in marriage. Fortunately, her preferred suitor, Bassanio, is willing to 'give and hazard all he hath' for Portia, as inscribed on the humble lead casket that he chooses (II.vii.9).

Whereas with *The Merchant of Venice* Shakespeare is working within the popular but stereotypical 'Turk play' of his era, in his tragedy *Othello* he transcends this genre's limitations. *Othello* is a play that has always been receptive to adaptations and postcolonial rewritings. As the Pakistani novelist Zulfikar Ghose observes in his book *Shakespeare's Mortal Knowledge*, Othello is a truly noble man, in contrast to the calumny of the 'lascivious Moor' with which Iago taints him (I.i.125). In fact, if Othello has a fault, Ghose suggests that it is his 'sexual frugality' (82), which leads him to make too great a distinction between body and spirit. This enables evil Iago to work both on Othello's jealousy over his wife and on the 'base racial instinct' (75) the villain shares with his fellow white Venetians. The consequence is that a 'beast with two backs' is created—not

through sexual union, but through the conjoining of Desdemona
and Othello in death (I.i.116; see also Ghose 73–103). With its
explosive cocktail of false friendship, cross-cultural love, racism,
military confrontation, and extreme sexual possessiveness, *Othello*
proves irresistible to many artists from postcolonial backgrounds.

This chapter explores some of the most notable global
reconfigurations of *Othello* through the lens of Bill Ashcroft et
al.'s notion of postcolonial 'writing back'. The texts under discussion
include Tayeb Salih's *Season of Migration to the North*, Toni
Morrison's *Desdemona*, Vishal Bhardwaj's *Omkara*, and Upamanyu
Chatterjee's 'Othello Sucks'. The rationale behind selecting
these particular postcolonial rewritings is, first, that there is an
equal number of Anglophone and non-Anglophone productions
(*Season of Migration to the North* was originally written in Arabic,
while *Omkara* is a Hindi film); and second, each text examines a
different aspect of Shakespeare's play: Salih thinks through the
play's representation of racism and sexuality; Morrison is similarly
interested in racism, but also in its imbrication with gender;
Bhardwaj transplants Shakespeare's concern with race onto caste;
and Chatterjee's characters are critical of Shakespeare being taught
in twenty-first century postcolonies. The chapter is divided into two
main parts. The first part focuses on the African diaspora, with the
locations of Sudan, black Britain, and the African American United
States taking centre stage. In the second, India is positioned as a
fulcrum for analysis of the history of *Othello*'s cinematic adaptations,
and there is also a close reading of Chatterjee's recent story about
Shakespeare's tragedy.

One of the key concerns of postcolonial critics has been to
interpret how authors from formerly colonized countries have
'written back' to classic novels from the English literary canon.
The phrase 'written back' is sourced from the title of the book
The Empire Writes Back (1989). Alluding to Salman Rushdie's pun

on the Star Wars film *The Empire Strikes Back* (Rushdie 'Empire'; Kershner), Australian academics Bill Ashcroft, Gareth Griffiths, and Helen Tiffin argue that postcolonial authors question and parody colonial ideas, writing back to the centre to contest accepted truths. In countering imperialist assumptions, the postcolonial writers discussed by these theorists also remake the English language and recast the form of the novel. However, Ashcroft et al.'s positioning of non-Western authors' challenge to colonial discourse actually tethers the creative writers to European ideas as the central stake they seek to uproot. In my opinion, Ashcroft et al. still accord too much attention to 'the West', even if the writers they analyse seek to dismantle its assumptions. Given this and other blind spots, several theorists have interrogated the terms 'postcolonial' and 'writing back' for their colonial baggage (Dirlik; A. Ahmad; Dabashi; Hauthal). However, I follow Mike Hill in striving to initiate a 'return to "writing back" in a new and different way' (62)—in this chapter's case, in a way that aims at decentring European thought and letters. I want to suggest that postcolonial recreations of Shakespeare have moved beyond 'writing back' to more creative and confident conversations across spaces and time periods.

African Diasporic Rewritings of *Othello*

In 1966, the Sudanese author, Tayeb Salih, published an Arabic-language novel, *Mawsim al-Hijra ila al-Shamal*. This novel was translated into English in 1969, the translation bearing the title of *Season of Migration to the North*, and is now a Penguin Modern Classic. In this landmark text for postcolonial literary studies, Salih depicts the cultural conflict that ensues when two rural Sudanese Muslims move to Britain and later return to Africa. Events in *Season of Migration to the North* are related by an unnamed narrator

who passed several years in Britain during the interwar period
pursuing a higher education. Returning to his seemingly timeless
village in rural Sudan, the narrator meets a mysterious older man
called Mustafa Sa'eed. Mustafa had also attended university in the
colonial metropole. We are told that during his time in Britain, he
seduced numerous white women, leaving behind a string of broken
hearts, suicides, and murder.

One of his lovers who takes her life, the married mother Isabella
Seymour, is enthralled by Mustafa's exotic blackness. Desdemona
to his Othello, she loves his outlandish stories of the landscape,
animals, and people of Africa. However, Mustafa is alert to the
racism underpinning her interest, as when she assumes he is a
cannibal. He plays along with her fantasies, inventing fictions
about the 'dark continent'. We are explicitly invited to make
connections between the novel and Shakespeare's play when
Mustafa declares, 'I am no Othello. I am a lie' and later, 'I am no
Othello. Othello was a lie' (33, 95). Later, during Mustafa's extreme
sadomasochistic relationship with the British woman Jean Morris,
he suspects infidelity and finds a man's handkerchief that does not
belong to him amongst her possessions. In contrast to the chaste
and submissive Desdemona, Jean is nonchalant, even defiant, on
being confronted with this evidence. She tells Mustafa it is his
handkerchief, and when he doubts this, she responds, 'Assuming
it's not your handkerchief [...] what are you going to do about it?'
Before long, Mustafa finds further belongings that are not his—'a
cigarette case, then a pen'—and the handkerchief is thus reduced
to a small piece in the larger puzzle of 'the tragedy [that] had to
happen' (162). Salih thus parodies and inverts *Othello*, not only by
exhibiting Mustafa's malevolence towards his white lovers, which
stems from anger at his colonial condition, but also by calling into
question Shakespeare's depiction of the 'noble Moor' (II.iii.121). In
doing so, he creates a web of intertextual references.[1]

Whereas *Othello* is situated on the periphery of Salih's text, later postcolonial writers have fashioned full adaptations of, or 'written back' to, the play. In her far-reaching work of literary criticism, *Playing in the Dark*, Toni Morrison argues that mainstream white American literature developed its own identity by casting African Americans in a shadow narrative. Morrison maintains that the notion of American individualism flourishes when cast against the stereotypical but inescapable bondage of slaves and their descendants. She writes of freedom that it 'can be relished more deeply in a cheek-by-jowl existence with the bound and unfree, the economically oppressed, the marginalized, the silenced' (64). In her 2012 play *Desdemona*, Morrison grafts her own discussion regarding the founding principles of the United States onto Shakespeare's seventeenth-century English context. The play, directed by American Peter Sellars and with music by the Malian singer Rokia Traoré, postulates that Desdemona's beauty and purity were partly facilitated by an almost-silenced figure in Shakespeare's work: her attentive African maid, Barbary. Desdemona was also invisibly aided by Iago's wife, the working-class character Emilia, who in Morrison's play is given lines in which she mimics the entitlement of the titular heroine: '"Unpin me, Emilia". "Arrange my bed sheets, Emilia". That is not how you treat a friend; that's how you treat a servant' (43). Morrison has several characters criticize Desdemona; despite this, she also intends to give Shakespeare's heroine a stronger voice. As Joe Eldridge Carney explains: 'Morrison's desire to create a more significant role for Desdemona came from her sense that Shakespeare's tragic heroine has been given insufficient attention, particularly in performances, a neglect that can be located in the critical tradition as well' (np.).

In Shakespeare's play, we only learn of Barbary's existence in Act IV, Scene III, when a heartbroken Desdemona tells Emilia that she is haunted by the Willow Song that her mother's maid sang while

dying after being jilted by a lover. Morrison assumes that Barbary
is a slave name, given that the word means 'Africa', so in *Desdemona*
she gives back the original appellation of Sa'ran that the woman
had had before slavery. Indeed, Sa'ran contradicts her mistress's
claim that they shared many experiences as young people and were
friends.[2] She tells Desdemona that they shared nothing and that
Desdemona misunderstood everything about Sa'ran, evidenced by
the fact that she didn't even bother to learn her real name:

> Barbary? Barbary is what you call Africa. Barbary is the geography
> of the foreigner, the savage. Barbary equals the sly, vicious enemy
> who must be put down at any price; held down at any cost for the
> conquerors' pleasure. Barbary is the name of those without whom
> you could neither live nor prosper (Morrison 45).

Sa'ran highlights the silencing and 'put[ting] down' of the African
presence in the West, while simultaneously drawing attention to
the indispensable nature of Africans' presence. This silencing is
partly achieved through violent acts of renaming. The play's very
first line reads 'My name is Desdemona', and the female protagonist
continues with a page-long soliloquy on the negative connotations
of her name, in which she explains that Desdemona means 'misery'.
She calls into question nominative determinism, declaring: 'I am
not the meaning of a name I did not choose' (13). Through this
statement, Morrison signals the importance of nomenclature in
establishing identity. In addition, 'Barbary' shares an etymological
root with 'barbarian', demonstrating the racially charged constitution
of the English language. By confronting Desdemona and her
'problematic posture of alleged "color blindness"' (Carney np.),
Sa'ran forces Desdemona to confront her own racism, especially the
way in which she renames and thereby colonizes others, producing
the dominant 'geography of the foreigner'.

In Morrison's 2012 play, Desdemona is a little older than the teenager envisioned by Shakespeare. She and her former servant, as well as Desdemona's murderous husband, meet in the afterlife and engage in conversation. By situating her characters in the liminal space between life and death, director Peter Sellars claims that Morrison 'create[s] a safe space in which the dead can finally speak those things that could not be spoken when they were alive' (Sellars 9). The white woman admits that in her childhood, Barbary was the only person who allowed her imagination to soar by telling her 'stories of other lives, other countries' (18). Therefore, in Morrison's act of 'writing back', it is Desdemona's female companion, as well as Othello, who inspire the girl with stories of faraway lands and their different customs. Towards the end of the play, Morrison's Othello articulates the rage felt by both Sa'ran and himself (and by the fictional Mustafa before them) that their story is 'cut to suit a princess' hunger for real life, not the dull existence of her home' (51). A self-absorbed character in Morrison's play, Othello criticizes his wife and claims: 'You never loved me. You fancied the idea of me, the exotic foreigner who kills for the State' (50). But the Nobel laureate also gives Desdemona some devastating lines where she censures Othello for his violent temper and misogynist views, most notably: 'I was the empire you had already conquered' (54).

Iago does not appear in Morrison's re-visioning of Shakespeare, and Peter Erickson points out that this serves to 'place [...] the emphasis on Othello and Desdemona as the makers of their own destinies and thus makes them logically the ones in the afterlife who are responsible for coming to terms with their own actions, with no recourse to blaming Iago' (np.). It also has the effect of making Morrison's play more female-centred than Shakespeare's original, with Desdemona and Sa'ran as the pivotal (non-romantic) pairing. Iago exists offstage and is only occasionally mentioned, as when Cassio declares: 'Now Cyprus is under my reign. I am the one who decides. Othello gone from life; Iago suffering in a police cell' (53). In live productions of the play, much of this dialogue is set to Traoré's ethereal score, with the lyrics projected onto screens and incorporated into the dialogue at times. The otherworldly music that accompanies Morrison's play intensifies the narratives of competing violence in *Othello*.

When Shakespeare's Iago proclaims: 'Men should be what they seem' (III.iii.127), he is, of course, dissembling. While gaining Othello's agreement as regards this truism, Iago also sets up the conceit that there are men who, despite appearances to the contrary, are not what they seem. In this way, he plants doubt in Othello's mind about Cassio and introduces the possibility that he and Desdemona are lovers. More broadly, by creating this white character who is so far from what he seems and Othello, the black man destructively duped by him, Shakespeare shadows forth a great deal about the lie that underpins racism. Many black and South Asian writers have pushed Shakespeare's central tenets in new and different directions to provide updated versions of his plays that reflect on our globalized world shaped by racism and structural inequalities.

Indian Rewritings of *Othello*

HAVING EXPLORED TWO AFRICAN DIASPORIC REWRITINGS of Shakespeare's *Othello*, I now turn to what Ania Loomba (2012) has called the 'made-in-India Othello fellows'. Put another way, I am interested in those Indian writers who, from Henry Louis Vivian Derozio (1809–1831) onwards, have looked to this play about love, jealousy, and race both for inspiration and to argue against. In her essay '"Filmi" Shakespeare', Poonam Trivedi defies accusations of 'bardolatry' (148) and colonial cultural cringe to trace the history of Shakespeare on the Indian big screen. She demonstrates that this filmic history goes back as far as 1935 with Sohrab Modi's *Khoon ka Khoon*, a cinematic re-rendering of an Indian stage version of *Hamlet*. In part because British colonizers laid emphasis on an English literary education for the Indians over whom they ruled (see Viswanathan), but also in some measure as appropriation and subversion of colonial presuppositions, there were many filmic versions of Shakespeare's plays. *Hamlet's* blend of politics and metaphysical mystery seems to have proven the most popular of the Bard's plays for Indian auteurs. In the early days of Indian cinema, indigenous directors found themselves between the rock of leaving Shakespeare 'pure and pristine' and the hard place of making him entirely 'bowdlerized and indigenized' (Trivedi 151). By the mid-twentieth century, the most successful adaptations relocated the plays to India in their entirety. Directors 'transcreated' the Shakespearean originals (Lal *Two*; *Seven*), borrowing ideas from their plots and themes rather than writing back to the plays in an overtly critical way.

The Bengali film *Saptapadi* (Kar) was probably the first piece of Indian cinema to namecheck *Othello*. In it, a pair of star-crossed lovers—a Brahmin boy and an Anglo-Indian Christian girl—fall in love during a performance of that Shakespearean play about a relationship transgressing social and racial fault lines. Then came Jayaraaj Rajasekharan Nair's *Kaliyattam* (1997), a Malayalam remake of *Othello*. It is set against the backdrop of Kaliyattam or Kathakali—a devotional Keralan form of folk theatre and dance which is also evoked in Arundhati Roy's *The God of Small Things*. In *Kaliyattam*, Jayaraaj shifts Shakespeare's racial concerns onto caste, since the plot revolves around a romantic pairing between a low-caste Theyyam performer and a Brahmin girl. Jayaraaj also exchanges Shakespeare's somewhat trivial, somatic device of a handkerchief—responsible for fuelling Othello's jealousy—with an opulent cloth that also serves as a consummation sheet for the two protagonists. In Ashish Avikunthak's short documentary-style film *Brihnlala ki Khelkali* or *Dancing Othello* (2002), he re-envisions Arjun Raina's dance theatre show *The Magic Hour* (2000). Like *Kaliyattam*, both of these contemporary adaptations use Kathakali—that art form mindlessly consumed by Western tourists to India—as a launch pad from which to discuss the Shakespearean play that is most concerned with what Graham Huggan (2001) calls 'the postcolonial exotic'.

The first of two Indian 'Othello fellows' whose work I want to discuss in detail is Vishal Bhardwaj. *Omkara* (2006) is Bhardwaj's second film in a twenty-first century Bollywood trilogy of Shakespearean retrofitting—the other two are *Maqbool* (2003), a remake of *Macbeth*, and *Haider* (2014), which relocated *Hamlet* to the Kashmiri conflict. In his essay 'Theorising *Omkara*', John Milton argues that Bhardwaj remains faithful to Shakespeare's tragedy, but makes it relevant to contemporary Indians. Issues of caste and biracial identity in colour-conscious India replace Shakespeare's interest in the people then known as 'blackamoors'. Omkara Shukla (played by Ajay Devgan) is the son of a Dalit mother and a higher-caste father. Known as Omi, he is repeatedly slammed as a 'half-breed' or 'half-caste'. Raghunath Mishra (Kamal Tiwari), who is father to Dolly (the Desdemona figure, played by Kareena Kapoor), is duly angry about his daughter's elopement with this swarthy gangster. Dolly is contrastingly Brahminical and has a pale complexion. Yet she is unperturbed by the gossip circulating and the accompanying claims that they are a mismatched couple, declaring, 'A crescent, though half, is still called a moon'. Othello's status as a general fighting against the Turks is altered in the film so that Omi leads a gang in Uttar Pradesh (Bhardwaj's home province), serving a shadowy political figure known as Bhai sahib (Naseeruddin Shah). This allows Bhardwaj to explore the endemic corruption that would later garner widespread attention with the

2011 to 2012 Indian anti-corruption movement led by Anna Hazare (see Sengupta np.).

The villainous Iago character is Ishwar Tyagi, who is known as Langda ('Lame') because he has a pronounced limp. Langda is portrayed memorably by Saif Ali Khan, who smoulders, plots, and swears his way through the film. To adapt Coleridge's famous phrase, if his felonies are not as 'motiveless' as Iago's are, he nonetheless exudes pure '[m]alignancy' (315). Langda has a motive that explains his proclivity towards evil—he is passed over for promotion in favour of a rival, Kesu Firangi (Vivek Oberoi). Omi chooses to replace himself with Kesu (the film's Cassio character) when he leaves his position as an underworld don to get involved with mainstream politics. In revenge for being passed over, Langda works on Omi's jealousy about his innocent bride. Dolly's father's words—'a girl who can deceive her own father can never be possessed by anyone else'—come back to haunt Omi, just as Brabantio's line—'She has deceived her father and may thee'—is a repeated leitmotif in *Othello* (I.iii.289). The idea that a deceitful daughter will become a wanton wife finds resonance in a South Asia where human beings, and specifically women, are often held hostage, and sometimes brutalized, in the name of family connections and arranged marriages. Ironically, though, a film that is relatively progressive in its treatment of caste and gender reverts to ableist stereotypes. Langda's disability is linked with his evil acts in a way that recalls the sinister hunchbacked Richard III of Shakespeare's history play. This grotesque stereotype reflects badly on the embodiment politics of the film and those of the society it seeks to entertain. In *Postcolonial Fiction and Disability*, Clare Barker reflects on the 'invisibility' of disabled people in South Asian biopolitics (140), although it is an encouraging development that twenty-first century activists and scholars such as Anita Ghai (2009) have acted as staunch critics of normative able-bodied discourse.

Omkara presents a range of views on women's rights, from the misogynistic to the progressive. The film usefully raises the issue of violence against women. There are some powerful scenes, such as when we see Langda's sexual violence towards his wife, Indu. (In the film Indu, unlike Iago's wife Emilia, is also Omi's sister, making Omi and Langda brothers-in-law.) Instead of a handkerchief, the film uses the device of a gold Indian waistband, which has sexual overtones in its suggestion of a chastity belt locking up a woman's 'honour'. Omi gives this priceless cummerbund to Dolly as a wedding gift, but Langda persuades Indu (Konkona Sen Sharma) to steal it, so as to mislead Omi into thinking Dolly has gifted the waistband to Kesu. When Omi sees Kesu's girlfriend, the dancer Billo Chaman Bahar (Bipasha Basu), wearing it, he goes out of his mind with jealousy. He has already been worked upon by Langda's suggestive remarks about Dolly's faithlessness, which he then cleverly appears to disavow, saying: 'Me and my filthy mind'. The auditory detail of the film's tragic final scene allows for even more pointed impugnment of men's cruelty to women. The audience is assailed by the stark creaking sounds of a swinging bed on which Omi strangles Dolly—foreshadowed by the repeated inclusion of swings throughout the film. The morbid swinging sound is accompanied by the song 'Jag Ja', which contains the repeated lyrics: '*Oh ri rani, gudiya, jag ja, ari jag ja, mari jag ja*', translated as: 'Oh my queen, my doll, come on wake up now'. These lyrics further insinuate that Dolly has long been treated as a plaything whose puppet-strings were pulled by the men in her life.

Indu, the Emilia character—Omi's sister and Langda's wife—makes a stirring speech near the film's end meditating on how the Hindu scriptures have painted women as temptresses and unfaithful. Mimicking Emilia in her 'proto-feminist' speech from *Othello*, Indu rails against the injustice that 'even after holy fires approve us, we're regarded as disloyal sooner than loyal'. On the other hand, the heroine, Dolly, has little agency, and when her father lambasts her relationship with Omi, she describes it as something over which she had little choice:

Papa… please forgive me. I can't live without Omkara. Don't trust what your eyes say. Your eyes will betray you. God knows how it all began, how I lost my heart to Omkara. I was in love… before I knew anything. I remember feeling like a blind bird plunging down an empty well. Everything seemed hopeless. And then I decided I'll end my wretched life. But then there was no point to it, when who I was dying for didn't even know why. Rajju will marry me dead. […] Let me confess… I'm yours and yours only. Put me down in your list of slain.

Dolly depicts herself as unintentionally losing her heart to Omi, adding to his 'list of slain', and thereby making him the warrior and possessor and she the conquered possession. Her only flashes of action are to consider suicide before dismissing this as pointless, and to maintain with some spirit that she would rather die than go through with her arranged marriage to fiancé Rajju. *Omkara* is outspoken for a Bollywood movie, but it is a shame that Bhardwaj did not see fit to allow Dolly to own her sexuality in choosing Omi as her partner. Shakespeare's Emilia stentoriously criticizes men as 'all but stomachs, and we all but food'. By contrast, in *Omkara* Dolly cloyingly tells Indu that a way to a man's heart is through his stomach. Indu to some extent challenges this, but only to counter with her grandmother's wisdom—that the way to keep a man is by keeping him sexually, rather than digestively, satisfied. That said, Indu does echo Emilia's lines—'They eat us hungerly, and when they are full, | They belch us' (III.iv.99-100)—when she states that women should leave their men somewhat hungry, otherwise 'the day they get satisfied, they'll puke you out like nobody's business'.

It is nonetheless telling that the seventeenth-century play is more vocal about women being treated as meat than the 2006 film.

This being a Bollywood film, songs and dances are a routine component. The songs are unusual in being written by Bhardwaj, who is a composer as well as a director, and limited to just two item numbers led by the provocative Bianca character, Billo. The first of these, 'Beedi' (Cigarette), contains the lines '*[b]eedi jalayi leh jigar se piya | Jigarmaa badi aag hai*', which in the subtitles are unromantically translated as '[l]ight your fag from the heat in my bosom' and elsewhere as '[l]ight your cigarette from the heat of my heart' (Rennam np.). In Hindi, however, the word used is '*jigar*', meaning 'liver'. Although the phrase may be literally translated as 'heat of my liver', it has connotations of intense, fiery passion. This is because in Hindi and Urdu letters, love and desire is said to originate in the liver, rather than the heart. The difficulties of translation are highlighted here, given that the South Asian and Western traditions pinpoint different organs as the seat of passion.

In some ways *Omkara* may be linked through intertextuality as much to *Kaliyattam* and *Dancing Othello* as to Shakespeare's *Othello*. All three productions use the 400-year-old story of jealousy to illustrate caste issues. Like *Kaliyattam*, *Omkara* replaces the handkerchief with a more substantial garment. As mentioned earlier, whereas Jayaraaj used a cloth, Bhardwaj deploys a jewelled waistband as the 'net | That shall enmesh them all' (II.iii.328–9). One possible reason for this repeated conversion of the handkerchief into more valuable artefacts is that the consummation sheet and waistband are visible metonyms of chastity in the Indian context. Also, the handkerchief as a garment is no longer seen as a prized possession with sexual connotations as it was in Shakespeare's day, so that Othello's interpretation of it as 'ocular proof' of Desdemona's infidelity can seem unconvincing to modern audiences (III.iii.361; see also Smith 4–8). *Omkara*, like its filmi predecessors, is an assured postcolonial adaptation that is neither derivative of, nor obsequious to, Shakespearean dramaturgy. Bhardwaj conveys a sense that Shakespeare belongs to everyone, so his work is open to both homage and critique.

Comic novelist Upamanyu Chatterjee contributed a short story entitled 'Othello Sucks' to the India issue of *Granta*, edited by Ian Jack in 2015. In it, as the story's title suggests, his characters are critical of Shakespeare, and their irreverence for the play and its context is highly entertaining. In the very first line of the story, Chatterjee uses metafiction to debate its generic conventions, which owe a debt to non-fiction, radio plays, and 'a comic strip in prose'. He also knowingly introduces the story's 'four principal dramatis personae' (169): Father, Mother, Elder Daughter, and Younger Daughter. The two daughters reluctantly study Shakespeare at their 'good right-wing south Delhi Punjabi' school (170). Younger Daughter declares that *Othello* sucks early on in the story, providing the story's title, while Elder Daughter retorts that she was lucky to avoid having to read *The Merchant of Venice* as the older sibling was compelled to. Younger Daughter objects to *Othello*'s wordiness and multiple meanings, and claims that Desdemona sucks even harder than Othello: 'No one in fact is sorry to see her strangled. It does improve the play' (175).

Father derides the educators who included Shakespeare in Indian children's curricula, rhetorically asking: '[D]o we want them as adults to speak in iambic pentameter when they apply for internships to CNN-IBN?' (170). Father is not objecting to the privileging of an English-language text over ancient Indian or Bhasha literatures, because CNN-IBN is an Anglophone news channel based in Uttar Pradesh where confident speakers of English are in high demand. Instead, he takes a utilitarian approach to education, desiring the inculcation in his daughters of a modern, tech-savvy English that will be useful when entering the job market. Above all, Father is troubled by what he sees as 'the fundamental assumption of the play that Othello is dumb because he is black' (175). Since A. C. Bradley's 1904 monograph, *Shakespearean Tragedy*, many critics have viewed Othello as a 'noble barbarian' who reverts to 'the savage passions of his Moorish blood' once he has been manipulated by Iago (186). If Father is correct about *Othello's* underlying racism, it is especially problematic in the girls' multicultural Delhi classroom. There, Cheik Luigi Fall (a biracial 'black guy' on whom Younger Daughter has a crush) and the dark-skinned teacher, Mrs Dasgupta, both come up against 'racist and skin-conscious' Indian assumptions (Chatterjee 171, 172).

In the story, Chatterjee reproduces a passage from Laurence Olivier's autobiography, *Confessions of an Actor*, on 'blacking up' for the role of Othello:

> Black all over my body, Max Factor 2880, then a lighter brown, then Negro No 2, a stronger brown. Brown on black to give a rich mahogany. Then the great trick: that glorious half yard of chiffon with which I polished myself all over until I shone ... The lips blueberry, the tight curled wig, the white of the eyes whiter than ever, and the black, black sheen that covered my flesh and bones, glistening in the dressing-room lights ... I am Othello (qtd. in Chatterjee: 175–6).

The quotation is well chosen. In it, Olivier explores with relish his metamorphosis by use of 'blackface', providing a detailed description of the layers of make-up he paints on himself and the gauzy material he uses to polish his skin to a shine. The actor's enchantment with his unfamiliar 'black, black' colour and stereotypically white teeth removes the culture from the figure of Othello and makes his race the primary preoccupation. Just as Olivier reduces the black general he plays to the particular shades of foundation and their accompanying brand names, so, too, the thespian makes Othello seem less than human through references to his sheep-like 'tight curled wig' and to the act of polishing, which produces a 'rich mahogany' akin to that found on expensive furniture. The cosmetics, with their precise shades of 'Max Factor 2880' and 'Negro No 2', are rendered attractive through the adjectives 'shone' and 'glistening'. Indeed, Olivier-as-Othello seems almost edible in the shape of those unnatural, vivid 'blueberry' lips. The berry image collocates with the 'Belgian chocolate' (174) comparison Younger Daughter reached for when describing Cheik Luigi Fall's skin. The two metaphors expose the racial fault lines both of 1980s Britain, from which Olivier writes, and the contemporary Indian society 'Othello Sucks' is set in.

But as Olivier's lively speech suggests, perhaps the most interesting ways in which Chatterjee's characters subvert Shakespeare is through their language use. Father frequently code-switches into Sanskrit phrases, such as '*Nirbhaya Bhavah*' (180; emphasis in original) or 'be free from fear', appropriates and alters hackneyed phrases such as 'Hell hath no fury like a man overlooked' (173), and quotes Shakespearean couplets freely. By contrast, the Daughters fall for an argot of speed: 'Communication is possible only by means of SMS, email or sign language' (181). All of the Indian characters speak with self-possession in a Hinglish that shows no sign of being browbeaten or colonized by Shakespeare's canonical English. Indeed, postcolonial confidence is the key attribute shared by these 'made-in-India Othello fellows' and other postcolonial writers, who borrow from the Bard to shed light on the concerns of twentieth- and twenty-first century Sudan, India, and the African American United States. They do so very successfully, and it will be interesting to see how adaptations of Shakespeare in general and *Othello* in particular develop and change as we move further into a twenty-first century already scarred by colonialism and its afterlives.

IN SUM, THIS CHAPTER HAS CHARTED how non-Western writers, most of them from formerly colonized countries, are turning their gaze back on Shakespeare. The decolonization of the English literary canon is only possible if scholars attempt to recover the voices of the conquered, while recognizing, with Gayatri Chakravorty Spivak ('Subaltern': 295), the 'fraught', contingent, and incomplete nature of this endeavour. My politicized version of writing back seeks to draw attention to overlooked texts by celebrated authors such as Toni Morrison, non-Anglophone narratives, and neglected aspects of well-known postcolonial novels, such as Salih's *Season of Migration to the North*. The subject of Shakespeare and his contemporaries' relationship with the Muslim world with which I opened this chapter has received a great deal of interest of late (see Brotton; Hutchings). What writers like Salih, Morrison, Bhardwaj, and Chatterjee emphasize, however, is the exotic way in which Shakespeare portrays 'Barbary' (IV.iii.25) and the Indian who 'threw a pearl away' (V.ii.343). This exoticizing gaze, as we have seen, is reversed by those who call Africa and India home. By turning the scrutiny back onto the West and its most prized author, these authors demonstrate that another way of seeing is possible. Displacement of Western hegemony and Shakespearean dominance is not likely and nor is it the objective of these authors, but what they do achieve is to offer supplementary valences that substantially change our readings of *Othello*.

NOTES

1. For more on Salih's transcreation of *Othello*, see Harlow; Calbi; Hassan 106–7.
2. Interestingly, an earlier text by Toni Morrison, the novel *Sula* (1973), is all about female friendship on a more equal basis. In an interview, Morrison said of this book: 'Friendship between women is special, different, and has never been depicted as the major focus of a novel before *Sula*' (Tate 157).

4

The Princess and the Priest:
Richard Dawkins' Attack on Fairy Tales

THE PROBABILITY OF A FROG turning into a prince is small. So small, in fact, that in 2014 evolutionary biologist Richard Dawkins spoke out against the fairy tale and others like it, asserting that we promote supernaturalism by telling these unlikely tales to our children (qtd. in Johnston np.). We shouldn't continue regaling our kids with these 'pernicious' narratives, he proclaimed, but rather encourage in them a spirit of 'scepticism'. It was a somewhat flippant statement and it is possible that he may have been misquoted (Weaver np.), though he has made similar comments in the past (Jones np.). But the whole notion of banning fairy tales smacks of an austere, quasi-fundamentalist worldview.

This is partly because Dawkins is taking an absurdly literal view of stories. Even my 7-year-old, still a devout believer in Santa Claus, doesn't think croakers are likely to metamorphose into crown princes just because his Ladybird Book makes such a claim. And that doesn't spoil his enjoyment of such stories in the slightest, because of their metaphorical dimension.

As children's author Lauren Child told Radio 4's *Today* programme, one moral to be found in *The Frog Prince* is that 'you shouldn't judge a book by its cover' and that ugly beings are often, in fact, beautiful once you get to know them. Accordingly, Disney's 2009 adaptation, *The Princess and the Frog* (Clements and Musker), turned this fairy tale into a predictably moralizing, but far from radical, fable about race and racism.

Yet you shouldn't judge this fairy tale by its cover either; it has a darker meaning about puberty and dread of female sexual maturation. The American confessional poet Anne Sexton explores this in her poem 'The Frog Prince':

Frog is as old as a cockroach.
Frog is my father's genitals.
Frog is a malformed doorknob.
Frog is a soft bag of green (164).

Far from encouraging supernatural beliefs, then, the tale encourages us to make sense of this world: superficial appearances are of less value than underlying characteristics, and girls (and boys) will come to terms with their desires (and sometimes absence thereof) over time.

Dawkins' attack on *The Frog Prince* reminded me that one of the charges against the controversial, beleaguered al-Madinah Free School in Derby (BBC np.) was that it 'banned fairy tales' (Owens np.). In both instances, the exhortation to stop recounting certain narratives is the same, even if the reasoning behind it comes from opposite extremes. As Zadie Smith shows in her novel *White Teeth*, families like the secular Chalfens, who are uncompromisingly scientific, atheist, and logical, affect children just as profoundly as Clara's religiously extreme Jehovah's Witness family. No matter what one's personal persuasion, coming down too hard on either side can warp young people who don't need contact with such absolutes too early on in their lives. There is enough space within the years of growing up for children to be exposed to a little magic and for them to escape unscathed from the exposure.

Far more dangerous than any potentially religious aspect of

fairy tales is when their lessons about gender roles are taken too seriously. Indeed, so much has been written about the 'princess myth' (see, for example, Smith 'Royal': np.) and its injurious allure for ever-younger females that I'm relieved I have boys. But this aspect doesn't seem to bother Dawkins, snug in his macho atheism.

As Arthur Bradley and Andrew Tate show in their path-breaking book *The New Atheist Novel*, authors like Ian McEwan, Philip Pullman, Martin Amis, and Salman Rushdie are indebted to New Atheist non-fiction writers such as Richard Dawkins, Sam Harris, and the late Christopher Hitchens. They share in common an urge to wage war on religion, and the belief that transcendence is only to be found in nature, love, and art. For most of these authors, literature is the pinnacle of art, so narrative—and its messiah, The Writer—is almost deified. Other idols include science and Enlightenment values, which the New Atheists often only partially understand or take on 'faith value'. Dawkins, of course, is embedded in the scientific community and its methods to a far greater degree than the other two; thus it is unsurprising that he has scorned the reverence for literature inherent in their creed and can expect a backlash even from these New Atheist high priests of the written word.

The Indian novelist Amit Chaudhuri writes: '[S]ecularism is a religion like any other, and its sacred texts are literary works' (np.). The only surprising thing about Dawkins' joyless opinion, therefore, is the attack he launches on one of New Atheism's shibboleths, literature. Stories are integral to culture and, as general public consensus will argue, shouldn't be prohibited, but nor should they be installed as secular totems, as some New Atheist writers try to do. It's perfectly possible to be sceptical of magic, while still believing in the enchantment of stories.

5

Journalists in Fiction and Reality

FROM THE SAFE CONFINES of my Paris hotel room, I watched helplessly as the attempted assassination of someone I know and admire unfolded live on Twitter. The Pakistani journalist, Raza Rumi, only narrowly avoided being sprayed with bullets on 28 March 2014. In response to the attack, he live-Tweeted that he had been 'dreading this day', acknowledging his anticipation of such an event. It is hard to believe someone would want to kill this gentle, erudite man, with his Sufistic approach to religion ('Rumi' is an adopted surname) and his laudably tolerant attitude (despite Pakistan's longstanding enmity with India, he has written an appreciative travel book about Delhi). His young driver, responsible for financially supporting several family members, was killed and his bodyguard badly wounded. Raza is now exiled overseas (as scholar in residence at Ithaca College in New York) and has been traumatized by these and similar events. Bina Shah summed up how I was feeling as I impotently read about the attack in Paris when she responded on social media to the attack: 'My heart sank and it still hasn't resurfaced.' Unlike Shah, I don't reside and make a living from my pen in Pakistan. But growing fear for the safety of my friends has caused me to feel more pessimistic about the nation's future than ever before.

Following this vicious attack on Rumi, even more (in)famously, the news anchor Hamid Mir was shot six times on 19 April 2014. His television station Geo accused the Inter-Services Intelligence

(ISI), the intelligence service of Pakistan, of being behind this attack. Geo faced governmental pressure and intense public criticism for this allegation. Despicable remarks were left on news comment pages as a result of the station's anti-ISI stance, which included the anti-Semitic conspiracist coinage 'Jew TV'. In response to this attack, the quotation I kept thinking of came from *Burnt Shadows* by Kamila Shamsie: '*How did it come to this*' (1; emphasis in original).

Reflecting on these atrocities, Pakistani journalist Mira Sethi wrote an impassioned, elegiac article, 'Age of Innocence', its title echoing both Edith Wharton and Moni Mohsin. In the piece, which is accompanied by faded family photographs, Sethi contrasts her own relatively carefree childhood with modern-day Pakistan, where a library has been named after Osama bin Laden, violence and securitization continues to escalate, and the mildest dissent is crushed. This might seem a rather nostalgic, selective vision of her early years in the 1990s, and, indeed, one online commenter urged her to 'remind yourself that that was the very worst period in Pakistan's history and one which helped lay the foundation for the problems being faced now'. Yet Sethi resorts to nostalgia knowingly; in the space of this short article, she recalls her uncle Shahid Sethi's kidnapping in 1997, as well as her father, the renowned journalist Najam Sethi's, similar abduction two years later. With bitter irony, she writes: '[T]hose were the good old days when the government picked you up and threw you in prison, but at least you got out alive.' This attitude finds resonance in Mohammed Hanif's dark humour in response to the journalist attacks, when he laments the passing of the days when the worst treatment journalists could expect from the ISI was 'light torture' ('Hamid Mir': np.). Sethi is well aware that today's 'country maddened by terror' (np.) has not been disgorged from a vacuum. Since her infancy, she has watched the harassing of family members for their political views and writings and understands that the current national climate is only an extension of what has come before.

Mira's brother, Ali Sethi, turns to fiction in writing about a journalist's travails during the same decade—the 1990s—in his novel *The Wish Maker*. But Ali Sethi also shows that the seeds of censorship and violence were sown in an earlier era, the 1980s of Zia's autocratic rule. (Another creative writer and journalist from an illustrious family, Fatima Bhutto, similarly highlights censorship as one of Zia's primary legacies in her memoir, *Songs of Blood and Sword*: 199–202.) Sethi's protagonist is a young man named Zaki, who has grown up in a Lahore household presided over by his liberal, widowed mother, Zakia. The latter edits a pioneering women's magazine and is described as 'an interventionist, a journalist who took risks and gave thrills' (121). This distinctive characterization ascribes several key attributes to the vocation of reporter and journalist: he or she should be politically involved, fearlessly confront hazards, speak truth to power, and always inform and entertain the public.

In Uzma Aslam Khan's *Trespassing*, one of the novel's four narrators, Daanish, studies journalism in Amherst, Massachusetts. There he discovers that the American 'freedoms' of expression and the press (the First Amendment of the United States Constitution) he hopes to be taught are deemed less important than the promotion of consumer confidence. During the 1991 Gulf War, Daanish keeps a journal charting his growing suspicion that the Iraqi invasion of Kuwait was actively encouraged by the US in order to justify an attack on its oil-rich former ally. Yet his coldly informal tutor shrugs aside this analysis as Daanish's 'tak[ing] pride in [his] own' (148)—in one phrase erasing the myriad differences between Arabs and Pakistanis, and reducing the contents of the journal to mere opinion (while hysterical American headlines about Saddam Hussein are curiously interpreted as factual).

Mumtaz, the femme fatale character from Mohsin Hamid's debut novel *Moth Smoke*, is an investigative journalist who writes under the pseudonym Zulfikar Manto. This name, with its resonances of one of the earliest globally recognized Pakistani–Anglophone writers (Zulfikar Ghose) and an internationally acclaimed Urdu short story writer and essayist (Saadat Hasan Manto), as well as its hint of politics (Zulfikar Ali Bhutto), indicates journalism's confluence of the creative with the political. The unnamed American in Hamid's next novel, *The Reluctant Fundamentalist*, may also be a journalist, depending on how you read this notoriously ambivalent text. There are possible links between the American interlocutor and *Wall Street Journal* reporter Daniel Pearl, who was brutally murdered by al-Qaida in Karachi in 2002.

In Kamila Shamsie's *Broken Verses*, the main character, Aasmani, takes a menial job in television soon after the 'cable TV explosion' of Musharraf's early 2000s government. The new media's strikingly female-dominated workforce idealistically seeks to bring 'youth culture, progressive thought, multiple perspectives, in-depth reporting' (4) to a Pakistani public previously accustomed to monochrome government propaganda. (As a side note, in her recent short story 'The Girl Next Door' (in Mahfouz 55–73) Shamsie takes up this issue of the female-led opening up of the Pakistani broadcast media though her portrayal of a make-up girl and a glamorous TV presenter against the backdrop of a wildly popular religious phone-in programme.) Although Aasmani isn't a journalist per se, the novel's detective elements, in which she tries to find out what happened to her mother and the latter's poet–lover may be read metaphorically as relating to the investigative work of the reporter.

The protagonist of Bina Shah's novel, *A Season for Martyrs*, Ali, also works in television, as a journalist. This book is set in Sindh and spans various eras—most prominently, 2007 to 2008, which

saw the Lawyers' Movement and Benazir Bhutto's return to, and
subsequent assassination in, Pakistan. It focuses on the way in
which Musharraf opened up the media only to effectively silence
it again during the lawyers' mass protests. A seasoned media figure
herself, Shah recognizes the artifice involved in the production of
television journalism. Indeed, as Ali's hard-nosed boss sees it: 'The
news was not about honest emotion, but about smooth edges and
the right sound bite' (30).

Journalists are in danger more than ever in today's Pakistan. The
perils they stare down, as well as broader debates about freedom
of speech and censorship, have long been represented in fiction.
This should not surprise us, because many creative writers also
work as journalists, and the two disciplines of journalism and
fiction share many common features. I believe that the press must
not be muzzled. Pakistan needs to foster a culture that invites
and encourages talking, listening, and arguing, as evinced in
the country's young but growing tradition of literature festivals.
Nothing will be settled by abuse, threats, shooting, and bombs.
Everything will remain unsettled.

II

PAKISTAN'S CITIES AND REGIONS

6

The Baloch Who Is Missing:
Representations of Balochistan in
Anglophone Prose

IN APRIL 2015, Pakistani entrepreneur, arts patron, and human rights campaigner, Sabeen Mahmud, was shot and killed by unknown assassins. At the time of the shooting, Sabeen was accompanied by her elderly mother, the redoubtable educationalist Mahenaz Mahmud, who took two bullets in the attack but survived. They were leaving an event—'Unsilencing Balochistan'—in Karachi, which the 40-year-old had organized to be held at her community arts space The Second Floor, widely known as T2F. It may be mere coincidence that Sabeen was killed immediately after the controversial panel discussion on Pakistan's battle-weary southwest province. However, not long before the event, the Lahore University of Management Sciences (LUMS) was prevented by governmental pressure from hosting 'Unsilencing Balochistan'. Sabeen, too, received numerous threats after stepping in with the offer of her space, T2F, to prevent the event from being cancelled altogether. While culprits supposedly 'confessed' to the murder as early as May 2015 (Tunio np.), two years later these accused men were appealing their conviction. One key witness, Ghulam Abbas—Sabeen's driver and a former policeman—had also been murdered less than five months after her killing (F. Khan 'Justice': np.). In light of this penumbrous history, it may be years before the

43

full truth emerges about the circumstances surrounding Sabeen's tragic murder.

I didn't know Sabeen, but many of my friends in Pakistan and its British diaspora knew her well and always spoke warmly of her. Her legacy is immense, but at what cost to her and her loved ones. Until April, I always imagined that I would eventually visit T2F and meet Sabeen in person. The realization that this is now impossible set me on a path of finding out more about Balochistan, its literary representation, and the reasons why the province needs 'unsilencing'.

The Baloch have long been known for their 'strong national consciousness' (Dashti 341), inter-clan rivalries, and practice of forming short-term alliances against a common enemy. During the Raj period, this made it easier for the British to exercise their classic destructive tactics of bringing particular leaders into the fold, excluding others, and exercising a strategy of divide and rule to accelerate the splintering of various factions. Not quite a princely state, officially a protectorate, the Khanate of Kalat (comprising the majority of Balochistan) was a loose federation of tribes and their sardars or chiefs.

In one of Rudyard Kipling's least impressive poems, a piece of woman-hating doggerel entitled 'The Story of Uriah' (1886), the British colonizers' attitude towards the 'hill tribes' is adumbrated. The poem centres on a hapless colonial administrator, Jack Barrett, whose superior officer has banished him to what is sarcastically described as 'that very healthy post' of Quetta (10). We learn that the officer has been having an affair with Jack's wife in the verdant hill station of Simla and therefore wants Jack out of the way. Within a month of his enforced transfer, Jack dies and his body is interred in a 'Quetta graveyard', whereupon Mrs Barrett 'mourned for him | Five lively months at most' (10). Easily discernible in this poem is a sneering British attitude towards the strategic base of Quetta as a remote, backward, and disease-ridden outpost.

There is scant more affection for the hilly landscape around Quetta in Bertram Mitford's *The Ruby Sword* (1899). Subtitled 'A Romance of Baluchistan', this is a *fin de siècle* colonial adventure story written by a scion of the aristocratic Mitford family. Its civilian hero, Howard Campian, is on his first visit to the region. He portrays its landscape as bleak, lacking in flora except uniform juniper bushes, and occasionally battered by vicious floods. Campian finds the terrain difficult to read; vast, indifferent, and alien:

> Here a smooth, unbroken slab of rock, sloping at the well nigh precipitous angle of a high-pitched roof—there, at an easier slant, a great expanse of rock face, seamed and criss-crossed with chasms, like the crevasses on a glacier. No vegetation, either, to relieve the all pervading, depressing greyness, save where a ragged juniper or pistachio had found anchor along a ledge, or fringed the lip of some dark chasm aforesaid. No turn of the road brought any relief to the eye—any lifting of the unconscious oppression which lay upon the mind; ever the same hills, sheering aloft, fearsome in their dark ruggedness, conveying the idea of vast and wellnigh [*sic*] untrodden fastnesses, grim, repellent, mysterious (16–17).

Campian compares the sharp tilt of a Baloch cliff to the comforting domestic image of Britain's sloping rooftops, and emphasizes the desert's climactic extremes through the glacier simile. Despite these attempts to make the landscape familiar, the featureless landscape depresses the spirit, troubles the eye, and afflicts the mind with its 'fearsome [...] dark ruggedness'. This uninviting depiction of Balochistan chimes with intrepid British travel writer Harry de Windt's 1891 book, *A Ride to India Across Persia and Baluchistàn*,

in which he claims that it is a 'standing joke' (220) that in all of
Balochistan there is just one tree.

In Mitford's novel, Campian settles down to an enjoyable Anglo–
Indian routine of hunting, drinking 'pegs' while having 'gup' with
other ex-pats (56, 30), and engaging in directionless flirtation with
a pretty young army belle. He quickly abandons these activities after
a chance encounter with his ex-fiancée, Vivien Wynier. At its heart,
this novel is about the rekindling of Campian and Wynier's love,
but this is embedded within a preposterous but enjoyable quest for
a precious sword lost in Balochistan decades earlier. Hook-nosed,
brutal Baloch characters pop up from time to time, almost always
intent on murdering our hero. The 'Pathan' servant, Bhallu Khan,
is portrayed as brave and loyal, but with the authorial proviso that
one never quite knows where one stands with 'Mohammedans'
(82, 160). The unlikeable British character Bracebrydge is overtly
racist towards the Baloch and Pashtuns, calling them 'niggers' and
sanctioning unprovoked violence against them (97). Yet even the
more sympathetic British characters, such as Campian and his host
John Upward, view the Baloch's 'religious fanaticism' and 'utterly
fearless, utterly reckless' temperament as pathological traits (21).
This widespread opinion accords with the racist martial race theory
to which most colonizers subscribed. In his 1933 work, *The Martial
Races of India*, Sir George MacMunn lumped Baloch together with
Pashtuns as having innately 'sporting, high-spirited, adventurous'
personalities (239).

When I am occasionally called upon to explain Balochistan's
post-1947 situation to British friends whose knowledge in
this area is lacking, I use two analogies. The first compares the
Baloch tripartite scattering between Pakistan, Afghanistan, and
Iran with that of their Kurdish neighbours between Iran, Iraq,
and Turkey. Kurds and Baloch can be identified, to adapt Luigi
Pirandello (1954), as two peoples in search of a homeland. Another

admittedly inexact parallel is between Balochistan and Bangladesh. Both regions were subsumed under the Pakistani nation-state following the 1947 Partition, but each had, and continues to have, proudly distinct cultural heritage, language, and loyalties. Whereas India eventually threw its weight behind the Bangladesh War of Liberation in 1971, Pakistan's hostile neighbour has never openly aided the Baloch struggle. Yet in her 2014 book *Capitalism: A Ghost Story*, Arundhati Roy claims that India covertly funds the rebels in Balochistan (88). Unlike the Bangladeshis', the Baloch's 1970s nationalist struggle did not meet with the same support or success. The bloody insurgency that lasted between 1974 and 1977 caused the deaths of approximately 5,300 ethnic Baloch and 3,000 Pakistani military personnel (Dunne np.). General Tikka Khan was known as the alliterative Butcher of both Bengal and Balochistan, and he wreaked terrible atrocities on both nations in the 1970s. As with the loss of Bangladesh, volatile Balochistan continues to trouble the idea of Pakistan.

In 1947, Balochistan was promised the status of an independent state, but after just nine months the first of four post-Second World War Baloch uprisings took place. Consequentially the Khan of Kalat signed an instrument of Balochistan's uneasy accession to the Pakistani state. After a revolt in the early 1960s that was partly influenced by Marxist–Leninist politics, a more serious struggle ensued between 1973 and 1977 in the western borderlands. Even Zulfikar Ali Bhutto's granddaughter, Fatima Bhutto, admits in her book *Songs of Blood and Sword* that there was 'no larger problem' that arose during her admired grandfather's tenure as Pakistani prime minister (between 1973 and 1977) than the repressive role he played in Balochistan, 'a province blighted by Pakistan' (115). The official government line, by contrast, is that the insurgency was the work of a few miscreants manipulated by powerful sardars.

It is the fractious period of the early 1960s to the early 1970s that the late Jamil Ahmad examined in his short story series, *The Wandering Falcon*. Ahmad's loosely interlinked short stories were written around the time that the major Balochistan conflict erupted, in 1973. According to Basharat Peer, 'Ahmad stashed away his first draft, leaving it untouched for three decades' ('Wandering': np.) and the book wasn't finalized for almost forty years. Three years before the author's death it found a publisher in 2011, when the region was again roiled by state violence against separatists. From a Baloch perspective, the Punjabi author Ahmad could similarly be cast as an interloper, alongside those earlier British authors, Kipling, Mitford, and de Windt. Yet because he worked for many years as a civil servant in the western borderlands and Northern Areas, his fiction has both insight and refinement. For example, Ahmad's characters convey a different view of the topography than the three Britons' impressions:

> [T]he land—their land—had seen to it that beauty and colour were not erased completely from their lives. It offered them a thousand shades of grey and brown with which it tinted its hills, its sands and its earth. There were subtle changes of colour in the blackness of the nights and the brightness of the days, and the vigorous colours of the tiny desert flowers hidden in the dusty bushes, and of the gliding snakes and scurrying lizards as they buried themselves in the sand. To the men, beauty and colour were rampant around them (21).

Rather than the 'depressing greyness' (16) that pervades Campian's depiction of Balochistan, the locals' trained eyes can make out hundreds of earthy hues in the parched landscape. Flora and fauna add still more colour to the vista.

Suffused with this understated iridescence, Ahmad's first story in the collection, 'The Sins of the Mother', is set near Balochistan's Siahpad Tribal Area. It concerns a young couple who elope from

Kurd Killa, have a baby together whom they name Tor Baz, and are eventually slain in an 'honour' killing—only the young child Tor Baz surviving. The settings of other stories in the collection include a waterhole belonging to the Mengals (a Brahui tribe) and the cross-Af-Pak routes of the nomadic Kharot tribe. The story collection loops northwards as it progresses, following the Bildungsroman of Tor Baz and his interactions with a shifting cast of other characters into Waziristan, a frontier area near Peshawar, then up to Chitral, dropping back down into the nomadic Gujjars' trekking routes, and ending in the Swat Valley.

The third story in the collection, 'The Death of Camels', is set in 1961, when the Durand Line between Afghanistan and Pakistan (first established in 1893) was officially closed. This had a deleterious impact on the Kharot nomads, 'whose entire lives were spent in wandering with the seasons' (37) and who, as a consequence, were (and still are) required to procure travel documents if they wish to traverse the frontier. In the short story, the Kharots allow one of their women to advance towards the border soldiers carrying a Qur'an on her head, since their Ryvaj tribal code dictates that this gesture will guarantee a cessation of violence (Ahmad 59; Lieven 353). This is disregarded by the soldiers, and '[m]en, women and children died. Gul Jana's belief that the Koran would prevent tragedy died too' (60). The shooting of the woman bearing a copy of the Qur'an also metaphorically communicates that Pakistan's creation myth as a state designed to protect the region's Muslims of all different ethnic, linguistic, and cultural backgrounds is a hollow promise. Ahmad's narrator criticizes the Pakistani government for its harsh treatment and corrupt manipulation of the Baloch and Pashtuns, as when twin brothers from the Wazir tribe are compelled to commit a robbery in order to pay a 2,000 rupee bribe extorted by government officials (88). Yet in this remarkably balanced collection, Ahmad also conveys, without judgement, the Baloch macho factionalism and their strong, corrosive sense of dishonour. The rough justice meted out by their jirga (assembly of leaders) has a devastating impact, especially on women, adulterers, and minority ethnic and religious groups.

In 1983, Salman Rushdie published his novel *Shame*, which in his memoir, *Joseph Anton* (2012), he describes as 'the second part of the diptych in which he [Rushdie] examined the world of his origins' (6). Following the triumphant publication of the mostly Indian-based *Midnight's Children* in 1981, *Shame* focuses on a country that is 'not Pakistan, or not quite' (29). In the text, Rushdie eventually gives his imaginary land the name Peccavistan, borrowing from the apocryphal declaration supposedly made by General Charles Napier (1782–1853): 'Peccavi', meaning 'I have Sindh/sinned' (88). Although Rushdie penned this novel in the early 1980s, the principal decade it examines is the 1970s. As several critics have noted (Almond 1146; Ben-Yishai 195; Strandberg 144), Rushdie explores the adversarial relationship between Zia ul-Haq (Raza Hyder in the novel) and his predecessor, Zulfikar Ali Bhutto (Iskander Harappa). Less commonly recognized is the emphasis that the novel places on the 'genocide in Balochistan' (70) between 1973 and 1977.

Much of *Shame* is set in the border town of Q., which, despite the narrator's insistence that 'Q. is not really Quetta at all' (29), has clear parallels with the frontier outpost depicted in Kipling's 'The Story of Uriah'. As with the nineteenth-century poem, Rushdie portrays the city in purgatorial terms, as 'some borderland of hell' (14) that is 'near the very Rim of Things' (22). Plagued by earthquakes like the one that tore apart Balochistan in 1935, Q. is fringed by the Impossible Mountains and the fiercely sought-after gas fields of the Needle Valley. The unforgiving 'noonday insanity of the sun' (12) in this region causes Zoroaster, the father of 'peripheral hero' (126)

Omar Khayyam Shakil's first love, to lose his wits. Zoroaster lives out his days as a customs officer, stark naked among the broken mirror shards and bollards that mark the border he is supposed to be guarding. Physically, the town of Q. is shaped like a dumb-bell: it comprises two ellipsoids, one the white cantonment area and the other the 'higgling and piggling edifices' of the South Asian area (11), with only the slightest point of tangency in between.

In the 'no-man's-land' (41) between Cantt and the bazaar live the Shakil family. The family is made up of Mr Shakil, who dies on the novel's opening page; the 'isolated trinity' (13) of his daughters, Chhunni, Munnee, and Bunny; and their shared son, Omar Khayyam. As in the colonial texts, there are few mentions of the southwest's indigenous peoples. On the rare occasions that these peoples are referred to, initially they are depicted in simultaneously ominous and homogenizing ways: these 'thin-eyed, rock-hard tribals' (23) belong to 'a culture of the edge' (24). The only individuated Baloch that readers encounter are the widow Farida and her brother, Bilal Balloch. They are stereotypically bent on revenge for the death of their loved one, the handyman Yakoob. He is suspected to have been poisoned by the Shakil sisters, after he built a dumb waiter for them so as to provide complete seclusion from the outside world. The Balloches' attempt at garlanding Omar Khayyam with a necklace of shoes is thwarted, and instead they accidentally festoon the apparently devout postman, Muhammad Ibadalla, with the insulting string of footwear. Soon afterwards, we learn that, unbeknownst to each other, both Farida and her best friend Zeenat Kabuli enter into affairs with Ibadalla. Conforming to the received image of the Baloch ruthlessness and penchant for blood feuds, the affairs end with Ibadalla, Bilal Balloch, and Zeenat's husband dying in a knife fight. Not unduly dismayed, the two women 'shack [...] up together instead' (45) and disappear from the narrative.

Rushdie's portrayal of Balochistan and its 'suspicious tribals' (5) therefore has many continuities with the nineteenth-century tales of the wild-eyed, feuding Baloch. But as a South Asian, Rushdie is simultaneously alert to the 'need and desire in primal fantasies' (Bhabha 118) that are at play in such stereotypes. He is also struck by the tragedy that in Pakistan religion is incapable of 'bind[ing] together peoples (Punjabi, Sindhi, Bengali, Baloch, Pathan) whom geography and history had long kept apart'. Rushdie therefore perceives the country with its metaphorical broken wings as a 'misshapen bird' (*Anton*: 60). He writes with sympathy, albeit in the abstract, about 'the guerrillas in Baluchistan' and castigates the Pakistani government's 'draconian punitive measures' against them in the 1970s (28, 101). Omar Khayyam's younger half-brother, Babar Shakil, joins these separatists, convinced as he is by a Baloch speech that he makes to him, while they are sitting together in a bar, about the Pakistani government stripping the province of its food, minerals, and gas, consequently 'screwing [the Baloch] from here to eternity' (131). Babar's end is swift. He is cut down by Raza Hyder's bullets, whereupon he is transformed into a seraph. Rushdie's portrayal of Balochistan culminates in the unveiling of eighteen shawls created by the scorned wife of Iskander Harappa (Bhutto's alter ego), on which are stitched the shameful details of his presidency:

What he did for the sake of no-more-secessions, in the name of never-another-East-Wing, the bodies sprawled across the shawl, the men without genitals, the sundered legs, the intestines in place of faces [...] *I have lost count of the corpses on my shawl, twenty, fifty, a hundred thousand dead, who knows, and not enough scarlet thread on earth to show the blood*, the people hanging upside down with dogs at their open guts, the people grinning lifelessly with bullet-holes for second mouths, the people united in the worm-feast of that shawl of flesh and death (194–5; emphasis in original).

In her field-defining book *Resistance Literature* (1987), US academic Barbara Harlow includes a short discussion of 'The Case of the Baluch' amidst exploration of the Palestinian, Sandinista, Mau Mau, and other liberation struggles. At the time Harlow was writing—under General Zia's 1977 to 1988 dictatorship—there existed an uneasy truce between the Pakistan Army and the Baloch, part of Zia's policy of 'non-provocative firmness' towards this region (Dunne np.). Yet the 1980s was also the decade in which vast numbers of refugees, fleeing the Soviet occupation of Afghanistan, crossed the porous border with Pakistan to seek sanctuary in Balochistan and the North-West Frontier Province (now Khyber Pakhtunkhwa). This caused diplomatic wrangling, resource squeeze, and ethnic and religious—Sunni and Shia—tensions between Baloch, Pashtun, and Hazara (Shaikh 56; Dunne np.). In Balochi poetry, Harlow perceives 'a sadness engendered by an ongoing struggle, a struggle not yet consummated' (41). Through readings of poems by Balach Khan, whom she terms a 'Baluch resistance poet' (43), Harlow makes the case against Punjabi hegemony and the stripping of the region's natural resources.

Focusing on the positive aspect of her argument, Harlow is in favour of the Baloch right to territorial self-determination. But Balochistan is no Palestine; it has had little experience of self-governance. What is more, unlike the Bengalis and Kurds, there isn't an established Baloch middle class or a history of political activity. Indeed, Anatol Lieven argues that independence would only bring 'a Somali-style nightmare, in which a range of tribal parties—all calling themselves "democratic" and "national"—under rival warlords would fight for power and wealth' (357).

Perhaps a solution can be found that bridges the gap between

Harlow's resistance and Lieven's pro-army stance. The creation
of a semi-autonomous Pakistani Balochistan, in which only its
currency, defence, and foreign affairs are the responsibility of
central government, might go some way towards assuaging the
Baloch grievances. Their complaints are mostly about the unequal
distribution of the region's rich resources: gold, copper, zinc, oil,
and natural gas. Balochistan is easily Pakistan's largest province,
but it has the least numerous, poorest, and most undereducated
population. A new bone of contention is the deep sea port of
Gwadar, which from the early 2000s onwards was developed as
part of Sino–Pakistani collaboration. Many Baloch feel that the
port has prompted another invasion of Punjabis to the area and
is doing nothing to help indigenous uplift. As Babar Ayaz argues:
'For over six decades Balochistan has been exploited. This has now
convinced many Baloch leaders that nothing short of independence
would solve their problems' (77).

The nationalist view that Balochistan is being colonized by
outsiders has become even more convincing since 2005. That
year Shazia Khalid, a doctor, was raped in Dera Bugti District,
reportedly by a Pakistani army officer (Cowasjee np.). Her assault
sparked an angry Baloch uprising, to which the government
responded with force. Since then, Balochistan has been in a state
approaching civil war. For the first time, nationalists have been
subjected to enforced disappearances. Sometimes they are released,
but are so badly tortured and frightened that they refuse to speak of
their experiences (Human Rights Watch 43). However, increasingly,
they are no longer released and instead are being murdered. The
bodies of the disappeared are then usually dumped in public places.

In 2013, Pakistani novelist and journalist Mohammed Hanif
wrote a short, generically indeterminate book about human rights,
or the lack thereof, in Pakistan. He conducted interviews with
relatives of the disappeared and wove them into the six loosely

connected, hard-hitting true stories that comprise *The Baloch Who Is Not Missing and Others Who Are*. From the father who is overwhelmed by excessive bureaucratic paperwork when his son disappears in 'The Baloch Who Is Not Missing Anymore', to the sister who puts her personal life on hold as she protests for her brother's release in 'A Sister's Vigil', these voices tell of the Kafkaesque bureaucracy and callous authorities these families are up against.

One particularly apt example of the injustice of the Pakistani authorities is demonstrated in 'The Journalist who Became a Uniform Contractor'. This short story centres on the character of Mohammed Bilal Mengal, who ekes out a living covering local events for a small newspaper called *Independent*. Through his journalism contacts, Bilal and his 22-year-old son, Khalid, make a little money on the side sewing uniforms for soldiers at Noshki Fort. Out of the blue, Khalid is forcibly disappeared by their previously friendly army employers. A soldier named Naib Subedar Ramzan ventured into the city without permission and was injured in a firing incident. Bilal and then Khalid come under suspicion of orchestrating the attack, even though neither man fits the physical description of the assailant. One Frontier Corps official admits frankly: 'Their man was ambushed in the city, what were they supposed to do? Sit quietly and tell their bosses they didn't know who attacked their man?' (22–3). Needing to make an arrest, the soldiers detain the nearest people to hand: 'their own tailoring contractor and his son' (23). Whereas Bilal is soon released, the younger Khalid remains in detention for over a year, his whereabouts unknown. Neither man takes much of an interest in politics; certainly, they are not the violent separatists portrayed by the military. For being the wrong ethnicity in the wrong place at the wrong time, they can be punished with impunity. The 2011 Human Rights Watch World Report, 'We Can Torture, Kill, Or

Keep You for Years', supports this account of the Balochistan situation: 'Those responsible for enforced disappearances [...] have not been held accountable' (5).

Hanif's rendering of the 2010s 'kill and dump' policy, Rushdie's depiction of the mass killings of the 1970s, and Ahmad's portrayal of both governmental and inter-tribal violence in this lawless region after the Second World War together demonstrate the severe and longstanding human rights problem in Balochistan. However, it is worth considering the poignant rhetorical question Kamila Shamsie poses of academic Mushtaq Bilal in his book of interviews with Pakistani authors: 'Where is the English language novel about Balochistan?' (*Writing*: 150). Although Balochistan was a popular setting for colonial writers such as Kipling and Mitford, until recently Baloch were missing from Pakistani prose writing in English. This may partly be accounted for by censorship (whether deriving from the state or writerly self-restraint). As the narrator of Jamil Ahmad's story 'A Point of Honour' observes:

> There was complete and total silence about the Baluchis, their cause, their lives and their deaths. No newspaper editor risked punishment on their behalf. Typically, Pakistani journalists sought salve for their conscience by writing about the wrongs done to men in South Africa, in Indonesia, in Palestine and in the Philippines—not to their own people. No politician [...] would [...] expose the wrong being done outside their front door (33).

Writing in the 1970s (although his book wasn't published until 2011), Ahmad made the bleak observation that the dead of Balochistan 'will live in no songs; no memorials will be raised to them' (34). This is starting to change. Although the songs are currently being sung by only a few weak voices and the memorials are makeshift and puny, they nonetheless create an impact. An increasing number of writers are turning their attention to this war-torn nation. Perhaps more will join their ranks in the wake of *littérateuse* Sabeen Mahmud's tragic murder.

In her 1988 essay, Gayatri Chakravorty Spivak famously argues that academics must not 'speak for' subalterns (303), but rather 'learn' from them, recognizing their 'heterogeneity' (Young *White*: 210, 215). In *Shame*, Rushdie similarly complicates his own legitimacy, as a diasporic outsider, in speaking for the frontier region of Quetta and doing so in 'Angrezi' to boot (38). 'You have no right to this subject', he chides himself, only to counter this with questions: 'Is history to be considered the property of the participants only? In what courts are such claims staked, what boundary commissions map out the territories?' (28). It is certainly disappointing that very little Balochi–Anglophone fiction exists, but it is heartening that a growing number of non-Baloch–Pakistani writers are venturing into the territory of this 'insufficiently imagined' (Rushdie *Shame*: 87) province. In 2011, Cara Cilano published a monograph about representations of the 1971 War in Pakistani writing. It is my hope that one day a scholar will find enough material to do the same for Balochistan.

7

Holy Women, *Waderas*, and 'Weapons of the Weak': Sindh in Contemporary Women's Writing

AFTER THE PUBLICATION OF CHAPTER 6—'The Baloch Who Is Missing: Representations of Balochistan in Anglophone Prose'—in the *Dawn* newspaper, a reader requested a further article—this time focusing on Sindh and its literary representations, because 'Sindh and Sindhis too are suffering in Pakistan'. In her article 'Who has Sin'd?', Ayesha Siddiqa makes a similar link between the troubled provinces of Balochistan and Sindh (np.). Responding to this reader-requested prompt, I delved into researching Pakistan's southeast, as depicted in fiction by four women writers.

In her book about post-Partition Sindh, Sarah Ansari shows that Karachi has long been a cosmopolitan city. However, rural Sindh has been stereotyped as a backward outpost, subject to outdated customs, and ruled by landlords, tribal leaders, and pirs. In fact, Ansari argues: 'Change, just as much as continuity was the order of the day' (17).

Social, economic, and political change (and conflict) accelerated with Partition. Of all provinces, Sindh took in the largest number of migrants from India in 1947. Amid the optimism of Pakistan's Independence, muhajirs were supposed to be greeted as 'new Sindhis'. Instead, the reception towards them became increasingly hostile as time passed. Many of the muhajirs who migrated were urban, wealthy, powerful, and held the view that Lucknow and Delhi were culturally superior to Sindh and Punjab. This caused immense animosity, but perhaps this was entirely natural, as Kamila Shamsie observes, 'in such extensive migration there are always clashes between indigenous peoples and newcomers' (qtd. in Chambers *British*: 219).

One famous example of a Sindhi Hindu who travelled in the opposite direction—to India—is Bharatiya Janata Party (BJP) leader and Ayodhya mosque-destroyer, Lal Krishna Advani. Advani was born into a Hindu family in Karachi, and he and his family fled the city in 1947. The horrors of Partition that he witnessed contributed to his opposition to the two-nation theory and disdain for Muslims.

Urdu poet Fahmida Riaz was born in Uttar Pradesh, but soon afterwards her family was propelled by Partition to move to Hyderabad in central Sindh. Her English-language story 'The Daughters of Aai' loosely fits into the genre of autobiographical fiction. In this short story, a group of village women make the journey to Karachi to seek help from the narrator, a well-known left-wing authoress. In their sector of society, women procreate at a young age; the main petitioner, Aai, is only 35 or 40 years old and yet she has sought out the writer to plead for the latter's help with her mentally disabled daughter, Fatimah, who is pregnant. Aai reveals that Fatimah has been raped, not for the first time, by an unknown assailant. It is too late for an abortion, but Aai fears an 'honour' killing may ensue if her condition is publicized. Eventually, a local landlord's new second wife, who has been faking a pregnancy to shore up her position, finds out about Fatimah's pregnancy and asks for the baby. When Fatimah returns to the village after the birth and secret adoption, the other women pretend that she was possessed by djinn and is now a holy woman.

This dénouement reminds one of Qaisra Shahraz's debut novel,

The Holy Woman, which takes as its protagonist a Sindhi virgin
called Zarri Bano. In this novel, when her brother dies suddenly,
Zarri Bano's father breaks off her engagement, since she is now his
heir. He forces her to marry the Qur'an and retain her inherited
land for the family's patriarchs. This cruel practice occasionally
occurs in parts of Sindh and elsewhere in Pakistan. The Prevention
of Anti-Women Practices Bill 2008 (passed in 2011) made the
practice illegal, but this does not stop it from intriguing writers.
Similarly, in Tariq Ali's *Night of the Golden Butterfly*, the Sindhi
character, Zaynab, marries the Qur'an to keep her inherited money
in the family. But Bina Shah, in her latest book *A Season for Martyrs*,
which I discuss later, describes Qur'an marriage as one amongst a
raft of myths associated with Sindhis.

In Pakistani–American Shaila Abdullah's debut collection,
Beyond the Cayenne Wall, the story 'Ashes to Ashes, Dust to Dust'
focuses on the 'dying fishing industry' in a fictional town 100 miles
outside Karachi (np.). The community portrayed are probably
makranis, Baloch–Sindhi fisherfolk. After protagonist Dhool's
husband loses his trawling livelihood, she becomes a ragpicker
in Karachi, scavenging for scraps she and her four children can
survive on. She leaves her husband when, keen to pay his gambling
debts, he accepts on behalf of their eldest daughter a proposal from
a much older man. Returning to their shack unaware that this
agreement has taken place, Dhool finds that the predatory groom
has carried off her barely pubescent daughter. Another short story,
'Demons of the Past', features a California-based, Karachi-raised
woman, Siham, who travels to interior Sindh to confront her
biological mother who gave her up for adoption. In the 'timeless
heritage' of her mother's house, which calls to mind 'a castle in the
fairy tales of Alif Laila', Siham demands to know the truth about
the man who impregnated her mother at 15 years old. Reluctantly,
the matriarch confesses that it was her own father who raped her,

so that Siham's grandfather 'was also [her] father!' (np.). In lively, sensationalist manner, Abdullah's stories give the impression of a Sindh throbbing with regular incidents of incest and child marriage.

Bina Shah's *A Season for Martyrs* unfolds in Sindh at different points in history, including the mid-eighteenth century world of poet–mystic Shah Abdul Latif, as well as 1843 when Sir Charles Napier allegedly wrote his victory joke '*Peccavi*', or 'I have sinned/ Sindh'. The contemporary storyline of 2007 to 2008 focuses on the assassination of Benazir Bhutto and its aftermath. Despite its wide-ranging historical strands, the narrative is defiantly modern, contrasting with earlier portrayals of Sindh as retrograde. The central character, Ali, is angered by the dominant media image of 'Sindhis as bloodthirsty plantation owners who kept their poor peasants in chains and raped the village girls and chased down runaway bonded laborers with dogs' (18). Ali recalls the year of 1990, when muhajirs in Hyderabad killed 130 Sindhis. His selective memory neglects the Sindhi reprisals against muhajirs that ensued. Sindh's diversity is evoked through Ali's girlfriend, Sunita, and his colleague, Ram, who are both Hindus. Readers are reminded of Muslims' and Hindus' long cohabitation in Sindh and the syncretism that sometimes led to joint worship at rural Sufi shrines. But this is no narrowly pro-Sindhi narrative, and Shah is clear-eyed in her depiction of 'the alphabet soup that made up Pakistani politics: PPP, PML, Q, N, F, ANP [Awami National Party], BNP [Balochistan National Party], MQM [Muttahida Qaumi Movement]—everyone jockeying for a piece of the very valuable pie' (35). What is more, despite her popularity throughout much of Sindh, Benazir Bhutto is far from idealized in this narrative, and Shah is alert to the late prime minister's flaws and corruption. The narrative voice concedes that travel to rural Sindh seems like a 'step […] back in time' (194), and *waderas* or landowners are a mixed bunch, some corrupt and lascivious, and others honourable.

A common thread that binds these writers' representations of Sindh is their interest in women's oppression and methods of protest. To varying degrees, the authors explore women's labour, participation in religious life, and place in feudal society. Riaz, Abdullah, and Shahraz treat rural Sindh as a backdrop and are critical of its patriarchal culture. In contrast, Shah brings the region to front and centre, and warns against accepting received ideas about Sindh.

Hope lies in these female protagonists' resourcefulness, ingenuity, and faith, which James C. Scott would call 'weapons of the weak' (Scott *passim*). Although Scott scrutinizes Malaysia and is concerned with class rather than gender, his identification of 'the tenacity of self-preservation—in ridicule, in truculence, in irony, in petty acts of non-compliance, in foot dragging, in dissimulation' (350) is applicable to Sindhi females' resistance to intersectional oppressions. In different ways, all four authors position women as the vehicle of empowerment, sovereignty, and human rights in Sindh.

8

'Lahore Lahore Hai': Bapsi Sidhwa and Mohsin Hamid's Urban Fiction

IN NOVEMBER 2013, an Indian television advertisement for Google entitled 'The Reunion' went viral on YouTube, garnering over 4 million hits from India, Pakistan, and the wider world in just five days (Associated Press; Google India). The advert pivots on the friendship of two boys from different religious backgrounds who were separated due to the partition of the Indian subcontinent in 1947. Now an old man living in Delhi, the Hindu boy, Baldev Mehra, reminisces with his granddaughter, Saman, about his younger years spent flying kites and stealing sweets in what is today's Pakistan. He recalls his best friend, Yusuf, especially fondly, and so, utilizing the Google search engine function, Saman traces this fellow septuagenarian and brings him to Delhi to be reunited with Baldev on the latter's birthday. The commercial generated largely positive reactions on both sides of the border, although Associated Press quotes one second-generation Partition migrant's observation that it is not so easy for ordinary people to travel between India and Pakistan amidst the ongoing enmity between the two countries.

For the purposes of this chapter focusing on the city as a simultaneously material and textualized space, what is most noteworthy about 'The Reunion' is that Yusuf lives in Lahore— the antique city which Baldev and his family fled, never to return.

Indeed, the way in which Lahore is represented in this tear-jerking advertisement is suggestive of the nostalgic diasporic lens through which the city is often depicted, especially in India. Its opening scene features the call to prayer from a red-brick, white-domed mosque. This is presumably intended to be the city's most famous monument, the Badshahi Mosque, commissioned in the late seventeenth century by the Mughal Emperor Aurangzeb (1618–1707). In the course of her research, Saman Googles Lahore's ancient history, parks, city gates, and sweet shops—all rich, culturally loaded, and recollective images of the city. In this short film as in much other cultural production, Lahore is made emblematic of Partition and the shared history of these two hostile subcontinental neighbours. As historian Gyanendra Pandey honestly states, Partition's legacy is 'an extraordinary love–hate relationship'. This relationship is split between on the one hand anger, hatred, and nationalism, and on the other 'a considerable sense of nostalgia, frequently articulated in the view that this was a partition of siblings that should never have occurred' (Pandey 2). The viral Google-sponsored advertisement tacitly supports, and helps to answer, this chapter's central concerns, namely: how are South Asian cities and regions imagined by their inhabitants—both elites and the poor—their diasporic communities, and their artists? Additionally, how does Partition and its aftermath continue to impinge upon such imaginings of the Punjab, the province that was most affected by the violence and population exchange that occurred in 1947? The emphasis in this chapter is on redressing imaginings that are shaped by what Salman Rushdie terms 'city eyes' (*Midnight's*: 81); that is, an inattention to the marginalized denizens of urban spaces.

The Punjab has long been an area of key importance to (pre-)colonial India and to postcolonial India and Pakistan. The two Punjabs experienced overlapping but distinct aftershocks from the advent of British imperialism, great trauma during Partition, relative economic vitality and hegemony within their nations, and centrality in the reinventions and imaginings of the postcolonial Indian and Pakistani nation-states. In an effort to enhance understandings of Punjabi literature, history, and anthropology, I examine depictions of the Pakistani Punjab, and particularly its ancient capital of Lahore, in texts by Bapsi Sidhwa and Mohsin Hamid—two prominent writers who are from that city and are among its most observant chroniclers.

However, these two writers have also lived for significant periods of time outside of Lahore—specifically, in the United States. Therefore, their perspectives on the city are to some extent moulded by what Dennis Walder terms 'postcolonial nostalgia'.[1] Sidhwa, born in 1938, is from the generation affected by India's partition and the creation of Pakistan, while Hamid was born in 1971, the year of a second partition after a bloody war of independence which resulted in Bangladesh seceding from Pakistan.

As well as exploring these authors' representations of the city's topographical, cultural, religious, and linguistic diversity, this chapter also examines a central but taboo locus of Lahore as depicted in novels by Sidhwa and Hamid. The iconic red-light district, Heera Mandi, stands incongruously close to a key religious site, the Badshahi Mosque. Heera Mandi is often frequented by powerful, wealthy, and religiously orthodox clientele, but the people who depend on it for their livelihood are urban outcasts (see Chakraborty and al-Wazedi 1–18). Notwithstanding the whiff of scandal surrounding this district, Heera Mandi is increasingly becoming a hipster playground of the rich, liberal, and not so liberal classes, who are happy to pay European prices for cappuccinos and curries overlooking the Badshahi Mosque. As the academic Louise Brown remarks: 'There's something exciting and illicit about coming here, something that makes respectable Pakistani pulses race' (6). There is a marked contrast between urban, urbane upper-middle class flâneurs, and the vulnerable streetwalkers. In her book *Hira Mandi*, Claudine Le Tourneur d'Ison and, similarly, her translator, Priyanka Jhijaria (in the English language version of the novel), express this diversity using language that is far from politically correct:

> The street resembled a court of miracles—handicapped beggars, cripples rolling in a ball on the ground, tramps in the last shreds of a shalwar kameez, and emaciated drug addicts [...] [W]ithin [the] misshapen walls looked like a junkyard for all of society's most depraved—dealers, prostitutes, pimps and of course, Shi'as, as rejected as the Christians. The only ones who dared enter here were the bourgeois in need of excitement, ready to mix with the riff-raff at the cost of their virtue, politicians who by day proudly brandished the Quran, and by night the bank notes that they showered on the dancers (88-9).

Le Tourneur d'Ison recognizes Heera Mandi's almost carnivalesque mix of those usually considered society's dregs—sex workers and their keepers, drug users and their suppliers, many of them Shia (a sect increasingly despised in frantically Sunni-izing Pakistan)—alongside those at the top of the social strata: patriarchs, politicians, and the pious.

In 'Re-evaluating the Postcolonial City', Graham Huggan and I argue that the recent outpouring of postcolonial urban studies research has tended to overlook rural experience and to neglect the structural asymmetries and social injustice found in what we term the 'global city' (786). Moreover, studies of South Asian cities have often focused on the urbanization of the city space, but not necessarily on the urban poor. A great deal of research from various disciplines has been conducted in relation to Indian cities, such as Bombay/Mumbai (see Hansen; Mehta; Prakash; and Patel and Thorner), Calcutta/Kolkata (S. Chaudhuri; Dutta; Gupta, Mukherjee, and Banerjee), and, to a somewhat lesser extent, Delhi (Kaul; Dalrymple; Hosagrahar). However, Pakistani urban environments have been grossly under-represented, with Karachi and especially Lahore receiving a small amount of scholarly attention in comparison with the vast archive on Bombay.[2] As such, Lahore is itself an 'outcast city' compared to others in South Asia. This chapter is an attempt, as it were, to re-cast this metropole and to make a literary contribution to urban studies.

I examine Sidhwa's work, paying special attention to her acclaimed Partition novel *Cracking India* (1991), alongside Mohsin Hamid's first three novels: *Moth Smoke* (2000), *The Reluctant Fundamentalist* (2007), and *How to Get Filthy Rich in Rising Asia* (2013). These texts are scrutinized for their textual descriptions of Lahore as a postcolonial city and as the heart of the Punjab—as well as of Pakistan more broadly. I then weave in the theoretical approaches of Fredric Jameson, Edward W. Soja, Michel Foucault, Michel de Certeau, and several other theorists, framing the same geographical locations as dynamic spaces of social and cultural contestations. My objective in doing this is, first, to highlight the precariousness of the urban poor (working-class women, for instance, occupy a doubly marginalized position) in the global city and its rural hinterland; second, I draw Lahore in to the twice-born fold of those highly scrutinized South Asian cities, such as Bombay/Mumbai, Calcutta/Kolkata, and Delhi.

Lahore has remained virtually invisible to literary and other humanities scholars, whereas other South Asian cities, such as Delhi, Calcutta, and Mumbai, have been loudly celebrated by critics. A first possible reason for this neglect is that Lahore is located in Pakistan, a country with a troubled and variable relationship with the West, and with its own internal problems apropos of scholarship.

Ever since Zia ul-Haq's regime, which was bankrolled by the US as part of its Cold War strategy, censorship has been at the heart of Pakistani governance. The media opened up dramatically albeit temporarily during Pervez Musharraf's military rule (1999–2008). However, Pakistani higher education institutions, particularly their arts departments, still chafe under restrictions and a lack of funding, both of which limit the research of the many brilliant scholars who work there. Second, Lahore used to be a popular destination along the hippie trail (loosely mapped onto the old Silk Route). After the Iranian Revolution of 1979 and the occupations of Afghanistan by the USSR and later the US, the majority of tourists could no longer enter or exit Pakistan's western gateways with ease. This means that fewer outsiders have had a chance to be inspired by the city's history and culture in the way that Indian cities have spawned their Mark Tullys, William Dalrymples, and Dominique Lapierres. Finally, in relation to urban studies, it is Karachi that appeals to researchers, in part because its megacity status dwarfs Lahore's, with estimated populations of 23 and 10 million respectively. Karachi's higher profile is also due to its disproportionately larger population of muhajirs (the migrants and descendants of migrants who fled from India to Pakistan during and after Partition) and attendant ethnic and political conflict, which attracts much scholarly attention (see, for example, Anjaria and McFarlane 298–337).

Yet Lahore, as an urban nucleus, could not matter more, given its history and hold on the South Asian imagination; its location and strategic importance as a hub in between India and the border with Afghanistan in Khyber Pakthunkhwa; and its economic productivity in the manufacturing and communications industries. As I show in this chapter, the city's close proximity to the almost impregnable Wagah border means that it is uniquely vulnerable when the two nations of India and Pakistan square up to each other. Uneasy peace between these countries periodically combusts, as in the nuclear stand-off of the late 1990s and the crisis following the Indian Parliament attack of 2001.[3]

More positively, Lahore is the cultural capital of Pakistan, even though it is just the political and administrative capital of the Punjab province. In 1940, it was in the city's Iqbal Park that Jinnah issued the Lahore Resolution, advocating the creation of Pakistan through an inchoate plan for 'autonomous national States' within independent India that would allegedly 'allow the major nations separate homelands' (Jinnah 55). Lahore's landmarks provide architectural testament to the many pasts which have overlaid the city, making it a palimpsest and a space of intersecting identities, pre-dating colonial India by centuries if not millennia. The metropolis has a strong arts scene, which, admittedly, has been defanged due to Partition, but is still clearly present.

Lahore also matters because it functions as a barometer of the political changes that are taking place in Pakistan, many of them especially damaging to the urban poor. Unlike Karachi, with its high numbers of muhajirs and incidents of ethnic violence, Lahore has until recently been a relatively peaceful city. However, the last decade has witnessed a sea change in relation to terror, sectarian violence, and international machinations. I argue that Sidhwa and Hamid trace the genesis of this transformation back to the class, gender, religious, and ethnic divisions that have always been present in Lahore and which were exacerbated by the creation of Pakistan.

For those who do not agree that Lahore, as an urban centre, in some ways functions as a synecdoche of Pakistan more broadly, it is worth thinking of Anatol Lieven. In a section of his book, *Pakistan: A Hard Country*, entitled 'Lahore, the Historic Capital', Lieven mistakenly writes: 'Pakistan is the heart, stomach and backbone of Pakistan. Indeed, in the view of many of its inhabitants, it *is* Pakistan' (267; emphasis in original). This tautological but revealing substitution of 'Pakistan' for 'Lahore' chimes with the saying Lahoris use, almost nonchalantly, to emphasize their city's distinctiveness: '*Lahore Lahore hai*' (Lahore is Lahore). The northeastern city is the cultural heartland of the country, with recorded history dating back to the seventh century AD, and a much longer oral, cultural, and communitarian presence. Its economic powerhouse status and the hold it has on the Pakistani imagination, channelled through the films of Lollywood (the nation's film industry, based in Lahore), have also generated large-scale migration from the rural areas to Punjab's capital in order to find work.

From the dire situation of many women in Lahore (which I explore at length later), to the intelligence, independence, and creative power of the city's women's movement, the picture revealed is extremely complex. Lahore is often seen as a pleasure city.[4] Mohsin Hamid—the first author under discussion—is interested in upper-class millennial Pakistan's voluptuary, ecstasy-taking social whirl, as well as more familiar scenes of violence and stark class divisions. According to Anita Desai ('Passion': np.), his debut novel, *Moth Smoke* (2000), was a turning point for subcontinental literature, in that it was one of the earliest twenty-first century novels to depart from the Indian magic realism fashionable in the 1980s and 1990s, and venture into darker and generically undecidable territory inspired by his hometown, Lahore. Indeed, for many, the metropolis represents pain, exploitation, and danger. Or, as Bapsi Sidhwa puts it in her anthology, *City of Sin and Splendour: Writings on Lahore* (2005), it is at once a city of sin and splendour. Even the Lahore of the late 1970s and early 1980s under the ruthless Islamization of the Zia ul-Haq regime, is portrayed in Sidhwa's fourth novel, *An American Brat*, as a city of 'paradoxes, where bold women of a certain class often wield as much clout as pistol-toting thugs' (192).

Tracery of Urbanization

LAHORE IS AN UNEVENLY DEVELOPED, international urban centre, which productively intersects with, and is cross-fertilized by, the well-irrigated rural hinterland in this 'Land of Five Rivers', so that the city is not easily separable from its outlying countryside. On first glance, this description might seem to be contradicted by Hamid's third novel, *How to Get Filthy Rich in Rising Asia*, in which the protagonist, 'you', comes from an archetypal Punjabi village. There, workers genuflect to zamindars or feudal landlords, women carry pots on their heads, and water buffalo are milked while they chew on fodder (8). Yet this rural setting is far from idealized. When the protagonist's father surveys it, instead of noticing the deliberately clichéd pastoral tropes, he sees 'the labor by which a farmer exchanges his allocation of time in this world for an allocation of time in this world [*sic*]. Here, in the heady bouquet of nature's pantry, your father sniffs mortality' (Hamid *Filthy*: 7). For these reasons of hardship and mortality, most of the novel's rural dwellers long, in the words of the opening chapter's title, to 'Move to the City', where they have heard that wages are high, but do not realize that expenses are equally lofty. The protagonist migrates to a city, which, it becomes clear, is Lahore (although places and people are unnamed in this novel, perhaps to lend it a universality that accords with its ironic structuring as a self-help book). During his relocation to the metropolis, the focalizer witnesses 'a passage of time that outstrips its chronological equivalent. Just as when headed into the mountains a quick shift in altitude can vault one from subtropical jungle to semi-arctic tundra, so too can a few hours on a bus from rural remoteness to urban centrality appear to span millennia' (13). This suggests that even though there is only a relatively short physical distance between the forelock-tugging, pitcher-carrying, buffalo-milking villagers and the city of pollution, dual carriageways, electricity, and advertising hoardings, culturally they are as dissimilar as jungle and tundra. Despite first impressions of this novel, Hamid complicated this seemingly bifurcatory picture of urban and rural Punjab when, in an interview I conducted, he stated:

> I think the rural/urban split is blurring, because all along Pakistan's many major roads, there's an urbanization taking place. If you drive around the GT Road, or any other large road in Punjab, little towns and shops have grown up around it. People live along those roads, have electricity, televisions, satellite dishes, and mobile phone coverage, and they watch the cars passing through. They are traders, selling things in their shops, and paying for services. They are not like the farmers. This network cuts across all of Punjab now, so it isn't as though there's an urban core and then periphery, but a tracery of urbanization that penetrates the periphery (Chambers *British*: 182–3).

Such a sketch is filled out in *How to Get Filthy Rich in Rising Asia* when 'the region that forms the economic hinterland to your metropolis' is described: 'The car approaches the outskirts of the city, passing the disinterred earth and linear mounds of vast middle-class housing developments. Rows of electricity poles rise in various stages of completion, some bare, some bridged by taut cables, occasionally one from which wires dangle to the ground' (81). This portrayal of the outskirts of Lahore dramatizes the 'tracery of urbanization' that Hamid outlined in more detail in the interview I undertook with him. His description of the exposed soil and incomplete electricity pylons suggests that this is an unfinished, in-between space that is neither urban nor rural, but fuzzy. This interstitial suburban area is seen as having neither the danger nor the promise of the city, while not possessing the fabled bucolic idyll or grinding poverty of the country. However, as rents and demand for urban space soar ever higher, urbanization is encroaching on the suburbs too. Cropland in the outer suburbs is increasingly being sold off to developers (*Filthy*: 82, 200), and the narrator acknowledges the porous nature of the city's borderlines: 'Your city is not laid out as a single-celled organism with a wealthy nucleus surrounded by an ooze of slums. [...] Accordingly, the poor live near the rich' (20). To some extent, then, Hamid recognizes, as does historian Ian Talbot, that 'Punjabi society [is] overwhelmingly rural' and that '[t]raditional rural customs and values lay just beneath the veneer of urban sophistication and culture' (Talbot 13, 15).

Similarly, in Hamid's debut novel *Moth Smoke*, Dilaram, a young village girl from rural Punjab—now the madam of a brothel in Heera Mandi—was repeatedly raped by her landlord and his relatives, causing her to flee to Lahore, where she ended up in bonded prostitution (50–1). Some doubt is cast over this personal narrative, however, as the protagonist, Daru, thinks Dilaram appears 'a little too well-spoken for an uneducated village girl, sounding more like a wayward Kinnaird alumna to me' (Hamid *Moth*: 51). Whether Dilaram really was an innocent peasant girl who got caught up in human trafficking and prostitution or, as Daru suspects, a sophisticated urbanite who attended a prestigious school such as Lahore's Kinnaird College for Women is never resolved.

La Whore: Gendering the City

THE NOVEL *MOTH SMOKE*, as intimated in the previous section, establishes Heera Mandi as a space in which young girls from both the country and city put their bodies on display, evade the police, and are exploited by predatory pimps. Even more extensively, in *Cracking India*, Sidhwa paints a vivid picture of Heera Mandi as a

place where poetry and music flourishes. The area was originally
built as a sanctuary for the illegitimate sons of Mughal emperors
and their *tawaifs*, also known as nautch girls or courtesans, who,
at least during the Raj era, were mostly Muslim women from
North India. The exploitation of women, many of them from the
countryside, went hand in hand with an attempt to dress up this
exploitation and, often, prostitution in glamorous ways. Ghazals,
frequently composed, recited, and sung in red-light districts such
as Heera Mandi, are also a typically Muslim poetic form. However,
the associations that ghazals have with royal courts, courtesans, and
dancing girls contributed towards these poems containing recurrent,
apparently un-Islamic images, such as the nightingale, wine, roses,
and the beloved, although these metaphors also reflect the Sufi
devotee's longing for God.[5]

Sidhwa's villain Ice-candy-man uses the elevated language of
ghazals in order to shower the kidnapped Hindu Ayah with praise.
There is a notable irony in his admiration of her dancing, since it
is he who has forced her into the dancing-girl profession he extols:
'She lives to dance! And I to toast her dancer's grace! | Princes
pledge their lives to celebrate her celebrated face!' (259). Despite
his most poetic efforts, Ice-candy-man's exploitation of Ayah is
evident in her diminished figure and downcast glance. As feminists
often point out, the flip side of idealization is a potential for abuse.

Heera Mandi is a central locus of Lahore's Walled City. The red-
light district is close to the Minar-e-Pakistan, a tower built in the
1960s to commemorate the 1940 Lahore Resolution. As previously
mentioned, it is also adjacent to Lahore's most famous landmark—
the enormous Mughal mosque, Badshahi Masjid. Other nearby
Mughal sites include Anarkali Bazaar, Shalimar Gardens, and the
Tomb of Jahangir. Analysis of the diverse history of this district
suggests that Heera Mandi can be read as a microcosm of the
city as a whole, and therefore of the Punjab more broadly, just

as Lahore can to some extent be read as the nation in miniature. Unsurprisingly, few in Pakistan are willing to recognize the 'female street' (Sidhwa *Bride*: 58) of Heera Mandi as analogous to the Pakistani nation. Fouzia Saeed observes:

> Identified by various names, it [Heera Mandi] represents one of the oldest flesh markets in the land, where prostitution and the performing arts are linked in a complex web of human relations. Hardly any informed citizen can plead ignorance of the residents of this area, but they are considered the least entitled to be understood by their fellow beings (vii).

In the red-light district, binaries are broken down, prompted by the contiguity of the nearby Badshahi Mosque, as well as the professed religiosity of many of the area's Shia sex workers. Sociologist Naheem Jabbar suggests that: 'The self-conscious piety of the women [in Heera Mandi] contradicts the idea that they are so generically typical of profanity (woman *qua* profanity)' (109; emphasis in original). The authors' representations of the heterogeneous nature of the people who congregate in the two very different areas of the red-light district and the mosque allow them to explore the metropole/hinterland dynamic. References to the mosque also necessitate discussion of the crucial and changing role of religion—the majority faith Islam and, to a lesser extent, the minority creed of Zoroastrianism, to which Sidhwa and the Parsi community belong—in contributing towards post-Partition Lahori identity. In an elegiac section of *An American Brat*, Sidhwa reflects on the exponential religification not only of Muslims in Pakistan, but of the formerly tolerant Parsi community: '[E]ducated custodians of the Zoroastrian doctrine were no less rigid and ignorant than the *fundos* in Pakistan. This mindless current of fundamentalism sweeping the world like a plague had spared no religion, not even their microscopic community of 120 thousand' (305-6; emphasis in original). It is essential to keep this perspective on the concepts of 'tolerance' and 'fundamentalism' in mind, rather than blindly accepting the widespread contemporary assumption that the rise of religious sentiment is limited to Muslims and mosques.

A sexualization of the city (La Whore) is perhaps best articulated in *The Pakistani Bride* (1983):

> Lahore—the ancient whore, the handmaiden of dimly remembered Hindu kings, the courtesan of Moghul emperors, bedecked and bejewelled, savaged by marauding Sikh hordes—healed by the caressing hands of her British lovers. A little shoddy [...] like an attractive but aging concubine, ready to bestow surprising delights on those who cared to court her—proudly displaying royal gifts (43).

Sidhwa alludes to the 'lovers' who have conquered Lahore, from the pre-Mughal 'Hindu kings' to the 'Mughal emperors', and implicitly from the Shivaji and Durrani Empires, the Sikh leader Ranjit Singh, and the British colonizers to the postcolonial Pakistani politicians who ruled over Lahore and West Punjab. Personifying the city as a fading but still attractive, somewhat tawdry figure, Sidhwa evokes Lahore's loss of its multicultural identity after Partition. This is also reflected in *Cracking India*: 'The garden scene has depressingly altered. Muslim families who added color when scattered among the Hindus and Sikhs, now monopolize the garden, depriving it of color' (249). Elsewhere in *The Pakistani Bride*, there is a sustained passage about Heera Mandi (57-65), which contains strikingly similar motifs to those found in Sidhwa's first novel, *The Crow Eaters* (130-8). Both depict men chewing betel leaves and proffering money; women in gaudy dress (churidar pyjamas, ankle bells, and heavy make-up) dancing in a 'mechanical' fashion while accompanied by harmonium, sitar, and tabla; and Heera Mandi's narrow streets, decrepit wooden buildings, trellises, and balconies. The recurring characters of a middle-aged madam, young girls of varying degrees of fairness, plumpness, and innocence, and sinister pimps in these novels signal that many features of Heera Mandi *qua* space have changed little over the last hundred years.

Space in Theory and the Imagination

MOVING FORWARD WITH OUR DISCUSSION of space and its many manifestations and constructions, I concentrate on one theoretical text in particular, Edward W. Soja's *Postmodern Geographies* (1989). Soja's positing of three manifestations of space is helpful in thinking about Lahore, and I would argue that it is borne out in the novels discussed in this chapter. Soja makes a tripartite distinction between 'space *per se*, space as a contextual given, and socially-based spatiality' (79). He is interested in the way in which space is primordially given, yet is also an effect of social production and imaginative construction. Soja's ideas come out of a theoretical perspective, from the mid-1970s onwards, to aver that Western accounts of history are incomplete, due to an excessive concentration on the temporal perspective, at the expense of the spatial dimension. Michel Foucault famously indicts the full spectrum of Western philosophy and theory for its inattention to geography: 'Space was treated as the dead, the fixed, the undialectical, the immobile. Time, on the contrary, was richness, fecundity, life, dialectic' (70). He identifies a dichotomy of thinking about time and space, suggesting that since the nineteenth century space has largely been ignored by philosophers, while time and history have been closely interrogated. Foucault's call for greater attention to space led to what many have summarized as the 'spatial turn' in the social sciences and humanities (Raju 1; Teverson and Upstone ix).

Returning to Soja, he argues, employing a common sense perspective, that space is a given, relatively unchanging physical reality that has a profound effect on its inhabitants. This is demonstrated in Lahore's status as a frontier city, just 30 miles away from hostile Indian territory, which positioning makes it would likely be the first urban location targeted in any nuclear war that erupted between the two countries. Hamid is alert to the impact this has on the city's residents, and in *Moth Smoke* 'if they nuke Lahore' is a frequent refrain (88, 91–2). Other sorts of violence in the city also have a levelling effect on Lahore's residents, both rich and poor, shaping their behaviour and fears and limiting their movements. After his mother is killed by a stray bullet while asleep on a charpoy on the roof during a baking Punjabi summer, Daru has a recurring dream in which he 'imagine[s] Lahore as a city with bullets streaking into the air' (Hamid 108). This prefigures the later stand-off between Pakistan and India over nuclear testing and the danger of possible retaliation in the form of nuclear war. Such a military confrontation is tensely felt in Lahore, as the municipality on the frontline between the two:

> The entire city is uneasy. Sometimes, when monsoon lightning slips a bright explosion under the clouds, there is a pause in conversations. Teacups halt, steaming, in front of extended lips. Lightning's echo comes as thunder. And the city waits for thunder's echo, for a wall of heat that burns Lahore with the energy of a thousand summers, a million partitions, a billion atomic souls split in half (Hamid *Moth*: 211).

The combination of exaggeration—'*entire* city'—together with mild humour—'teacups extended'—undercuts the implicit reference to Nagasaki and Hiroshima, as well as Lahore's own holocaust of Partition. Clearly, even space that appears to be a stable, de facto entity is actually socially constructed. Although space is more likely to be a problem for urban outcasts, it can also be turned against the tea-sipping middle classes, engulfing them in violence and terror.

Therefore, according to Soja, the second understanding of urban space is as a socially manipulated, changeable material that is produced as much as it produces and involves 'social translation, transformation, and experience' (79-80). Both Soja and his theoretical forerunner Henri Lefebvre develop persuasive theoretical accounts of the ways in which urban planning is intimately related to ideology and methods of social control. They also recognize that the attempts of the powerful to monopolize the social production of space are never entirely successful. The intentions of town planners are modified or subverted by the uses locals make of their space 'on the ground', and city dwellers have varying degrees of agency to transform their surroundings.

We need only look at the depiction of Lahore's Lawrence Gardens (now the Bagh-e-Jinnah) and other locations in Sidhwa's *Cracking India* to see that space can be radically reconstructed by its residents. The nanny, Ayah, who is in many ways a gendered personification of independent India (*Bharat Mata* or Mother India), meets her admirers in Lawrence Gardens on the Upper Mall near Charing Cross. At first, her beauty unites members of various religious groups; they sit together in relative harmony, discussing current events and gossip under a Raj era monument, a statue of Queen Victoria. In contrast to this statue, which is 'cast in gunmetal, [...] majestic, [...] overpowering, ugly', Ayah is described as resembling 'the Hindu goddess she worships' (Sidhwa 28, 12). Everything about her is depicted as soft, attractive, and fertile. Ayah is an allegorical representation of the youthful promise of Indian Independence in comparison with the austere decay of the old British order, and in the park she subverts the colonial space around her. Later, when this harmonious group shifts from meeting under the statue of Queen Victoria—the symbol of the British Raj—to meeting at a wayside restaurant, their unity disintegrates, suggesting that existing tensions between different religious groups are exacerbated once the common enemy has departed. As the accord between Ayah's courtiers breaks down and a more vicious struggle begins for her approval (and, by implication, for control over her body), it becomes evident that the city is splintering along ethnic lines. The conflict between the different religious groups now makes it impossible—and, indeed, undesirable—for this group to meet peacefully in the spaces they previously occupied with ease.

The third way in which Soja argues that we experience space is through its construction in the imagination. This is what Fredric Jameson terms 'cognitive mapping' ('Cognitive': 353–6), through which he argues that we all have our own mental maps of the cities in which we live. Jameson emphasizes the social, collective nature of this mental cartography, asserting that each of us positions our subjective consciousness within 'unlived, abstract conceptions of the geographic totality' ('Postmodernism': 90). These conceptions may, however, be 'garbled' or distorted reflections of cultural biases ('Cognitive': 353). Jameson's cognitive mapping serves as a reminder that space is as much created by the imagination as by civic leaders and planners. William Glover, the pre-eminent scholar on Lahore as an urban space, concurs: '[A]ny city is constituted as much imaginatively as it is physically of bricks and mortar' (xv). Anatol Lieven stresses this visionary aspect in relation to Lahore when he writes that it 'is a city of the imagination, in a way that bureaucratic Islamabad and dour, impoverished Peshawar cannot be' (268).

A disjuncture between this city of the imagination and the metropolitan world of lived materialism discussed earlier is illustrated in Hamid's second novel, *The Reluctant Fundamentalist*

(2007). The text's protagonist, Changez, muses on the city's Mughal past and historic texture to a sceptical and materialist American businessman:

> I said I was from Lahore, the second largest city of Pakistan, ancient capital of the Punjab, home to nearly as many people as New York, layered like a sedimentary plain with the accreted history of invaders from the Aryans to the Mongols to the British. He merely nodded. Then he said, "And are you on financial aid?" (Hamid 7).

William Glover's research accords with Changez's imaginative view that Lahore is a palimpsest in which British architecture is grafted onto the strata of pre-Mughal, Mughal, and Sikh history. According to Glover, there is a surprising quantity and frequency of movement between Lahore's bustling Old City and the white civil station, which was intended to be spatially quarantined from the Indian areas during the Raj era. For example, from the year of the Indian Rebellion (1857) until 1891, St. James's Church found itself formally consecrated and housed in Anarkali's Tomb, the last resting place of a Muslim dancing girl (Glover 19). Anarkali is said to have been the Mughal Emperor Akbar's courtesan, but when his son, Prince Salim, fell in love with her too, Akbar was so enraged that he buried the dancing girl alive in a wall located within the bazaar.

However, Lahore's passionate, hybrid past constantly rubs against the bathos of financial realities. These are tersely introduced by the US official above when he barks: "'And are you on financial aid?'" Fiscal restraints are also apparent in Sidhwa's *An American Brat*, in which the young migrant, Feroza, has her pride in her education and aristocratic Lahori background undermined when she tries to enter New York's Kennedy Airport and finds that a 'sallow, unsmiling officer' handles her Pakistani passport with contempt, quizzing her

on her financial means and the length of time she plans to stay in
the United States (Sidhwa *Brat*: 54). There are, thus, barriers to the
movement of even the most Mughal prince- or princess-like upper-
class Lahori. Michel de Certeau's theory of 'walking in the city' is
significant to an understanding of contemporary Lahore. Writing
in 1980, de Certeau lyrically describes the 'ordinary practitioners
of the city', who are said to live '"down below"' (93), and whose
raison d'être is apparently *flânerie* or walking. Interestingly, he begins
his account of the ordinary walkers in the city from a panoramic
vantage point at the top of the World Trade Centre. The post-9/11
reader may find chilling presentiment in his description of New
York as 'a universe that is constantly exploding' (91) and the World
Trade Centre occupant as anticipating 'an Icarian fall' (92). This
resonates strongly with the famous passage in Hamid's *The Reluctant
Fundamentalist* in which Changez admits that his first reaction to
the Twin Towers' destruction was to smile, 'caught up', as he was, 'in
the *symbolism* of it all, the fact that someone had so visibly brought
America to her knees' (73; emphasis in original).

As soon as de Certeau descends 'down below' to the street, he
argues that walking is 'an elementary form of this experience of
the city; they are walkers, *Wandersmänner*, whose bodies follow
the thicks and thins of an urban "text" they write without being
able to read it' (93; emphasis in original). Hamid and Sidhwa
unsettle these assumptions, showing that walking is not an
'elementary form' common to the experience of all cities. In *The
Reluctant Fundamentalist*, Hamid writes:

> [T]he newer districts of Lahore are poorly suited to the needs
> of those who must walk. In their spaciousness—with their
> public parks and wide, tree-lined boulevards—they enforce an
> ancient hierarchy that comes to us from the countryside: the
> superiority of the mounted man over the man on foot. But [...]

[in] the congested, maze-like heart of this city—Lahore is more democratically *urban*. Indeed, in these places it is the man with four wheels who is forced to dismount and become part of the crowd (32; emphasis in original).

Some parts of Lahore are difficult to walk in because they are spread out and lack pavements, while in other places, especially the Walled City areas, class distinction is inverted and it becomes the envehicled person who is at a disadvantage. This is the only instance in Hamid's representations of the divided city where the poor are sometimes privileged over the rich. In contrast to this context-specific privileging, various binaries are set up in his other novels— between the classes who are able to afford air conditioning and their own generators and those who are unable to do so in *Moth Smoke* and those with access to bottled water and those without in *How to Get Filthy Rich in Rising Asia*—which are unvaryingly positively weighted towards the rich and powerful. As such, Lahore's Old City has a reverse effect on class hierarchies. De Certeau mentions barriers to movement like the obstacles encountered in the quote from Hamid when he writes of 'interdictions (e.g. [...] a wall that prevents one from going further)' (98). Such barriers are prevalent and marked in postcolonial cities such as Lahore, with the Wagah border merely a short car ride away, but partitioned India almost impossible to travel to easily for Pakistanis.[6]

From a gendered perspective, walking in the city is shown to be even more difficult for women (Elkin; Sizemore). In Sidhwa's *An American Brat*, Feroza observes that 'there were so few women, veiled or unveiled, on the streets of Lahore, that even women stared at other women, as she did, as if they were freaks' (106). This description of the self-alienation of women indicates that walking around outside is a hazardous act for Feroza, even in one of Pakistan's most sophisticated cities, as she encounters a cavernous gender gap on the streets.

In *Cracking India*, Lenny is constrained in her ability to walk in the city not only due to her gender, but also because of her disability. She has suffered from polio and is lame as a result, with a fallen arch in one of her feet. Ayah confines her to a pram for movement until well past the age at which this is considered socially acceptable. Once she begins corrective surgery, Lenny worries that her foot will 'emerge […] immaculate, fault-free', thus forcing her to compete with other children 'for my share of love and other handouts' (18). In the context of this story concerning Independence, and considering that the girl's lameness is arguably an indirect legacy of British rule (25), it is hard not to read Lenny and her calipers as the infant Indian nation preparing for the difficulties (and rewards) of standing on its own two feet. As Clare Barker writes:

> Echoing a problematic conflation of individual and national bodies that was apparent in nationalist discourses in this period, the text performs a discomfiting oscillation between materialist constructions of disability as a social presence and the deployment of disability as a prosthesis standing in for colonial disablement and the mutilated—partitioned—body politic (95).

Pakistan is known to be a hard place for wheelchair users and other disabled people, both in its urban areas and rurally. As well as a lack of ramps and lifts to aid their movement (Farid np.), there is also a widely reported lack of cultural awareness about disability. Further impediments to de Certeau's blithe Western-oriented analysis of 'walking in the city' in Lahore include the threat of rape and kidnapping, which becomes a central issue for women during the Partition so graphically depicted in *Cracking India*. Moreover, the workers of Heera Mandi are prohibited from moving around freely, except between the hours of 11 p.m. and 1 a.m., because of draconian and extortive police tactics enforced in this area.

Historically, perhaps spatial theorists have overlooked barriers to the act of walking, particularly when these relate to various forms of oppression in previously colonized countries. Accompanying the 'spatial turn' over approximately the last four decades of social sciences and humanities research, since 9/11 there has been increasing interest in analysing the post-secular city.[7] The idea behind the post-secular turn is to take account of religion, war, and terror's impact on twenty-first century cities. This is clearly a timely examination, especially in the light of cities such as Cairo, Benghazi, Damascus, Aleppo, and Homs becoming sites for revolution— to varying degrees religiously inflected—in the Arab Spring (or Arab Winter). I am intrigued to learn what this new post-secular direction in scholarship will bring to the study of devastated post-Arab Spring cities. In the meantime, it is hoped that this chapter has shed light on Sidhwa and Hamid's depictions of Heera Mandi's important place within Lahore, itself of inestimable significance to the Punjab and the Pakistani nation.

Lahore is a highly multifaceted space, constituted by sedimented histories, uneven capitalism, rural and urban continuities and discontinuities, and cultural nostalgia. Notwithstanding these noteworthy features, the city remains deplorably under-researched compared with Indian conurbations (and to a lesser degree, compared with research into Pakistan's former capital and largest city, Karachi). As a palimpsest of various accreted histories and the nation's artistic and cultural capital, Lahore is Pakistan's heart (and stomach and spine, to recycle Lieven's metaphor). However, Sidhwa and Hamid—both writing from the diaspora—reveal the tangled skein of this city, repudiating the binaries that are seductively omnipresent in representations of Lahore. Hamid is keen to trouble conceptual borders between Lahore and its pastoral hinterland, demonstrating how the urban is invading the rural in the guise of industrialization, while the rural encroaches on the urban via the figure of the erstwhile village dweller seeking a livelihood. Sidhwa adds a gendered dimension to the city through her representation of the plight of sex workers in Heera Mandi in almost all of her novels to date. Turning to the theoretical thrust of this chapter, the social sciences, literary, and postcolonial theory together provide three broad understandings of space: as a physical reality, a socially constructed entity, and a place that is imagined through cognitive mapping and the textualizations of fiction, life writing, and non-fiction. De Certeau's 'walking in the city' helps us to see ways in which the city is imagined, but also how its physical manifestations and social manipulations can thwart the imaginer's assumptions and dreams.

NOTES

1. Hamid returned to live in Lahore in 2009, which may affect the future trajectory of his fiction.

2. The main scholarly monographs on Lahore are Glover (2007) and Suvorova (2012).

3. Both of these incidents—the nuclear race and the Indian Parliament attacks—are foregrounded in Hamid's fiction (*Moth*: 88–93; *Reluctant*: 121, 126–8, 143).

4. The term 'pleasure city' comes from the title of a neglected novel by Kamala Markandaya (*Pleasure City*). Heera Mandi is also referred to as a 'Pleasure District' in the subtitle to Louise Brown's book, *The Dancing Girls of Lahore* (2006).

5. For more on the ghazal form, see Matthews, Shackle, and Husain (32–7).

6. This point could also be extended to Palestine and the notorious Separation Wall.

7. See, for example, Beaumont and Baker; Knott 'Religion' and 'Cutting'.

9

Literary Peshawar: From Kipling to the Present Day

I HAD INTENDED TO BEGIN 2015 with a lively article for *3 Quarks Daily* about the history and literature of the British curry house (see Chapter 28, 'In Praise of the Chapaterati', for this article). Then, just as my sons were getting dizzy with excitement at the prospect of new Xbox games in their Christmas stockings, the Army Public School in Peshawar was attacked by gunmen affiliated with the Tehrik-i-Taliban, Pakistan (TTP).

From 1993 to 1994, I briefly taught at Fazlehaq College in Mardan. The college had been established by General Fazle Haq, Zia ul-Haq's right hand man in Khyber Pakhtunkhwa, around ten years before my arrival. It is modelled on a British public school and many of its (all-male) pupils come from army families. At the tender age of 17 years old and something of a hippie, I felt out of place as soon as I arrived at this august institution, with its bore cannon on display and Rudyard Kipling's 'If' inscribed proudly on a playground wall.

Unsurprisingly, it wasn't long before my friend Kate and I moved (or, what is closer to the truth, fled) to Islamia Public High School located in Peshawar's University Town. This was a day school with much lower fees and a more diverse student body than Fazlehaq College. About a third of the pupils were Afghan. As refugees, some of the Afghan students were substantially older than their Pakistani classmates. They knew only Pashto and Dari, and so had to catch up with their Urdu. One young man was almost six feet tall, with a ratty moustache and acne, and the poor thing had to almost fold himself in two to fit at his desk in the 9- and 10-year-olds' class to which he was allocated. Some of the pupils were so poor that three siblings would share a single pencil. At least, that's what they told this teenage English teacher from Yorkshire. It may have been an excuse to get out of class, and 'Miss, brother; Miss, pencil' became a common refrain even amongst kids I suspected didn't have a sibling attending the high school.

To my relief, this school taught girls and had no military regalia. Kate and I taught there for the best part of a year; a highlight being when we organized the older girls to write and produce a play of the fairy tale *Cinderella*. During my time at Islamia Public High School, I noticed that the small number of girls present tended to be significantly more middle-class than their male peers. In these cases, their brothers had been sent to impressive public schools like Fazlehaq College, and when questioned several of the girls disclosed that they were lucky to be receiving any education at all.

Kate and I lived with the headmaster—a dry, twinkling Punjabi—and his family for the duration of our time in Pakistan. His brother, a youth not much older than me, vacated his bedroom for us and, without complaint, spent the whole year sleeping on a charpoy on the roof. I joined him and two servants up there for a few nights during the summer, when the heat seemed to radiate up through my bedframe, but the choking air did little to help me sleep. During our time there, Kate and I visited Saddar Bazaar, Qissa Khawani, and the smugglers' bazaar at Hayatabad to buy shalwar kameez and toiletries. Every evening we would walk from the house to the adjacent school's office to watch *The Bold and the Beautiful* and *Santa Barbara*, and soon Kate and I were as hopelessly addicted to these soaps as the headmaster. His father—the tall, devout Haji Sahib—sometimes had cause to come into the office, and his usually dignified son would lunge, panic-stricken, to change the channel to innocuous, halal state television.

When I heard about the massacre of children in Peshawar at Christmas time it was especially painful, because as a result of my youthful experience, I could picture the scene exactly. I don't want to add to the commentary on this landmark atrocity, which has been written by others more knowledgeable about, and closer to, the situation than I am. Instead, I want to focus on the endlessly fascinating literature of Peshawar.

Kipling, whose iconic poem 'If' served to alienate me during my stay in Mardan, writes of Peshawar in *Kim* that it is an 'insalubrious city' (36). More famously, he describes it as 'the city of evil countenances'. In his essay of the same name, he cements many stereotypes of Pashtuns; that they are warrior-like, vicious, oppressive to women, and highly sexualized:

> [Peshawar's] main road teems with magnificent scoundrels and handsome ruffians; all giving the on-looker the impression of wild beasts held back from murder and violence, and chafing against the restraint. The impression *may* be wrong; and the Peshawari, the most innocent creature on earth, in spite of History's verdict against him; but not unless thin lips, scowling brows, deep set vulpine eyes and lineaments stamped with every brute passion known to man, go for nothing. Women of course are invisible in the streets, but here and there instead, some nameless and shameless boy in girl's clothes (137; emphasis in original).

No wonder then that in her novel *A God in Every Stone*, Kamila Shamsie challenges the Orientalism of what her character Viv calls 'Kipling's Peshawar! The North-West Frontier! Where even the finest hotel in town was a whitewashed barracks, a reminder

that the world of guns lurked beneath every veneer' (84). Shamsie
pushes back against the meretricious European myth of Pashtuns
as a warrior race. Instead, she concentrates on Peshawar's pre-
Islamic past, the brutal British massacre of Pashtuns in Qissa
Khawani Bazaar in 1930, and the city's neglected treasure trove
of a museum.

Peshawari poet Farid Gul Momand recuperates another, more
positive epithet—the 'city of flowers'—only to demolish it in his
portrayal of Peshawar as a metropolis in which 'those who've
monopoly over God | […] Could preach nothing | But hatred on
your soil'. In another poem, Momand blames himself and his people
for allowing these monopolizers entry into Peshawar:

> They ruined my schools
> Raped my dolls
> Orphaned my children
> Widowed my sisters
> And we kept silent—like stones or tombs.[1]

Peshawar has also made an indelible impression on poets with
Pashtun heritage from the diaspora. Like turning a corner on a
pockmarked road in Khyber Pakhtunkhwa and taking in the Swat
Valley for the first time, I find Pakistani–American poet Shadab
Zeest Hashmi's 'Passing Through Peshawar' simultaneously
breathtaking and invigorating. Hashmi is interested in Peshawar's
domestic life, modes of transportation, and nature, pointing out the
poplars and willows, tanga horses, 'the breaking open of a walnut
in a door-hinge' (36), and the smell of Lux soap. British–Pakistani
poet Nabila Jameel remembers Peshawar's maze of alleys, the sound
of the Pashto language which 'drizzles confetti' on her listeners' ears
(115), and the taste of kahwa green tea. For these women diasporic
poets, the city is noisy, sensual, and much missed.

Pakistan's severe East–West divide is responsible for conflict and division, such that Britain's Foreign and Commonwealth Office now blandly advises tourists 'against all travel to […] the city of Peshawar and districts south of the city, including travel on the Peshawar to Chitral road via the Lowari Pass' (FCO np.). Accordingly, I haven't been back to the city since my formative stay in the early 1990s, even though I have returned to Pakistan on three occasions and hope to visit again in 2018. Instead, this frontier city, with its vista of lush mountains and peopled by green-eyed children, comes to me in dreams, and in news reports. With Farid Gul Momand, I '[y]earn […] for peace. | All this for you, my city, my sweetheart'.[2]

NOTES

1. This work is as yet unpublished and was emailed to the author by the poet.
2. This is from another unpublished poem by Farid Gul Momand.

10

On a Hair Trigger: Images of Kashmir in Literature

KASHMIR IS OFTEN REPRESENTED in literary texts as a paradise lost. Before its contemporary period of ongoing violence and unrest, Kashmir was frequently represented almost as an earthly heaven. The region is mountainous and its capital, Srinagar, boasts the beautiful Dal Lake. British tourists flocked to this lake for holidays, staying in houseboats in order to avoid paying tax on landed accommodation. However, Britons were not the first to find in Kashmir a summertime refuge from the searing heat of the plains. The earlier Mughal rulers were also highly appreciative of the valley. The Mughal Emperor, Jahangir, is said to have written a couplet that took inspiration from older verses on Kashmir and loosely translates as: 'If on earth there is a garden of bliss | It is this, it is this, it is this.' He adored Kashmir so much that he built the Shalimar Gardens there, and was rumoured to have died with the words 'Only Kashmir!' on his lips.

The area's strategic importance, as well as its splendour, proved a bone of contention between Pakistan and India from Partition onwards. As the Maharaja of Kashmir, Hindu ruler Hari Singh was allowed to choose which country he wanted the Muslim-majority princely state to belong to. After some prevarication, and threatened by the incursions of a group of Pashtun looters, he plumped for India. Pakistan owns about a third of the land, known as Azad (or 'Free')

Kashmir. India holds the rest, which happens to be the most visually stunning part. In 1948, United Nations Security Council Resolution 47 called for a plebiscite on Jammu and Kashmir's future, a call that has been repeated several times over the years. This plebiscite on Kashmiri independence was never held, and three wars and many skirmishes have been fought between India and Pakistan.

In 1988, Indian author Amitav Ghosh published his novel *The Shadow Lines*, an elegiac reflection on the social bonds severed in Europe by the Second World War, and throughout the subcontinent by Partition. Critics often overlook that the riot in Dhaka that kills the narrator's uncle, Tridib, is due to the temporary disappearance of the Prophet Muhammad's (PBUH) sacred hair from the Hazratbal Mosque in Kashmir in 1963. The narrator meditates on the exceptionally resilient connections that prompted the amassing of peoples on the streets in East Bengal in response to an event over 2,500 kilometres away. He concludes, somewhat paradoxically, that the episode proves the continuing connections within the Indian subcontinent in spite of Partition: 'Dhaka and Calcutta were [never] more closely bound to each other than after they had drawn their lines' (233).

Ghosh's optimism about Kashmir as the central point of an inclusive circle encompassing other South Asian cities such as Dhaka and Calcutta is shown by contemporaneous events to be misplaced. It was around 1988—the same year as the publication of his novel—that concerted strikes and insurgency began in Kashmir, following an unfairly steep electricity price hike and, more significantly, a disputed election. The Indian regime ramped up human rights abuses against ordinary citizens, as well as against those guerrillas starting to mobilize in the valley. As Basharat Peer openly confronts us with in his extraordinary non-fiction piece published in *Granta* entitled 'Kashmir's Forever War': '[C]ivilians continue to be killed and described as terrorists' (79). Over the

ensuing brutally destructive years, it should also be said that Pakistan,
Kashmiri separatists, and especially the Islamist groups have not
escaped morally unscathed. Tariq Ali rightly calls the Islamists and
the Indian Army the 'neither-nor' (7) of Kashmiri politics.

A few years later, during his time spent in hiding, Salman
Rushdie, himself from a Kashmiri background, took up the historical
theft of the sacred hair in his work of fiction 'The Prophet's Hair'
from *East, West* (1994). In this short story, a courtly and complacent
moneylender finds a vial containing the holy relic in Dal Lake.
Attracted by the vial's aesthetic and financial value, the man seizes it.
Although the moneylender confesses that he does not want the relic
for its religious significance, after appropriating it he is overcome
by uncharacteristic religious zeal. He forces his family to pray five
times a day, burns all books in the house apart from the Qur'an,
and orders his daughter, Huma, to enter purdah. Unhappy, Huma
engages the services of a thief to steal it while her father is sleeping.
Jolted awake, the moneylender murders his daughter instead of the
burglar. Overcome with remorse, he then kills himself. The thief is
shot by a policeman while trying to escape. The story closes with the
return of the sacred relic, which 'sits to this day in a closely guarded
vault […] in the heart of the valley which was once closer than any
other place on earth to Paradise' (57).

Rushdie returns to Kashmir in *Shalimar the Clown*—a novel
in which he follows Ghosh in the idealization of Kashmiriyat (a
transcendent Kashmiriness) and its Hindu–Muslim syncretism,
while playing down Indian occupation. The novel opens with an
apt Shakespearean epigraph—'A plague on both your houses' (qtd.
in Rushdie *Shalimar*: vii)—and at regular intervals this sentiment
of Kashmiri disdain for both India and Pakistan is reiterated:

Freedom! A tiny valley […] and [i]ts inhabitants had come to the
conclusion that they didn't much like India and didn't care for

the sound of Pakistan. So: freedom! Freedom to be meat-eating
Brahmins or saint-worshipping Muslims, to make pilgrimages to
the ice-lingam high in the unmelting snows or to bow down before
the prophet's hair in a lakeside mosque, to listen to the santoor and
drink salty tea, to dream of Alexander's army and to choose never
to see an army again, to make honey and carve walnut into animal
and boat shapes and to watch the mountains push their way, inch by
inch, century by century, further up into the sky. Freedom to choose
folly over greatness but to be nobody's fools. *Azadi!* Paradise wanted
to be free (Rushdie *Shalimar*: 253).

Yet this politically laudable free indirect discourse, with its antipathy
to both sides and well-worn images of Kashmiri syncretism, is
swiftly dented by a withering intervention from Shalimar the
clown's brother, who points out that freedom does not come
without cost and that '[t]he only paradise that's free that way is a
fairy-tale place full of dead people'. In combination with references
to 'the crazies [getting] into the act' of Kashmiri liberation and
to Kashmir's small size and 'preindustrial' civilization (Rushdie
Shalimar: 253), the impression given is of freedom as a fool's
paradise and Indian rule as the least worst option for the valley.

Agha Shahid Ali, in his poetry collection *The Country Without a
Post Office* (1997), similarly brings together stereotypically verdant,
heavenly Kashmiri images, such as saffron, paisley, and paradisiacal
gardens, all of which derive from various religious and secular
traditions. However, unlike Rushdie and Ghosh, Ali does not balk
at recognizing Islam, especially its mystical component, as the most
influential of the valley's many cultural strands. For example, in
the poem 'I See Kashmir from New Delhi at Midnight', Ali takes
a section of W. B. Yeats's 'Easter 1916' as his epigraph: 'Wherever
green is worn, […] | a terrible beauty is born' (Yeats 24, qtd. in Ali
24). Here, he singles out the colour green as that associated with

the Emerald Isle *and* Islam, so as to suggest a point of comparison between the Irish and Kashmiri conflicts in the aftermath of British imperialism.

The Collaborator by Mirza Waheed is set in Kashmir during the early 1990s. In this novel, the Kashmir conflict has finally reached the isolated village of Nowgam, close to the Pakistan border. One by one, four of five teenage friends cross the border and join the insurgency. The novel is narrated by the unnamed fifth boy, son of a headman, who is left behind near the Line of Control with his memories of cricket matches, music, and budding romance. The headman has forbidden his family to leave, so the son has little choice but to become the titular 'collaborator'. Employed by the Indian Army, he collects valuables from the bodies of so-called militants, dreading the day he will encounter the corpse of a friend. As the narrator watches his malevolent employer drinking heavily and behaving badly, he thinks: 'I'm beginning to get used to this. That's worrying' (9). The narrator makes a gradual transition from revulsion at the sight of the cadavers to communing with them and finally no longer noticing them as he becomes hardened to the horrors. This novel makes demands on its readers, again recalling Yeats's 'a terrible beauty is born'.

Basharat Peer wrote the memoir *Curfewed Nights* and the screenplay for *Haider*—Bollywood director Vishal Bhardwaj's Kashmir-located *Hamlet*—as well as the article, 'Kashmir's Forever War'. In Peer's essay, he recounts going to meet the family of Manzoor Bhat, the Kashmiri who fought alongside a Pakistani in the Indian Parliament attack of 2008. Peer is curious to learn what caused this young man to leave his successful career as a painter and decorator to join Lashkar-e-Taiba. He learns that Bhat was radicalized when a peaceful protest he was taking part in was attacked by Indian forces, resulting in a bloodbath. Peer encounters relatives of other slain Kashmiris, including a man dubbed the region's 'oldest militant' (79) by the Indian press. No wonder, then, that Peer paints a picture of Kashmir in the first decade of the twenty-first century as 'silent and seething, crouching like a wildcat' (74).

As I have so far delineated an exclusively masculine world of representations of Kashmir, I close by turning to Sudha Koul's memoir, *The Tiger Ladies* (2000). Early on in his novel *Midnight's Children*, Rushdie describes the grandfather, Aadam Aziz, praying against the spectacular backdrop of the Kashmiri mountains of the Himalayas and the Pir Panjal Range. Comparably, Koul begins her memoir with a similar but matrilineal invocation of her Kashmiri grandmother, Dhanna, who churns buttermilk and smokes a hookah in an earlier, tranquil period for the region. Like Rushdie, Koul reflects that amidst the trauma of Partition, it was the 'shared life in the valley' that gave succour to Kashmiris from various religious backgrounds. 'We revel', she writes, 'in one another's mysteries and legends and resort to them when required, which is frequently' (30). She reports meeting fellow Kashmiri, Pandit Jawaharlal Nehru, when he attended a play at her school in the early 1960s, accompanied by his adult daughter, Indira, and her two sons. The memoir ends with the author, now exiled in New Jersey, reflecting on Kashmiris' hopes for political resolution to the conflict. As she muses, there are elusive moments of peace, but before long there is always a riot or kidnapping, 'and reality stares us again in the face' (218).

This cycle of peace and violence, which Koul compares to the inane rotation of a dog's tail, must eventually come to an end. Through the will of its people, Kashmir shall again come close to the earthly paradise imagined by Jahangir. How much more bloodshed this already saturated region will take remains a matter for conjecture.

11

Isloo and Pindi on Page and Screen

ISLAMABAD WAS CREATED under Field Marshal Ayub Khan's military governance in the early 1960s by a team of developers led by Constantinos A. Doxiadis, an architect and town planner from Greece. Doxiadis is also known for overseeing the construction of Karachi's Korangi Township. His Greek nationality contributed significantly towards his nomination to manage the formation of Islamabad, his career-defining project, because it placed Doxiadis at one remove from the Euro-American neo-colonizers of whom many Pakistanis were highly suspicious. In his recent book *Islamabad and the Politics of International Development in Pakistan*, Markus Daechsel shows that although Pakistan's capital is not as famous as the South Asian planned city of Chandigarh, designed by Le Corbusier (see Prakash *Le Corbusier*), its story is no less interesting. The new city was originally planned for the outskirts of Karachi, but was eventually located near Ayub Khan and the military's stronghold of Rawalpindi. Doxiadis called his credo of the built environment 'Ekistics', in which he privileged Muslim folk culture over top-down town planning. He was a proponent of clean lines, modernity, and what could sometimes be a coercively Eurocentric brand of development.

Amit Baruah, diplomatic correspondent for *The Hindu*, summed up the city accurately and succinctly in *Dateline Islamabad*—a book about his time spent in the city: 'Islamabad is a nice, sleepy, picturesque town. Situated at the foot of the Margalla Hills, it is divided into residential sectors—E, F, G, I—with the neatness that is the hallmark of a planned city' (xv). Less diplomatically, Islamabad also has the unfortunate reputation of being a boring place; as the strapline for Hammad Khan's film *Slackistan* quips, this is '[t]he city that ~~never~~ always sleeps'. Despite its alleged safe tedium, Islamabad is affectionately drawn in *Slackistan*. The city might almost be regarded as the sixth character in this film about young, affluent friends Hasan, Shehryar (given the appropriately louche nickname Sherry), and Saad, as well as their female companions Aisha and Zara. Hammad Khan explained that the '[c]ity was true protagonist of @SlackistanMovie'.[1] Indeed, in the film and most of the other texts examined in this chapter, Islamabad is no mere backdrop, but an active player.

Although the film's clever title led reviewers to make connections with Richard Linklater's 1991 movie *Slacker* and the slacker genre more broadly, *Slackistan* perhaps fits more closely with mumblecore's naturalism and low-budget, dialogue-heavy traits. If characters' code-switching exchanges are often indistinctly heard in the film, space is delineated with precision. In *The Poetics of Space*, Gaston Bachelard writes: 'For a knowledge of intimacy, localization in the spaces of our intimacy is more urgent than determination of dates' (9). Accordingly, we know little about when *Slackistan* is set, beyond a single conversation between Hasan and his father, which viewers are witness to, about 'Mr Ten Per Cent' (probably a reference to Asif Ali Zardari, who was Pakistan's president from 2008–2013). By contrast, we find out a great deal about what Bachelard terms 'the spaces of [the characters'] intimacy'. Captions flag up 'The Best DVD Shop in Town', 'The Busiest Hospital in Town', and various cafés and basement lounges. In a tender moment, Hasan and Aisha take in the quiet beauty of a sunset near the Margalla Hills, and later he meets her ABCD (American-Born Confused Desi) boyfriend, Owais, at a cactus-lined coffee shop in the hills.

Over the sound of birdsong, Owais, who works in renewable energy in the US, casually leans against the balcony of a lookout area, telling Hasan: 'You live in a beautiful city'. 'It used to be better', retorts lovesick Hasan. In a voice-over, he then confides in the audience: 'I can't even see the city any more. All I see is a reflection: an image of failure, fake dreams, and just a dead, empty space'. This solipsistic evocation of the protagonist's lack of success and the synthetic 'simulacra' (Baudrillard 166) he sees around him flows through the movie as a whole. When Aisha departs to go and live with Owais in America, she leaves a card for Hasan containing a photograph of herself on the back of which she has felt moved to write: 'This is a real image'. This slightly disconcerting note suggests to the viewer that several characters have a hard time distinguishing between genuine and fake things in Pakistan's hi-tech capital city.

Slackistan opens with a tracking shot of the backs of 'a couple of random guys' walking down one of Islamabad's tree-lined dual carriageway central reservations amidst free-flowing traffic. They both wear black t-shirts, blue jeans, sport 'funky haircuts', and one of the guys nonchalantly smokes a cigarette as they discuss the relative merits of McDonald's burgers, the 'kebab in a bun' served in local restaurant Munchies, and chicken chow mein. Their contrasting opinions about what should count as a burger and about the 'little differences' between national cuisines recall Quentin Tarantino's famous 'Royale with Cheese' scene from *Pulp Fiction*. Another film that is intertextually referenced in *Slackistan* is *Zibakhana* (Hell's Ground), directed by Omar Ali Khan in 2007. This was Pakistan's first slasher horror film and, like *Slackistan*, it centres on the travails of a group of well-educated young inhabitants of Islamabad.

At the end of *Slackistan*'s opening scene, the men's upper bodies are captured in freeze-frame, as a languid voice-over explains that the pair are moneyed and knowledgeable, but still can't decide what to eat: 'It doesn't matter if it's American, desi, or Chinese. If they can't [...] make up their mind and choose what they want, they'll end up with nothing'. This signposts the picture's deeper substratum about cosmopolitan, Westernized twenty-somethings residing in Pakistan. This demographic group, the film suggests, faces confusion about the direction their lives should take as the country becomes increasingly contorted with violence. Hasan—whose voice it is, as we discover at the end of the opening scene—is an 'Isloo wallah' (S. Khan *City*: 134). He relates some of Islamabad's history, calling (unspecified) Ayub Khan's vision for his city a perfect 'masterplan'. Hasan's confident tone dissolves into hesitancy as he tacks on the disclaimer: 'in theory, anyway'. A split screen flashes up with the caption 'Good Sector' over a still of a well-heeled area, atop the lower screen, where the words 'Bad Sector' are superimposed on the image of a slum district. Halfway through *Slackistan*, Hasan makes a rare trip outside his air-conditioned milieu into a poor Christian colony. There, he is confronted with open drains and children playing on a hazardous trampoline near a skip overflowing with rubbish. So much for Doxiadis's perfectly planned grid system for Islamabad, which he hoped would 'keep much of everyday life in as safe and intimate spaces as possible' (Daechsel 218). Hasan acknowledges—again in a voice-over—that Islamabad was built so that 'the diplomats, the bureaucrats, the VIPs could all live in their comfort zones without being too disturbed by the masses'. Yet there was a fatal design flaw: '[T]hose who cooked for, cleaned after, served these people had to live nearby. I guess that's why the masterplan could never be perfect.'

In Sorayya Khan's stunning new novel *City of Spies*, the fractious contours of a divided city and the perilous lives of servants are projected onto a 1970s backdrop of General Zia's coup against, and subsequent execution of, Prime Minister Zulfikar Ali Bhutto. Signalling the city's thematic centrality from the outset, this novel is dedicated to '*Nadeem and our Islamabad*' (S. Khan np.; emphasis in original). Readers are then presented with an epigraph from Intizar Hussain's Partition novel *Basti*: '*[T]hey carried their cities with them, as a trust, on their shoulders*' (Husain 102; qtd. in S. Khan np.; emphasis in original). The protagonist, Aliya, is a pre-pubescent girl who attends the American School of Islamabad and lives in a relatively 'good sector' with her Dutch mother, Pakistani father, their servant Sadiq, and his small son. The varied colours of car number plates announce the segregated nature of this city. From her perspective as a young child, Aliya relates: 'My parents drove a car with black licence plates, not the yellow ones sporting special codes of numbers which announced their foreign embassy and rank' (54). Aliya's comfortable Pakistani district is far less opulent than the diplomatic enclaves many of her friends live in. However, even if she feels insecure as a middle-class 'half-and-half' (*passim*), the racial and class-based indignities she suffers are nothing compared to Sadiq's humiliation and pain. Each day, this manservant struggles to run errands on his bicycle as he is compelled to traverse dangerous, potholed roads. He regularly has to swerve to avoid the spit-balls lobbed at him by raucous American boys from the bus that carries Aliya and other children between the separate 'universe[s]' (27) of school and home. A self-hating, goraphile part of Aliya thinks Pakistanis deserve to be spat on by the international school pupils (27). One ill-fated day a white woman mows down and kills Sadiq's son in a hit-and-run accident. In this 'city of spies', Sadiq himself begins spying on his son's killer as his mental health unravels.

Islamabad and its environs house Pakistan's nuclear facilities, while camps have sprung up near the city for the training of Kashmiri insurgents. Little wonder, then, that the capital is a hub for intelligence work. In November 2016, Pakistani authorities accused eight Indian diplomats of spying for India (Abbas 'FO Reveals': np.); however, espionage has a much longer and more involved provenance in the city. During the Cold War, the USSR and US covertly confronted each other on Islamabad's streets, and Pakistan 'was but one playground where both superpowers spread mischief' (S. Khan *City*: 1). In the novel, Sadiq spies on his son's inadvertent murderer in this city 'full of secrets' (156), children play 'I Spy', Aliya's family are watched around the clock by motorcycle spies, Iranian SAVAK secret agents lurk in the shadows, and the father of Aliya's American best friend is an emissary who speaks Urdu and uses the pretence of work as a malariologist as a cover for his espionage activity.

This subterfuge is mostly hard to spot, and at a surface level, Islamabad remains calm and clean. It is a relatively small, bureaucratic city, portrayed in the novel as distinct from other Pakistani metropolises, such as Lahore. Aliya is familiar with the Punjabi capital, as her childhood home is located within Islamabad—specifically, Five Queen's Road (also the title of Sorayya Khan's second novel). Khan contraposes the two cities through sensual images of slumber and smell; 'Islamabad was quiet, asleep in a way Lahore never was' (189), and 'Lahore stank and Islamabad did not' (129). Notwithstanding this last olfactory shortcoming bluntly articulated by Aliya, her grandfather sees Punjab's capital as greatly superior to Islamabad, whose 'restrictions', he claims, such as the ban on rickshaws and horse carts, 'forever separated it from the rest of the country' (133)

Not only is this city internally demarcated along social and racial lines, therefore, but it is also cut off from the rest of the nation. '*Nothing* ever happens' in Islamabad, Aliya tells her father (165; emphasis in original). That is to say, until something does happen (237)—namely, the allegedly CIA-sanctioned hanging of Zulfikar Ali Bhutto in 1979. In the same tumultuous year, Khan reminds us, Afghanistan was invaded by Russian troops, Saddam Hussein came to power in Iraq, American hostages were held in Iran (Mr Hill, Aliya's school principal among them), and the Grand Mosque in

Mecca was seized for two fraught weeks at the end of the year. The
Grand Mosque seizure was accompanied in Pakistan by spurious
rumours of US involvement. The American Embassy in Islamabad
and other Pakistani cities deflagrated in response. Violence and fear
now reach Aliya's hermetically sealed school, once the only place in
Islamabad where it was impossible to hear the call to prayer (131).
Aliya and her friends find themselves under siege from a violent
mob roiled by the burning of the American Embassy. Islamabad
finally joins the rest of the country in shame and suffering. Similarly,
Aliya feels 'suddenly Pakistani' (186) amid her American classmates'
hasty exit from the country aboard a disguised bus. Thus, when
Islamabad awakens finally to its inevitable conjoining to the nation,
the narrator astutely observes (208) that relationships between
countries often come to operate like a game of Klackers—that
vintage American game in which two glass beads are slammed
together on a single string. The year 1979 was a momentous one
when it became clear that 'the world was a small place and what
happened in one place affected the other' (208). Indeed, in many
ways the last year of the 1970s was more of a turning point for
Pakistan than 9/11.

The novel concludes with evocative explorations of other earth-
shattering years: 1989, when the Cold War ended; 2001, which
heralded the inception of a new Afghan War after the World
Trade Centre attacks; and Benazir Bhutto's assassination in 2007
(222–3). After all this historical change, present-day Islamabad is
almost unrecognizable: rebuilt and overcrowded. Its diplomatic
bailiwick is now a fortified 'Red Zone' replete with checkpoints,
bodyguards, and security gates. On the novel's final page, Khan's
narrator eloquently laments the situation:

My home is a barrage of headlines. You see, my country is at war.
My cities are burning. My capital is a police checkpoint. My sector

borders the Red Zone. My road is a sandbag bunker. My hills, my beautiful Margalla Hills, are an airplane crash site. My Kohsar Market is the site where the Punjab governor was gunned down. Later today, tomorrow, or not until next week (if we're lucky), the list of headlines will have grown.

The Islamabad of my childhood is so remote there was only one way to keep it alive.

I wrote my home (238).

Here, Khan refers, first, to the assassination of the twenty-sixth Governor of Punjab, Salman Taseer, for opposing Pakistan's blasphemy legislation (Walsh np.), and, second, to the domestic plane crash that killed 152 people, due to pilot error (Ellick np.; Dawn np.). These two Islamabad-based tragedies both unfolded in the early 2010s. What Khan does not mention is a slightly earlier and more famous incident that occurred in the city: the Red Mosque siege. The Lal Masjid mosque 'had become a base for militants who were launching vigilante raids on video stores and Chinese-run "massage parlours"'. Because the Masjid is 'less than 2 miles from the presidential palace and the parliament' (Lieven 417), the government was forced to act. In July 2007, President Pervez Musharraf controversially ordered troops to storm the mosque, and over 150 people, including women and children, were killed in the ensuing carnage.

Khan also confidently embraced the task of setting her debut novel, *Noor* (2004), in blood-spattered, conflict-ridden 1970s Islamabad. Partly set in 1971, eight years earlier than *City of Spies*, against the backdrop of the Bangladesh Liberation War, *Noor* is about hatred and love, disability and artistic genius. Ali is an ageing estate agent, who built a house in the shadow of the Margalla Hills during Islamabad's early days. This house is known locally as 'Ali's Sector', because its modular structure reflects the lines of the city.

Out of guilt for his role as a West Pakistani soldier, at the end of the 1971 War Ali adopted Sajida, the 5-year-old daughter of a dead Bengali woman. As a young woman, Sajida marries a suitor named Hussein. The couple have two healthy sons, before Sajida gives birth to a girl. Throughout this third pregnancy, Sajida is convinced that her unborn daughter is different in some shape or form. Noor, her daughter, has an undiagnosed mental disability. She does not notice pain; refuses to leave the home, which is her whole universe; and has a revealing fear of lines or borders, as well as an almost preternatural gift for painting other people's dreams and reminiscences.

Noor's skill disturbs her grandfather, Ali, who has until now successfully repressed his memories of the atrocities he and his fellow soldiers committed in Bangladesh. After the war, he takes pains to avoid the half-constructed empty houses strewn around the city, 'which existed in a strange tandem of being there and not being there' (34). Ali is haunted by the knowledge that these dwellings belonged to East Pakistanis killed in, or forced to flee after, the war. The ghostly domiciles sit oddly next to the exuberant urban growth and rampant corruption that exists in the capital city during these early years. Over time, the sublime view of the hills from Ali's Sector is impeded by construction works and the sprouting of 'massive pillars and mansions' out of the scrubland (38). Yet it is the city's pastoral origins that are most strongly called to mind in this novel. Sajda remembers 'the mountains of shrubbery and streams that broke so abruptly from the plateau' (94), while Hussein recalls a tryst with Sajida at the Daman-e-Koh viewpoint before the pair were married: 'They'd parked their cars pointing down toward the city of Islamabad, which unfolded like a planner's blueprint from where they sat on boulders perched high above. Below, the main sector avenues ran like airport runways and cut the city into now unimaginably precise rectangles' (85). Khan uses a similar architectural exactness to the 'planner's blueprint' in describing the city in *Noor*. She portrays Islamabad's most iconic landmark, the sleek white Faisal Mosque, as startling against the Margalla Hills' splendour and as remarkably 'spaceship-like' (71)—a simile that is repeated in *City of Spies* (S. Khan *City*: 112).

In an interview appended to the American edition of *Noor*, Cara Cilano poses a question about place to this spatially alert writer: 'Is place-based-ness a move toward looking into the domestic?' Khan responds to communicate that location is the point of departure for her: '[T]hat's my lens. When I'm thinking about narrative, it springs from location.' As in the film *Slackistan*, Khan talks of Islamabad's 'scripted' design, while acknowledging that '[i]t didn't turn out that way because growth is uncontrollable; it's sprawl' (217). She is less convinced by Cilano's intimation that location allows her to explore domesticity. Yet I would agree with the American academic that Khan's two Islamabad novels put across a stronger sense of the unassailable attachments of place (see Lefebvre; Tuan) than of the freedom and excitement of space so often denied to Pakistani women.

The final Isloo novel under examination in this chapter, Sophia Khan's *Dear Yasmeen*, is set in snowy New York state for the duration of the novel's first half, while the reader is treated to glimpses of Islamabad in its second half. This is, in many ways, a campus novel, and it features another mixed-race family. Crawford, NY, is depicted as a masculine space, where teenage protagonist Irenie's Irish-heritage professor father, James, broods distantly on the mysterious disappearance and death of her Pakistani mother, Yasmeen. By contrast, Islamabad is a kaleidoscope of chaotic, female interior spaces:

> Petticoats of six different colours adorn every surface and blouses loiter adulterously over petticoats with which they don't belong.

Jewellery cases spill over on the dressing table, gold lengths a
gleaming mess around stern, solid bits of stone. A clutter of
half-filled perfume bottles march over the bureau and cosmetic
implements of every type are scattered here and there. Ashtrays and
undergarments lie forgotten on the floor where stiletto heels with
sharp, cruel points endanger every step (219–20).

The womanly milieu that Khan outlines here chimes with fellow
Pakistani–American writer Sara Suleri's Lahore-based *Meatless
Days*. The memoir's famous first line reads: 'Leaving Pakistan was,
of course, tantamount to giving up the company of women' (1).
Khan similarly conveys an almost claustrophobically feminine
world in Islamabad. She paints a picture of the disarray and detritus
of wedding preparations, recalling the toilet scene from Alexander
Pope's epic poem *The Rape of the Lock*, in which readers are invited
to behold Belinda's vanity:

The Tortoise here and Elephant unite,
Transform'd to *Combs*, the speckled and the white,
Here Files of Pins extend their shining Rows,
Puffs, Powders, Patches, Bibles, Billet-doux (Pope I.l.35–8; 31;
emphasis in original).

Just as Pope sneaks in the Christian holy book to his last, alliterative
line, so, too, does Khan allow the dangerous adverb 'adulterously'
entrance into her seemingly innocuous list of clothing, jewellery,
and cosmetics. This is especially significant, given that the novel
quickly establishes that Irenie's mother deserted her family due to
an extramarital affair.

American-born Irenie finds herself relatively sequestered when
she spends time in Islamabad, her containment seemingly due
to security fears, which were held well before the events of 9/11.

She sees little more than the interiors of houses and views from chauffeur-driven cars: 'Now and again an overloaded white van passes by, undecorated but for a decal on the back window depicting a female eye peering seductively through a plastic shade' (192). Soon after arrival, she sees a huge sign broadcasting Quaid-i-Azam (Father of the Nation) Muhammad Ali Jinnah's idealistic slogan 'UNITY FAITH DISCIPLINE' on a hill near the airport (192). In *Slackistan*, this well-known landmark is ironically juxtaposed with a wall emblazoned with an Urdu graffito, translated in the subtitles as 'No More American Enslavement'. Irenie's relatives draw her attention to the buildings they pass: 'the Saudi Pak Tower, the prime minister's house, a garish new skyscraper' (192), but the car does not stop and she is thus unable to take in much of note. Hers is very much a touristic gaze (Urry), since her cousin Shamim 'prides herself on coming up with new entertainments in this city where there are only about four things to do, three of which involve eating' (268). Again, this inadvertently echoes *Slackistan*, in which aspiring filmmaker Hasan bemoans that 'there are a hundred restaurants and not a single cinema in this town'. Once Irenie has visited the forlorn zoo, rowed on Rawal Dam, and climbed Mount Happiness, the only tourist attraction left to explore is the Itwar bazaar or Sunday market. Irenie possesses a Western, decidedly Orientalist perspective, which is made apparent when she attempts to imagine the bazaar she is preparing to visit: 'Marrakesh and Bombay and camels pulling loads. [...] If not odalisques and hashish pipes, at least open-air market places full of brilliant things' (269). Instead, she discovers that:

Itwar bazaar proves quite unlike the movies [...]. The small stream we cross to get there indeed glitters, but with broken glass and plastic bags. I suspect sewage flows beneath the trash, though once

we get into the chickens I can't smell it anymore. They're stuffed
into cages, feathers escaping like spaghetti through a sieve (269).

More than the tourist sights and attractions that Shamim valiantly
takes Irenie to see, it is the clear sounds of strange animals and
birds, the call to morning Fajr prayer, and the view of a beautiful
young bride on a dais that have the most impact on her.

Stark contrasts are to be found in Islamabad's much older sister
city, Rawalpindi. Like Islamabad, it has a stiflingly hot climate in
summer and the winters are surprisingly cold and wet (Ashraf
199). However, there the similarities between the two cities
end. Rawalpindi is located southeast of Islamabad, nearer to the
Khanna plain—where the British colonizers used to hold horse
races—than to the lush banks of Rawal Lake. Whereas, as we
saw, Islamabad was hastily constructed from the 1960s onwards,
'Pindi's history dates back to the first millennium BC. It is one of
Pakistan's longest continuously inhabited cities, and is situated less
than twenty miles from Taxila—an archaeological site rich with
Buddhist and Hindu ruins.

Turning to the 1993 edition of the India Lonely Planet, John
King writes: 'The two cities, 15 km apart, are really a single mega-
town with bazaars at one end and bureaucrats at the other' (217).
King is right to identify 'Pindi's close association with bazaars.
Indeed, in Sorayya Khan's *Noor*, Ali goes to a bazaar in Rawalpindi
to buy parrots for Noor. It is also in this neighbouring commercial
centre that Isloo wallahs procure marble (42) and sweetmeats (57).
In addition to its significance in terms of shopping and bazaars,
'Pindi has long been the Pakistan Army's key garrison city. In
comparison with Islamabad's reputation for secure monotony,
Rawalpindi therefore tends to be viewed as a pugnacious, edgy
municipality. The two are night and day, and they endure a fraught,
if close, relationship. This is illustrated in *Dear Yasmeen* when a

member of Irenie's Pakistani extended family says of an aunt that she is so desperate to perfect a wedding outfit '[s]he's even been to Pindi' (301). In *Slackistan*, Aisha takes a pleading phone call from Zara, who is stuck at a local Islamabad café, the Hot Spot. As Aisha relates to her male friends: 'Pindi boys are circling her [Zara] around and she sent her driver away... Can we go rescue her?'

If contemporary Isloo wallahs construct Rawalpindi as a city one would visit or live in only as a last resort and whose denizens are threatening outsiders, the colonial, pre-Islamabad generation saw the metropolis differently. As a young journalist, Rudyard Kipling (1865–1936) was sent to Rawalpindi in 1885 to report for the *Civil and Military Gazette* on 'a move in the […] political chessboard' (in Moran 153) of the Great Game between Britain and Russia. This 'move' was a meeting that was scheduled to take place between the British Viceroy Lord Dufferin and Abdur Rahman, Amir of Afghanistan. In an early dispatch from the city entitled 'The Rawal Pindi Camp', Kipling stated, 'Pindi is […] fearfully and wonderfully martial' and remarked that the city 'swarms with wandering officers' (in Moran 123). Here and in the articles that comprise 'To Meet the Ameer', 'The Rawul Pindi Durbar', and 'The Rawulpindi Camp', written over March and April 1885, Kipling charted the area's topography, albeit limited to a British outlook from the civil lines. He described the Pindi Club, the mall, and the military camp—the latter jadedly depicted as turning into a 'swamp' in the pouring rain (in Moran 145, 151, 158).

Kipling's increasing frustration at the Ameer's delayed arrival on this, his first substantial journalistic mission, overspills into his reportage about 'Oriental notions of etiquette', the Ameer's tactic of making the Viceroy wait, and his 'lavish' rider of sherbets, fruits, and spices (in Moran 128, 130). He compares this 'oriental potentate'[2] with a 'wayward child', and encounters 'utter futility' (in Moran 127, 132) as he tries to obtain reliable information about the

Ameer's whereabouts: 'Verily, the way of Easterns [*sic*] are strange
and past finding out' (in Moran 132). The Ameer dismantles the
Raj's pomp and circumstance and in its place creates a comedy of
manners amidst interminable postponement. Kipling performs
some hand-wringing over the durbar's observance in wet, muddy
'Pindi: 'If it had *only* been in Lahore!' (in Moran 152; emphasis
in original). Yet it is in Rawalpindi that his path crosses with an
enigmatic personage who 'looks more like a wild Irishman than
anything else, commands troops and gives rise to innumerable vain
tales concerning his nationality' (in Moran 154). Could this be a
source of inspiration for Kipling's peripatetic, charismatic character
Kim, whose national identity for much of the 1901 novel appears
indeterminate, but who is, in fact, of Irish parentage? Overall,
Kipling portrays 'Pindi as a city at the centre of things during
the Raj's heyday, even if it is also associated with the 'dust and
confusion' (in Moran 132) that Kipling sees as an inevitable part
of life in the Orient.

This view of Rawalpindi's centrality is reinforced by *The
Postmaster* by Saad Ashraf (a former civil servant who also happens
to be Bapsi Sidhwa's brother). The novel's protagonist, Ghulam
Rasool, works as a loyal postmaster for the British. In the mid-
1920s, he and his family are relocated to Rawalpindi, a city which
is portrayed as bureaucratic, backbiting, and routine-bound.
There, he serves an unusually long six-year term as postmaster
in a largely white, racist organization. He is valued by his boss,
Herbertson, to such an extent that he is given sole responsibility
for operations when a cholera epidemic breaks out in the city.
The Englishman acquires the sour nickname 'Herbert the Wog'
for allowing his Indian employee to serve an unprecedented two
tenures in Rawalpindi. As in Kipling's writing, a cultural preference
for Lahore is expressed, exhibited by the fact that no sooner has
the narrative arrived in the Potohari city than it veers off to focus

its attentions on Lahore's Heera Mandi. Whereas in the red-light
district, women are pawns and men players, 'Pindi is portrayed
from the outset as a distinctly female space. It is in the zenana
or women's area of a hospital in the city that Ghulam Rasool's
wife, Sara, gives birth to their second child, a little girl. Soon after,
Ghulam's forthright and witty mother, Noorani Begum, disembarks
from a second-class women's carriage to look after her daughter-in-
law in her confinement. Sara is not sorry to leave Rawalpindi when
her husband is eventually appointed to a postal job in Amritsar, for
she hates the city's 'cold, dark winters'. However, to her friends and
relatives in Delhi she plans to 'praise the town sky-high' (212), as
she hopes to impress the majority of them who have never set foot
outside the Indian capital.

Not long after Independence, an incident known as the
Rawalpindi Conspiracy occurred. In 1951, Major General Akbar
Khan allegedly banded together with other left wing military
officers and some civilian Communist Party activists to attempt
a coup against Pakistan's first prime minister, Liaquat Ali Khan.
The group of civilian activists supposedly included the authors
Sajjad Zaheer and Faiz Ahmed Faiz, who were both involved with
the Progressive Writers' Association. In her essay 'Faiz Ahmed
Faiz and the Rawalpindi Conspiracy Case', Estelle Dryland traces
Faiz's growing disillusionment with the fledgling state of Pakistan.
Liaquat's signing of the Objectives Resolution—ensuring the
country became 'a citadel of Islam' (qtd. in Dryland 176)—quashed
Faiz's hopes for Pakistan's grounding on secular socialism. This rude
awakening will be familiar to readers of Faiz's poem 'The Morning
of Freedom: August 1947', with its famous lines:

This stained light, this night-bitten dawn—
This is not the dawn we yearned for.
This is not the dawn for which we set out

Hoping that in the sky's wilderness
We would reach the final destination of the stars (102).

Faiz, Zaheer, and the others denied all the charges against them.
Dryland contends that there had been some talk between the fifteen
conspirators of a coup, but this was abandoned as unworkable.
Nonetheless, all were imprisoned, apart from the sole woman,
Begum Akbar Khan, who was released. The male prisoners faced
a summary death penalty for this treason indictment. A trial
eventually took place, but it was held in camera in Hyderabad,
Sindh. Faiz was released in 1955, but not before he wrote 'some of
the finest resistance poetry to have ever come out of Pakistan' (Jalal
81). In response, the state embarked on a vicious cleansing of left
wing activity throughout the country.

In 1988, an Afghan mujahideen ammunition cache exploded
in Rawalpindi, killing at least 100 people. Tariq Mehmood moves
beyond the sensational newspaper headlines to chillingly fictionalize
this disaster in *Song of Gulzarina* (2016). Mehmood's intelligent
thriller partly unfolds in the northern English settings of Bradford,
Shipley, and Manchester, but its protagonist, Saleem, also repeatedly
returns to his Pakistani home village near 'Pindi and to its western
neighbouring city, Peshawar. During the War in Afghanistan, he
briefly disappears over the border, where he witnesses a bomb attack.
When he was working as a journalist in Pakistan, Mehmood was
one of only two people who ventured into the Ojhri Camp, which
was used as an ammunition depot, even as the rockets were still
intermittently taking off and causing havoc. Communicating via
email, he described it as nothing less than 'a scene from hell'. Rafia
Zakaria also examines the Ojhri Camp incident in her non-fiction
work *The Upstairs Wife*, which is at once a memoir, an account of
women's social history, and a history of Pakistan. In her writing

about Ojhri, Zakaria proves a contention made in *Slackistan* that Pakistan is a country where conspiracy theories come true:

In the days that followed, more stories and even more bodies were extracted from beneath the shattered glass and twisted pieces of metal, bits of flesh still stuck to them. Tales of the dead were smuggled to newspaper offices, where editors published them in bits and pieces. One official body count was one hundred. The body count based on these unofficial accounts was estimated to be anywhere between one thousand and four thousand people, felled by weapons intended for another place altogether. The Ojhri Camp massacre showed ordinary Pakistanis just how little they knew about the deals their military rulers reached with the United States (125).

This visceral and mistrustful description indicates that Rawalpindi's military status has not been beneficial for ordinary dwellers in the city.

To conclude, the three Khans—Hammad, Sorayya, and Sophia— are perspicacious Isloo wallahs. The auteur Hammad Khan's panoramic *Slackistan* centres on men roaming around the city and going for expansive, if aimless, drives. By contrast, Sorayya and Sophia Khan's Islamabad novels tend to focus more on domestic spaces, interiors, and occasional, supervised trips to viewpoints such as the one mentioned earlier, situated at the Margalla Hills. All three convey truths about men and women, the home and the world, in Pakistan's youthful capital city. There are fewer representations of 'Pindi in literature and film, and what there is tends to have a historical slant. The then contemporary history of the Raj is portrayed in Kipling's 'Rawul Pindi' dispatches, and British rule is looked back on from a millennial vantage point in Saad Ashraf's *The Postmaster*. Both Mehmood and Zakaria recall the 1980s and one of Pakistan's most notorious man-made disasters. Rawalpindi

has been overshadowed by the abutting capital Islamabad and
darkly shadowed by the scandals of the Conspiracy and Ojhri. If
a wider range of art is set in Islamabad, despite the capital's young
age, 'Pindi is still a popular location for representations of military
derring-do and Kafkaesque bureaucratic structures.

Notes

1. This comment was made in Twitter communication between Khan and me;
   see H. Khan 'City': np.
2. Kipling was remarkably random and inconsistent in both his orthography
   and capitalization, as we see from his fungible use of 'oriental' and 'Oriental',
   as well as his various renditions of 'Rawalpindi'.

III

HUMAN RIGHTS AND INHUMAN WRONGS

II

HUMAN RIGHTS AND
INHUMAN WRONGS

12

Torturing the 'Other': Who is the Barbarian?

Towards the end of J. M. Coetzee's *Waiting for the Barbarians*, his protagonist, the Magistrate, speculates on how much pain he—an ageing, out-of-shape man—will be able to withstand. He is about to be tortured at the hands of the Empire. Despite years of loyal service, his antagonist, Colonel Joll, believes that the Magistrate has betrayed the Empire, because of his romantic entanglement with a girl from the enemy 'barbarian' community.

This particular section of Coetzee's novel encapsulates torture's most distinctive attributes. While the Magistrate's anxieties revolve around what degree of pain he can tolerate, the level of the pain inflicted is not the central purpose behind the act of torture. Through their torture, the Magistrate's tormentors reduce him to a body or a thing that is incapable of thought or political opinion. Coetzee conveys this in part through his use of the third person singular gender neutral pronoun 'it': '[I]ts head is gripped and a pipe is pushed down its gullet and pints of salt water are poured into it till it coughs and retches and flails and voids itself' (154). The diction here drives home the elaborate, quasi-medical, inventive methods that torturers use on their victims. Coetzee emphasizes that the central event of torture—the interrogation of the prisoner—is, in fact, a cover story: a huge lie. The Magistrate has prepared 'high-sounding words' to answer the interrogator's questions about his dealings with the barbarians. But there is no conversation, no questions, and no single interrogator; instead, 'they came to my cell to show me the meaning of humanity, and in the space of an hour they showed me a great deal' (154). What 'they' demonstrate to the Magistrate is that when his body is in severe pain, he is incapable of thought, language, or ethics.

Five years after the publication of Coetzee's novel, in 1985, the literary critic Elaine Scarry published *The Body in Pain*. In this seminal philosophical discussion cum cultural critique, she explores what happens to people who are physically agonized. In the most important chapter for our purposes, 'The Structure of Torture', Scarry examines what the consequences are when we inflict pain on others, both for the inflictor and the afflicted. She argues that torture pivots on a display of agency, which frequently involves the victim being confronted with, or 'being made to stare at' (27), an outlandish and often outsized weapon.

Scarry asseverates that torture is not only physical, but also verbal. The spoken component is the interrogation, which is almost always integral to the process of torture. Interrogations provide a justification for torture, in that the necessity of information gathering propels the violence. However, torturers' questions are usually irrelevant or even meaningless. All that matters about the questions that are asked is the tone in which they are spoken and the unequal power relations that they articulate. As the afflicted is broken down, both physically and mentally, they become increasingly quiet and preoccupied with their body. The torturer, in contrast, becomes exponentially verbose and concerned with justifications and explanations. Eventually, if the victim says anything, they submit to using the torturer's language, since their own has ceased to exist.

Whether questioning or hurling assertions, abuse, and orders, interrogators do not uncover important information. Instead, they produce the interrogation as a performance that takes centre stage in what Scarry terms 'the structure of torture'. Scarry goes on to argue, using language that chimes plangently with *Waiting for Barbarians*:

> For the prisoner, the sheer, simple, overwhelming fact of his agony will make neutral and invisible the significance of any question as well as the significance of the world to which the question refers. Intense pain is world-destroying. In compelling confession, the torturers compel the prisoner to record and objectify the fact that intense pain is world-destroying (29).

Confronting severe anguish, the prisoner finds that questions and answers fade into the background and seem trivial and inconsequential. Towards the end of this excerpt, Scarry twice uses the term 'world-destroying' to describe pain's effects. This resonates with her larger thesis running through the book, which is that pain is destructive and unmakes the world, whereas the creation of life is constructive and makes the world—hence, *The Body in Pain* is divided into two parts, 'Unmaking' and 'Making'.

When undergoing torture, the pain inflicted is so intense that a confession is almost inevitable. Despite this, both those who are pro- and anti-torture share a veiled contempt for confession. Confession tends to be interpreted as a betrayal of one's people, politics, and principles. Yet it is impossible either to betray or remain true to something that no longer exists. During the act of torture, the world shrinks to merely that which is contained within the space of the torture chamber and even language ceases to exist, despite the torturer's incessant chatter. Nothing else is real other than the room, torturer, tortured person, and weapon. As Scarry puts it: 'The body is its pains, a shrill sentience that hurts and is hugely alarmed by its hurt; and the body is its scars, thick and forgetful, unmindful of its hurt, unmindful of anything, mute and insensate' (31). Confession is also often unreliable (see Constanzo and Gerrity 182–4). For example, the misleading revelation that Saddam Hussein trained al-Qaida in the use of weapons of mass destruction and was in possession of these weapons—famously used as justification by the US and UK for the second invasion of Iraq in 2003—was elicited by means of torture and later retracted (Finn np.).

Scarry draws a comparison between the pain of the prisoner and that of the dental patient having a tooth drilled, the religious penitent who self-flagellates, or the old person experiencing aches and discomfort as a daily reality. The dentist's act of drilling a tooth is a short-lived, if admittedly unpleasant experience. One knows how long to expect the pain from this sort of procedure to last and takes painkillers to militate against its shrill agonies. With torture, one has no idea what its duration will be, whether any relief will be provided for the injuries afterwards, or whether and when the torture will recommence. The person who mortifies their body out of religious conviction regulates the pain level and can stop it at any time, whereas the torture victim has no such control. Both of these types of pain—oral pain brought about by dental work and self-inflicted physical pain prompted by spiritual belief—also have a rationale and future orientation, and thus are submitted to on that basis. Even the elderly person, whose suffering may seem more random and is not chosen, can take comfort in looking back on a long life, which self-same life has led to the body's natural state of decay and death.

Scarry links torture to a juxtaposition of Self and Other, which I discuss further in Chapter 33, 'The Barbarians Are at the Gate: On Self-Construction and the "Other"'. To be able to torture someone else, one has to disregard that person's humanity. If one recognizes a spark of consciousness in the Other, it becomes more difficult to inflict pain on them, since one can imagine, and therefore empathize, with how they feel and what they think about treated in this cruel way. Scarry recalls the German–Jewish political theorist Hannah Arendt's evaluation in *Eichmann in Jerusalem* of how the Nazis were able to starve and murder their concentration camp victims. They did this by inverting the direction in which the pain was believed to flow. Rather than focusing on the suffering they made others undergo, instead they convinced themselves: 'What horrible things I had to watch in the pursuance of my duties, how heavily the task weighed upon my shoulders!' (Arendt, qtd. in Scarry 58).

The connection that Scarry makes between torture and the denial of the Other's humanity is extended in Tzvetan Todorov's *The Fear of Barbarians*. Todorov calls torture 'a gangrene on democracy' (11) and a 'mark [...] of barbarity' (24). He agrees with Scarry's point that non-admission of the Other's humanity leads to torture, but argues that paradoxically it is a simultaneous recognition of the Other's sentience that shapes the nature of torture. '[T]he others are like us', he writes, 'they have the same vulnerable points as us, they aspire to the same good things' (21). If we are able to put ourselves in the enemy's shoes, we will be all the more adept at placing pressure on their weak spots. Todorov also highlights the sense of unlimited power that committing acts of torture gives the torturer. Unlike murder, which is finite, torture goes on and on, making its instigator 'feel close to the gods' (125). Torture is therefore, according to Todorov, worse than murder.

Article 5 of the Universal Declaration of Human Rights clearly states that: 'No one shall be subjected to torture or to cruel, inhuman or degrading treatment or punishment' (UN np.). This is not to say that torture ceased to occur after the Universal Declaration was adopted and proclaimed in 1948, but rather that governments at least moved to try to hide it if they undertook acts of torture.

However, during the 'War on Terror' and its toxic half-life, what
Todorov calls 'the adoption of torture as a legitimate practice' (113)
was implemented by the United States and its allies.

Todorov's *The Fear of Barbarians* was completed in 2007, but in
its English edition, published in 2010, the French–Bulgarian critic
reflected on the release by Barack Obama in 2009 of secret torture
memos written during George W. Bush's administration. These
memos revealed the way the US sought to change the definition of
torture after 9/11, so that 'cruel, inhuman or degrading treatment'
(Todorov 114–15), such as being played loud music, waterboarding,
humiliation, sleep deprivation, and so on, would be categorized
as 'increased pressure', rather than torture (CIA counsel, qtd. in
MacAskill np.). Since *The Fear of Barbarians'* publication, more
information has emerged with respect to the cover-up of torture
by the White House and US intelligence agencies. As recently as
December 2014, the United States Senate published a shattering
report on the CIA's torture regime (Rushe et al. np.). This report
exposed that prisoners were forced to stand on broken limbs, a man
died of hypothermia after sitting all night naked from the waist
down on a cold floor, and rectal interference caused permanent
physical damage to prisoners. The prisons of Abu Ghraib in
Iraq, Bagram Airbase in Afghanistan, and Guantánamo Bay in
Cuba remain bywords for terror, neglect, abjection, and violence.
Following up on campaign trail bluster that 'torture works', early
in his presidency Trump issued a draft order revealing that his
administration was scoping the possibility of bringing torture
back and that the aim was to bring new captives to Guantánamo
(Serwer np.).

The most common justification for torture is known as the
ticking bomb scenario. The thought experiment, dramatized in
the television show *24* (Cassar), is that a terrorist has planted a
bomb which will explode in an hour's time, but its whereabouts are

unknown. The utilitarian argument is advanced that the torture of a single terrorist is necessary in order to save the lives of hundreds, perhaps thousands of innocent civilians. Todorov denigrates the extreme implausibility of this set-up. In any case, as Scarry shows, confession is unreliable, because a person will say anything when the body is in pain. The notion that torture helps win wars is also faulty. It might bring a few short-term gains, but in the long run, the torturers' reputation is tarnished, vast numbers of opponents are created, and people are radicalized because of the injustice. Another reason for torture is simple revenge, but as Todorov observes: 'Terrorizing the terrorists also means that we are prepared to become their mirror image—to become even more hardened terrorists than they are' (124). The metaphor of the mirror in the context of torture underscores Todorov's broad thesis, which is that terrorizing the terrorists makes 'us' terrorists, and that it is the fear of barbarians that turns us into barbarians.

Let us now take a contemporary 'real life' example (from which an autobiography was subsequently produced)—the experience of Moazzam Begg. Begg is from Birmingham and has muhajir Pakistani heritage. As a young man in the 1990s, he worked for charities and as a political activist in such war zones as Bosnia and Chechnya. When 9/11 happened, Begg was working to set up a girls' school in Kabul. After the American invasion of Afghanistan, he moved with his family to Pakistan. There, he was seized from his home by security forces in 2002, and imprisoned first in Bagram and then in Guantánamo Bay.

In the infamous legal black hole of Camp X-Ray in Guantánamo Bay, Begg was detained without charge for three years, interrogated over 300 times, and tortured repeatedly. After this ordeal, Begg worked with journalist Victoria Brittain to write his autobiography, *Enemy Combatant* (2006). The book's title is significant: the US created a new category—enemy combatants—to refer to the people who were picked up in Afghanistan and Pakistan after 9/11. Rather than referring to these individuals as 'criminals' or 'enemy soldiers', both of which categories are covered by existing laws, the neologism 'enemy combatants' meant that security officials didn't have to treat the prisoners humanely.

When he was first arrested, Begg had a certain degree of awareness from keeping abreast of current events and popular culture about what was in store for him: 'hoods, beating, electric shocks [...], false accusations, death threats'. Yet nothing prepared him for the 'naked aggression' (110) he encountered. Not only was he falsely accused before being forced to don a hood, but he was also yelled at, kicked, abused, humiliated (his clothes were removed and photos were taken of his naked body), he underwent cavity searches, and his head and beard (a symbol of Muslim male religiosity) were shaved. The cruelty that upset him the most was psychological. Night after night he was played a recording of a woman screaming; convinced that it was his wife, he almost suffered a breakdown.

While Todorov identifies 'an eye for an eye and a tooth for a tooth' as one of the motivations for torture (92), Begg similarly found that the cells at Bagram Airbase are so named due to a revenge motive. These bullpens were named after terrorist atrocities perpetrated by Islamists, such as *USS Cole*, *Twin Towers*, and *Pentagon*. And just as Scarry describes the Othering of the prisoner that enables the torturer to break his body, so, too, a Christian guard confided to Begg that the only way he could fulfil his duties was to 'convince myself each day that you guys are all subhuman—agents of the Devil' (165). Eventually, Begg was so traumatized by the punishments meted out to him that he promised to tell his torturers whatever they wanted to hear, illustrating again the shakiness of the evidence produced in torture situations.

Torture is barbaric, in Todorov's sense of the failure to acknowledge that others are like us. It leads to an increase rather than a diminution of terror. Turning to the present, several credible sources (see Chulov np.) suggest that the occupation of Iraq and torture of people in Abu Ghraib were significant recruitment tools for Daesh. Although Hilary Benn's lauded speech during the UK Parliament's debate about Syrian intervention in 2015 was, in my opinion, overrated, he was right to point out that Daesh holds Britain and 'British values' in contempt (Benn np.). In that sense, Daesh is barbaric, as well as being terrifyingly ruthless. It should be loudly proclaimed, though, that Bashar al-Assad has done far more damage in Syria. But if Britain and the United States had stayed true to their alleged values and not colluded in rendition and torture over the last fourteen years, Daesh's propaganda would have fallen on deaf ears.

13

Culture and the Arab Spring

WHILE THE INITIAL ARAB SPRING REVOLUTIONS OF 2011 are well over, this pivotal event of the early twenty-first century continues. After the first revolutionary successes, which included the rapid and ignominious fall of Tunisian President Zine El Abidine Ben Ali; rousing scenes of protest in Egypt's Tahrir Square, leading to the departure of President Hosni Mubarak; and the ousting and repellent murder of Libya's Colonel Muammar Qaddafi over the spring and summer of 2011, the movement towards unseating Arab dictators is now taking on a darker aspect. The clear binary that could be identified earlier between, on the one hand, the initial protesters' dignity, courage, and good humour, and the authorities' disproportionate retaliation and violence on the other, gave way to something altogether more terrifying and incomprehensible. The conflict in Syria has continued for over six years, making it the bloodiest and most protracted of the Arab rebellions. This led to a 2012 intervention by the UN calling for all sides to adhere to international humanitarian and human rights law. However, full-scale genocide through the unmitigated use of barrel bombs, sarin, and chlorine gas has continued to be perpetrated on the Syrian people with ever increasing confidence by the murderous dictator, Bashar al-Assad. Assad's Russian allies then initiated their own self-styled 'War on Terror' with greater impact on the Free Syrian Army and other resistance fighters than on their declared enemy, Daesh. Yet their actions did not receive anything like as much media coverage or leftist critique as the US's War on Terror, even when the Russians deliberately targeted four hospitals on 16 February 2016. That same month, the UN released a damning report, in which they found Bashar al-Assad's government, al-Nasra, and Daesh guilty of murder, torture, and war crimes. The government, they held, was easily the worst culprit, having additionally perpetrated the 'crimes against humanity of extermination, [...] rape or other forms of sexual violence, [...] enforced disappearance and other inhuman acts'. In the report, the UN investigators also pointed out that the victims are often vulnerable, and certainly innocent civilians, who are not even involved in the war:

> While the overwhelming majority of the victims who perished while detained in Government-controlled prison facilities were men, the commission has documented cases of women and children as young as seven years old dying in the custody of State forces. One of the earliest documented cases of death in detention is that of a 13-year-old boy, arrested during a protest in Sayda (Dara'a) in late April 2011. His mutilated body was returned to his family in May 2011. Women, boys and girls, as well as the elderly, have been subjected to torture and brutal prison conditions and have suffered physical and mental trauma. They too have been the victims of, as well as witnesses to, deaths in custody (UN Human Rights Council np.).

A tectonic shift in the region's power play occurred with the unopposed fall of Aleppo in December 2016, even if Trump fired an impetuous salvo against Assad and the Russians with his bombing of Homs' Shayrat Airbase in April 2017. No wonder that amid all this turmoil some people now refer to the chill of an 'Arab Winter' (see, for example, Byman np.).

From an academic perspective, it is difficult to narrate the rapidly unfolding story of the Arab Spring. Ziauddin Sardar locates the revolutions within what he describes as our current 'postnormal society', meaning 'an in-between period where old orthodoxies are dying, new ones have yet to be born, and very few things really make sense' (435). Hamid Dabashi similarly argues that the Arab Spring quickly moved beyond 'race and religion, sects and ideologies, pro- or anti-Western' (xvii). He uses the term 'post-ideological' to describe the uprisings (11, 13, 155–70). Sardar's term, 'postnormal', and Dabashi's use of 'post-ideological' suggest that people are cumulatively challenging the previously pervasive idea of a clash of civilizations (Huntington 'Civilizations'; *Civilizations*). Hamid Dabashi even goes so far as to question if the current situation in the Middle East signals the end of postcolonialism. Building on this, he argues optimistically that—for all their problems, tensions, and uncertainties—the Arab revolutions are neither straightforwardly secular nor religious, and that the revolutionaries and rebels are proving that the region 'is no longer the middle of anybody's East' (6).

When they began, the uprisings that swept Tunisia, Egypt, Libya, Yemen, Bahrain, and Syria surprised many commentators in the West and amongst the Middle East's ruling classes, as they were accustomed to stereotypes about Arabs, Muslims, and the working classes as backward, obedient, and craving authoritarian rulers. These received ideas were stoked by the region's autocratic rulers. '[T]he government', writes Ahdaf Soueif wryly, 'knew the people and knew what they wanted and would supply the bits of it that it saw fit' (*Cairo*: 10). As late into the revolution as April 2012, former Egyptian Intelligence Chief and Vice President, Omar Suleiman, claimed that Egyptians were not ready for democracy (al Hasan np.)—and, indeed, many Western and non-Western newspaper and magazine articles made similarly incorrect claims.[1]

However, these revolutions, each one seeming to ignite another, revealed a very different image of Muslim Arabs as progressive, politically informed, and independently minded. Arab people occupied a position outside the ambit of mainstream history for decades, so these revolutions re-injected a real sense of dynamism. The significance of the Arab Spring bears comparison with the fall of the Berlin Wall in 1989, the (albeit very different) revolution in Iran in 1979, and even the rapid post-war decolonization of the British Empire. However, it also led to unprecedented bloodshed and displacement. Groups like Daesh and the al-Nusra Front jockeyed to fill the power vacuum caused by the collapse of corrupt regimes, most of whose so-called 'stabilizing' dictators had been armed and supported by the US. This has led to Arab civilians' serious, and justifiable, fears and anxieties about the future.

Since December 2010, the faces and voices of Arab people—rather than the abstractions 'Arab' and 'Muslim'—involved in the protests began being broadcast globally on television, computer, and phone screens. As British–Syrian author and media commentator Robin Yassin-Kassab puts it, the wider world became privy to the fact that 'the people in the Middle East in all their variety, as opposed to financial and military conspirators, are [...] crucial actors' ('Nobody': np.). On television channels such as Al Jazeera and through social media including Facebook and Twitter, viewers watched as the uprisings spread from Tunisia to Egypt, Libya, Syria, Bahrain, and Yemen, and as citizen–journalists, with their mobile phones and cameras, fed on-the-ground reports to the mainstream media. Meanwhile, intellectuals and journalists, many of whom hail from the aforementioned Arab countries, offered background knowledge and analysis of events, mostly through television interviews.

But technology does not a revolution make. The sheer number of protesters, their persistence and bravery, the fact that they are made up of as many women as men, and all their organization, creative, and communication skills are pointers to a history of protest and resistance in the Arab states, much of it suppressed. This is a history that includes many feminist protesters—some secular, some practising Muslims, some devotees of other religions—who have claimed and continue to demand freedom from oppression due to gender. In the uprisings that began in North Africa, women were prominent among the protesters in publicly voicing their demands for long overdue economic and political reforms. However, there was also significant backlash. A photograph of a woman stripped of her abaya by army men became a social media phenomenon, as her exposed blue bra was retooled as a symbol of resistance. Bloggers, Tweeters, and Facebookers criticized the country's Supreme Council of the Armed Forces (SCAF) and the Egyptian establishment's use of sexual harassment to keep women protesters in check.

Ironically, given the claims of Western nations to champion oppressed Muslim women, the importance of women activists in the uprisings has been neglected relative to the attention given to men in the Western media. Journalists Juan Cole and Shahin Cole write that '[w]omen have been aided by […] the rise of the Internet and social media. Women can assert leadership roles in cyberspace that young men's dominance of the public sphere might have hampered in city squares' (Cole and Cole np.). Indeed, the Yemeni Tawakkul Karman was one of three women awarded the Nobel Peace Prize in December 2011 for her journalism and activism against the Yemeni regime. Intense anger and suffering continues to animate Muslim women who are active in the cause of women's emancipation. Amina Wadud argued, in a different context, that what is needed is a 'gender jihad'—in other words, a struggle for the rights of women, as well as a religious striving, and a battle to overcome dictators.

Cultural production and art not only reflected, but also anticipated resistance. For example, the Egyptian film *Sarkhet*

Namla (Abdelaziz; Ant Scream), which deals with poverty and protest, prefigures the revolution: it was released around the time of the Tahrir Square demonstrations, but was completed in October 2010. Alaa al-Aswany, the Egyptian author of *The Yacoubian Building* (2002) and *Chicago* (2007), made some prophetic statements, collected in his book of essays, *On the State of Egypt* (2011). In 2009, more than a year before the Tahrir Square protests, he wrote: 'The time has come for us to leave our seats in the auditorium and create the next scene ourselves. Democracy is the solution' (*State*: 6). This reads like a call for revolution, and the author's words proved prescient. Al-Aswany was also instrumental in bringing about Prime Minister Ahmed Shafiq's resignation after only a month in power after he attacked Shafiq on television in March 2011 for being a Mubarak regime holdover, thus providing an example of writers directly influencing political events.

Turning to the medium of art, graffiti is street-level art calling for change. Particularly in Egypt, many witty placards, signs, and graffiti could be seen on display threatening the regime to get out and stay out. Yassin-Kassab even saw a 'mobile nuts-and-seeds stall' in Cairo soon after the fall of Mubarak with the words 'Social Justice' stencilled onto it ('Tahrir': 20). In Syria, the cartoonist Ali Ferzat was picked up by thugs hired by Bashar al-Assad and had his hands broken—the same hands that had produced great satirical art. His cartoons had shifted from veiled criticism of the regime to explicit ridicule of Assad and his cronies. One of his cartoons depicts President Assad sweatily clutching a suitcase as he tries to hitch a ride with Colonel Qaddafi of Libya, who is driving a getaway car. Cartoons openly criticizing the regime proved a step too far, so al-Assad tried to silence him, as regimes often do to defiant artists who agitate for justice.

In music, the group Eskanderila formed a few years ago to sing protest songs. The existence of the group was of questionable

legality until Tahrir Square erupted, when, according to Ahdaf
Soueif, their music could be heard openly on Egyptian streets for
the first time; their song 'Regaiyeen' ('We're Coming Back') was
especially influential. In Leila al-Shami and Robin Yassin-Kassab's
rapier-like analysis in their book, *Burning Country*, they explore
other forms of music, including hip hop and heavy metal, which
were adapted to attack the oppressive Assad regime (175–6).

In the Muslim world and beyond, the arts are less likely to be
compartmentalized and therefore ignored or considered elitist as
they are in the West, and instead are likely to be an integral part
of everyday life. In Arab countries and the nations of the Indian
subcontinent, for example, many of the great poets have had
their verses set to music and sung by popular musicians (think,
for example, of Noor Jehan singing Faiz Ahmed Faiz). This
often surprises Westerners; it's as though John Ashbery's poems
were being sung by Rihanna. Robin Yassin-Kassab explained to
me in an interview: 'Working-class Arabs have as much access
to poetry as the higher-class people. In the Middle East, poets
like Mahmoud Darwish and Nizar Qabbani become towering
nationalist figures, in a way that's almost unheard-of for poets in
the West' (qtd. in Chambers *British*: 205–6). Artists have therefore
used their popularity to push for change during the last two years
of revolution. In his book on the status and function of art during
the recent uprisings, *The Naked Blogger of Cairo*, Marwan M. Kraidy
gives us the useful term 'creative insurgency':

> If publics gather around concentrations of attention-grabbing texts,
> then revolutionary art is exemplary of the kinds of lures that attract
> publics. At once whimsical, grim, and heroic, insurgent art is chock-
> full of stylistic features that attract attention […]. Inventiveness
> is vital to rebellion, but revolutionary publics place politics above
> aesthetics. Creative insurgency uses art to shape revolutionary

political identities and promote cross-border solidarities, but it is not limited to art making. It is in the seesaw of bodies-in-pain and bodies-in-paint, in the cycle of artful protest and protest art, and in the debate about art that creative insurgency unfolds (206–7).

In light of art's inventiveness and political resonance, it is little wonder that oppressive regimes are quick to supress creative insurgency. In Syria, an amateur poet, Ibrahim Qashoush, who wrote the revolutionary song 'Get Out Bashar', had his vocal cords ripped out and was then murdered by Assad's henchmen (al-Shami and Yassin-Kassab 175). The actress Fadwa Suleiman led many Syrian demonstrations against Assad, despite being from the same minority Alawi sect that Assad comes from (al-Shami and Yassin-Kassab 89, 113). This was helpful early on in the conflict in minimizing sectarian violence against the Alawis, who make up almost 10 per cent of Syria's population.

Writers, artists, and filmmakers have been, and still are, at the forefront of revolutionary activity, but also, as we have seen, are being sickeningly punished for their courage and far-sightedness. Yet what is the role of literature in this conflict? Aside from the direct political activism undertaken by Alaa al-Aswany, the imagination has an essential role to play in revolutionary activity. Sinan Antoon, an Iraqi poet and novelist who was exiled to the US after the Gulf War of 1991, but who returned to Iraq in 2003 to perform in the film *About Baghdad*, argues that the Tunisian and Egyptian revolutions were sparked by poverty and oppression, and fuelled by 'poems, vignettes, and quotes from novels [which] were all there in the collective unconscious. The revolution introduced new songs, chants, and memes, but it refocused attention on an already existing, rich and living archive' (qtd. in Plum np.). In the same interview with Hilary Plum, Antoon extols some verses from 1934 by the late poet Abu al-Qasim al-Shabbi—'To the

Tyrants of the World'—which were used as a slogan almost a century later in al-Shabbi's home country of Tunisia and spread to Egypt and beyond:

> Hey you, the unfair tyrants
> You the lovers of the darkness
> You the enemies of life
> You've made fun of innocent people's wounds; and your palm covered with their blood
> You kept walking while you were deforming the charm of existence and growing seeds of sadness in their land
> Wait, don't let the spring, the clearness of the sky and the shine of the morning light fool you
> Because the darkness, the thunder rumble and the blowing of the wind are coming toward you from the horizon
> Beware because there is a fire underneath the ash (qtd. in Adib-Moghaddam 53).

Al-Shabbi's use of the second person pronoun serves to construct the poem as direct and accusatory, its tone insulting and full of righteous anger. The apparent calm of the spring belies the coming apocalyptic weather and an ominous, fiery future rising out of the ashes of the tyrants' destruction.

In relation to prose, Egyptian–British novelist Ahdaf Soueif was one of the most famous protesters against then President Hosni Mubarak in Tahrir Square. In her memoir, *Cairo: My City, Our Revolution*, she explains that on 25 January 2011, she was in Jaipur attending the literature festival. Quickly apprehending that something important was happening, she rushed back to her country of birth to participate in the action. By 28 January, Egypt erupted in protest, and Soueif describes being at the mouth of Tahrir Square, with smoke and gunfire ahead of her. A new solidarity emerged as strangers came to the collective realization that this was a battle for country's soul: '[W]e stood our ground and sang and chanted and placed our lives, with all trust and confidence, in each other's hands' (Soueif *Cairo*: 23). Soueif experienced a strange cocktail of revolutionary enthusiasm, laced with fear for the safety of her son and nieces, who were also present in the crowd. Elsewhere in her writing, she describes a thriving popular art scene in Egypt, including street art, jokes, and placards, concluding that '[t]his revolution is so organic, so personal, so real, it has exploded reservoirs of creativity' ('Protesters': np.). Turning to 'high' art, she argues in an Al Jazeera interview that even though it is easier to perceive poetry's role in rousing revolution, fiction 'keeps certain ideas alive and therefore keeps the ground fertile for revolutionary thoughts to take root' ('Political': np.). Imaginative texts galvanize because they make people understand that they are not alone in their thoughts and emotions.

Soueif holds that '[o]ptimism is a duty', but comments that the fight will take longer and prove more difficult than was first thought ('Political': np.). This British–Egyptian novelist found herself in the position of having to act as a commentator during the revolution. At first, she felt frustrated at her inability to experience in their fullness the eighteen days of the Tahrir protests. But as civilians were clearing rubbish, plumbers were constructing impromptu bathrooms, and doctors were treating the wounded, Soueif came to the conclusion that everyone had to do what they could. Her job became the business of interpreting, contextualizing, and representing: 'In revolution, you can't not be a participant' ('Political': np.). Even the book she produced about the revolution, *Cairo: My City, Our Revolution*, is described by Soueif as a revolutionary act. It was conceived of, written, and published with the intention of furthering the aims of the revolution, rather than simply commenting on it. To convey the dynamic nature of the

Egyptian movement, she even invents a verb: 'I tried to "revolute" and write at the same time' (xiv).

On the same Al Jazeera programme in which Soueif was interviewed, novelist Hisham Matar modestly claimed that authors are of equal or less use-value as bakers during civil wars, including the long and violent one that his nation of Libya has been suffering from, on and off, since 2011. Like Soueif, he suggests that everyone has their duty during the revolution—the baker to bake bread for the revolutionaries to eat, and the writer to represent the struggle (Matar 'Political': np.). Matar's father was taken from his home by the Mukhabarat (secret police) in 1990 and is still missing, presumed dead. Perhaps because of his traumatic experience, Matar played a central role in broadcasting the Libyan pro-democracy struggle to the West. His fiction, too, foreshadows many of the Arab Spring's concerns. His debut, *In the Country of Men* (2006), is a 'dictator novel', which holds up the figure of Qaddafi, Libya's 'Guide', to ridicule, horror, and condemnation. Matar's second novel, *Anatomy of a Disappearance* (2011), discusses the differences between the disappearance of an individual compared with a straightforward death: when someone disappears there are no mourning rites to help the relatives face their loss and move on. Finally, in 2016's *The Return*, he turned from fiction to autobiography to tell his father's story less obliquely.

Not only is Matar preoccupied with despotic regimes, but he also portrays the disorientation felt by the refugee or asylum seeker, who 'cannot leave and cannot return' (*Return*: 2). This is important, because the Arab Spring has prompted a tremendous migrant wave. The UN's High Commissioner for Refugees believes that in most Muslim countries, despite the significant size and subsequent repercussions of the uprisings, 'protection space inside countries of the region has not been substantially degraded. Traditions of Islamic and Arabic hospitality towards refugees endure' (UNHCR

'Refugee': np.). Libya is an especially alarming case, however, because it is the only North African country to have refused to sign the 1951 Refugee Convention and its 1967 Protocol. During the initial conflict between supporters of Muammar Qaddafi and rebels against his regime (supported by NATO forces), sub-Saharan African residents were most in need of protection, partly because of ongoing Arab racism towards them, and partly because they were associated in people's minds with mercenaries, or soldiers who get paid to fight for the regime.

Another Anglophone text that foreshadows the Arab Spring and limns dictatorships and repressive regimes with subtlety and black humour is *The Road from Damascus* (2008) by Robin Yassin-Kassab. In it, the British–Syrian author discusses multiculturalism, racism, and radicalization in Britain, as well as the larger conflicts present throughout the Middle East, via the story arcs of Sami, a British–Syrian, and Muntaha, his Iraqi-born wife. The novel examines tensions between religious and secular concepts of Arab nationhood, and comments on the use of state terror by totalitarian regimes. During a trip to Damascus, Sami discovers an uncle who had been the victim of prolonged imprisonment and torture. Deeply disturbed, Sami returns to his wife but retreats from their strained relations, disappears from the home, and falls into rapid but thankfully shortlived decline. The narrative builds in London during the aftermath of 9/11 and focuses on Muntaha's traumatic childhood, including her escape to Britain from Iraq with her father and brother. At its heart, *The Road from Damascus* is about the dogmatism that exists in both secularist and religious ideologies.

At present the least hospitable place for Arab Spring refugees is much of 'Fortress Europe'. Then the UK's Foreign Secretary, William Hague—who said the Arab Spring was more significant than 9/11 and spoke in 2011 about extending the 'hand of friendship' to Arab countries (Stourton np.)—nonetheless argued that Europe must be 'tough' on migrants trying to enter the EU in order to escape the conflict (Peck np.). More recently, the celebrity Lily Allen was vilified as a bleeding-heart liberal in several tabloid newspapers for apologizing on behalf of Britain to refugees in the 'Jungle' camp in Calais. Teenage migrants to the UK were threatened with dental checks to verify their ages. David Cameron employed unpardonable collective nouns for describing refugees—namely, 'a swarm of people' and 'a bunch of migrants'. He may have been a little more conciliatory following the emotional outpouring that followed the affecting photograph and naming of deceased toddler Alan Kurdi in Kos in September 2015. However, his feelings as a 'deeply moved […] father' (qtd. in Dathan np.) only led to a promise to take in a total of 20,000 migrants over five years (compared to the 1 million Germany took in 2015 alone, due to Angela Merkel's more humane policy on refugees). The signs of Theresa May's premiership point to even greater strictness than that of her fellow Tory predecessor (Travis np.). This should be a matter of national shame. Creative artists based in Britain, such as Ahdaf Soueif, Robin Yassin-Kassab, and Hisham Matar, are holding successive British governments to account for their (in)action in the Middle East, while artists on the ground in countries affected by the Arab Spring continue to risk everything for their creative insurgency.

Note

1. For two illustrative examples, see A. Green (np.) and Arabic News Digest (np.).

14

Advocacy Without Footnotes: Pakistani Cultural Production and Human Rights

R ECENT PAKISTANI CULTURAL PRODUCTION has shown a distinct turn towards human rights discourse. Writers and filmmakers are increasingly representing minorities' precarious position in contemporary Pakistan, and many of them also explore fierce debates about human rights, Islam, and cultural relativism. Therefore, in this chapter I examine how fiction, film, poetry, and theatre put the 'human' into 'human rights'.

Over a mere few months of 2013 alone, Pakistan witnessed the murders of Shia Hazaras and non-governmental organization (NGO) activists. Arson attacks against Christians in Joseph Colony, Lahore, shocked the nation, and Ahmadis continued to find themselves under attack, as they have done exponentially since Zulfikar Ali Bhutto amended the constitution in 1974 to label them 'non-Muslims'. It is unsurprising, then, that Pakistan was described by the Asian Human Rights Commission (np.) as having 'one of the most serious' human rights predicaments in Asia.

Human rights groups challenge the widespread persecution of minorities, but their views are seen by many as being alien to, or incompatible with, Pakistan and the wider 'Muslim world'. The allegedly 'Universal' Declaration of Human Rights is often perceived as a coercive, secular product of the West—another stick with which to beat Coca-Colonized nations. Islamic scholar Abdulaziz Sachedina unequivocally supports the enforcement of human rights, but argues that notions of democracy, pluralism, and human rights cannot be unanimously agreed upon 'without taking into consideration contextual and communitarian interpretations imposed upon the inclusive language of secular and religious texts' (4). Ann Elizabeth Mayer, author of the 1991 book *Islam and Human Rights*, argues for a similarly context-specific approach when it comes to Muslim attitudes towards human rights:

> A survey of this literature [produced in the 1980s by Muslims dealing with human rights] will quickly disabuse anyone of the assumption that there is a monolithic Islamic cultural standard. Muslims presently do not have a common belief about the Islamic position on human rights or where Islam stands regarding international human rights norms. Muslims have taken many differing positions on human rights, including the unqualified endorsement of international human rights standards as fully compatible with their culture and religion (10).

It is worth keeping in mind Sachedina's and Mayer's sensitively critical slant on human rights and Muslims' views.

Ron Dudai begins his piece 'Advocacy with Footnotes: The Human Rights Report as a Literary Genre' (2006) with the following statement:

> The human rights movement has given us a new vocabulary, new standards, new mechanisms and a new literary form: the human rights report [...]. Not a journalistic report, not a peer-reviewed academic piece, different from a legal brief, not quite a non-fiction documentary, and aiming at being something other than the old-

fashioned political pamphlet: it is a whole new kind of publication, with its own rules of style and presentation (783).

Based on my reading of human rights reports on Pakistan by groups including Amnesty International, Human Rights Watch, and the Office of the United Nations High Commissioner for Human Rights (OHCHR) Committee on the Rights of the Child, I agree with Dudai's playful point that the human rights report constitutes 'a genre of its own'. That said, there is enough variation between individual reports to argue that it is a flexible form. Writing for a particular audience and using its unique terminology, authors of human rights reports employ a fact-finding, legalistic style—often replete with scholarly footnotes—to establish credibility.

Fiction and Film

HOWEVER, THE HUMAN RIGHTS REPORT also has points of productive overlap with a number of creative mediums, such as films and fiction. This is especially evident in the report's inclusion of testimony—its sole vehicle through which emotions are allowed to penetrate measured, quasi-academic arguments. Similarly, films such as Sharmeen Obaid-Chinoy's and Daniel Junge's Oscar-winning documentary *Saving Face* about acid attacks on women, as well as novels such as Bina Shah's *Slum Child* and Mohammed Hanif's *Our Lady of Alice Bhatti* (both of which deal with Christian communities in Karachi), highlight individuals' articulation of their own experiences and those of the minority groups within which they belong. What these varied texts share is a sense of responsibility to the story of human rights violation, but also to the person (real or imagined) whose story it is. Sometimes these two responsibilities clash, as evidenced by the acid attack victims' accusation that they had not given Obaid-Chinoy permission to broadcast their story in Pakistan and also because one of them (Rukhsana) brought legal action against the filmmaker in response (F. Mirza np.).

Arguably one of the first South Asian texts to link literature with a nascent idea of human rights was the Indian Progressive Writers' Association Manifesto, drafted in London in 1935 by several leftist writers and intellectuals from British India. The manifesto's main argument was that 'the new literature of India must deal with the basic problems of our existence today—the problems of hunger and poverty, social backwardness and political subjection, so that it may help us to understand these problems, and through such understanding help us to act' (Anand np.). The Progressive Writers' Association (PWA) and its manifesto have had, and continue to have, profound implications for the arts and human rights throughout the subcontinent because of the connections they made between aesthetics and emancipatory politics. In her one-act play, *Behind the Veil* (1932), for example, progressive writer Rashid Jahan's representations of purdah, arranged marriage, polygamy, and childcare are forward-looking. The play follows the conventions of the Progressive Writers' Association's manifesto by advocating social change, although it, and the PWA collection *Angaaray* in which it was originally published (Shingavi), also alienated many Muslims with their anti-religion stance.

Moving forward to President Zia's 1980s regime, the *We Sinful Women* poetry collection published in 1991 (Ahmad) responded to the period's Islamization, suppression of women's human rights, and censorship with searing anger. Candid and penetrating, it contained iconoclastic poems by Fahmida Riaz, Kishwar Naheed, and others (and was translated from the Urdu by Rukhsana Ahmad).

More recently, Jamil Ahmad, in the sparse but powerful chapter 'Sins of the Mother' from his linked short story collection

The Wandering Falcon, depicts an unnamed couple who have eloped and are on the run. After sheltering for many years with bored soldiers assigned to a remote military outpost in Balochistan, the couple fall victim to an 'honour' killing. Rather than allowing his lover to be condemned by the Siahpad tribe's extra-judicial laws, the man kills the woman himself, before being stoned to death. Only their child escapes in this evocative story about hospitality, vengeance, gender, and sexuality.

Yet it is important not to pin the blame for Pakistani women's manifold problems solely on religion. In her essay '*La Femme Pakistanaise victime de l'Islam, un discours qui se vend bien*' ('The Female Pakistani Victim of Islam, a Discourse that Sells Well'), Maha Khan Phillips argues that '*[l]es poids qui pèsent sur les Pakistanaises sont la corruption rampante, le féodalisme profondément enraciné, le tribalisme, les clivages ethniques, voire l'héritage culturel*' ('[t]he issues that let women down in Pakistan are rampant corruption, deeply entrenched feudalism, tribalism, ethnic divisions, and even cultural legacy')—rather than Islam, as is often supposed in the West ('La Femme': np.; my translation).

Mohammed Hanif, the author of *A Case of Exploding Mangoes* and correspondent for both the BBC and *Dawn*, wrote an outspoken book, *The Baloch Who Is Not Missing and Others Who Are* for the Human Rights Commission of Pakistan in 2013. The non-fiction accounts in this volume are based on horrifying stories by relatives of some of the thousands of Baloch who have 'disappeared' in recent years, allegedly due to the clandestine involvement of Pakistan's intelligence agencies. In a passage on the banality of evil revealed through legal processes, Hanif reports that one of the relatives of the missing 'did what everyone in Balochistan with an abducted family member does' and went to the police station to file a First Information Report (FIR). Yet when it became clear that he intended to name the intelligence agencies as his relative's kidnappers, the police refused to file the FIR. Laconically, Hanif continues: 'He went to the High Court. The court ordered that an FIR be registered. No FIR was registered' (41). Director of the Human Rights Commission of Pakistan Zohra Yusuf writes in the collection's foreword that Hanif's conversations with relatives of the disappeared were 'moving—and disturbing—in a way that statistics can never be' (Hanif *Balochi*: 1). This chapter shows that Yusuf's claim holds water for cultural texts more broadly. Lacking the human rights report's footnotes, literary texts and films successfully touch audiences' emotions due to their creative advocacy of humanity and humaneness.

Theatre

IN THE ABOVE-MENTIONED ARTICLE, 'Advocacy with Footnotes', Dudai writes that 'all the [...] tensions and contradictions' of the human rights report can leave the reader feeling unsatisfied. However, he poses a momentous question: '[D]o we have anything better' (793) than human rights discourse with which to tackle the abuse and murder of innocent civilians, and to effect change globally. The tensions and contradictions that Dudai refers to include the human rights report's disjuncture between the scientific, 'fact-finding' (793) style of the main text and the poignant language of the victims' testimony contained therein. I indicated earlier that literature and film could serve as the 'anything better'—but so too could theatre. This suggests that the current form of the human rights report is not necessarily the most effective form we have through which to combat violence and discrimination.

From a wider, global perspective, human rights are the abstract rules outlined in the Universal Declaration of Human Rights (UN), and the legal instruments that come out of it, which are often seen as being deeply flawed. The Universal Declaration was made in 1948, shortly after the Partition of India, the beginning of apartheid in South Africa, and the creation of the state of Israel, all of which stemmed from the influence, control, and reach of the British Empire. In *Race and the Right to Be Human*, Paul Gilroy therefore derides human rights talk for continuing colonialism under a new guise; for a Eurocentric, secularist approach to individuals and 'freedom'; and for capitalist prioritization of property, resources, and the nation-state. Another aspect of this is Pankaj Mishra's observation that 'the universalist religion of human rights seemed to be replacing the old language of justice and equality within sovereign nation states' (169). However, without worrying too much about semantics, human rights at the micro-level are principles which many people hold dear and try to live by. Articles 3–5 concern the rights to life, to not be enslaved, and to live outside slavery. These are basic rights, but many examples from Pakistan, Asia, and the wider world indicate the egregious impact on individuals and communities when these rights are violated. We remember Parveen Rahman, the head of the Orangi Pilot Project, who was shot dead by four gunmen in March 2013. And if we were in danger of forgetting ongoing human rights abuses at Guantánamo Bay, the hunger strikes in 2013 and the release of Shaker Aamer in October 2015 served as troubling reminders.

In 2004, London-based writers Victoria Brittain and Gillian Slovo wrote the play *Guantanamo: Honor Bound to Defend Freedom* to address this human rights black hole. Brittain's and Slovo's play explores human rights and focuses on what Gilroy, in another context, describes as 'the critical figure of the person who can be killed with impunity' (*After*: 52); in this case, the person in question is the Guantánamo Bay detainee. The play is based on testimony from so-called enemy combatants, including Moazzam Begg and Jamal Al-Harith, their relatives and legal defenders, politicians, and other involved parties, including the brother of one of the almost 3,000 people killed in the World Trade Centre attacks. Brittain and Slovo unsettle the widespread Western assumption that Afghanistan is backward and lacking in human rights while the West is the model for progress and civil liberties. This is a point made by the solicitor, Gareth Peirce, in the play:

> The [boys] are three young British lads who are like all our children—they're people who are very familiar, very easy to feel immediately comfortable with. And yet the story they tell is one of terrible stark medieval horror... [of] being tortured in a prison in Afghanistan, being interrogated with a gun to your head, being transported like animals to a country you don't know where you are, and being treated like animals from start to finish for two years (51–2).

Peirce's emphasis here on the 'knowability' and ordinariness of 'the Three' is contrasted with the extraordinary, almost inhuman treatment they received from the Americans and their allies in Afghanistan and Cuba.

For reasons of safety, dignity, equality, and remembrance, I believe that everyday lived human rights have inalienable value. In his book *Theatre and Human Rights*, Paul Rae writes: '[P]resuming an *inherent* sympathy between making theatre and safeguarding human rights does neither—and no one—any good' (2; emphasis in original). I would describe the relationship between theatre and human rights not, as the Brazilian founder of the Theatre of the Oppressed Augusto Boal grandly describes it, as 'a rehearsal for the revolution' (98), but as effecting smaller, local change.

To a great extent, there are symmetries and sympathy between producing theatre and safeguarding human rights. One of the main connections between the two, as Rae recognizes, is that both are concerned with 'who did what to whom' (14). In human rights discourse, this is about getting to the bottom of who committed what kind of abuses to which individuals or groups. The theatre is similarly interested in plot, which concerns characters, action, and resolution. It can thus be an ideal vehicle through which to air views about rights and to promote action and activism.

Not long ago, I led a tutorial on theatre and human rights at the University of York, and one class member, a human rights defender from a troubled African country that shall remain nameless, told the group that her work involves using theatre and puppetry to spread the word on human rights violations in a coded way, and to encourage adults and children to enter into discussion about the issues raised afterwards. However, the student acknowledged this is politically very risky when living in a dictatorial regime like hers. Therefore, censorship of the theatre can itself be a human rights issue. That said, Article 19 on 'freedom of expression' is one of the most controversial articles of the Universal Declaration, and more open to discussion than unarguable human rights such as the right to life. There are also tensions between theatre and human rights when directors or writers are thought to tread close to hate speech. In Britain, a production of Gurpreet Kaur Bhatti's play *Behzti* was cancelled in 2004, because Sikh activists disputed the play's use of religious icons and negative representations of the Sikh community.[1] English PEN lobbied the government in support of Bhatti and in opposition to proposed religious hatred legislation (Niven et al. np.), using human rights arguments concerning freedom of expression. Yet in cases such as the *Behzti* affair and protests over the filming of Monica Ali's *Brick Lane* in Spitalfields, the working-class communities being criticized did not have the same right identified in Article 19 to 'seek, receive and impart information and ideas through any media' (UN np.) as existed for the educated, media-savvy Bhatti and Ali.

In 1984, Peter Chelkowski wrote the article 'Islam in Modern Drama and Theatre', in part to challenge the assumption, common throughout the West, that 'Islam was completely antagonistic to drama and the theatre' (45). He found many examples of theatre thriving in the 'Muslim world', including Persian puppetry and pantomime, and came to the sensible conclusion that 'Islam is not generally opposed to drama and theatre' (69).

While Chelkowski dismissed Pakistan in less than a sentence as 'an Islamic country par excellence' (66) and had nothing to say about the nation's drama, one gets a vibrant impression of Pakistani performing arts from Claire Pamment's and Fawzia Afzal-Khan's later research. In *Comic Performance in Pakistan*, Pamment situates the comic performers of the folk theatre the *bhānd*—including the itinerant comedian, the *ranga* or straight man, and the *bighla* or clown—within a long and syncretic Hindu–Muslim history. By contrast, Afzal-Khan explores the 'secular alternative theatre' (*passim*) that emerged in response to President Zia's rule, and which continues to address 'issues of human rights and gender equity within the larger political realm of Pakistani society' (5). Afzal-Khan refers to *Dukhini/Woman of Sorrow* (Nadeem)—an Ajoka play about the trafficking of Bangladeshi women into prostitution in Pakistan, which is also described in a Human Rights Watch Global report—and to Lok Rehas's play *Saar*, adapted from the famous 'Saima love-marriage' case (see Toor 261–7). Theatre groups intervening in high-profile human rights cases in this way is highly significant, because dramaturgy can make a difference when human rights are at stake, using song, dance, and physical gestures to convey complex situations to ordinary people in an accessible, affecting way. However, the theatre companies' funders, their links with NGOs, and their underlying political ideologies also matter, and can lead to particular drama initiatives being compromised.

Hajrah Mumtaz argues that what used to be called 'parallel theatre' (np.) has lacked political direction post-Zia.

In Tehrik-i-Niswan's YouTube clip 'I am a Woman', an actor describes a female as follows: 'She is a wife... She is a daughter'; an actress subsequently responds: 'I am a human being. I am... a woman' (Tehrik-i-Niswan and Kirmani np.). The implications of this scene for our understanding of women's rights are profound, encouraging empathy for the individuated female subject. Theatre groups such as Lok Rehas, Tehrik-i-Niswan, Dustak, Bang, and Ajoka stage human rights as a crucial battleground on which Pakistan's future identity is being fought. With the YouTube ban instated in response to *Innocence of Muslims* only recently lifted (Reuters np.), years after the offensive film's 2012 release, we wait to see whether Pakistani theatre and the arts may be allowed to flourish as democratic, oppositional forces.

NOTE

1. For a useful survey of *The Guardian*'s reportage of this Sikh cultural flashpoint, see http://arts.guardian.co.uk/behzti. For an academic article that pays close attention to the Sikh context and perspective, see G. Singh.

15

The Ugly Face of Attacks: Facing Up to Acid Violence in South Asian Writing

Although Acid Violence might seem a more apt subject for examination by criminologists and human rights scholars, this chapter discusses the issue in relation to its treatment in literature and film. South Asian cultural production has long dealt with 'honour' killing, but acid attacks in creative writing comprise a subset that has not yet been thoroughly explored by critics.

Perhaps the best known of these outputs is Sharmeen Obaid-Chinoy and Daniel Junge's provocative Oscar-winning documentary, *Saving Face* (2012). Rukhsana was 25 years old when she was portrayed in the documentary. She had been doused in acid by her husband, following which her sister-in-law threw gasoline at her, while her mother-in-law lit a match. Rukhsana's husband claimed that she was mentally ill and brought the damage on herself. Despite her abuse at the hands of this family, penury compelled Rukhsana to move back in with her husband. Despite her victimhood, Rukhsana's scarring was considered disgraceful and, as a consequence, she seldom spent time in public, not even venturing out in a full-face veil. Despite her fears of being seen and of public speaking, she eventually found the courage necessary to exhort a conference on acid violence: 'Someone must stop these brutal people, who turned us into the living dead' (Obaid-Chinoy and Junge np.).

Acid survivors may still be alive, but after an attack they come to envy the dead. Suffering psychological as well as physical scars, they report feelings of fear and exhibit symptoms of trauma. They also endure victim-blaming and ostracism. Forced by their disfigurement into self- or socially imposed purdah, they are likely to become dependants. Some are ashamed and view themselves as a drain on their innocent families. Others, as in Rukhsana's case, are forced to live with their abusers. Depression is widespread. It is common for victims to commit suicide, thus escaping their torment. Rehabilitation is difficult, since survivors need expensive, risky, and painful reconstructive operations.

The earliest fictional representation that I am aware of is found in Indian author Manohar Malgonkar's 1964 novel, *A Bend in the Ganges*. In this text about Gandhianism, Indian Independence, and Partition, the formerly peaceful character Basu joins the Hindu Mahasabha after a Muslim mob throws acid-filled bulbs at his wife. Basu exclaims: 'Would you remain non-violent if someone threw acid at the girl you loved?—Would Gandhi?' (291). Shortly afterwards, a prostitute called Mumtaz angers the sinister Shafi Usman by leaving him when Debi-dayal rescues the girl from the brothel where she works. This enrages Shafi, who lobs acid at her, severely injuring Debi-dayal's hand as he reaches out to protect her (311).

Acid crime is not just a problem restricted to the global south and nor, as Malgonkar's dubious depiction suggests, is it a problem uniquely perpetrated by Muslims. In Britain, the best-known acid violence survivor is Katie Piper. She was burned when industrial-strength sulphuric acid was hurled at her on the streets of London by a goon hired by her ex-boyfriend. Piper, who is now a vocal spokesperson on scars, burns, and healing, shares in her memoir: 'I was sure [...] I'd never be attractive to anyone again' (12). In June 2017, Jameel Mukhtar and his cousin Resham Khan were attacked with acid in Beckton in an Islamophobic hate crime, seemingly in retaliation for the London Bridge and Manchester attacks. Mukhtar powerfully told Channel 4 News: 'If this was an Asian guy like myself going up to an [...] English couple and acid attacking them, I know for a fact, and the whole country knows, it'd be straight away classed as a terrorism attack' (np.). Sarah Marsh describes the pair's life-changing injuries and traces the recent rise of acid crime in Britain, while Masuma Rahim agrees with Mukhtar's assessment that there was a lack of coverage of his and his cousin's maiming due to institutional bias in the mainstream media.

Such violence has a long history wherever women are in an unequal position, there is discrimination against members of minority groups, and acid is available. So: everywhere. It becomes more virulent in countries where access to acid is unregulated and legislation is non-existent or ineffective. The motive tends to be revenge, frequently for turning down sexual advances or over a financial disagreement. Offenders are almost always known to the injured parties, often intimately. Despite the fact that such attacks happen around the world, one can detect a saviour complex in certain Euro–American analyses of the violence as a phenomenon that happens 'out there' in the non-West (see, for example, Swanson). Would-be rescuers to some extent play down the primary activism of local NGOs. In South Asia, organizations such as Depilex Smile Again in Pakistan and Acid Survivors Foundation (founded in Bangladesh and now a pan-subcontinental outfit) are undertaking significant work tackling the crisis and helping survivors.

The short telefilm *Ayna* (The Mirror) is written and directed by Kabori Sarwar and produced by the Acid Survivors Foundation.[1] Its subject matter is acid violence in the Bangladeshi context. The film opens with a joyful song and dance sequence centring on the young protagonist, Kushum, and her hopes for the future. But Kushum soon becomes a child bride and the joyful rhythm is replaced by melancholy music, accompanying, as it does, the bitter lyrics: 'My feet are chained to the society. Always I have to stir the pots'. Next, as the subtitles communicate, the 'dark ages' come to the village, when Kushum is badly burnt in an acid attack. Shahinoor Akter, an unscathed actress, is replaced with a victim of acid violence, Jahanara Akter, who acts expressively as Kushum for the rest of the film. She lies prostrate in agony on the ground, and fellow villagers rush to her side with pained expressions. As she rises, a voice-over intones:

> I, Kushum, go to the mirror, but there is no mirror. [...] I see a face, but I don't know whose face that is. I see a face of death. The darkest dark spreads its long hair. From the mountains and valleys of my heart the shadows of the darkest dark capture my everything—I don't know what shadow is that. [...] I swear to fight this darkness till my death. I go to the mirror—but there is no mirror. I have broken the mirror in pieces and throw it away. I will not suffer my death before my death (Sarwar np.).

As is the case for many acid victims, the mirror, which once reflected beauty and, thus, pleasure, is now a symbol of suffering and society's gaze. In *Ayna*, the shattering of the mirror and imagery of light and dark represent Kushum's breaking free of the chokehold that patriarchy has had on her until this moment.

In Monica Ali's *Brick Lane*, protagonist Nazneen's Bangladeshi-based sister, Hasina, is friends with a woman who almost dies in an acid attack. As a household servant, Hasina needs permission from her employer, Lovely, to visit the victim. Hasina writes to Nazneen in England: 'Cheek and mouth is melt and ear have gone like dog chew off' (269). Lovely is initially disgusted to hear about these injuries. When the woman dies and Lovely learns that she had a

son who was also maimed, the latter opportunistically profits from
the information, making her name as the head of a new charity
emotively titled 'Acid Innocents' (408). Lovely's saviour fixation is
propelled by her hope that rescuing children will allow her to climb
the ranks of Dhaka's fashionistas and philanthropists.

Pakistani actor, filmmaker, and human rights activist Feryal Ali
Gauhar takes a feminist approach to the War in Afghanistan in *No
Space for Further Burials* (2007). Gauhar makes a searing attack on
vitriolage in her novel through her study of a schoolteacher, Sabir
Shah, who has acid flung in his face by the village mullah. Sabir
is accused of blasphemy and communism, but this accusation is a
cover for his real 'offence' of educating local girls. The acid 'mak[es]
the flesh around his jaw fuse with his neck' (18). Consequently,
from the time of the attack onwards, his face *'would frighten children
and the faint-hearted even in daylight'* (79; emphasis in original).

The protagonist of Mohammed Hanif's *Our Lady of Alice Bhatti*
is an attractive Christian nurse who works in the fictional Sacred
Heart Hospital in Karachi. Labouring in the emergency room,

> there was not a single day—not a single day—when she didn't see a
> woman shot or hacked, strangled or suffocated, poisoned or burnt,
> hanged or buried alive. Suspicious husband, brother protecting his
> honour, father protecting his honour, son protecting his honour,
> jilted lover avenging his honour [...] [M]ost of life's arguments, it
> seemed, got settled by doing various things to a woman's body (96).

At the novel's end, Alice falls prey to this misogynist violence
when her husband pours acid on her. He is told by an enabler that
'[t]his is the only thing that'll hurt as much as love hurts' (211),
and loftily thinks: 'I only want justice. [...] If I can't have her, then
nobody should be able to have her' (210). After the fatal onslaught,

her father and some bystanders believe they see Alice triumphantly ascending to heaven dressed in Virgin Mary blue.

Acid crime is not just a problem for women, as men are also increasingly becoming victims. In 1990, most vitriolage victims in Bangladesh were women, but a decade later nearly a quarter were men, according to an Acid Survivors Foundation executive (John Morrison, qtd. in Swanson np.). To take another British case, Andreas Christopheros was left partially sighted after opening his door to a man who threw acid on him in what appears to have been a case of mistaken identity. Christopheros chose to stay away from his toddler son for two months, so as not to distress the boy while he was having operations to rebuild his face and save his vision. As soon as the boy saw his father, 'he put his arms out and held on to me for three quarters of an hour', Christopheros recounted afterwards, describing this embrace as 'the best feeling I think I've ever had' (BBC 'Acid': np.).

It is important to recognize that acid crime is not simply a socio-economic issue. Even the rich and seemingly powerful can be victims of burning and find themselves disbelieved and smeared. Piper comes from a middle-class family and has a glittering career, as do many victims. These codicils notwithstanding, it would be wrong not to recognize the preponderance of sufferers who are women and the fact that, more often than not, this is gendered violence. Due to a range of factors, including deprivation, lack of education, freely available acid, and a toothless judicial system, it is more common in the global south, in rural areas, and amongst poor, minoritized communities.

Given the range of victims and the complexity of the problem, sociologists Farhan Navid Yousaf and Bandana Purkayastha rightly argue (2016) that an intersectional approach is needed to prevent future assaults and reintegrate victims. Activists should fight the horizontal and vertical workings of power, from class, caste, and religion to race, age, and gender. Novelists and filmmakers must continue to draw attention to the problem and add flesh to the bare bones of media reportage. In the future, we must hope that all are free from the fear of entering what Achille Mbembe (40; emphasis in original) calls a '*death-world*' and of having 'conferr[ed] upon them the status of *living dead*'.

NOTE

1. I am grateful to Dr Aroosa Kanwal, Assistant Professor of English at International Islamic University of Islamabad, for recommending this source.

16

'The Reality and the Record': Muslim Refugee Stories

THIS CHAPTER EXAMINES selected works of fiction from the last decade that focus on refugees, asylum seekers, and migrants from the Muslim world. In 1995, political scientist Astri Suhrke wrote a noteworthy essay entitled 'Refugees and Asylum in the Muslim World', in which she observed that two-thirds of the world's refugee population were Muslims or refugees in Muslim states (457). Writing in 1992, at the height of the Yugoslav Wars, poet and translator Rana Kabbani put the proportion of Muslims among refugees even higher at over 75 per cent, identifying approximately 2 million Bosnians as the latest entrants to a long list of displaced Muslims. Kabbani controversially concluded that '[i]f Bosnian Muslims have become the new Palestinians, all Muslims have become the new Jews of the world' (qtd. in Malik 20). Her point is, to some extent, borne out by Sander L. Gilman's argument that beneath the veneer of European secularism lie the centuries-old prejudices held by Christians towards Jews and Muslims, in unreconstructed or sublimated forms. Moreover, Gilman recognizes that anti-Muslim rhetoric has been exacerbated by 9/11, 11/3 (the Madrid bombings of 2004), and the 7/7 London attacks. (We can, of course, now add the Paris, Brussels, and Berlin atrocities, among others.) As Yosefa Loshitzky argues: 'Europe's traditional resistance to nonwhite migrants, its racial selectivity, is [now]

tainted by religious tones' (4). The Muslim refugee is thus doubly
(even triply) stigmatized by Islamophobia, 'immigrant-bashing'
rhetoric (and, in the case of women, patriarchal discourse). We see
this scaremongering against mostly Muslim refugees writ large in
Donald Trump's executive order, which aims to prevent Muslims
from seven countries entering the United States.

Although the figures remain disputed, the undeniably high
proportion of Muslim asylum seekers leads Suhrke to trace the
religious origins of Muslims' perspective on migration. As is well-
known, the Islamic calendar begins with Muhammad's (PBUH)
flight to Medina, where the city's warm welcome 'enabled the
Prophet to regroup and successfully lead a holy war (jihad) against
Mecca' (457). In 622 AD, Muhammad (PBUH) and his followers
were compelled to flee Mecca for Medina due to persecution, in
what became known as hijra, or migration. Due to this history of
forced migration (from non-Muslim to Muslim countries, or the
dar al-harb to dar al-Islam), the hospitable treatment of refugees
is viewed as a sacred duty that good Muslims should perform
whenever the need arises. Migration continues to be central to the
sacred geography of many Muslims, even in recent decades when
the free mingling of different groups of people within the ummah
(global Islamic community) has been increasingly restricted by
nation-state borders, fears of migrants 'swamping' the 'host' society,
and post-9/11 securitization processes.

The word 'muhajir' comes from the same root as 'hijra' and means
'immigrant' or 'refugee [...] for the sake of belief' (Lieven 309).
Rushdie discusses the muhajir in a seminal passage on migration in
Shame, but the religious aspects of the term are little acknowledged,
either in his argument or its subsequent serial redeployment by
postcolonial critics. 'I have a theory', Rushdie declares, 'that the
resentments we *mohajirs* engender have something to do with our
conquest of the force of gravity' (84). Yet, despite his subsequent

detailed explanation of the cosmic tree Yggdrasil from Norse mythology, Rushdie shies away from describing the religious origins of the term muhajir.

Similarly, in discussions of diasporic literature more broadly, questions of faith and religious identity have tended to be neglected in favour of analysis of such categories as ethnicity, nationality, and race. Amin Malak suggests that the relative neglect that postcolonial theory has shown to religion may be partly due to its unwitting valorization of 'a secular, Euro-American stance' (17). An example of this is to be found in Leila Aboulela's novel *The Translator*, within which one of her characters points out that '[e]ven Fanon [...] had no insight into the religious feelings of the North Africans he wrote about' (109). This chapter attempts to redress the critical imbalance, while guarding against the urge to overcompensate and privilege religion at the expense of other components of identity (see Lewis xiii–xv). Using insights drawn from anthropology and religious studies, I consider the important and dynamic role of Islam and Muslim cultural identity in contributing towards the literary practices of writers in relation to what may be termed 'Muslim asylum'.

Some of the most famous muhajir groups throughout modern history include, first, mostly Urdu-speaking Muslim refugees from India, who migrated to Pakistan in 1947. The Partition of India was the largest population exchange in history, during which approximately 14 million people were shunted across the new frontiers. The event's reverberations continue today, seventy years later. For example, at least half of the population of the southern Pakistani port city of Karachi are muhajirs, and conflict between this group, indigenous Sindhis, and Pashtun internal migrants was fierce during the 1980s and 1990s, persisting into this twenty-first century. Another famous muhajir group is some 4.8 million Palestinian refugees, the majority of them Muslim, who were forcibly expelled from the land that became Israel, and today live in neighbouring countries, especially Jordan and Lebanon, as well as the occupied territories of Gaza and the West Bank. This group is so large and lives in such parlous conditions that an entire agency is dedicated to its welfare—the United Nations Relief and Works Agency for Palestine Refugees in the Near East (UNRWA)—the only UN group assigned to refugees from a specific area or conflict. In his documentary film *Shebabs of Yarmouk*, French director Axel Salvatori-Sinz traced what happened to the young people in Syria's biggest Palestinian refugee camp before and after the Syrian War broke out, showing that Palestinian refugees based in Syria have now been doubly displaced.

Afghan refugees are a third well-known group of muhajirs: they fled from Afghanistan in the years following the Soviet invasion of 1979 until the United States' apparent conquest of the Taliban in 2001, after which many refugees returned home, creating a new problem of excessive numbers of 'returnees'. The Gulf Wars of 1991 and 2003 contributed significantly to the large number (over 3 million) of Iraqis identified by the UN Refugee Agency (UNHCR) as 'persons of concern', either as Internally Displaced Persons (IDPs) within Iraq or as refugees in other countries. Finally, the intractable conflict means that by the mid- to late 2010s the Syrian had become the prototypical refugee in the global imaginary.

Contrary to the doomsaying of right wing individuals, groups, and media organizations in the West, the vast majority of refugees find asylum in other Muslim countries, with relatively few entering Europe, Australasia, or North America. Since the Afghan War, for instance, over 1.5 million Afghans have fled across the porous border with Pakistan, many of them taking refuge in one particular province, Khyber Pakhtunkhwa. In the Syrian case, the pressure on other Muslim-majority countries has been even starker. Ian Lesser observes: 'Newspapers across Europe and the United States have been dominated by images, both heartening and horrifying, of Europe's worsening refugee crisis. In reality, the crisis is not acutely European, but rather a global crisis felt most dramatically in Syria's neighbors' (1). Robin Yassin-Kassab and Leila al-Shami express this pressure more vividly in their book, *Burning Country*:

> By July 2015, half the population [of Syria] was no longer living at home—four million had fled the country and 7.6 million were internally displaced. Many were displaced multiple times as the violence spread. Families were torn apart; communities fractured. [...] Of the just over four million who managed to get beyond the border, as of early 2015, 35.1 per cent were in Turkey, 34.5 per cent in Lebanon, 18.7 per cent in Jordan, and 6.9 per cent in Iraq. As of July 2015, by official United Nations numbers, 1,805,255 refugees were in Turkey, 1,172,753 were in Lebanon, 629,128 were in Jordan, and 241,499 were in Iraq. The mass migration to these neighbouring countries placed a huge strain on their resources, stretched services to breaking point, and caused increasing insecurity. The host countries were largely left to carry the burden alone; wealthier states failed to provide sufficient assistance or to resettle significant numbers of refugees (154–5).

They divulge the staggering statistic that over a million Syrian refugees seeking asylum in Lebanon makes up well over a quarter of the country's population—the equivalent of more than 16 million people entering the UK (157). As the UNHCR's Lebanon Crisis Response Plan 2015–2016 reports: 'Lebanon has been persistently bearing the brunt of the Syria crisis with increasing economic, social, demographic, political, and security challenges' (np.).

When one takes into account the issue of Internally Displaced Persons or IDPs, the picture becomes further complicated. Like the refugee, an IDP is a person who is compelled to leave their home; but in contrast to the refugee, an IDP is displaced within their own nation. At the end of 2008, there were thought to be 26 million IDPs in over fifty countries, with Africa the most affected continent, but South and Southeast Asia the regions with the fastest-growing IDP populations.[1] It is beyond this chapter's scope to discuss the recent upsurge of IDPs within such Muslim-majority nations as Pakistan, where heavy fighting in the Swat district in 2009 and the catastrophic floods of 2010 created displacement reminiscent of Partition (Hanif np.). However, a conference was held at the National University of Singapore in October 2011 that aimed to explore and interrogate the existing division between internal and international migration research and 'to bring these two bodies of literature into engaged scholarly conversation with one another' (Yeoh et al. np.). This indicates a rising tide of scholarly interest in the overlap between international and internal displacement.

In the post-War on Terror world, as in the 1990s when Suhrke and Kabbani were reflecting on the Balkan crisis, there is a disproportionate number of Muslims that make up the world's refugee and asylum seeker population. Suhrke singles out Palestinians, Afghans, and Bosnian Muslims as particularly vulnerable groups, to which in the post-Gulf War world of the 2011 Arab Spring, we can add Iraqis, Libyans, Yemenis, and Syrians, among others.

One key text that represents Muslim asylum with subtlety and black humour is Iraqi refugee Hassan Blasim's short story collection, *The Madman of Freedom Square* (2009). This book harrowingly depicts the perils, trauma, and abuse suffered by those who leave Iraq, as well as those who stay, in the wake of two Gulf Wars. The only text discussed here that was originally written in a language other than English, this collection raises the complex issue of translation, which Gayatri Spivak (herself an adept translator of

Jacques Derrida and Mahasweta Devi) hails as 'the most intimate act of reading' ('Translating': 94). One of Hassan Blasim's most pertinent insights into asylum for the purposes of this chapter relates to language and translation. The narrator of the first story in the collection confesses that many refugees are compelled by immigration law to speak two languages, 'the real one and the one for the record' (1). This doublespeak crops up throughout the story 'The Reality and the Record', the collection as a whole, and other literature that takes as its focus Muslim asylum. The story that asylum seekers narrate 'for the record', is necessarily a tactical one about trauma, persecution, and likely death if the refugee does not leave their country. By contrast, the 'reality' of what happened 'remain[s] locked in the hearts of the refugees, for them to mull over in complete secrecy' (1). Yet, as David Farrier observes, '[t]he difference between "life as experienced" and "life as text" is not so easily delineated when life depends to such a degree on the *reception* of the narrative' (130; emphasis in original). The difficulty of drawing a line between 'official' and 'private' asylum accounts is exemplified at the end of 'The Reality and the Record', where the protagonist, after spinning an enthralling tale of kidnapping, murder, and duplicity, suffers mental collapse and tells psychiatric workers his 'real' story: '*I want to sleep*' (11; emphasis in original).

Similarly, the 2007 novel for which Jordanian–British author Fadia Faqir is best known, *My Name Is Salma*, deals with Arab asylum, in Britain rather than in mainland Europe. The novel's protagonist, the Bedouin woman Salma, struggles to find the correct words to speak to the immigrant officer she encounters when entering Britain for the first time. He becomes impatient when she informs him that she wants to go to '[t]he river meets sea', rather than 'Exeter' (Faqir 20). In this troubling encounter, it becomes clear that asylum seeking is about performativity, which itself, as Judith Butler puts it, entails 'neither free play

nor theatrical self-presentation [...] [but] a regularized and
constrained repetition of norms' (95). Clearly, a person is not born
an asylum seeker, but becomes one. There are several parallels
between performativity and Muslim experiences of asylum in
the UK (especially in the post-9/11 era). For example, there are
many competing requirements for refugees to perform or renounce
particular (stereotyped) notions of 'Muslim' identity. These acts
of performativity often involve the decision of whether or not
to adopt visible signifiers associated with Islam, such as veils
for women or beards for men. Religious language more broadly
is imbued with a sense of spectacle: Muslims 'perform' namaz
(prayer), hajj (the pilgrimage to Mecca), and other religious rituals.
North African migrants whom Salma meets in Devon are adept at
the kind of iteration Butler describes. They pretend to be French
in order to gain entry to Europe, although this leads to paranoia
when they suspect Salma of being an MI5 agent spying on their
movements and interactions. Salma, too, learns to speak English
fluently (even enrolling in a university course on literature), to
bury her feelings and any desire to communicate them, and to
open conversations with remarks about the weather. She imagines
her mother admonishing her: 'Illiterate: you are not any more. In
trouble: you are. Speaking different tongues does not lessen the
burden of the heart' (77). Hakim Abderrezak identifies a subgenre
of '*illiterature*' about North African migration to Europe, the
francophone *il*-literature playing on its resonances with illegality,
illness, insularity ('île'), and masculinity (461–9; emphasis in
original). This converges productively with her mother's imagined
jibe, which indicates that conquering illiteracy has not mitigated
Salma's problems with the law, patriarchy, mental illness, and
homesickness.

The performative nature of asylum accounts is most clearly
exemplified in Zanzibari–British author Abdulrazak Gurnah's

carefully structured 2011 novel, *The Last Gift*. One of the protagonists, Maryam, takes a job at the local refugee centre in order to support her bedridden husband. This plot development allows Gurnah to continue his exploration of the predicament of asylum seekers, first begun in his 2001 novel *By the Sea*. Moreover, her son, Jamal, is doing a PhD at the University of Leeds, focusing on the effects of asylum. His research entails analysing EU policies, statistics, and migration trends, but he comes to realize that 'each one of the dots on his chart had a story that the graphs could not illustrate'. At the end of the novel, his mother helps to articulate this understanding when her refugee centre puts on a play dramatizing the stories of these asylum seekers' 'disrupted lives' (87, 269-70). On a 'makeshift' stage at the centre, Maryam directs the actors—women and children, most of them Muslims from Afghanistan, Eritrea, and Somalia, or Roma from Eastern Europe—who perform in a series of interlinked narratives conveying their migration journeys. Similar theatrical pieces have recently been developed (see Woolley) to convey asylum seekers' experiences of seeking sanctuary.

If it is possible to divine other shared themes in this body of literature about asylum seekers who are of Muslim descent, one would be that the work draws attention to the apparent invisibility of these subjects, in a Europe nonetheless dependent upon their cheap labour. In parallel with the experience of the refugee, perceptions of the Muslim are tangled up with issues of visibility and invisibility (the Muslim refugee doubly so). As Yvonne Yazbeck Haddad and Jane I. Smith point out: 'Ironically, while Islamic dress (long skirts, long sleeves, and the scarf) renders most of the female figure invisible to the eyes of strangers, it also serves to dramatically raise the visibility of women who choose to wear it' (xiv). This 'particular visible invisibility' (Anderson 44) at once conceals (the body) and exposes (one's religion), in a way that recalls Edward Said's punning on the word 'covering' (1) to denote both the media's coverage of, and enshrouding the truth about, Muslims. It is possible to demonstrate even stronger connections with invisibility as an element of contemporary Muslim experience, when compared with Said's pre-9/11 and 7/7 text. The matter of being seen or not seen (whether passed over or concealed by hijab or niqab) is now a prominent aspect of Muslim experience, particularly since the London bombings of 2005, the subsequent shooting of innocent Jean Charles de Menezes, and the thunderous crescendo to already voluble debate around the requirement or banning of wearing the veil. Without suggesting a simple homogenization of different experiences of migration—as mentioned in my introduction, there is a *compound* effect at work here—nonetheless, in recent decades Muslims have been on the receiving end of, at once, great scrutiny and unprecedented misinterpretation. As anthropologist Emma Tarlo observes:

> Heightened visibility is [...] a fact of life for British Muslims who wear distinctive forms of dress and can undoubtedly have negative consequences. But it should also be acknowledged that for many Muslims who choose to wear clothes which indicate their religious belief and affiliation, being recognizable as Muslim is not simply an unfortunate by-product of their appearance but also an essential element of it (10).

Faqir's Salma claims asylum in the UK because she gave birth to a child outside of marriage and her brother and fellow villagers have threatened to 'shoot [her] between the eyes' if they find her (81). Despite early optimism about her move to Britain, she has to learn to cope with the exclusion and invisibility she faces as an asylum seeker. Yet both Salma and her Pakistani–British friend Parvin (herself an internal refugee who has escaped a forced marriage) derive a certain level of empowerment from their position of concealment from mainstream society:

> In the early evening the city belonged to us, the homeless, drug addicts, alcoholics and immigrants, to those who were either without a family or were trying to blot out their history. In this space between five and seven we would spread and conquer like moss that grows between the cracks in the pavement. [...] 'You know, Salma, we are like shingles. Invisible, snake-like. It slides around your body and suddenly erupts on your skin and then sting, sting', Parvin said and laughed (25).

These images of viruses and invasive plant species spreading, and of migrants ultimately triumphing and becoming menacingly visible due to their 'snake-like' cunning, represent an enabling inversion of the dominant diction of natural calamity that is often used in discussions about immigration to Britain.[2] Accordingly, Salma survives, securing a job in Exeter as a poorly paid seamstress, and thus continuing the themes of weaving and fabrications explored in Faqir's second novel, *Pillars of Salt*.

Abbas, the sexagenarian protagonist of *The Last Gift*, collapses from undiagnosed type 2 diabetes near the start of the novel. His wife, Maryam, prior to taking on the position at the asylum centre, was a foundling apparently of Muslim heritage, who was fostered by a number of families all of whom treated her with varying degrees of neglect and cruelty, until she met and ran away with the 34-year-old Abbas while still in her teens. She notices Abbas's return from work just before he collapses; usually quiet and reserved, his noisy entrance makes her jump. He subsequently suffers several strokes, and his incapacitated state encourages him to reassess the life he now considers 'as useless as a life can be' (9). The 'last gift' of the title is a voice recording Abbas has made that is discovered after his third and fatal stroke. In it, Abbas reveals to the family his previously undisclosed childhood in Zanzibar, his secret first marriage to a countrywoman he got pregnant, his abandonment of her for life as a sailor, and his bigamous marriage to Maryam. It becomes clear that the process of migration has transformed the adventurer into a quiet man, almost invisible to his family, who, it turns out, do not really know him at all.

Yet, many of the migrants and asylum seekers rendered in the novels under discussion desire to make themselves more invisible still, by assimilating or blending into the 'host' society. Abbas's daughter, Anna (born Hanna), is ostensibly the most assimilated family member. She has discarded her childhood identity as a 'daddy's girl' and second-generation immigrant and now works as a teacher in London, where she lives with her white boyfriend, Nick, and tries to be English. Over time she discovers that this is impossible because of the inherent racism of Nick and his milieu. Not only are they uncritical admirers of Orwell, Forster, Conrad, and Kipling, but Nick's vicar and his sister's boyfriend also taunt Anna with the insult 'jungle bunny' (118). Anna eventually discovers that Nick, an academic, has been having an affair, lying to Anna with the excuse of attending conferences. Despite the betrayal, she feels nothing but relief when she terminates their relationship. In dreams that recur until the breakup, Anna talks with, and explains herself to, an inaudible and invisible person. This penumbrous figure is not Nick, but rather may be her father—a migrant who has made secrets and silence his currency.

Faqir's Salma also wants to slough off her identity like a snake discarding its skin and longs to become a white woman with pale, unobtrusive nipples. She variously fantasizes about becoming a rebellious Gothic teenager or a blonde Englishwoman, and self-destructively considers plastic surgery to expunge her Arab identity: '[j]ust like that I would disappear' (140, 38, 46-7). There are clear mental health concerns behind Salma's wish to become white, and she claims a 'severe psychological disorder' in order to claim asylum in Britain (87). Contrary to Salma's belief, this is no trumped-up excuse. She begins hallucinating, imagining that she sees her brother, Mahmoud, hiding in the shadows wielding a gun wherever she goes, and is eventually put on medication to control her post-traumatic delusions.

Nowhere are the mental health problems engendered by the refugee's desire to assimilate more starkly exemplified than in Blasim's story, 'The Nightmares of Carlos Fuentes'. This story follows the trajectory of Salim Abdul Husain, who moves to the Netherlands from war-torn Iraq and tries to 'bury [...] his identity and his past' by learning fluent Dutch, adopting rabid anti-immigration politics, marrying a Dutch woman, and trying to forget 'misery, backwardness, death, shit, piss and camels'. He assumes the name Carlos Fuentes, taken from a literary magazine, because a friend advises him that it is better to have any other 'brown name' than an Arab moniker in Europe (78–9). This, of course, has intertextual significance, because Blasim, like Fuentes, breaks with the idea that the material world can be rationally understood, and strives for formal experimentation, including the incorporation of indigenous beliefs and folklore. Carlos's successes disintegrate when he begins to have horrifying dreams, at first of losing his hard-won Dutch identity, and later of car bombs and accusations of terrorism. He appears to revert to a primitivism of 'secret rituals', such as wearing a coat to bed, sleeping with his face painted like a Native American, and shunning sweet potatoes because of their connection to roots, when in fact these tactics all come from advice he finds in Western books on dream control. The short story ends with one of Carlos's lucid dreams—he decides to slaughter all the Iraqis in his nightmare so that he can return to his untroubled life in the Netherlands. In the dream, he also meets his younger self, Salim Abdul Husain, who looks at him and derisively chants: 'Salim the Dutchman, Salim the Mexican, Salim the Iraqi, [...] Salim the Pakistani, Salim the Nigerian...' (84). This equation of his Dutch self with the 'wretched of the earth' causes Carlos to panic, and he jumps out of the nearest window while still asleep. Dying instantly, he is remembered against his earlier desires as an Iraqi who committed suicide and was buried in his home country. His highly visible act of self-definition is first misinterpreted, and then erased, rendered non-existent by his 'host' society.

The narrator of Rushdie's *Shame* rather optimistically describes the migrant's desire to cut free from his home country and its incumbent ties and prejudices as translating into the ability to 'float [...] upwards from history, from memory, from Time' (87). I established earlier that the muhajir passage in *Shame* is often invoked to describe postcolonial diasporic theories, without any reference to its religious overtones. A recuperation of the religious associations underpinning the passage in Rushdie's novel communicates that, for these writers on Muslim asylum at least, weightlessness is not achieved by crossing borders, especially when the migrant does this to escape 'too much past' (Faqir *Salma*: 108). Whereas Rushdie's narrator argues that the 'worst thing' about being a migrant is 'the emptiness of one's luggage' (*Shame*: 87), Salma is described by Parvin as 'a Bedouin woman with baggage', her heavy suitcase containing an exquisite dress she has embroidered for the baby daughter she left behind in Jordan (289, 259).

In *The Last Gift*, Jamal helps an elderly neighbour who faints outside a supermarket, mirroring Abbas's earlier collapse. This neighbour, Harun, is also an immigrant, although unlike Abbas he is a Ugandan of Yemeni background. Initially, he appears to have shed his roots; this is demonstrated by the framed picture he keeps of an unknown woman belonging to the previous owners of his house. As if owning up to a crime, he furtively reminisces to

Jamal about his passionate relationship with a friend's wife, so that the younger man realizes Harun has merely been 'play-acting [his] non-existence' (Gurnah *Gift*: 213).

In Blasim's story, 'Ali's Bag', the eponymous travel bag contains the skull of his dead mother, which refugee Ali al-Basrawi is hoping to bury safely in Europe. After refusing to be parted with the bag during his months of travel, even talking to his mother's skull when he thinks no one is watching, Ali literally 'loses his head' in an altercation with border guards in a forest on the Turco–Greek border. Rarely has the issue of migrants' excess baggage been so starkly exemplified. Ali's bag now contains the rest of his mother's bones, some grooming products, a Qur'an, and a picture of Imam Ali (beloved to Shia Muslims). Salma takes a similar bag filled with her belongings from Jordan to Britain in *My Name Is Salma*; it holds 'a reed pipe, cloth sanitary towels, a brown comb with a few of the teeth missing, a Qur'an, a black madraqa, my mother's shawl' (61). The inclusion of the Qur'an with all the other belongings intimates that Islam is not viewed in abstract terms by the majority of Muslim asylum seekers, but as a concrete, practical, and indispensable part of ordinary life. Sure enough, in other stories in *The Madman of Freedom Square*, characters recite the Throne Verse during stressful moments,[3] perform prayers, swear by the Qur'an or Allah, and attend mosque. However, they are far from being uniformly religious; for example, soon after the end of the bloody Iran–Iraq War, the protagonist in the short story 'The Composer' becomes increasingly truculent in his atheism and causes conflict by composing songs that are derogatory towards Islam and human existence itself. Even though Salma believes that she has 'never thought about God' before coming to Britain, what she finds most difficult to understand in her new life is that 'religion is as weak as the tea in this country' (121, 44). Yet her Islam is of the everyday, lived variety, mixing sacred concepts with the profane.

Salma thinks, 'I was a [...] Muslim and had to be pure and clean', as she performs her ablutions, while Parvin admits that being Muslim is 'complicated' (16, 253).

Even though Blasim, Faqir, and Gurnah do not obfuscate the complicated nature of Islam, with its multifarious sects and modes of practice, faith provides some of their characters with hope amid the poverty, discrimination, and uncertainty of the asylum seeker. For instance, in *The Last Gift*, Hanna/Anna is ashamed of her immigrant past, which she regards as 'pathetic and sordid'. In contrast, her more optimistic brother, Jamal, reacts to his hidden past by researching the 'desperate flight' (196, 73) of migrants and joining an Islamic reading group. The group proves to be a humane debating society, which helps him come to terms with his past in a more fruitful and enlightened manner than Anna, who has internalized racism to a greater extent.

This chapter has illustrated that there is no single story in these writers' depictions of either Islam or asylum. By removing both migrants and Muslims from the position of 'Other', these authors assert their right to explore asylum and religion, but equally to disregard, satirize, challenge, and celebrate these issues. The burgeoning quantity (and quality) of texts describing Muslims' experiences of asylum illustrates that Suhrke's two-decade-old point that the majority of refugees are Muslims is still relevant today. Through textual analysis of an under-attended body of writing, this chapter intervenes in the emerging corpus of criticism on asylum literature. While it would be reductive to impose a pattern on this body of writing because heterogeneity is its strength, there are certain important themes that recur (especially performativity and invisibility), which resonate for both asylum seekers and Muslims. What is gained by grasping an understanding of asylum through accounts of specifically Muslim experience is, first, an awareness of the asymmetric number of asylum seekers from Muslim backgrounds in the world population and, second, an understanding of the additional layers of discrimination faced by Muslim asylum seekers in the current era of anti-immigrant, Islamophobic 'coverage'.

Notes

1. For this, and earlier, information on asylum and IDPs, the UNHCR website is useful: http://www.unhcr.org

2. Peter Gatrell argues that the use of Biblical diction, including "'flood", "deluge", "wave", "avalanche", "lava flow" and "plague"', dates back to the Tsarist state of 1915, when the Russians coined the term 'refugeedom' to denote a state of being permanently exiled, which mostly referred to Others, such as Armenians and Jews (Gatrell 32).

3. Thought by many to be the Qur'an's most excellent verse, the narrator of 'The Reality and the Record' recites the Throne Verse, or Ayat-ul-Kursi, while terrified for his life after he has been kidnapped. Similarly, in 'The Truck to Berlin', a young man in a lorry carrying frightened migrants to Germany keeps repeating the same surah (3, 72).

IV

MUSLIMS, ISLAMOPHOBIA, AND RACISM IN BRITAIN

17

We Are Here Because You Were There

THE EARLY MIGRATION HISTORY and literature of Britain's largest religious minority, the Muslim community, is diverse and fascinating, especially given that scholarship on migration and diasporic writers tends to have a contemporary bias. This community now makes up approximately 2.7 million people or 5 per cent of the British population (Office for National Statistics np.). These numbers have risen dramatically since the 1960s, mostly due to the aftermath of the British Empire and the post-war demand for manual labour. However, it is vital to recognize that Muslims have visited, lived, and worked in Britain for hundreds of years. As Sukhdev Sandhu observes:

> Blacks and Asians tend to be used in contemporary discourse as metaphors for newness. Op-ed columnists and state-of-the-nation chroniclers invoke them to show how Englishness has changed since the end of the war. That they had already been serving in the armed forces, stirring up controversy in Parliament, or helping to change the way that national identity is conceptualized, often goes unacknowledged (*London*: xviii).

New Right individuals and institutions consistently erase the contributions of Muslims, Asians, Blacks, and other marginalized peoples from British history, portraying migrants in Britain as constituting an unwelcome post-war invasion. They nostalgically recall a mythical 'Englishness', which was apparently lost with the arrival of these strangers. By contrast, Black and Asian anti-racist protesters in the 1980s formulated the slogan 'we are here because you were there', proving that 'here' and 'there' are not so easily separated in this island nation, with its long history of imperialism and exploitation.

Probably the earliest book-length account by a Muslim conveying experiences of life in Britain is Mirza Sheikh I'tesamuddin's *The Wonders of Vilayet: Being the Memoir, Originally in Persian, of a Visit to France and Britain in 1765*, first published in 1780. This travel book is in many ways emblematic of the experiences and cultural production of these early Muslims to visit Britain. Mirza Sheikh I'tesamuddin (c. 1730–1800) was raised in Panchnoor, West Bengal, in a cultured Sayyid family who predominantly worked in the fields of administration and the law. I'tesamuddin himself became a tax collector and then a munshi—a scholar of the Persian language at the imperial court. In the mid-eighteenth century, as the East India Company and Robert Clive battled to establish their Raj in India, an opportunity opened up for I'tesamuddin to travel to the West. Evoking Allah, as he did at intervals throughout the volume, he departed for England.

I'tesamuddin undertook an exciting six-month sea voyage to England via such countries as Mauritius, Cape Town, and France. En route, he claimed to have seen cannibals, Muslim converts, slaves, mermaids, and flying fish. His ship eventually docked at Dover, where I'tesamuddin and others were detained because one of their fellow passengers had brought contraband fabrics into the country. Despite this inauspicious start, I'tesamuddin was generous in his praise for what he often referred to as the 'hat-wearing Firinghees' of 'Vilayet' (22, 25, 29, 44, 46, 87, 118). He wrote that Europeans had 'attained astonishing mastery over the science of navigation' and that British women were 'lovely as houris' (30, 53).

He was occasionally modest about his own abilities ('my life so far has gone by aimlessly, and so will what remains of it' (52)), but more often self-confident, as when he maintained that he taught the famous Orientalist William Jones much about India. About the various nations and cultures of the world, though, he was mostly even-handed and humanistic. I'tesamuddin's welcome to English society was mixed: people had never seen an Indian wearing such opulent clothing because they were only used to poorly dressed lascars, so there was much gawking. He was even expected to dance for a group that mistakenly assumed he was some type of entertainer or performer. However, he claimed over time to have received 'great kindness and hospitality' from the English and to have been treated by many 'as an old acquaintance' (53–4).

One of the most striking things about this book is the way I'tesamuddin constantly compared England to India, just as Nadeem Aslam's later immigrant characters in *Maps for Lost Lovers* also translate northern England into subcontinental terms (see Chambers 'Recent': 180–1). For example, I'tesamuddin reached for the right words to praise London and asserted that '[l]ike Calcutta it straddles a river that falls into the sea' (56).

A true tourist, he visited St. Paul's Cathedral, the Tower of London, Westminster Abbey, and King George III's palace. He described the palace with a hauteur common to many upper-class Indians of the period, who compared British monuments, lifestyles, and customs with their Indian equivalents and found them wanting. To him, it was 'neither magnificent nor beautiful' and could easily be mistaken for the house of 'a merchant of Benares'. However, he conceded that friends told him that the palace's interior design was splendid: '[T]he suites of rooms and the chambers of the harem are painted an attractive verdigris' (59). Modern readers may find it comically incongruous that he described George III's private quarters as his 'harem' (he also memorably called Oxford University a 'madrassah').[1]

Britain was also shown to have its fair share of distressing attributes, as I'tesamuddin was left shocked by the chasm separating rich and poor. He depicted northern England as 'a place where it is dark night for nine months of the year and broad daylight for the remaining three months' and where the ice crumbled 'like so much *papadom*' (66). Similarly, he presented readers with a now commonplace trope of the migrant's first glimpse of snow; I'tesamuddin described it as being 'like *abeer*, the powder Hindus sprinkle on each other at the Holi festival, only instead of being coloured it is a brilliant white' (76). With images of ice cracking like *papadom* and the snow as powdery as *abeer*, I'tesamuddin warmed up the glacial British landscape with rich subcontinental similes.

At times he trained a quasi-anthropological gaze on local habits, discussing Vilayet's class system and lack of social mobility (141–3), its custom of 'love marriage' (78–9), and the grams and pulses used in farming. One chapter, 'On History and Religion', explored Muslims', Jews', and Christians' views on halal, kosher, or permissible food, and outlined the anti-Semitism rampant in Europe at the time. Similarly, whereas in many European nations a Muslim would be 'instantly burnt at the stake' for openly practising his or her religion, I'tesamuddin argued that the English were mercifully 'free of such bigotry' (91). Yet he criticized the English for the scant importance they accorded to religious observances: 'Many of them regard prayer as optional'. This scepticism was an anathema to him: 'Allah save us from such misguided ideas' (4).

How, then, should we read and examine texts such as *The Wonders of Vilayet*, and to what extent is it possible to recover an authentic voice from I'tesamuddin's text? This book, and others like it by such travellers as Sake Dean Mahomed and Mirza Abu Taleb Khan, should not be taken as *the* authentic voice of Muslims in Britain in the late eighteenth and early nineteenth centuries. They are the traces left behind by elite individuals with the power to inscribe themselves on history, not the majority of working-class migrants analysed in Rozina Visram's wonderful book, *Ayahs, Lascars and Princes*. However, this does not mean they are not revealing. In I'tesamuddin's travel writing we witness both hostility and acts of kindness from the 'host' community. The traveller's backward gaze towards the home country infuses his descriptions of Vilayet with subcontinental imagery, producing something new. There is much that resonates here—not least the lack of comprehension between I'tesamuddin and Vilayatis on the matter of religion—with the depiction of migrant writers of the late twentieth and early twenty-first centuries.

NOTE

1. I'tesamuddin (71). For more on Persian-language writers' experiences at the Universities of Oxford and Cambridge, see N. Green.

18

Early Twentieth-Century Muslim Women's Travel Accounts of Britain

IN THE PREVIOUS CHAPTER, I began exploring the written accounts of early Muslim migrants to Britain through an examination of Mirza Sheikh I'tesamuddin's *The Wonders of Vilayet* (1780). Over a century later, we encounter two early examples of Muslim women travel writers in Britain, Atiya Fyzee and Shahbano Begum Maimoona Sultan.

Atiya came to Britain as a single woman aged nearly 30 to study at the Maria Grey Teacher Training College from 1906 to 1907. Here, she wrote letters to her sisters about her European experience. These letters were serialized in an Urdu women's journal, published as a book in 1921, and reproduced as Siobhan Lambert-Hurley and Sunil Sharma's comprehensive English translation, *Atiya's Journeys* (2010).

Five years later, Maimoona Sultan departed for England by steamship from Bombay, making stops in Aden and France, and glimpsing a Sicilian volcano during the journey. Just 14 years old when she published her book, *A Trip to Europe*, Maimoona could trace her lineage back from a line of women travel writers. She made her journey to England with her mother-in-law, Nawab Sultan Jahan Begum of Bhopal, who had written an account of her pilgrimage to Hijaz in 1903–04. Unsurprisingly, given her mother-in-law's royal status, the purpose of Maimoona's 1911 trip was more highfalutin than Atiya's pursuit of education: Maimoona and Her Highness were to pay their respects at George V's coronation.

The Fyzees were from an aristocratic Sulaimani Bohra Muslim background. Atiya's father had a strong Turkish mercantile connection, and she was born in Constantinople, raised in Bombay, and died in relative poverty in Karachi. The Afghan-born Maimoona Sultan was born in Peshawar and brought up in Bhopal from the age of 5 by the Nawab Begum. Both of these authors demonstrate the porous borders between India, Afghanistan, Turkey, and modern-day Pakistan, just as many of the eighteenth-century male travel writers confirmed strong links between India and Persia.

Writing just a few years after the death of Queen Victoria, Atiya was a recognizably modern and independent traveller. This was reflected in her middlebrow modernist style, which was often frivolous and hyperbolic. She wrote of a trip into central London a few months after arriving in Britain: 'How many lights! What costumes! Such fashionable women!' (Lambert-Hurley and Sharma 151). Her narrative was punctuated with the humorous exclamations, 'oho!', 'uf!', and 'ahahaha!' (see, for example: 113, 134, 121). On the other hand, writing in the immediate pre-war period, Maimoona used a ponderous, Victorian style when reconstructing George V's coronation through second-hand accounts (she was in purdah, so had to rely on her mother-in-law's and newspaper reporting). She solemnly and archaically wrote: '[A] shout of "God Save King George", springing from loyal hearts, rent the air' (Sultan 78). This difference in timbre can be accounted for, first, by the fact that Maimoona was half Atiya's age and exhibited the earnestness of an over-protected teenager. By contrast, Atiya was worldly and did not lack for male attention—from poets Maulana Shibli Nomani and Allama Iqbal, no less. Second, Maimoona's royal blood marginally trumped Atiya's pedigree, but smothered her with rules about purdah. '[T]he sequestered Maimoona', write Lambert-Hurley and Sharma devastatingly, 'gave the impression that she saw little more than the inside of hotels and curtained motor-cars' (5). Maimoona was stranded in London's suburbs, rather than being close to the capital's action as was Atiya.

The greatest impact on Maimoona was the Nawab Begum, whose influence is easily discernible in this travelogue:

> Her Highness says that Turkey has yet many things to learn and to do, the Turks being in almost all respects a long way behind Europe. Her Highness admits that owing to their religious training they are not wanting in Islamic civility and hospitality, but it is very sad that they have begun to show a sort of indifference to religion. Her Highness was specially struck with this religious remissness (118).

The repetition of 'Her Highness' at the beginning of each of these three sentences suggests that the Nawab Begum's opinions have permeated Maimoona's reportage.

Atiya was influenced by her relatives' unusual approach to women's veiling, travel, and seclusion. Rather than 'going native' and adopting Western dress, Atiya wore a family version of the veil, the Fyzee charshaf, which was a Turkish women's floor-length cloak worn with a head-covering and gloves. Instead of the 'oppressive' veil—which has remained a Western obsession—it was a liberating garment that could be adapted to its context, as Atiya showed by teaming it with 'good walking shoes' (151) and lining it with warm materials to keep out the cold. This modest dress enabled Atiya to travel where and with whom she wanted. Moreover, British women of the period equally had their own restrictive practices as regards dress. When Atiya went to see the famed English contralto Clara Butt sing, she pitied her:

Regarding the waist, I remembered this line of poetry:

> *divan men khali hi jagah chhod di main ne*
> *mazmun hai bandha teri nazuk kamari ka*
> I left a blank spot in my book of poetry,
> When I created an image of your delicate waist.

God knows how she can bind herself and sing in such a constricted state, and that too with a smile. These people bear all kinds of tortures for the sake of appearance (143; emphasis in original).

In observing the cinched-in waist of the singer, Atiya was reminded of the ever-tinier waists of Urdu poetry's beloveds, which comparison shows that she astutely understood women's oppression across cultures.

Both women retained their pluralist Islamic faith while travelling in Europe and were not seduced by the various brands of Christianity and secularity they encountered there. Atiya's distinctively Muslim sensibility was clear when she compared the new Underground railway to 'the workings of a jinn' (158). Maimoona was sceptical of a shrine in Cairo that was rumoured to possess healing properties, but joyous when the Turkish Sultan gave her mother-in-law a relic said to be a hair of the Prophet Muhammad (PBUH).

Yet the two writers frequently rubbed up against fixed ideas about 'Mahomedans' in imperial London. Atiya attended a talk at which Muslims were described as a backward-looking and 'slothful' community. Remarkably, she found herself in agreement: 'Dear sisters, he spoke the truth, if we feel bad that's our choice' (163). Thus it is apparent that these women were probably too willing to accept Orientalist criticism of Muslim societies. Indeed, Maimoona argues that 'it is wrong not to tell one's co-religionists their weak points', censuring the Turks, for example, for not having any 'lady doctors' (126), despite their Muslim faith and concomitant belief in gender segregation.

Both women were sold on the significance of education, which they regarded as the only route to women's and Muslims' uplift. As Atiya the budding teacher argued: '[H]igher education is a heavenly thing' (127). Her Highness also valued learning, telling Maimoona that education is 'a jewel, whose lustre can never fade' (10). Importantly, though, Atiya speculated on when there would be universal education for South Asian girls (207).

Even at the beginning of the twentieth century, Atiya and Maimoona were debating this ongoing and seemingly intractable problem of how to benefit from a Western education while simultaneously maintaining South Asian ways. In what became Atiya's homeland, Pakistan, only 29.2 per cent of girls attended secondary school in the period from 2008 to 2012 (as compared with 39.7 per cent of boys; UNESCO np.). But in their travels and writings, these women writers encapsulated the saying of the Prophet: '*Seek knowledge even as far as China*' (Netton vii; emphasis in original). They continue to educate us with their texts, observations, and the bold spirit in which they lived.

19

Disorientation as Loss of the East: Muhammad Marmaduke Pickthall's Fiction

MOST CONTEMPORARY MUSLIMS only encounter Muhammad Marmaduke Pickthall through his explanatory translation *The Meaning of the Glorious Qur'an*. His trailblazing role as an early Muslim convert and his extensive, albeit uneven, oeuvre as a novelist have been almost forgotten, even though he wrote a total of twenty-five books between 1900 and 1930. Two early novels, *All Fools* (1900) and *Saïd the Fisherman* (1903), and two short stories, 'Karàkter' (1911) and 'Between Ourselves' (1922), especially merit a closer look, as they bookend his 1917 conversion and depict Muslims in Britain.

Marmaduke was born in 1875 and grew up in Suffolk and London. He passed an unhappy few years at Harrow, with Winston Churchill as a contemporary. While he possessed a flair for languages, his poor numeracy prevented him from entering conventional careers. Instead, Pickthall spent two formative years learning Arabic and travelling around Palestine, Lebanon, and Syria. In the Arab world he was tempted to convert to Islam, but a Damascene religious leader encouraged him to wait until he was older, so he delayed his declaration of faith. In 1896, his mother persuaded him to come home. Settling back into British life, Pickthall now saw his country through Arab eyes, in an instance of self-Othering that would prove fertile for his fiction. He began working to establish himself as a writer of short stories, novels, and, increasingly, political essays. In 1907, he rekindled his love affair with the Middle East, travelling to Egypt, Lebanon, and Turkey. Unlike his peers, he wore local dress, studied other languages, and tried to understand people whose worldview was different from his own.

During the First World War, Pickthall's allegiance lay with Turkey rather than Britain. Because of their shared Turkophilia he started making alliances with other British Muslims, most of them from India. In 1917, he became a convert to Islam at the age of 42. After the war, Pickthall's political interests shifted from Turkey to India. He spent the last fifteen years of his life in Hyderabad, working for the Nizam and as a journalist. He returned to England in 1935, where he died a year later and was buried in Brookwood's Muslim cemetery near Woking.

All Fools exhibits its author's scattergun contempt for his characters and lack of artistic control over his material. However, the novel is worth mentioning because of its London setting and the appearance of a religiously ill-defined Indian character, 'Brown Geegee', a corruption of 'Baraoniji' (36). Here, Pickthall probably took inspiration from the early twentieth-century British–Asian politician Mancherjee Bhownagree, who was from a Parsi background and served as an MP in the Houses of Parliament from 1895 to 1906. The character Brown Geegee is a racist portrayal of a 'comedy' Indian who cannot speak English properly. The young Pickthall turned almost as negative an eye on his countrymen, possibly due to his new sense of alienation on arriving 'home' after a charmed stay in the Middle East. Moreover, while he had attained insight into the perspective of Arab peoples, he had not yet developed sympathy for Indians, resulting in this sad caricature.

Remarkably, Pickthall soon followed up this flop with his sophisticated second novel, *Saïd the Fisherman*—an Englishman's attempt to represent an insider's view of both Islam and Arab culture. This is probably the first Anglophone novel to describe the life story of a Muslim (the titular Saïd), at least part of which is set in Britain. Saïd is a rogue whose sins in Syria eventually catch up with him. He flees retribution by stowing away on a boat bound for London. On arrival, he is drugged, robbed, and beaten. Living in the gutter, tormented by homesickness, he eventually suffers mental collapse. Moved by Saïd's plight, a missionary working in the psychiatric hospital to which he has been admitted sends him home, where he is subsequently killed in the 1882 Alexandria riots. Free indirect discourse references to 'the horror' and 'the noiseless horror' (288, 301) suggest that Pickthall had read Joseph Conrad's *Heart of Darkness*, published four years earlier in 1899. In this novel, however, the horror glowers from the centre of the Empire, rather than at its dark margins.

Saïd the Fisherman represents Pickthall's serious attempt, before his conversion, to portray the centrality of Islam to the everyday life of ordinary, rather than saintly, Muslims. Listening to the engines throbbing on the steamship transporting him to England, Saïd personifies the sound as 'an imprisoned jinni toiling with bitter sobs' (269). Britons' racist treatment of him once in London makes Saïd long for the company of fellow Muslims. He finds it difficult to accept English speech, with its failure to evoke the name of God.

Pickthall compassionately portrays the migrant's experience of disorientation in the West. Saïd is dazzled by the traffic and street lights, bemused by people's unfriendliness, and deafened by the city's roar. Far from Indian diasporic author Kamala Markandaya's idea that migrants have productive 'double vision' ('Pair': 23) and can turn their gaze on both hostland and homeland, Saïd is almost sightless in dull, colourless Britain. His vision only returns amidst the Arab world's sunshine: 'Scales seemed to fall from his eyes so that he saw distinctly' (293).

Pickthall's two short stories have in common an interest in Arabs who make the journey to Britain, and in how their initial mimicry of the British is transformed by racism and ill-treatment into rebelliousness. In 'Karàkter', an Egyptian farmer petitions a local British official to help him send his 14-year-old son, Ahmed, to the most prestigious school in the colonial centre. He wants Ahmed to learn 'karàkter', of which the English alone are said to possess the secret. Ahmed acclimatizes after a period of initial torpor upon arrival in Britain and overcomes the abuse he initially faces at public school. When he returns to Egypt for a governmental job, Ahmed joshes with his English master as though the two were equals. The master, who until then had been friendly, upbraids him for his insolence. Ahmed is mortified and resigns from his post to become a nationalist. The story concludes with his father's lament that the 'karàkter' he was so desirous that Ahmed learn has been his undoing.

'Between Ourselves' is structured as a frame narrative; Sir Charles Duclay—an Orientalist and one of Egypt's rulers—tells some companions a tale to illustrate the hypocrisy of British rule. In his allegedly true story, Abbâs, a young Egyptian, tells Duclay of his admiration for British rule and promises support. However, Arabic newspapers publish a poisonous and false article about Abbâs. He believes that British libel law will help recuperate his reputation, but Duclay 'expound[s] to him the real nature of the British Occupation and its history; how we were there for our own ends, and not the good of Egypt' (63). Thus enlightened, Abbâs travels to London. There, he becomes an anti-imperialist speaker and '[r]epresentative of the Egyptian nation' (64). Yet some rivals reignite the slander against Abbâs and, disillusioned with Britain, he goes into exile in Paris, becomes a terrorist, and is finally imprisoned. This fascinating incident, so emblematic of the period, invites further contextual analysis. Pickthall is concerned with the rise, in the immediate post-First World War period, of Egyptian nationalism. In this story within a story Pickthall intimates to his fellow Britons, 'between ourselves', the dangers of allowing bright young Egyptians to be encouraged into radicalism by mistreatment and racism.

For most of his career, Pickthall was a perceptive chronicler of the disorientation of the Muslim migrant in Britain. Unfortunately, he was pessimistic about the possibility of reorientation. *All Fools'* Brown Geegee is simply a figure of fun, Saïd flees to Egypt and is subsequently killed after only a short time spent in England, while the short stories' disorientated characters are 'mimic men' (Naipaul), who try but fail to rebel. For all his fine qualities as an author, Pickthall does not seem capable of imagining for any of his characters the empowerment that he himself seems to have found in a state of in-betweenness.

20

From 'England-Returned' to 'Myth of Return' to the Point of No Return

I HAVE BEEN WORKING on my monograph (*Britain Through Muslim Eyes: Literary Representations, 1780–1988*) and related projects for over a decade, since the revelation that three of the four 7/7 bombers hailed from my home city of Leeds. Following this horrific event I realized that, despite researching South Asia for years, I had little knowledge of the experience of those on my doorstep. Thus, I decided to rectify this lack of knowledge about Muslims in Britain, my prior expertise being predominantly in Indian literature. As I delved into the archive in an effort to produce the most comprehensive history possible of writing by Muslims, it yielded engrossing travel writing, memoirs, and fiction by Muslims in Britain from the eighteenth, nineteenth, and early twentieth centuries. I realized I would have to divide the material into two books, and am currently working on a sequel.

My aim in this two-book study is to discover what Britain looked like to the Muslims who increasingly visited and lived in the country from the late eighteenth century onwards. What I discovered from writing *Britain Through Muslim Eyes* was that most of the pre-1980s authors were elite, 'England-returned' sojourners, whereas in the later period a more permanent 'myth of return' class of writers emerged. 'England-returned' is a term used in South Asia to refer to people who have been educated all over the United

194

Kingdom, not necessarily just in England. This elite class of early travel writers included princes (like the scribbling Persian brothers, Reeza, Najaf, and Taymoor Meerza, who came to Britain in 1836), religious leaders such as the Aga Khan III (who wrote about his 1898 European tour in *The Memoirs of Aga Khan: World Enough and Time*; see Shah *Memoirs*), and future prime ministers, including Malaysia's Tunku Abdul Rahman Putra Al-Haj (whose sojourns from the 1920s to the 1940s are documented in his collected newspaper columns; Tunku).

For this elite, transient, sheltered group of people, cultural prejudice was veiled and rarely experienced head-on. Thus, for the most part, England-returned writers were positive about Europe in general and the UK in particular. That said, their admiration was often mixed with an alertness to British irreligiosity, hypocrisy, and self-contradiction. These traits were easier to perceive through the gaze of a stranger, although the longer these writers stayed in Britain, the more they came to view their culture from an alternate perspective. Bear in mind, however, that the majority of Muslim travellers to Britain came from proletarian backgrounds. Rozina Visram highlights the centrality of ayahs, lascars, servants, soldiers, and pedlars to pre-Second World War British life. I focus on the elite end of the migrant spectrum—princes, travellers, and students—because these people were most likely to have written about their experiences.

In 1979, Pakistani academic Muhammad Anwar coined the phrase 'myth of return' to describe the predicament of those working-class South Asians who travelled to Britain in large numbers from the 1960s onwards. In his book, *The Myth of Return*, Anwar explained that these migrants assumed that they would work hard in Britain and soon save up enough money to become powerful 'England-returned' success stories back in their home country. Dreams of a triumphant homecoming were gradually dashed as the (initially more male than female) immigrants discovered that their wages would not come close to offsetting their high overheads. They also began to marry, have children, and put down roots in Britain, making it harder to leave. Return became a myth, but it was still something to cling to when traversing the often hostile and usually damp streets of Britain. Most migrants maintained links to South Asia, and many sent substantial amounts of money home and sponsored relatives or friends to come over. For this emerging precariat, racism and discrimination were daily realities. Understandably, the perspective of Britain from these permanent settlers tended to be more critical—sometimes bitterly so.

There is no direct equivalent for 'England-returned' and 'myth of return' in Arabic or any of the other languages (such as Persian and Kiswahili) spoken by the non-South Asian authors of Muslim descent who came to Britain. Yet, during the 200-year period examined in *Britain Through Muslim Eyes*, it is also generally true that Arab, Persian, East African, and other Muslim writers, like the South Asians, initially came to Britain for extended stays, but in the post-Second World War period and accelerating from the 1980s onwards the tendency was for them to stay there permanently.

I have been newly awakened to the significance of these waves of migration in the light of the current refugee crisis. In the peregrinations of the early voyagers, the indefinite and often precarious stays of the 'myth of return' migrants, and the perilous journeys of refugees, never has the slogan 'we are here because you were there' been more relevant. It is notable that the refugees' routes to Europe, and those of the less desperate travellers before them, often follow the pathways of colonization. Maghrebi refugees tended to head for France and authors from western North Africa historically wrote about the French, just as Britain was the most popular destination and imaginative terrain for inhabitants of the UK's former colonies. Recently, this pattern of movement has changed as migrants have become aware of Germany's positive open door policy towards refugees.

The stigmatization of refugees, which has become increasingly virulent this century, is wrong. Muslim travellers and migrants have hugely enriched British life over the centuries, as my research has demonstrated at length. Not only have they created a body of literature worth celebrating, but they have also changed the nature of music, sport, British cuisine (for evidence of this, see Chapter 28, 'In Praise of the Chapaterati'), business, and science. I hope that the monograph and now the present essay collection do them justice.

21

'Islamophobia': Orwellian 'Newspeak' or Racially Inflected Hatred?

RECENTLY, A PAKISTANI WRITER FRIEND based in London challenged me to tackle an issue he often hears me ranting about: the institutionalization of Islamophobia, and how this is explored and challenged in literary texts. As my friend knows, Islamophobia has become a pressing topic for me, especially since reading Salman Rushdie's *Joseph Anton*. This memoir is perhaps best summarized by Matthew Hart: '[Much] like his career to date [the book is] great until about halfway through' (np.). However much one might wish to contest some of Rushdie's arguments, there is no denying the literary and emotional power of the early sections. Yet as *Joseph Anton* progresses, it becomes increasingly pompous, celebrity-obsessed, and misogynist.

More interesting from my perspective, though, is the way in which Rushdie denies the existence of anti-Muslim hatred. He writes: 'A new word had been created to help the blind remain blind: *Islamophobia*' (344; emphasis in original). Shortly afterwards, he co-opts George Orwell's *Nineteen Eighty-Four* to relegate the term to 'the vocabulary of Humpty Dumpty Newspeak' (346). (It's revealing that Rushdie should cite Newspeak's creators' name for their torture chamber, the Ministry of Love, in support of his argument, but fail to mention Muslims' experiences of the doublespeak of 'extraordinary rendition', 'shock and awe', and 'detention'.)

But what is Islamophobia? Is it a species of loathing akin to homophobia, misogyny, anti-Semitism, and racism? Or is religion, as some secularists believe, a set of ideas that should be robust enough to shake off even the most strident criticism? Islamophobia is a new, imperfect idiom still finding its place in mainstream discourse. First coined as the French 'Islamophobe' in the early twentieth century (Allen 5), it didn't make its way into English until 1985, when Rushdie's friend, the distinguished Palestinian Christian writer Edward Said, presciently pointed out 'the connection [...] between Islamophobia and anti-Semitism' ('Reconsidered': 8–9).

Chris Allen describes the 'first decade of Islamophobia' (3) as truly beginning in the 1990s. In 1997, Britain's Runnymede Trust published its foundational report *Islamophobia: A Challenge for Us All*, which led to the term entering public policy for the first time, and sought to explain the word's meaning by tabulating eight 'closed' and 'open' views of Islam. For my money, though, the best definition comes from Nasar Meer and Tariq Modood, who describe Islamophobia as 'anti-Muslim sentiment which simultaneously draws upon signs of race, culture and belonging in a way that is by no means reducible to hostility towards a religion alone' (70). Whereas Rushdie seeks to make a distinction between attacking ideas and attacking people, Meer and Modood dismantle this common argument that religion, unlike skin colour, gender, and sexuality, consists of private beliefs that one chooses and can equally abandon. Instead, they suggest that both religious and secularist beliefs actually tend to be rather fixed, context-specific, and inherited. It is not just 'ideas' that anti-Islam zealots are attacking, but people—and in the West, these people often belong to vulnerable and impoverished minorities.

Having defined Islamophobia, it next behoves us to ask whether this racially and culturally constructed anti-Muslim sentiment actually exists. Two Internet storms from a single month (July 2013) indicate that Islamophobia is real and aggressive. Writing in *The New York Times* about Mohamed Morsi's fall, David Brooks suggested that undifferentiated Islamists are embroiled in a 'culture of death', concluding, in high Orientalist style: 'It's not that Egypt doesn't have a recipe for a democratic transition. It seems to lack even the basic mental ingredients' (np.). On Twitter, American author Joyce Carol Oates mused: 'Where 99.3% of women report having been sexually harassed & rape is epidemic—Egypt—natural to inquire: what's the predominant religion?' (qtd. in Bury np.). Oates later half-apologized for the comment, but first the Moroccan–American novelist Laila Lalami riposted: 'Sexual assaults and rape are epidemic in the U.S. military. What is the predominant religion there?' (np.). No wonder researchers Alana Lentin and Gavan Titley describe Islamophobia and related prejudices as a 'toxic gift that keeps on giving' (1).

In the UK, there was a spike in the number of hate attacks against Muslims after the 2013 murder of Lee Rigby in Woolwich. Yet when a small group of English Defence League (EDL) supporters protested in Rigby's name outside York Mosque—in my picturesque (and quite monocultural) city of work—the mosque members welcomed the bigots with tea and biscuits, provisions with quintessentially British (and Pakistani) cultural resonances. This incident, which *The Guardian* called an attempt to 'open a dialogue' (Czernik np.), demonstrates that many Muslims, far from cultivating a 'victim mentality'—a charge often levelled at them by the anti-Islamophobia brigade—in fact employ reason, humour, and toleration to combat hatred.

How does anti-Muslim sentiment make its way into writing by authors from Muslim Pakistani backgrounds? One of the earliest writers to consistently explore the issue is Aamer Hussein, whose short story about the First Gulf War, 'Your Children', was published soon after the 1990 invasion. Along with another story, 'The Book of Maryam'—which recalls the tense atmosphere in London around the time of the Second Gulf War—it evokes the ethical and political concerns raised for Muslims by US-led raids. As a character in 'Your Children' remarks, the Gulf War 'isn't a Muslim war' (49).

Daniyal Mueenuddin and Kamila Shamsie almost casually mention Islamophobia experienced in post-9/11 America. Mueenuddin's elite Pakistani émigrés in *In Other Rooms, Other Wonders* are described as apologizing daily for the crime of 9/11 (149), despite their great philosophical distance from al-Qaida's politics. In Shamsie's *Broken Verses*, a character accounts for his return from New York to Karachi with a familiar litany: 'The INS. Guantanamo Bay. The unrandom random security check in airports' (46). In *Burnt Shadows*, another character says: '[E]veryone just wants to tell you what they know about Islam, how they know so much more than you do, what do you know, you've just been a Muslim your whole life, how does that make you know anything?' (352). In *The Reluctant Fundamentalist*, Mohsin Hamid explores Islamophobia through the Pakistani character Changez, who is aware of countrymen being beaten and arrested in post-9/11 New York, and is himself ostracized for adopting the potent visual symbol of a beard (130), eventually propelling his return to Pakistan. H. M. Naqvi's novel *Home Boy* similarly recounts the story of well-integrated Pakistani–Americans Shehzad ('Chuck') and his two friends, who are arrested on terrorism charges in the fearful post-9/11 climate. Twenty-first century Islamophobia in Britain is scrutinized in Hanif Kureishi's *Something to Tell You*. The novel depicts religion coming to the fore in London just after 7/7, when Ajita, a previously secular character, tries to reorient herself by sporting a burqa. More convincing is Kureishi's image of London as 'one of the great Muslim cities' (10) and his exploration of a Britain where Muslims' 'fortunes and fears rose and fell according to the daily news' (14), and 'Mussie' and 'ham-head' (320) are new insults.

This riveting and substantial body of writing suggests that the pen is among the best weapons minority Muslims have with which to fight racially inflected religious hatred. Like Scheherazade telling stories to stave off violence, these Pakistani writers dispute common stereotypes of Muslims and distract from the dominant narrative with wit, passion, and empathy. Their voices add gradation to the 'not-for-prophet' New Atheist movement's hollering. Rushdie might do well to study some of these novels, so that he can learn what Islamophobia is from those qualified to define it from experience as well as theory.

22

'Colour-Blind' Nigel Farage Lives in a White-Washed World

'I DON'T ACTUALLY, but if I did talk to my children about the question of race, they wouldn't know what I was talking about', declared then UKIP leader Nigel Farage in 2015 (qtd. in Grice and Morris np.). His daughters were born in 2000 and 2005. For older children to be unaware of race is surprising. However, when your father is a UKIP politician and you live in the leafy hamlet of Single Street in Kent, it makes more sense. It's easy to be colour-blind when you're dazzled by the whiteness around you.

In 2015, Farage caused a furore by saying he would scrap much of Britain's racial discrimination legislation. He made his sweeping claim during a Channel 4 interview (qtd. in Phillips *Things*: np.) with former Chair of the Equality and Human Rights Commission Trevor Phillips. Attempting damage control after Farage's public statement, UKIP candidate Winston McKenzie went on Radio 4's *World at One* programme to deny that demolishing anti-discrimination law was the party's aim. Instead, he argued (inasmuch as you can call it an argument) that Farage's comments were actually about the issue of nationality. Many Black Britons, he claimed, were losing out on jobs to foreign workers, so it was UKIP's aim to protect them.

The 1960s saw racial discrimination legislation emerge, alongside a tightening up of Britain's rules on immigration. In 1960, Harold

Macmillan's Conservative government announced that new laws would clamp down on immigration to the UK. In order to 'beat the ban', there was a dramatic uptick in migrant arrivals during in the early 1960s. According to Trevor and his brother Mike Phillips, in their book *Windrush* (189), in 1959 only 16,000 West Indian immigrants came to the UK, but by 1961 the number rose to over 60,000 per year. The Commonwealth Immigrants Act came into force in 1962. It was introduced to combat the influx of migration from the Caribbean and South Asia. Members of white settler colonies of the Commonwealth, such as Australia and Canada, were still allowed into Britain, because they were 'patrials' whose forebears came from Britain (Phillips and Phillips 245). On the other hand, non-settler colonies, such as those of the Caribbean, South Asia, Africa, and the Middle East, 'only' had a connection with Britain because their countries had been occupied and plundered during colonial rule.

So-called 'coloured immigrants' were dismissed as a problem community, supposedly causing crime and overpopulation, whose numbers needed to be reduced. Their low rates of unemployment and solicited input into the National Health Service, transport, and the broader economy were conveniently forgotten, in much the same way that Farage, Paul Nuttall, and UKIP regularly overlook immigrants' contributions to the UK today (see, for example, Mason np.).

A little later, under the Labour government of Harold Wilson, racial discrimination legislation began to be introduced. The first Race Relations Act was passed in 1965. It outlawed public discrimination on the basis of colour, race, or ethnic or national origins. It was followed in 1976 by another, more detailed Race Relations Act. This legislation applies to Great Britain, but not Northern Ireland. It specifically covers employment, the provision of goods and services, education, training, and welfare. According to political activist Christine Burns, these legal initiatives 'echo[ed] similar forms of protection introduced in the United States a decade beforehand' (np.). In other words, these moves were positive but belated attempts at ensuring equality and justice for British citizens. They were the carrot to the stick of 'Fortress Britain's' constricted immigration policy. Now Farage wants to remove the carrot, while sharpening the stick.

Farage's declaration that UKIP is a colour-blind party is just as curious as his position on discrimination law. Critical race theorists in the US, such as Kimberlé Crenshaw and Blake Emerson, argue that colour-blind interpretations of the law actually foster white privilege and racism in the workplace. Legal colour blindness has a complex history. Emerson shows that in 1896 Justice Marshall Harlan evoked the idea that the American constitution was colour-blind in order to justify segregation in the state of Louisiana. In the middle of the twentieth century, civil rights activists used the colour-blind argument to fight Jim Crow legislation. But in recent years, those who have used and benefitted from claims to colour blindness are those who are opposed to affirmative action.

Farage is wrong to suggest that it is positive, even anti-racist not to notice a person's colour. According to critical race theory, colour blindness actually works to conceal racism, ignore historical oppression, and imply a meritocracy where none exists. My children are four years younger than the Farage girls. They go to schools in northeast Leeds where ethnic diversity is well above average. They know what race is and despise the unfairness of discrimination on this basis. Maybe Farage and his minions wouldn't be so quick to use 'colour-blind' as a term to prove their antipathy to racism if they knew it was a dirty word in US race relations. What is needed to create a socially just society is not colour blindness, but race consciousness and anti-racist activism.

23

Freedom as Floating or Falling

NINE DAYS AFTER 9/11, on 20 September 2001, President George W. Bush responded to the World Trade Centre attacks by addressing a joint session of Congress. He lamented that in the space of a 'single day' the country had been changed irrevocably, its people 'awakened to danger and called to defend freedom'. The murders of almost 3,000 people generated anger and a drive for retribution. The attackers, whom Bush termed 'enemies of freedom', were apparently motivated by envy as well as hatred: 'They hate what they see right here in this chamber: a democratically elected government. Their leaders are self-appointed. They hate our freedoms: our freedom of religion, our freedom of speech, our freedom to vote and assemble and disagree with each other' (np.). In this passage alone, 'freedom' is utilized in four instances, and in the approximately 3,000 word-long speech from which it is taken, the word 'freedom' is invoked thirteen times. Given that the speech was a major statement of Bush's intent following the wound of 9/11 and that the US government used the code name 'Operation Enduring Freedom' to describe its war in Afghanistan, it is clear that freedom is a crucial concept to the US and its allies. This is unsurprising, since the Statue of Liberty on Liberty Island in New York Harbour has long served as a symbol of freedom and the vaunted American myth of social mobility.

But what does freedom consist of, is it a universal value, and does everyone—men and women, and people from different classes, races, or religious backgrounds—experience it in the same way? In 2014, Bangladeshi-born writer Zia Haider Rahman published his captivating, if very masculine, debut novel, *In the Light of What We Know*. The book deals in part with 9/11 and its aftermath. One of Rahman's two main protagonists, Zafar, takes a job in Afghanistan soon after the outbreak of war in 2001. He asserrts that the American occupiers 'justify their invasion of Afghanistan with platitudes about freedom and liberating the Afghani people' (325). Having studied law and worked for a US bank, Zafar is in some ways part of the American 'relief effort'. And yet he is simultaneously not part of it, due to his Bangladeshi background and brown skin. Because of this, coupled with his working-class origins, he sees through the rhetoric of freedom as platitudinous.

Later, Rahman's Zafar describes a raucous, sexually charged UN bar in Kabul, concluding: 'It was a scene of horror. This is the freedom for which war is waged' (360). Here, he unpicks what Americans mean by 'freedom'. It bathetically involves a person being free to drink alcohol and explore their sexuality—whether they are married or single is unimportant. To the occupiers, freedom is about individual choice in the free market. This means little to the majority of Afghans. The influx of new bars and nightclubs during the occupation is a popular, positive development in the minds of the local elite class but, as Zafar points out, 'the poor are disgusted' (368).

From freedom's sister word, liberty, comes the verb 'liberate', another word for saving. This idea of liberation and saving brings us to Lila Abu-Lughod's book, *Do Muslim Women Need Saving* (2013). The anthropologist tackles ideas about freedom in relation to the realms of race, class, and gender. A feminist with heritage partly in the global south, Abu-Lughod suggests that Western feminists see themselves as 'saving' their benighted Muslim sisters. Abu-Lughod also scrutinizes the repercussions from one notion of freedom being extolled above all other values. She questions whether women's clothing can symbolize freedom or unfreedom, and whether forces that put limits on every individual's free will mean that, as Wendy Brown puts it, 'choice [...] is an impoverished account of freedom' (qtd. in Abu-Lughod *Saving*: 19). Abu-Lughod seems to suggest that the binary opposition of free and unfree lies at the heart of twenty-first century versions of Orientalism. She argues that American feminism is deceived by the 'powerful national ideology' (20) of freedom and fails to recognize the unequal power relations that underpin this ideology.

Rather than accepting the premise that Western freedom contrasts with imprisonment by Islam, Abu-Lughod deftly communicates that believing Muslims have their own ideas about, and goals for, liberation. The Islamic scholar Abdal Hakim Murad, also known by his birth name of Tim Winter, similarly writes that Islam represents 'radical freedom, a freedom from the encroachments of the State, the claws of the ego, narrow fanaticism and sectarian bigotry and an intrusive state or priesthood' (np.). Abu-Lughod's delineation of a dominant narrative of freedom recalls a statement made by Salman Rushdie regarding the World Trade Centre attacks:

> The fundamentalist believes that we believe in nothing. [...] To prove him wrong, we must first know that he is wrong. We must agree on what matters: kissing in public places, bacon sandwiches, disagreement, cutting-edge fashion, literature, generosity, water, a more equitable distribution of the world's resources, movies, music, freedom of thought, beauty, love. These will be our weapons. Not by making war, but by the unafraid way we choose to live shall we defeat them ('Attacks': 393).

This somewhat tongue-in-cheek list is a salad of trivial things, ideals, and rights. It also neatly illustrates that many apparent freedoms are culturally specific shibboleths that might alienate not just 'fundamentalists', but a good number of non-Western, non-Christian, non-male people (not to mention that many Western vegetarians, including me, would be put off by the bacon sandwiches). It becomes apparent that ideas of freedom are culturally located. Notwithstanding Rushdie's claims, liberty does not equate to wearing miniskirts rather than burqas.

Shifting focus slightly to discuss Muslim women writers' ideas about freedom in Britain, Attia Hosain immediately springs to mind. Hosain is well-known for her short story collection, *Phoenix Fled*, and novel, *Sunlight on a Broken Column*, which are both set in India. Few people realize that she also wrote a promising putative novel about diasporic Britain, *No New Lands, No New Seas*. Hosain worked on this novel from the 1950s through to the 1970s but eventually abandoned it. This was probably because the virulent racism of the late 1960s onwards (typified by Enoch Powell and the National Front) dissuaded her from completing it on the grounds that her novel's focus on the migrant experience was painful to contemplate (Habibullah 13–14). Her central migrant character, Murad, experiences a minor breakdown in the paradoxically crowded and yet isolating capital of London. He frequently expresses the idea that he has been unmoored, sure that his thoughts should be 'pegged down, hammered to solidity or he would fly into space, dissolving all matter into formlessness' (28). Murad remembers that when he first arrived in London 'he floated away with a wild incredulous sense of freedom' (55). Perhaps the most interesting instance of Hosain's portrayal of freedom—as a version of what David Bowie unforgettably described as 'floating in a most peculiar way'—is this passage:

[H]is happiest moments were in the in-between world where he was free yet not free of intrusive presences, as when at a concert his submerged thoughts would float above the music and cover it with a drifting film until he pushed it away, and under the sounds to which he forcibly attached his mind until the music emerged clearly as if he, with every nerve-end vibrating, were himself one of the instruments (29).

Although at certain moments, Hosain's novel represents freedom as floating in an unnerving way, in this particular passage Murad's thoughts soar above the music, until he almost coalesces with the instruments themselves. They are then brought back to earth by a 'drifting film'—a metaphor of feathery lightness that nonetheless weighs down, and of the film's transparency that still manages to ground the character again.

This notion that happiness can emerge from an in-between realm that at once represents freedom and bondage is illuminating. It's a notion that women, especially, can appreciate. The Cairo-born London-resident writer and activist Ahdaf Soueif once shared in an interview on her writing process that she feels most free when she is writing on her own in a room, but can hear her family busy with happy activities not far away. She finds contentment in being free and yet not free. Although Hosain's ideal is a sublime freedom coexisting with unfreedom, breaking down the binary that Abu-Lughod so dislikes, the novelist recognizes that a mundane version of freedom as individual choice is the one that prevails. Murad and his friend Isa together investigate 'the areas of liberty that London had given them' (33). The narrator opines that this liberty is initially 'mostly in respect of women and wine, then through pubs and prostitutes to the poetry of freedom and friendship without the taboos of tradition, the constraint of custom and duress of duty' (33). It is a similar version of freedom to that which Rahman criticized: a prosaic lack of restraint in relation to 'women and wine'. Alliteration underscores the glibness of Murad's free indirect discourse on freedom.

Formlessness, lack of solidity, freedom, and loneliness: these motifs echo again through the pages of Sudanese author Leila Aboulela's London novel, *Minaret* (2005). Hosain's notion of flying or floating up into space is inverted in *Minaret*. Aboulela describes her Sudanese protagonist Najwa's metaphorical 'fall' through space due to an encounter with the vertiginous liberties of the West. What makes *Minaret* distinctive as a novel of Muslim experience is that it centres on a character's propulsion towards religion, rather than away. Many Anglophone novels about the British Muslim experience from the 1990s and early 2000s focus on young Muslims discovering 'freedom', usually in the shape of a secular life and independence from familial or kinship ties. In contrast, Aboulela's novel traces the Westernized protagonist, Najwa's, downwardly mobile fall from her privileged position as a Sudanese minister's daughter, to exile in London when a coup dislodges her father from power, and eventually life as a domestic servant to a wealthy Arab family in the former imperial capital.

During this descent, an unfurling religious identity nourishes Najwa through her losses. The supportive ties that Najwa discovers in her mosque are starkly contrasted with the supposed 'freedoms' of the non-religious world, which Aboulela portrays as being constrictive rather than liberatory. The notion of liberty in Western thought since the time of Hobbes's *Leviathan* has meant a freedom from external constraints and the right of individual self-determination. In Arab and South Asian thought, by contrast, freedom—*hurriyya* in Arabic or *azadi* in Urdu—typically possesses political, communitarian connotations. It would be wrong to assume that Muslims have not hotly debated the concept of freedom over the centuries. In the Sufi tradition, freedom has been compared to 'perfect slavery' (Bostom np.), which indicates not only that slavery in the Arab world was, in Amitav Ghosh's words, a relatively 'flexible set of hierarchies' (*Antique*: 260), but also that the institution was often used as a metaphor for understanding 'the relationship between Allah the "master" and his human "slaves"' (Bostom np.). Aboulela provocatively challenges Western perceptions of what freedom entails when she constructs a protagonist who expresses a desire to become her employer's family slave or concubine:

> I don't explain […] my fantasies. My involvement in Tamer's wedding to a young suitable girl who knows him less than I do. She will mother children who spend more time with me… I would like to be his family's concubine, like something out of *The Arabian Nights*, with life-long security and a sense of belonging. But I must settle for freedom in this modern time (215).

The issue of clashing cultural understandings of liberty highlighted by this passage is particularly pertinent in the light of Abu-Lughod's analysis of the rhetoric of 'freedom' used to justify the War on Terror. With her evocation of *The Arabian Nights*, Najwa communicates that feminism has typically overlooked non-Euro–American traditions when defining 'women's lib'. Yet Najwa's wish is itself problematic, especially since later she chooses to perform hajj, rather than marry Tamer. This internal monologue smacks of lugubrious, even masochistic, propensities.

Najwa has been brought up in a broadly Western tradition: she comes from an elite family that only pays lip service to Islam. Her early life, while affluent and sheltered, is nonetheless depicted as lacking some essential component. Within conventional limits, Najwa has considerable freedom in her dress, education, and sexual relations. Yet she feels uneasy when men she is unfamiliar with openly appraise her body, and her only sexual relationship—with a Marxist exile in London—is sordid and guilt-ridden. After the leftist coup in Sudan leads to her father's imprisonment and eventual execution, her family is described as 'falling' through space. This image of descent evokes the 'horror' inherent in too much liberty. Of course, it also suggests the 'Fall' common to both Judeo–Christian and Qur'anic doctrine, whereby Adam and Eve/Hawwa were banished from the Garden of Paradise to live on earth. Najwa's fall is complete once her brother, Omar, is imprisoned for possession of drugs and her mother dies. Freed from her duties as caregiver, Najwa supposes that she should feel a sense of emancipation, but instead observes: 'This empty space was called freedom' (175).

The War in Afghanistan has led to the privileging of a Western dichotomy of freedom versus unfreedom. Lila Abu-Lughod interrogates and genders this binary. Hosain anticipates these debates in her novel fragment written between 1950 and 1970, while in a post-9/11 context Aboulela robustly challenges them. We should not forget, though, that ideas of political freedom are more crucial in the Muslim world now than ever before. This is easily perceptible in the advent of the Arab uprisings. A chant against the Egyptian regime that Soueif evokes clearly encapsulates and calls forth that ever elusive and changeable idea of liberty: 'They said trouble ran in our blood and how'd we dare demand our rights | Oh dumb regime | understand | what I want: | Liberty! Liberty!' ('Liberty': np.).

24

Writing Muslim Lives

D URING THE FIRST SEMINAR of a module on postcolonial
writing in a recent academic year, I used an icebreaker exercise
which involved each student introducing themselves by revealing
their name and what sort of books they enjoyed reading. One
18-year-old male English literature student memorably replied:
'I don't really like reading. ... Maybe sporting biographies?' While
some might interpret his comment as philistinism, I prefer to see
it as exemplifying the current popularity of the (auto)biography.
Sportsmen and women, celebrities, cultural icons: anyone who's
anyone has written (or employed a ghost writer to pen) an (auto)
biography. Indeed, many unknowns are at it too, as the rise of
interest in books and courses about 'life writing' indicates. Yet,
Hanif Kureishi—himself the author of a thoughtful (auto)
biography about his relationship with his father entitled *My Ear
at His Heart*—discusses:

> the falsity, or impossibility perhaps, of an autobiography, of the belief
> that one can say, 'I am speaking the truth', and be sure that that is
> what one is doing. [...] It might have to be admitted that the 'truth'
> of an artist is more likely to be discovered in their fiction than in
> other direct witness ('Mad': 261).

This statement pinpoints that the autobiography as a form is not
separable from fiction without difficulty. Autobiographies and

novels both fuse fact with fiction and blur distinctions between narrator and author, so that often readers are dependent on the authors' and marketers' choice of label. For example, Ahdaf Soueif's *In the Eye of the Sun* is categorized as a novel, while Sara Suleri's *Meatless Days* is categorized as a memoir; it could almost as easily be the other way around.

It is important that critics try to ascertain what 'truths' or 'fictions' are conveyed in popular autobiographies by individuals from Muslim backgrounds. Many autobiographical texts written by women from Muslim backgrounds veer towards categorization as misery memoirs, describing the abuse, forced marriage, or kidnapping of the passive, oppressed Muslim female. In her ghostwritten autobiography, *The Caged Virgin: A Muslim Woman's Cry for Reason*, for instance, Somali-born, Dutch, and now US resident Ayaan Hirsi Ali makes the dubious claims that Muslims view the Prophet Muhammad (PBUH) as being infallible, and that Islam is dominated by tribal Arab sexual morality. She also describes her experiences of abuse apparently sanctioned by Islam:

> When we were living in Ethiopia my mother did not want my sister or me to attend school. We were going to be married off within a few years anyway, so what good would all that knowledge be to us? [...] But my father insisted that we go to school. [...] He also declared himself dead set against our circumcision. What he doesn't know is that my grandmother secretly arranged to have it done behind his back (70-1).

It should not escape our notice that doubt has been cast on Hirsi Ali's forced marriage asylum claim in the Netherlands (see Shah 'Wolf': np.). Moreover, female genital mutilation, which Hirsi Ali alleges is carried out 'in the name of Islam', is a cultural practice undertaken in non-Islamic African cultures too, but rarely practised by Muslims outside of Africa and some parts of the Middle East.

In Maha Khan Phillips' satirical novel *Beautiful from this Angle*, the protagonist, a wealthy Pakistani socialite from Karachi, tries her hand at writing a novel in the style of 'woe is me' narratives (Gilmour 210) such as Hirsi Ali's:

> When I announced that I would be going to uni, my father screamed for two weeks and told me they had already found me a husband. [...] (Note: Research has shown that there are two types of oppressed women—the ones who are princesses in their own countries, and the ones who are foreigners suckered into entering a Muslim country and are never able to leave. Oppressed women trapped in Pakistan always come from either Birmingham or North England. Look on the Internet for some Birmingham street names) (36).

The character's 'research' correctly identifies two common trends within life writing that tackles the nature of Muslim lives. First, there is the theme of the kidnapped Arab princess. Gillian Whitlock calls this type of book 'the veiled best-seller', which she defines as 'popular and romantic biographies of Muslim women' that sell well, in large part due to their harem setting (88). This is a locale that also features in 'desert romance' fiction, featuring the sexy but authoritarian sheikh, probably inspired by the framing narrative of King Shahryar and his beleaguered wife, Shahrazad, from *The Arabian Nights*. British–Syrian novelist Robin Yassin-Kassab observes that 'the "Arab World" sections of many Gulf bookshops could be renamed "Harem Fantasy for Whites", concentrating disproportionately on more or less fraudulent revelations of the "Princess" variety' ('Gulf': np.).

Khan Phillips also gestures towards another common strand

in Muslim life writing: the forced marriage plot, which involves the British protagonist being tricked and sent back to the subcontinent to face an unwanted marriage with a stranger. To these two dominant genres, we can also add the memoir about domestic or sexual abuse, such as 'Anon Beauty's' *Not Easily Washed Away: Memoirs of a Muslim's Daughter*, and the Christian conversion narrative, such as Bilquis Sheikh's autobiography (which continues the trend for long titles), *I Dared to Call Him Father: The Miraculous Story of a Muslim Woman's Encounter with God*. Amongst male autobiographies, another mini-subgenre is developing, which documents the author's flirtation with extremist Islam, often while away at university and in the initial throes of adult life, and his growing disenchantment and eventual departure from the movement. This is exemplified in Ed Husain's *The Islamist* and Russell Razzaque's sensationally titled *Human Being to Human Bomb*—both of which are books by British–Bangladeshi authors that deal to greater and lesser degrees with their brushes with Hizb-ut-Tahrir while attending universities in London.

Tacitly countering the Islamist subgenre is a small number of memoirs about the wrongful imprisonment of supposedly radical Muslims in Guantánamo Bay and other legal black holes, of which the most famous is Moazzam Begg's *Enemy Combatant*, which I discussed in Chapter 12, 'Torturing the "Other": Who is the Barbarian?' There are also well-known autobiographies by Sarfraz Manzoor, Shelina Zahra Janmohamed, Rageh Omaar, Yasmin Hai, Imran Ahmad, and others; writers now in their late thirties or early forties, many of them with a background in journalism, who were children in the 1980s, young adults in the 1990s, and came of age when 9/11 made them increasingly conscious of their religious background. For the most part, these texts exemplify 'Indo-chic' (Huggan 59, 67), or, more accurately, what I would call 'Muslim Cool', placing discussion of music, fashion, night life, and university study alongside analysis of identity politics, Thatcherism, the Rushdie affair, 7/7, intergenerational conflict, and Islamophobia.[1] Many of these writers criticize abuses that are committed in the name of Islam or are linked to particular Muslim cultures, while remaining alert to stereotypes of the religion from the outside.

Life writing by Muslim-identified authors is, then, a genre with various subcategories, including the wrongful imprisonment memoir, the literary memoir, and the subgenre I identify as 'Muslim Cool'. In many of the misery memoirs in particular, Islam is presented as an undifferentiated monolith. As we have seen, writers such as Hirsi Ali seem to have a clear and absolute concept of what they believe Islam is, and it usually appears inimical to women. More recently, however, subtler autobiographies, such as Shelina Zahra Janmohamed's *Love in a Headscarf*, are emerging, which pivot on the narrator's journey towards Islam as a civilization or a religion, rather than towards 'freedom' and secular life.[2]

Note

1. My use of the term 'Muslim Cool' is adapted from two sources: first, 'Cool Britannia', the media brand name used in late 1990s Blairite Britain, and 'Asian Kool', a documentary film by Paul Moseley about the bhangra music scene at the turn of the millennium. Other thinkers have used terms such as 'Mipster' (meaning a Muslim hipster; see Sheikh Bake and Herding) and 'Generation M' (see Janmohamed *Generation M*).

25

Who Do YA Think You're Representing? Diversity in Young Adult Fiction

THE POOR STATE OF DIVERSITY in young adult (YA) fiction is nothing short of embarrassing. In 2013, less than 3 per cent of children's and YA books depicted non-white characters (Flood np.). Young adult author Malinda Lo writes that those YA novels that represent diversity in relation to ethnicity, sexuality, or disability tend to prompt several predictable reactions. Trade reviews regard these books as 'scarcely plausible', and think readers may be surprised by the sheer volume of issues that they bring up, which are 'a lot to decode' (np.); read: any young adult book that ventures beyond engaging with white, heterosexual, able-bodied characters and themes will unsettle expected norms and alienate its readership.

Fortunately, an emerging group of British–Asian young adult writers is successfully challenging these mainstream assumptions, about race at least. The most senior among them, Tariq Mehmood, was born in Mirpur in 1956 and came to Britain as a young man. Living in Bradford, he became a respected leftist political activist, film-maker, and writer of literary and children's fiction. He has a PhD in creative writing from Lancaster University and now teaches at the American University of Beirut. In conversation at London's School of Oriental and African Studies' literature festival 'Cultural

Confluences' in March 2015, Mehmood divulged that when he visits Pakistan, he always finds himself defending Christians; by contrast, when he visits Britain, he speaks up for Muslims. Simply put, this is a writer who is on the side of scapegoated minorities.

This is clearly apparent in his YA novel, *You're Not Proper*. The book alternates between the perspectives of two 14-year-olds living in a divided northern English town. Biracial Kiran is also known as Karen, while her arch-enemy is the hijab-wearing Shamshad. Reacting to peer pressure from her white friends, Kiran insults Shamshad, calling her a 'scarfie' (4). As her faith increases in intensity, Shamshad likewise disapproves of Kiran, insisting that Kiran is not a 'proper' Muslim due to her mixed heritage. As well as exploring the issues of racial in-betweenness and a rise in religiosity in racist Britain, Mehmood also explores the fallout from the War in Afghanistan. In another plot line from the novel, Dex is a white British soldier from the girls' town, who has gone missing while on deployment in Afghanistan. Dex's plight inspires demonstrations by the far right group, the English Defence League or EDL. If this particular narrative arc seems unfinished, that is due to Mehmood's intention to take up this plot trajectory of the missing soldier in his next YA novel—marking the first time he has focused on a white character.

Also from Yorkshire, Sufiya Ahmed published her award-winning *Secrets of the Henna Girl* with Puffin Books in 2012. Its epigraph is the hadith: 'Obtain the virgin's consent before you marry her'. The YA novel centres on a 16-year-old girl, Zeba Khan, who is being forced by her parents into marriage with a cousin. Set in both northern England and Pakistan, this is a story of girls' rights and empowerment. Ahmed decided to write the book when she was working as a parliamentary researcher for an MP in the 2000s. It was through her work in Parliament that she met a group of Asian women activists who were campaigning to raise awareness of the issue of forced marriage as an ongoing problem in these communities. Some of these activists were also campaigning to make forced marriages illegal in the UK. The legislation to categorize forced marriages as illegal was subsequently passed in 2014 (Erlanger np.). Ahmed makes a clear distinction between arranged and forced marriage, arguing that unlike an arranged marriage, a forced marriage will never yield a successful union. She is now writing a book about acid attacks on women in India; thus, it is apparent that this is a writer with a strong commitment to women's human rights. In the light of arguments about Western 'saving discourse' (Abu-Lughod 'Really': 788-9; Cilano 157), it is conspicuous that Ahmed writes about these issues with sensitivity. She is not so simplistic in her fiction as to blame female oppression on Islam. Indeed, her first book—*Zahra's First Term at the Khadija Academy*, which was shortlisted for a Muslim Writers Award— might be justifiably categorized as what Karin van Nieuwkerk terms 'pious art' (van Nieuwkerk 172-6). *Zahra's First Term at the Khadija Academy* is set in a girls' Islamic boarding school and features an indomitable hijab-wearing heroine.

A weighty oeuvre of literature has been published that focuses on Partition, but little that is written explicitly for the teen market. Irfan Master's *A Beautiful Lie* (2011) is therefore an unusual YA novel, in that it deals with the traumatic events of 1947. Master's father is from Gujarat, India, where the novel is set, and his mother comes from Pakistan. The novel's central premise is that the 13-year-old protagonist, Bilal, lies to his dying father, who like Gandhi is known as Bapuji, in order to convince him that Partition is not taking place. This plot line, coincidentally, finds a presage in the 2003 German film *Good Bye Lenin!* (Becker np.), in which an advocate of East Germany slips into a coma prior to the fall of the Berlin Wall. When she awakes, her family pretend that the Wall hasn't come down and reunification hasn't occurred. Perhaps this exploration of lies and pretence around cataclysmic events is currently part of the zeitgeist because of heightened awareness of politicians' subterfuge in our post-WikiLeaks, Trumpian world. Given the context about which Master is writing—Partition, with its political rhetoric of secularism and irredeemable enmity—the theme of lying and deceit seems peculiarly appropriate. Fiction itself is a kind of lie; and historical fiction, with its intermixture of true events and fabrication, makes it difficult to distinguish fact from fiction. Indeed, this YA novel questions the whole notion of truth and asks whether it is worth telling hard truths to vulnerable people who will only be hurt by them. Bilal's brother is a proponent of Pakistan's creation and is in favour of telling their father about Partition. Bilal hectors him:

> What would you know about the truth anyway? What truth do you represent, Bhai? Smashing somebody's head in with a stick isn't any kind of truth I recognise. Is that the truth you want me to tell Bapuji about? I've seen what's going on with my own eyes. If that's the truth, I don't want it (240).

Despite his tender age, the younger brother is more clear-sighted about Partition than the adults, who have been corrupted by various political ideologies.

For the rest of this chapter I focus on vampire fiction by a contemporary British writer of South Asian descent, Sarwat Chadda. In 2008, Chadda signed to Penguin Books' children's imprint Puffin, with whom he published two teen novels—*Devil's Kiss* (2009) and *Dark Goddess* (2010)—featuring the mixed-race protagonist Billi SanGreal. I primarily concentrate on *Devil's Kiss*, as its vampire theme is particularly pertinent for the post-War on Terror era (*Dark Goddess* is indebted to Sir Arthur Conan Doyle's *The Hound of the Baskervilles*, and focuses on werewolves). As

Chadda himself acknowledges, his debut novel contains echoes of both Joss Whedon's *Buffy the Vampire Slayer* television series and Dan Brown's *The Da Vinci Code*. Like Dan Brown's 2003 bestseller and other novels in the conspiracy/historical mystery genre, *Devil's Kiss* focuses on the activities of an offshoot of the medieval Order of the Knights Templar still operating furtively in contemporary society. Yet, perhaps because of his South Asian background and years spent in the Middle East, Chadda is suspicious about the role played by these so-called Poor Fellow-Soldiers of Jesus Christ and of Solomon in both medieval and more recent crusades.

This is evident in the sympathetic protagonist, Billi's, marginalization from the Templar group, which stems partly from her resistance to the Order's ruthlessness. Billi's full name is Bilqis, which evokes heroism, nobility, and wisdom: it is the Arabic name for the Queen of Sheba, a figure common to the Abrahamic traditions. Billi's mother, Jamila, was a Pakistani migrant killed in mysterious circumstances, but whom Billi mistakenly believes may have been murdered by her English father, Arthur SanGreal (this name is, of course, straight out of Arthurian legend). Under her mother's influence, Billi spent her early years loving Allah, but as she approaches puberty she is taught to worship Jesus, because Christianity forms the main focus of Templar religious life. Yet she retains aspects of her Muslim upbringing, exemplified by the fact that she cannot bring herself to eat pork and feels an instinctive empathy towards oppressed peoples, partly due to her familial link to British–Pakistanis—a marginalized group in multicultural Britain.

As a second-generation migrant of mixed heritage, Billi does not inhabit what Homi Bhabha describes as a productive and enabling 'third space' (Bhabha 36–9, 116), so much as cultural confusion grounded on oppressive experiences. Her Muslim heritage creates a sense of isolation from the Templars. She has virtually no power within the Order, even though she is expected to risk her life with, and for, them. She is emotionally and physically abused by her father, has few friends, and appears resigned to a life ostracized from wider society except the group she unwillingly belongs to. Moreover, while Buffy and Billi are strong, adept warriors, in Chadda's text there is a stronger emphasis on the physical vulnerability of Billi. Her encounters with demons, vampires, and her apparent Templar allies more often than not leave her bloody, bruised, and traumatized. There is a sense in which Billi's body (like that of her mother before her) becomes the site on which the novel's various metaphysical, cultural, and religious battles are violently enacted.

If Billi's mixed heritage is often a source of pain and conflict within the novel, then there is also a sense in which she embodies a fluid and redemptive hybridity. This becomes more apparent in the second Bilqis SanGreal novel, *Dark Goddess*. In the following exchange, Billi, conversing with a psychic Russian girl, Vasilisa, has compared the Templars to the Russian Bogatyrs:

> 'The Bogatyrs were great knights [says Vasilisa]. My mother told me stories about them. They fought dragons, evil witches, the Mongols, the Muslims. All the evil people.'
> Billi laughed. 'My mother was a Muslim.'
> Vasilisa went red. 'Are you?'
> Billi shrugged. She could pray in Latin, Greek and Arabic. She knew the direction of Mecca and the psalms. Did God really care? (Chadda *Goddess*: 58–9).

The child's unthinking Islamophobia is offset by Billi's comfortable mixing of faiths and her confidence in a beneficent deity that is unconcerned by sectarian divisions. Billi goes on to explain to Vasilisa that after centuries of fighting Muslims, the Templar

Knights eventually reached out and united with them, replacing the 'holy war' against Islam with the 'Dark Conflict': 'Instead of fighting other men, we fight the Unholy. Monsters like werewolves. Ghosts. The blood drinkers' (59).

In Chadda's teen vampire slayer fiction, Islam emerges as one of a number of potent cultural and religious forces engaged in a Manichean struggle against evil, which draws upon, but significantly renegotiates, the premise of Joss Whedon's cult favourite, *Buffy the Vampire Slayer*. Another significant difference between the two is that *Devil's Kiss* relocates its vampires and slayers from the rather bland, racially homogenous community of Buffy's American suburb of Sunnydale to the hybrid space of contemporary London. London offers Billi (as it did for another mixed-race British–Asian protagonist, Karim, in Hanif Kureishi's *The Buddha of Suburbia*) 'new kinds of community and ways of living' (Moore-Gilbert 125). What appeals to Billi about London is its multiculturalism, the 'kaleidoscope of cultures and races' (Chadda *Devil's*: 130). She eagerly sets about learning several different languages so that she can communicate with recent migrants to the city. What is clear here is that Billi identifies with the hybrid, postcolonial city of the immigrant poor—the city of orphans, poor labourers, and refugees. Indeed, there is a clear sense in which Billi's British–Muslim identity is a *Londoni* identity that aligns her explicitly with marginalized groups, often invisible to privileged white society, who are nevertheless mandatory for the economic and social functioning of the city. The fact that this mixed-race heroine saves a metropolis unable even to recognize the true nature of the danger it faces can be read as a potent metaphor for the unacknowledged enrichment achieved by the marginalized (and often abused) citizens of postcolonial London.

In a context in which migrants generally, and Muslims in particular, tend to be demonized and their contribution to British

society underplayed if not obviated, Chadda's work emerges as
radically counter-cultural. Consider, for instance, the extent to
which vampyric mythology surrounds Muslim immigrants in
Europe and North America. Muslims are seen as draining the
continents' resources, the process of creating halal food is often
regarded as involving animal cruelty (because it involves the
slow bleeding of the animal), and Muslims are seen as predatory
outsiders, acting as a fifth column. For comic purposes, American
humourist Stephen Colbert imagines the figure of the 'Muslim
vampire' who communicates not through sleeper cells, but through
'sleeper-in-coffin cells'. He exhorts his audience with mock hysteria:
'Protect yourself from Muslim vampires by making your neck non-
halal: rub it with pork sausage' (qtd. in Edwards np.; emphasis in
original). Within this broader cultural context, Chadda's reworking
of the contemporary vampire-slayer narrative deserves to be taken
very seriously.

'Children narrators', argues the postcolonial critic Sujala Singh,
'function as bridges, as interpretive filters informing and educating
the reader about violence "out there"' (14). The child narrator is a
common device in explorations of violent events in South Asian
adult literature, such as Indian Arundhati Roy's *The God of Small
Things*, Sri Lankan Shyam Selvadurai's *Funny Boy*, and Pakistani
Bina Shah's *Slum Child*. The British–Asian authors discussed in
this chapter transplant the child narrator successfully into the new
ground of YA fiction. They give us stereotype-quashing, critical
novels about religion, gender, violence, and families. Taken together,
these novels sound a melodious, authentic note that cuts through
the monotone voices coming out of YA writing today.

26

Laughing At Ourselves

IN NOVEMBER 2013, the UK's Attorney General, Dominic Grieve, made allegations that corruption is 'endemic' amongst British–Pakistanis, whereas British–Indians and 'white Anglo-Saxons' (his appellation) are said to be less crooked (Brogan np.). This flagrantly speculative, prejudiced comment led to a barrage of criticism which prompted Grieve's eventual apology (Malnick np.). It reminded me, however, of a joke I inadvertently heard a couple of years ago when Pakistan came close to topping a poll taken of Asia's, as well as the world's, most corrupt countries (see Transparency International np.): 'But we're so good at corruption', goes the apocryphal response from an imagined Pakistani, 'and we can't even win at that!'

These allegations and the half-remembered joke triggered consideration of the complex relationship between stereotypes and humour. Cliché demands that stereotypes contain a grain of truth, but I think they reveal more about the person or society that holds the stereotype. This argument that stereotypes are in the eye of the beholder is confirmed by the fact that different cultures often have vastly different preconceptions about a single community. For instance, Pakistanis may be seen by Americans as cabdrivers or terrorists, by Turks as hashish smokers, and by Sri Lankans as cricketers. And that's just the women! Stereotypes also metamorphose over time, so that the British caricature of Russians as Cold War paupers, for example, is now being bedaubed with a new myth of extravagant Russian billionaires. Similarly, the early

1980s British stereotype of Pakistani migrants as a hard-working, parsimonious 'model minority' community has been all but replaced by the bogeyman of the 'enemy within', the figure of the suicide bomber, or the apparently oppressed veiled woman.

Another stereotype has emerged since the Rushdie affair and gained traction following the Danish cartoons and *Charlie Hebdo* controversies: this is the myth that practising Muslims are opposed to comedy. Several comedians and sketches have sought to repudiate such views of the 'humourless Muslim', including the US troupe Allah Made Me Funny. Of course, *some* Muslims oppose comedy in general and especially material that is perceived to be bawdy or religiously sensitive. But this is true of religious communities more broadly. From 2005 to 2006, a television show based on the musical *Jerry Springer: The Opera* (Orton) was targeted by a well-organized Christian campaign, which used online complaints forms and British blasphemy legislation in an attempt to petition the removal of this show from the air (Tryhorn np.).

As Andrew Stott explains, given its reliance on plot-driven narratives, comedy inevitably often creates types, rather than well-rounded characters:

> Comic characters are traditionally one-dimensional in the sense that they are apparently unable to learn and change [...] What makes [Bugs Bunny] funny is the weightlessness of his character, the fact that he is not anchored within an orthodox system of selfhood or responsibility [...] [C]haracter types are so rigidly defined that their behaviours are entirely predictable within given situations. The miser will always be miserly, and the braggart will always boast (39–40).

As such, to demand subtle characterization or verisimilitude from comic theatre, film, television, and literature is to commit a category mistake. However, it is not wrong to probe the use of stereotypes in comedy and question whether they are being used excessively or lazily.

Contrary to the dominant image of dour, cheerless Muslims, the production and consumption of comedy among Pakistani diasporic communities has a rich history, and 'Muslim comedy' is becoming increasingly popular and moving into the mainstream. From the late 1970s and early 1980s onwards, Hanif Kureishi wrote about South Asian Muslims for page, stage, and screen in groundbreaking, hilarious ways. He celebrated and satirized migration, sexuality, pop culture, and intergenerational tension, inspiring a younger crop of British–Asian writers to join what the indie band Cornershop extolled in song as the 'Hanif Kureishi Scene'. One of the 1990s' and early 2000s' most well-known British–Asian comedies, *East Is East*, was written by Ayub Khan-Din, who began his career by playing Sammy in Kureishi's 1987 film, *Sammy and Rosie Get Laid*. Mainly comic in tone, *East Is East* is set in 1970s Salford, in the context of Enoch Powell's racist repatriation policies and the 1971 War. The script is semi-autobiographical, and focuses on a mixed-race British–Pakistani family as they negotiate tensions between religions and generations, as well as between Pakistani and northern English culture. However, it raised eyebrows for its one-dimensional characterization—particularly in Damien O'Donnell's cinematic rendition—in which largely 'salt-of-the-earth' northerners are problematically juxtaposed with the dictatorial Pakistani father, George Khan.

In 2010, non-Muslim director and comedian Chris Morris produced a rigorously researched, funny film about Muslims in Britain, *Four Lions*, which was well received amongst young British–Pakistanis. It centres on five would-be martyrs, who are soon reduced to four after their bomb-making specialist, Fessal (Adeel Akhtar), trips over a sheep and blows up. The remaining jihadis are led by Omar (Riz Ahmed), the cleverest member of the group, and include his best friend, Waj, who is described in the script as being 20 years old (Morris, Armstrong, and Bain 1) and self-admittedly 'thick as fudge'. Following Omar's and Waj's ignominious militant training in Afghanistan and various arguments and rifts, the group decides to stage suicide bombings at the London Marathon. The attacks don't go to plan, and what begins as a humorous sequence of accidental detonation set pieces becomes a chilling reflection on what happens when an intense combination of religion, politics, and friendship spirals out of control.

In recent years, the BBC comedy *Citizen Khan*, co-written by and starring Adil Ray, has moved to prime time. This series references British situation comedies of the 1970s, whereby, for example, Mr Khan's anguish at an extended visit from his mother-in-law evokes the chauvinist working men's club comedy of that era. The programme received numerous complaints (Sherwin np.), especially for its portrayal of daughter Alia, who employs an outwardly religious persona complete with voluminous hijab as cover for an active social life. In a cluster of articles focusing on the television show in the journal *South Asian Popular Culture*, it was dubbed 'citizen can't' (Huq, Abbas, and Dudrah) and 'last of the dinosaurs' (T. Abbas) for what some scholars saw as its institutionalization of Pakistani stereotypes on British TV. Yet I would argue that, as with Kureishi's early work, Ray alters our perceptions and widens our understanding of 'Britishness'. In *Citizen Khan*, Birmingham's Sparkhill district is the 'capital of British Pakistan', and self-appointed community leader Mr Khan directs inverted racism at a homogeneous group of ginger Daves—mosque officials who are converts from the white Brummie community. As a ploy to discourage his mother-in-law from outstaying her welcome in their home and in Britain, Khan tells her that Pakistan has 'got much better since you've been here. It's got a Nando's now'. Despite his selfishness, each show usually ends with Khan reluctantly doing the right thing and upholding (admittedly unorthodox) family values. For example, after almost losing his mother-in-law on a shopping trip, he agrees she can stay with the family for an indefinite period. Although it knowingly works with stereotypes of the Asian, white, and African communities in Britain, the show's politics are at a far remove from the often racist 1970s sitcoms that it is influenced by and takes elements from. *Citizen Khan* seems to me symptomatic of an increasingly confident diasporic Pakistani community willing to laugh at itself. Muslims and British–Pakistanis not funny? Who are you trying to kid!

27

Banglaphone Fiction: British Sylhetis in Writing by *Londoni* Authors

I N T H E 1940s, around the time that the British Raj was disintegrating, an abundance of Bengalis began migrating to Britain. (However, ever since the seventeenth century, smaller numbers of Bengali migrants had flowed in to Britain.) Many of them hailed from Sylhet, in what is now northeast Bangladesh. Some of these new residents had previously been lascars, working as crew or cooks on ships. Settling in areas such as East London's Spitalfields, Sylhetis pioneered Britain's emerging curry restaurant trade, laboured for long hours and with few rights in the garment industry, and worked as mechanics. Geoff Dench et al. demonstrate the hard graft of those who occupied this particular part of London and a stark contrast with the development of the City:

The East End of London is the backside of the City. As the City of London evolved over six centuries into the centre of global capitalism, the areas on its eastern fringe evolved too in symbiotic differentiation. At first they supplied food for the emerging urban community, then as the City concentrated increasingly on the pursuit of profit it gradually exported its less valuable and more polluting trades to just outside the City walls—where the benefits accrued without offending the dignity of the City itself. Leather trades, clothing, furniture, shipping and distribution were expelled in turn, and established to the east. As the City became wealthier and more important, the contrast between it and the East End grew sharper (1).

The fact that the East End first distributed food and later clothes to the nearby City demonstrates the former area's somatic function; cooking and the textile industry are two standout themes that pervade writing from this part of London. The contrast between the deprivation of the East End and the wealth of the City is so stark that Dench et al. use the bodily image of a 'backside' to describe the East End; accordingly, poverty is another significant preoccupation.

Sylhetis have made an inestimable contribution to the fabric of British life over more than three centuries. This is most frequently recognized in their association with Brick Lane, the popular road of curry houses in East London. Indeed, too often their contribution to literature is reduced to one novel, *Brick Lane*—Monica Ali's 2003 debut about the famous street and its denizens. While I explore Ali's text, this chapter seeks to broaden the focus to English-language literature from authors writing about Britain who come from across the Bengaliyat. This word 'Bengaliyat' signifies national and cultural continuities between East and West, Hindu and Muslim Bengal.

As I discuss in my book *Britain Through Muslim Eyes*, the first book written in English by a South Asian author was Sake Dean Mahomed's *The Travels of Dean Mahomet* (Fisher). Although Mahomed grew up in Patna, Bihar, he claimed to be related to the Nawabs who governed Bengal, Bihar, and Orissa between 1740 and 1854. He is often thus categorized as a Bengali–British writer. *The Travels of Dean Mahomet* is an epistolary account of his journey through northern India, drawing on conventions of sentimental fiction and Western travel writing. Written to an imaginary English 'sir', these letters describe 'Mahometan' habits and customs, such as circumcision, marriage, and death rites.

Although his book focuses on India, Mahomed's travels took him far from the subcontinent. From 1784 to 1807, he lived in Cork, where he married a Protestant gentlewoman, Jane Daly, converted (on paper at least) to her religion, and fathered the first few of what would turn out to be a family of at least eight children. While in Cork, he had a chance encounter with another sojourner, Mirza Abu Taleb Khan, who was on a brief visit to Ireland in 1799 and was also a skilful travel writer. Whereas Mahomed cast his gaze eastwards to India for the benefit of a Western audience, Khan primarily wrote about Europe in Persian for his fellow Indians. Probably due to a withdrawal of his patronage in Ireland, creating economic and social pressures, Mahomed and Jane relocated to London in 1808. In the capital they set up the first Indian restaurant in Britain—the Hindoostane Coffee House—in 1810. London's high overheads and Britons' then timid taste buds meant that it went bankrupt in 1812.

Reinventing himself again, Mahomed moved his family to Brighton and began offering Indian massages, eventually being appointed 'shampooing surgeon' to George IV and William IV. Mahomed styled a multi-layered identity for himself; his job title (and thus identity) of 'shampooing surgeon' was a hybrid confluence of the Hindi word 'shampoo' (champo, from champi, 'to massage') together with the European, scientific connotations of the word 'surgeon'. In 1822, he published another book (Mahomed *Shampooing*)—this one a quasi-medical tract on the benefits of massage and bathing.

Dean's grandson, Frederick Akbar Mahomed (1849–1884), was to achieve great renown as a doctor of Western medicine who pioneered a 'collective investigation' of diseases through the use of patient questionnaires. He was also responsible for discovering a number of reasons as to why people develop high blood pressure. It was recently reported that the most popular name for a doctor in Britain is Khan, with Patel in second place, Smith and Jones third and fourth, Ahmed coming in sixth, and Ali ninth (Kennedy np.). This hints at one of the many ways in which South Asian Muslims like Dean and Akbar Mahomed contributed positively to making Britain what it is today. Their lives illustrate how settled, how integrated in British life Muslims have been for several centuries, and what great contributions they have made to this nation.

Two centuries after Mahomed, we are witnessing an efflorescence of Anglophone writing from the two Bengals about Britain. In his 1988 novel, *The Shadow Lines*, Calcutta-born Amitav Ghosh was an early writer to explore South Asian East London in fiction. Before coming to Britain, the novel's unnamed narrator imagined Brick Lane to be composed of 'small red-brick houses jostling together, cramped, but each with its own little handkerchief-garden and flowers in its window sills' (100). When the narrator finally arrives at Brick Lane in the 1970s, he finds instead that the urban landscape of the imperial centre is being radically altered by migrants. Few shop signs are in English, the narrator hears 'a dozen dialects of Bengali' as he passes through, and advertisements for the latest Hindi and Bengali films proliferate. Fly-posters adorning the 'walls of aged London brick' are indicative of how this area of London is changing (100). The narrator is surrounded by a palimpsest of posters, where 'stern grey anti-racism' notices—presumably posted there by the predominantly white members of left wing organizations—are half covered by a colourful 'riot' of Hindi film posters. The narrator can almost imagine himself in Calcutta. People hurrying down the road cheerfully hiding their fingers in their jacket sleeves to keep warm remind him of 'shoppers at Gariahat on a cold winter's morning'. He is also amazed to see a shopfront that is almost an exact replica of one in Gole Park, but grafted onto 'a terrace of derelict eighteenth-century London houses' (100). The intermingling of Bollywood posters with earnest Marxist publicity materials indicates that this space is socially pliant and in the process of moulding to the changing composition of its residents.

The unruly collage of flyers serves as a useful metaphor for the changing face of Spitalfields, the district of London in which Brick Lane is located. Historically, Spitalfields has been known for housing immigrants and refugees, from the Huguenots in the eighteenth century and Jewish and Irish settlers in the nineteenth century, to post-war Bengali migrants. Bangladeshi-origin people now make up over 40 per cent of Spitalfields' population. Ghosh alludes to the various stages of migrant history when the narrator's love rival—the British character, Nick—comments that the local mosque 'used to be a synagogue when this place was a Jewish area' (*Shadow*: 101). In a review of Monica Ali's *Brick Lane*, Sukhdev Sandhu traces the many configurations of the Jamme Masjid, which began as a Huguenot church, was transformed into a Methodist chapel, then a synagogue, and finally morphed into the Bangladeshi-majority mosque ('Hungry': np.).

However, Jane M. Jacobs's research (1996) suggests that immigration to the Spitalfields area has proved a far from liberatory experience for Bengalis. Overcrowding, housing insecurity, and racial harassment have dogged Bangladeshi settlers since the 1970s. Large-scale development projects and gentrifying schemes to renovate the area's Georgian houses forced many Bengalis out of their homes or businesses in the 1990s, even though the same developers claimed to speak and act in their interests. In the 2010s, the meteoric rise of nearby hipster area Shoreditch is another push factor behind the uprooting of South Asians from the area (Peek np.).

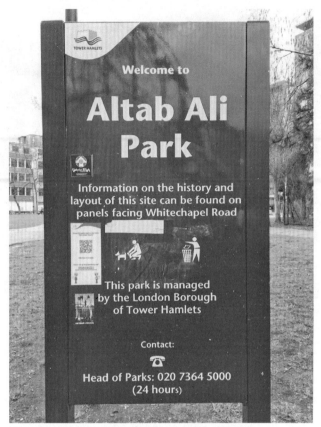

Figure 1: Altab Ali Park, East London, March 2017.
Source and copyright: Claire Chambers.

In 1978, the murder of a Bengali clothing worker, Altab Ali, served to politicize the plight of the Bengali community. A park near Aldgate East Underground station was named after him (Figure 1) and there, too, stands a smaller replica of the Shaheed Minar memorial to the fallen of the Bengali Language Movement in Dhaka (Figure 2).

The British National Party, and later the English Defence League and Britain First, made Brick Lane a target in their far

Figure 2: Smaller replica of Dhaka's Shaheed Minar, East London, March 2017.
Source and copyright: Claire Chambers.

right campaigns of racial hatred. The left has seen the tensions
in Spitalfields as representing an opportunity to consolidate local
support. Socialist organizations moved in, claiming to act on
behalf of the Bengalis in the face of racism and the incursions of
big business. In Bethnal Green and Bow constituency, Respect
leader George Galloway was elected in 2005 after a dirty
campaign against Labour's MP Oona King (n.a. np.). In 2015,
Bengali politics in Tower Hamlets came under the spotlight when
the mayor, Bangladesh-born Lutfur Rahman, was ousted from
his post. He was found guilty of electoral fraud—a charge he
contested. Rahman's Tower Hamlets First party, established in
2014 and popular amongst many Bangladeshi Britons, has also
been removed from the register of political parties due to claims
of financial irregularities.

In light of this background, it is apparent that Ghosh accurately delineates how space is fought over by combatants with different residential ideals and competing visions of Britain. *The Shadow Lines* may be seen as an early precursor of fellow Calcuttan novelists Neel Mukherjee's *A Life Apart* (2008) and Amit Chaudhuri's *Odysseus Abroad* (2014). While they don't specifically depict Brick Lane or its environs, these twenty-first century novels also demonstrate a fascination with Sylhetis in London and their material and spatial culture. In the post-9/11 political climate, there has been significant interest in the ways in which non-Muslim, white writers like John Updike, in *Terrorist* (2006), Martin Amis, in *The Second Plane* (2008), and Ian McEwan, in *Saturday* (2005), have examined Islam and Anglo-American Muslims. Less attention has been paid to the South Asian writers from other religious backgrounds who have also examined this topic. One exception is British Sikh author Sunjeev Sahota, whose debut novel, *Ours Are The Streets* (2011)—about terrorism, identity, and radicalization— has garnered scholarly criticism (Sánchez-Arce). Yet other South Asian writers have written about the quotidian texture of Muslims' lives in Britain with a greater understanding both of Islam and the pernicious effects of deprivation, racism, and Islamophobia on Muslim communities.

For instance, Amit Chaudhuri's quiet masterpiece is an often humorous, modernist slant on the everyday events of one London day in July 1985. As fellow novelist Neel Mukherjee observes in *The Guardian* review of *Odysseus Abroad*: 'Nothing […] happens […] everything happens' (np.). The novel is focalized through the eyes of Ananda, a dilatory student of English literature. Like Chaudhuri, he is preoccupied by twentieth-century writers' focus on 'modern man—strange creature!' (63). Ananda has a 'retinue of habits, like getting on to buses, secreting the bus ticket in his pocket, or going to the dentist' (63–4). He and his uncle,

Rangamama, contemplate taking a bus through London, both of them expressing their pleasure at the view of the city it avails from the upper deck. For convenience, they settle on taking the Tube to King's Cross. Although readers aren't quite privy to the minutiae of characters' dental check-ups, they do learn of Ananda's frustration with European literary heroes who 'had no bodily functions'. Each morning, both Hercules and James Bond 'didn't bother to brush their teeth; they jumped out of bed in pursuit' of villains (128). Nor are these giants ever shown interrupting their activities in order to take care of bodily functions. By contrast, we learn much about the physical woes of *Odysseus Abroad*'s heroes. Rangamama once lost a tooth in a reckless altercation with some skinheads in Chalk Farm. He puts up with the unsightly gap in his smile in anticipation of a health tourism trip to India to avoid Britain's high dentistry costs. Even the prosaic domain of the toilet isn't off limits for this unobtrusively experimental fiction. When Ananda goes to answer nature's call, Rangamama expresses an interest in whether his nephew is going 'for big job or small' (134). With wicked humour, Chaudhuri proceeds to depict Ananda's 'small job', as he aims his urine stream at a cigarette butt left behind in the bowl by his chain-smoking uncle.

Ananda, who like Ghosh's narrator is from a Hindu background, nonetheless has 'covert Sylheti ancestry' (66). His parents and uncle came from Sylhet, but moved to Shillong in India after Partition in 1947. They later shift to East Bengal's capital, Kolkata, where they purposefully gentrify their Sylheti accents into 'standard Calcutta Bangla' (232). His parents never take Ananda to visit his ancestral district, a decision about which he has no regrets. Yet in London he feels some sense of kinship with the waiters in establishments like the Gurkha Tandoori on the edge of Bloomsbury. This is despite the fact that, as he ruefully admits to himself, there was a chasm between the two communities, at least from the perspective of upper- and upper-middle class Bengali Hindus: 'In prelapsarian undivided Bengal, […] the Bengali Hindus were called "Bengalis", the Bengali Muslims just "Muslims"' (232). His uncle is nonetheless struck by the fact that the inapt name of the Gurkha Tandoori's waiter is Iqbal, like the famous poet and architect of the creation of Pakistan. Ananda is charmed by Iqbal's accent, with its rural Sylheti inflections and overlay of flat cockney vowels.

Another interesting text about Bengalis in Britain is Neel Mukherjee's *A Life Apart*. Mukherjee was born in Calcutta and moved permanently to the UK at the age of 22. His first novel, *Past Continuous*, was published in India in 2008. It came out in the UK as *A Life Apart* in 2010, where it was well received. He became better known as a novelist with the publication of his second novel, *The Lives of Others*, which won the Encore Prize and was shortlisted for 2014's Man Booker Prize. However, given this chapter's focus, it is his first novel that is examined. *A Life Apart* is in some ways a rewriting of Rabindranath Tagore's *The Home and the World* from the perspective of the minor British character Miss Gilby. In a highly metafictional fashion, the novel's central character, Ritwik—a Hindu Indian migrant to Britain—is writing a novel within which he constructs a version of Miss Gilby that we catch glimpses of at intervals throughout the text (flagged by bold type).

In the light of the appalling news reports about the global refugee crisis that have spread like lava over the last few years, *A Life Apart* seems all the more timely and important. Ritwik studies at Oxford University, and after graduating, he has little choice but to allow his student visa to expire and become an illegal immigrant, moving outside the 'vast grid of the impeccably ordered and arranged first-world modern democratic state' (218). The novel exposes the Third World that exists within the First World, the migrant as a ghostly figure, and the pipe dream of the better life that supposedly exists in Europe.

A primary concern in both of Mukherjee's novels to date, and in Bengali–British fiction more broadly, is education. Mukherjee explores the differences between an English- and a Bengali-medium education, and how this creates the haves and have-nots of language usage. *A Life Apart* features the hybrid proto-language Benglish, while *The Lives of Others* contains a large glossary of Bengali terms. Ritwik, an orphan from a modest background, wins a scholarship to study English literature at Oxford. His fellow students see his home country as 'exotic, [...] wild [...] And all that mysticism and stuff, it's spiritual' (34). In his turn, Ritwik struggles to eat bland English dishes like toad-in-the-hole, and even thinks a strongly accented Liverpudlian classmate is speaking in German. His classmates are baffled that an Indian should study for an English degree:

> He surprises them by revealing that English Literature, as an academic discipline, was first taught in India, not in England; English administrators and policy-makers thought that the study of English Literature would have an ennobling and civilizing effect on the natives. They are thrown a bit, even a little embarrassed by this. [...] 'It's a strange thought, isn't it, thousands of Indians poring over Shakespeare and Keats', Declan says. Now that Ritwik has it pointed out to him by an outsider, it becomes unfamiliar, shifts patterns and configurations (84).

Here, Ritwik alludes to the fact that in the Raj period and beyond, the British realized the importance of establishing themselves in the imaginations of their colonized peoples as being worthy of allegiance. In place of controversial religious doctrine, they used an almost deified Literature as one tool of persuasion. As Gauri Viswanathan identifies in her pioneering study *Masks of Conquest* (1989), English literature as a subject was closely linked to colonialism, and the study of English literary culture was instituted in Indian schools and universities before it became an established discipline in Britain. Ritwik chafes against what he calls 'this business of other cultures, other countries' (154), in which the British neo-colonizers recalibrate those territories they colonized using their own gauges. He suddenly sees his compatriots' bookish tastes cast in an outlandish light as he notices his British classmates' racially-tinged 'embarrass[ment]' that Indians were the first to study English literature's 'greats'.

Unlike Amit Chaudhuri, Mukherjee doesn't focus on British–Sylhetis, but he does portray other Muslims in Britain. He describes in detail a successful British–Pakistani family, the Haqs, who live near Ritwik in a house that is 'a teeming, heaving slice of the subcontinent' (205). Mr Haq has made his money in import–export, but when newly illegal Ritwik asks him for a job, he receives an ambiguous reply. At first, Mr Haq tells him that they usually hire 'other Pakistani families who are in England', but then seems to change his mind, explaining: 'In this country, we need to stick to each other and have our own community' (210). Ritwik is unsure whether this response means that he will secure a job with the firm, or is a way for Haq to say that the Hindu boy is not part of his Muslim Pakistani community. He leaves the house with a 'strange, lonely feeling of unbelonging' (211).

Manzu Islam's short story collection, *The Mapmakers of Spitalfields* (1997), and his novel, *Burrow* (2004), were probably the first Anglophone fictions about Britain to come out of Bangladesh and its diaspora. In *The Mapmakers of Spitalfields*, four stories— 'Going Home', 'The Mapmakers of Spitalfields', 'The Tower of the Orient', and 'Meeting at the Crossroads'—are set in Britain. That said, they often 'drift [...] into another world' (59), swerving away from London locations, such as King's Cross station and the Sonar Bangla café, to imagine the imaginary homeland—a remembered

Bangladesh of tigers, sadhus, and water, water everywhere.
Characters are equally difficult to contain within particular
stories. For example, both 'Going Home' and 'The Mapmakers
of Spitalfields' are told from a first-person perspective, as well as
featuring minor characters named Badal and Shafique. (Badal also
appears in 'The Fabled Beauty of the Jatra', set at a folk theatre
play in Bangladesh.) It is striking that all the writers discussed in
this chapter on Banglaphone writing cannot be confined within
a purely British location. Not one of the authors discussed here
(Mahomed, Ghosh, Chaudhuri, Mukherjee, Islam, Rahman,
Ali, Gupta, and Anam) construct an exclusively British setting.
Even the most British among these texts, such as Chaudhuri's
Odysseus Abroad, Islam's 'Mapmakers', and Ali's *Brick Lane*, provide
flashbacks to their characters' previous homes in South Asia. These
are highly transnational authors, whose characters are similarly
mutable wanderers.

As we saw in Chapter 20, 'From "England-Returned" to "Myth
of Return" to the Point of No Return', working-class South
Asian Muslim migrants in the post-war period saw themselves
as transients and were motivated by the 'myth of return'. They
planned to save, send money home, and go back to their home
countries as soon as they had made enough. However, as Pakistani
scholar Muhammad Anwar pointed out in 1979: '[I]n reality,
most of them are here to stay because of economic reasons and
their children's future' (ix). As more and more family members
migrated and began reuniting in Britain, they became interested in
building self-sufficient communities. Several of the academics who
theorize the myth of return, such as Anwar and Badr Dahya (1974),
specifically discuss the Pakistani, rather than the Bangladeshi,
diaspora. However, the model of migration is similar—the migrant
populace tends to predominantly come from particular locations

(Mirpur in Pakistani Kashmir and Sylhet in Bangladesh) and to involve mostly working-class populations.

Several of Islam's short stories and his novel *Burrow* provide subtle, shaded depictions of the myth of return. Bangladeshi critic, Kaiser Haq, rightly points out that this is mostly a male phenomenon. Haq writes that in diasporic Bangladeshi literature, 'the men dream of return, but not the women, who even as second-class citizens enjoy rights denied them in the mother country' (np.). As might be expected, 'The Tower of the Orient', a rare story by Islam told from a female perspective, is about a reverse illusion and subsequent disillusionment. In this short story, the protagonist, Soraya—a young wife—has daydreamed at length about 'taking off from Dhaka airport for this destination of fabled fortunes' (84). The chimera she chased was of a Britain in which she could buy her own home with husband Munir and feel a sense of belonging. Yet the poverty of 'damp, creeping rot and a riot of rats' (84) and the racism that she eventually encounters there dash her sketchy notions of T. S. Eliot and the beauty of an English April (87).

In *Burrow*, Islam makes apparent that one of the reasons why return migration fails to occur and eventually becomes a myth is that parents desire an education at British schools and universities for the younger generation. There, the changes that they undergo, such as the protagonist Tapan Ali coming to despise the Bangladeshi grandfather he had once revered, show that it would be hard to go back. Tapan's family makes an enormous financial sacrifice to send him to study in Britain, so understandably enough they see accountancy as a more lucrative course for him than the arcane discipline of philosophy that he loves. At a political demonstration, Tapan meets British-born Nilufar, who later becomes his lover. Her parents had been proud when she began her higher education, but as they discover that the hard-won BA degree is not helping her to secure her a husband they are so disappointed that they almost

disown her. Just as Tapan becomes estranged from his grandfather,
Nilufar's parents are alienated by 'the foreignness of her ideas and
her feringhee style' (45).

Zia Haider Rahman's novel, *In the Light of What We Know*
(2014), is structured within a complex epistolary and intertextual
architecture. To list just a few of the different types of documents
employed in this novel, it packs in dialogue, stories, and diary
entries, as well as many anecdotes about topics including the global
financial crash, the Bangladesh Liberation War, mathematics, and
the British class system. (A rare blind spot is gender, which is not
discussed with anything like the same precision of focus as race
and class.) In the novel, a conversation between two 'philosopher-
carpenters' (164), Bill and Dave, who the protagonist Zafar works
with briefly as a young man, is revealing. Bill tells Dave that their
new colleague, 'Paki-man' (159), is adjusting well to the demands of
their high-end house refurbishment business. They quickly realize
Zafar has overheard the racial slur and, without missing a beat, the
two intellectual handymen begin debating the term. Discovering
that Zafar is from Bangladesh rather than Pakistan, Bill apologizes,
instead calling him, in a coinage that resonates with this chapter's
title, 'Anglo-Banglo' (163). Wryly returning to this incident from
the vantage point of the early 2000s, Zafar is surprised that it took
place before the Rushdie affair of 1989. He suggests that the fault
lines of identity, racism, and 'offence' exposed in the exchange with
the handymen will increasingly define British cultural life from
this moment on.

In a perceptive review (2014), James Wood maintains that
Rahman's novel is all about knowledge and its limitations.
However, the text's title offers up a hint that it is equally about
'light'—or religious knowledge, vision, and optics. Sylhet-born
Zafar turns away from the Islam of his upbringing and becomes
attracted to Christianity because he believes that 'meaning counted

for more than the rewards of ritual' (184). He dislikes the lack of understanding his South Asian co-religionists have for their Arabic-language sacred text the Qur'an. Yet he also exhibits a Joycean–Forsterian scepticism about the church's airy clarities and its endeavour to make God in its own image:

> [H]ere was a very local rendering of a religion that had come from a part of the world that the proud Englishman could only look down upon. The Christianity before me was English, white, with Sunday roasts and warm beer and translation into the English, the language [*sic*]. Even the Bible at its most beautiful, the King James version, was in a language that asserted and reassured its readers of their power. [...] The English Christ was [...] an English God under an English heaven (187–8).

Ultimately, Zafar's quests for meaning at Oxford, Harvard, at church, or in the bed of his icy aristocratic English lover, Emily, each prove equally illusory. The light of religion may contain greater profundity than constructed knowledges, but the numinous and the material world interpenetrate, each contaminating each other. From such a perspective, '[e]verything new is on the rim of our view, in the darkness, below the horizon, [...] nothing new is visible but in the light of what we know' (320).

The novel's unnamed narrator, who pieces together Zafar's story through the latter's voice recordings and writings, is an elite Pakistani, the son of highly successful academics, who attends Eton and Oxford as a matter of course. The narrator's father sees no contradiction in attending mosque each Friday, while regularly drinking and 'lik[ing] his bacon crispy' (110). Such a relaxed view would be anathema to Zafar's family, who are from a much more precarious social class and do not have the cosmopolitanism of the frequent flyer set. For a while in his youth, Zafar lived in a squat where rats caused regular upset, and even his temporary job as a carpenter immediately marks him out as coming from a humbler background than the narrator and Emily. With his inquisitive, scientific mind, Zafar is dissuaded from Islam by a book his parents bought from an East End shop and gave him for Eid. Its title, *How Islam Predicted Science* (182), and its trite, uninformed certainties alienate the maths-obsessed boy for whom Gödel's Incompleteness Theorem is akin to religious lore.

What might seem like a grab-bag set of texts on closer inspection yields overlapping insights. Most of these male writers portray characters who have been educated to at least undergraduate level, with parents' wish for their children to acquire a British or at least an English-medium education, and the travails of university life as common themes. Home and belonging are also intertwining and recurrent motifs. Mahomed made a home for himself first in Ireland and then England, carving out a space of belonging through self-exoticization (as Hindoostane Coffee House proprietor, 'shampooing surgeon', and then travel writer). His descendants, such as his celebrated doctor grandson and two great-grandsons who fought in France during the Second World War, needed no such self-exoticization and made equally fine contributions to the nation as British-born individuals. Ghosh represents inhabitants of Spitalfields Indianizing the area through both concrete changes and the mind's eye; Chaudhuri's Ananda hears the accents of home in a Bloomsbury 'Indian' restaurant; Mukherjee's Mr Haq creates a Pakistani enclave in his London residence; and Manzu Islam's imagination is rarely detained in Britain for long, looping as it does across national borders. Finally, the authors engage with the often contentious issues surrounding religious belief and praxis. Mahomed's religious identity is fluid; he plays down, without denying, his Muslim identity (despite his overtly 'Mahomedan' name) and subtly links himself with the 'clean [...] and fine' Hindus in his 1822 tract, *Shampooing, Or, The Benefits Resulting from the Use of the Indian Medicated Vapour Bath*. Through his allusion to 'prelapsarian undivided Bengal', Chaudhuri not only refers to Christian theology of the Fall and the religious strife of Partition, but also exposes the class and religious prejudice that caused many Bengali Hindus to reduce Muslims to their religion, rather than accepting them as fully Bengali. Mukherjee gestures towards discrimination on a religious basis through Mr Haq's ambiguous remark to Ritwik, while Haider depicts Zafar's scepticism towards 'unscientific' Islam and a certain attraction to Christianity despite its colonizing tendencies.

A somewhat different tonal palette emerges out of the women's writing I will now explore. In her novel *Brick Lane*, Monica Ali mostly evokes life in Britain, with only occasional and usually analeptic descriptions of Bangladesh. By contrast, Sunetra Gupta's *Memories of Rain* is at once intercontinental, urban, and stateless— often all within a single sentence. Tahmima Anam establishes an alternative strategy again, choosing, in *A Golden Age* and *The Good Muslim*, to abjure representations of Britain, in favour of a concentrated focus on the Bangladeshi nation.

No text exemplifies more clearly the contrast between the England-returned and the myth of return migrants (see Chapter 20, 'From "England-Returned" to "Myth of Return" to the Point of No Return') than *Brick Lane*. If we examine a resonant passage near the beginning of *Brick Lane*—Monica Ali's 2003 novel that, like Neel Mukherjee's *The Lives of Others*, was shortlisted for the Man Booker Prize—we are confronted with an arresting example of 'Going Home Syndrome':

'This is another disease that afflicts us', said the doctor. 'I call it Going Home Syndrome. Do you know what that means?' He addressed himself to Nazneen. [...]

'[W]hen they have saved enough they will get on an aeroplane and go?'

'They don't ever really leave home. Their bodies are here but their hearts are back there. And anyway, look how they live: just recreating the villages here. [...] But they will never save enough to go back. [...] Every year they think, just one more year. But whatever they save, it's never enough'.

'We would not need very much', said Nazneen. Both men looked at her. She spoke to her plate (Ali 22).

The quotation illustrates that the 'disease' is caused by the desire to return to the homeland, and Dr Azad claims that it afflicts many Bangladeshi migrants. This concatenates into another strand in the novel about the migrant's sense of being out of place, which can lead to mental illness, such as Nazneen's collapse due to 'nervous exhaustion' (315; see Santesso 61–82).

Probably the most important means by which migrants either try to assimilate in the host country or turn away from it towards the homeland is through education. At first, Nazneen's husband, Chanu, imagines himself to be immune to Going Home Syndrome, and tries instead to make a life for himself in Britain. When he arrives in England, the sum total of Chanu's possessions is the usual few pounds in his pocket, along with the significant additional item of his degree certificate. In England he zealously takes classes in everything from nineteenth-century economics to cycling proficiency, and acquires further certificates. These he frames and displays on the wall of his and Nazneen's poky Tower Hamlets home, as a talisman of his hopes of promotion at work and the consequent acquisition of a comfortable life in London. Yet his dreams remain unrealized, whether because of institutional racism at his workplace or his own incompetence is never made clear. Chanu's fortunes then take an embittered turn when he aspires to become an England-returned success story. He clings ever more desperately to the fantasy of returning to Dhaka in financial and social triumph. However, as we have seen, for migrants this hope of return migration often proves to be a myth, especially because men begin to feel inclined to put down roots in their new country when they get married and start having children. Nazneen and especially their young daughters, Shahana and Bibi, fear the realization of their father's longed-for homecoming. The rationale for going back to Dhaka is tenuously based on Chanu's saviour complex (see Abu-Lughod)—to rescue Nazneen's sister, the vulnerable ingénue Hasina, whose unwittingly alarming letters to Nazneen about sexual grooming and exploitation pepper the narrative. However, despite Hasina's increasingly worrying communication, the three women— Nazneed, Shahana, and Bibi—now have firm roots in Britain. They decide to stay on. Trailing clouds of defeat more than glory, the patriarch Chanu returns home on his own.

A decision in reverse, whereby the wife moves back to the subcontinent while her husband stays in Britain, is described by Sunetra Gupta. A Bengali–Hindu author who writes about life in London and elsewhere in southern England, Gupta's day job is as an epidemiologist at the University of Oxford. Perhaps her most compelling work of fiction is *Memories of Rain* (1992). This debut novel centres on the young, dreamy protagonist Moni's furtive plans to return home to Calcutta. The choice has been made for her by her husband Anthony's passionate and drawn-out affair with a slim, green-eyed Englishwoman named Anna. Languorous, even lachrymose free indirect discourse conveys Moni's acute sense of her own beauty and intelligence and her refined disappointment at her husband's womanizing. Indeed, the narrative voice recalls that of another Bengali woman writer, American-resident Bharati Mukherjee, who in early works such as *The Tiger's Daughter* (1971) expressed the similarly elitist ennui of the upper-class exile.

Gupta's Moni works as a translator for the National Health Service, interpreting the medical problems of poor Bangladeshi migrants for their health care professionals. Despite sharing a language and ethnicity with these mostly Muslim inhabitants of Britain, she feels that they have little in common. This lack of connection has more to do with the British–Bengalis' modest social class and destitution than their religion. Repelled by 'the pits of squalor that they called their homes' and with a Brahminical distaste for their 'dense smell of spice trapped in winter wool, of old oil and fungus, poverty and filth' (170, 83), Moni exhibits significant condescension towards her co-regionalists. In the course of the plane journey back to Calcutta, she encounters a bourgeois British–Bengali of unclear religious identity who tries to engage her in conversation. Her sense of upper-class superiority is again exposed, as she refuses to listen to the specificities of his potted biography:

[H]e is going back to do his medical elective at the hospital where his father was trained, it will be an experience, he was a child of two when his parents left, she knows their story, she has heard it many times before, of how they had landed upon English soil with a mere five pounds to their name, the first difficult years, on weekends they had shared curried shad with other couples and reminisced of hilsa fish, cradling their children, they had rubbed their eyes in the damp heat of the coin-operated gas fires, and absorbed heavy texts, and now they basked in their hard-earned success, in detached suburban homes, their children amassing A-levels, she remembers a damp day [...] when an unmistakable East Bengal accent drifted through the spangled wire, you will not remember me, her father's distant cousin, they had urged her to spend a day with them, and the following evening [...] in the oppressive heat of their home she had met his kind wife, the smell of fried spice hung dense in the overheated hallway, the wife, her aunt, took her coat [...] (Gupta 186).

This passage is worth quoting at length because it demonstrates how the unnamed Bengali and his family are rendered generic by her dismissive aside: '[S]he knows their story'. What could have become a novel in itself—the tale of a Bengali couple starting out with little money to overcome the hardship and hostility of Britain through hard work and community support—is reduced to less than a sentence. Moni is familiar with this narrative trajectory, due to her aunt and uncle—Hindu migrants who presumably moved from East Bengal because of Partition. So, she, somewhat selfishly, refuses to listen, and turns her attention back to her own family in West Bengal. Further information about Gupta's writerly concerns is made manifest at the level of the 595-word run-on sentence, of which I have quoted only an excerpt. With their breathless, iterative comma splices and literary impressionistic intertwining of actions with memories and thoughts, Gupta's never-ending sentences engage in neo-modernist provocation and transcend their everyday subject matter.

The construction of Gupta's sentences also allows the novelist to convey that Moni never truly gets to know England. Each time the narrative starts to explore the country, her character's memories and tastes cause it to swerve off into descriptions of India, more specifically Calcutta. Another example comes when the well-worn trope of a migrant taking the Tube transmutes, at Gupta's hand, into reminiscences about an English teacher back in Calcutta. In the space of a single, however protracted, sentence, Moni quickly abandons London's autumnal streets for the overheated cocoon of a train. On the wall of her carriage is a verse by Keats, part of a 'Poems on the Underground' promotion (146). Reading this poem leads the upper-class character to think, with a mixture of contempt and compassion, about a temporary lecturer who taught Keats at her Calcuttan college and whose broad Bengali accent she and the other girls had mocked. This cognitive and spatial dissonance, which prevents the narrative from dwelling on the London Underground or Romantic poetry for long, is characteristic of much of the Banglaphone writing I have examined so far, even if it is especially exaggerated in Gupta's prose.

Another Bengali woman writer based in London, Tahmima Anam, has a different literary approach. Whereas Ali employs occasional flashbacks to Bangladesh and Gupta tightly interbraids her present-day British life with Calcuttan memories, Anam chooses not to represent Britain at all. Her first novel, *A Golden Age*, was published in 2007 and focused on the 1971 Liberation War, which, after India's military involvement, led to Pakistan's defeat and the creation of the new nation of Bangladesh. As with *Brick Lane*, the plot is conveyed through a third-person narrative interspersed with occasional letters. *A Golden Age*'s protagonist, Rehana, is an Urdu-speaking widow who strives to protect her teenage children, while simultaneously supporting the Mukti Bahini—the Bangladesh Liberation Army—in its war effort.

The action of *The Good Muslim*—Anam's second novel in her planned Bengal Trilogy—mostly unfolds during the 1980s, a decade when the Islamic Right became increasingly powerful in Bangladesh. Focalization is transferred from *A Golden Age*'s Rehana to her daughter, Maya, now in her early thirties, and occasionally to Maya's older brother, Sohail. These siblings react very differently to 'the Dictator' Hussain Muhammad Ershad's military rule. Sohail joins the Tablighi Jamaat, an austere, revivalist religious movement, while Maya keeps faith with the secular, left-leaning nationalism that sustained them both during the war years—an era of political idealism she remembers with exponential nostalgia as she and her brother grow apart.

In 2013, Anam was named one of Britain's best young novelists by *Granta* magazine (Freeman np.). When interviewed and in her journalism she not only focuses on Bangladeshi politics and cultural production, but also discusses 'making a home in London' (Vogel np.), the (somewhat dull) details of her weekly delivered vegetable box, and her earlier life as a PhD student in the US (Anam 'Thank You': np.). One would not know about this life in the West from her fiction, set in Bangladesh or, in the case of her new novel *The Bones of Grace*, the Bangladeshi diaspora in Dubai and the US. Yet this expansive focus is to be welcomed, while Anam's fiction is simultaneously welcomed into the fold of British literature. As with many of the writers explored here, she is a global thinker, a nationalist who is not easily confined within national boundaries.

As this chapter has made clear, 'Banglaphone fiction' is currently experiencing a boom in both production and popularity. Depictions of Bangladeshis, especially Sylhetis, in London, their cuisine, and other aspects of popular culture form an enduring fixation, among Hindu Indian as well as Muslim Bangladeshi authors. An increasing number of women writers, with heritage from Calcutta as well as Dhaka, are adding their voices to the chorus of Banglaphone fiction. Ali, Gupta, and Anam have the confidence to focus on Britain, shift attention away towards memories of the subcontinent, or ignore Britain altogether. What future women novelists will do with these very different models remains to be seen.

28

In Praise of the Chapaterati

IN 1810, SAKE DEAN MAHOMED (whose travel writing was explored in the previous chapter), by then a 51-year-old, opened the first Indian restaurant in Britain—the Hindoostane Coffee House. It catered to retired colonial administrators, whose Indianized tastes were no longer satisfied with bland British food and manners. At the Coffee House, these nostalgic epicures lounged on bolsters, smoked hookahs, and ate various spiced dishes. Mahomed was ahead of his time, though, as curry restaurants would not take off for more than a hundred years, with the founding of the high-end London establishment Veeraswamy in 1926. After just two years, he went bankrupt. Earlier, in 1793, he had published a book, *The Travels of Dean Mahomet* (Fisher). This book was unique for having been written in English, so as to give European readers a glimpse of his Indian homeland. The writing and subsequent publication of this book probably formed part of the author's attempt at integration in County Cork. He had lived there for over twenty years after marrying his Irish wife Jane Daly, who then moved to London and then Brighton with him and their large family.

As proprietor of the first, admittedly short-lived, curry restaurant in Britain, Mahomed must take some credit for this cuisine's enduring popularity. Curry is often hailed today as Britain's national dish. In what became known as his 'Chicken Tikka Masala Speech', Robin Cook (former Foreign Secretary) remarked on its 'national' importance and assimilatory tendencies:

Chicken Tikka Massala [*sic*] is now a true British national dish, not only because it is the most popular, but because it is a perfect illustration of the way Britain absorbs and adapts external influences. Chicken Tikka is an Indian dish. The Massala sauce was added to satisfy the desire of British people to have their meat served in gravy (np.).

Curry's centrality to British popular culture is underscored in one of the most darkly comic jokes from Hanif Kureishi's novel *The Black Album* (1995). Against a backdrop of the racial and religious tension surrounding the Rushdie affair, Kureishi's Marxist lecturer Brownlow pronounces: 'I could murder an Indian' (180). Accordingly, curry houses are a dominant setting in much writing by authors of Muslim heritage in the UK. This should not surprise us because, as Ben Highmore points out in his article about the history of the British curry industry (185), 'the predominant food culture of the high street restaurant is Bengali (Bangladeshi)'—a nationality which is mostly Muslim. As a scribbling Indian restaurateur, Mahomed was a pioneer, and his culinary experiences have even inspired a self-published crime novel by the British writer Colin Bannon, *The Hindostanee Coffee House* (2012).

Later in the nineteenth century, an important figure to both British history and the literary imagination is Queen Victoria's Munshi, Abdul Karim. Victoria was very close to this servant from Jhansi, and as with Victoria's previous beloved servant, John Brown, the two of them were rumoured to be having an affair. Karim came from the ranks of the many South Asian Muslim servants who travelled to Britain in the nineteenth and early twentieth centuries. He caused consternation by worshipping at Britain's first purpose-built mosque in Woking, and was disliked and distrusted by the Queen's household due to the influence a man of his race, religion, and lowly origins had on the Crown. One of the ways

to the Queen's heart was through her ample stomach. She had a
deep affection for Karim, the man who introduced her to curries.
Food historian Ivan Day explains that Queen Victoria's love for
curry made Indian dishes 'very fashionable' in the late nineteenth
century, since she had 'an Indian staff who cooked Indian food
every day' (qtd. in Jahangir np.). Victoria bestowed many honours
and substantial tracts of land on Karim for her curry cookery tuition
and Hindustani language lessons. Despite his loyal service, after the
Queen's and later Karim's deaths, royal emissaries systematically
dispossessed his family of the land and almost all the records of
Victoria's Hindustani lessons and personal letters that passed
between the Queen and Karim.

As I discussed in Chapter 23, 'Freedom as Floating or Falling',
Attia Hosain wrote an accomplished but incomplete novel about
diasporic Britain, *No New Lands, No New Seas* (begun in the 1950s).
One of the fragment's most interesting insights concerns the post-
war contributions to material culture—particularly food—that
South Asian Muslims made to Britain. In his influential 1964
article, 'Institutional Completeness of Ethnic Communities and the
Personal Relations of Immigrants', Canadian sociologist Raymond
Breton coined the term 'institutional completeness'. The expression
stands for migrants' establishment of halal butchers, restaurants, and
grocery stores to create for themselves a home from home in the
foreign land. These often food-based institutions in part operate to
shore up and continue the migrants' traditions and culture, but also
cater to, and change, the palates of indigenous Britons.

Accordingly, in Hosain's novel, migrants track down outlets
that serve their 'own kind of food'. The narrator points out
the importance of sociable cooking and eating in South Asian
culture. (By contrast, Britons allegedly erect barriers of books and
newspapers to prevent social interaction during meals.) Murad's
favourite restaurant sells 'cheap, wholesome and tasty' meals (55).

The eating establishment has gone through several name changes. Before the Second World War, it was known as the 'Great British Indian Restaurant'. In 1942, responding to the rise of nationalism, its proprietor, Chaudhary, changed this to 'Great Indian Restaurant'. After Partition, patrons fiercely debate the politics of this name, until Chaudhary calls an uneasy truce by renaming it the 'Great Indo–Pakistan Restaurant' (57). Aiming to please everyone, the nomenclature impresses no one, and Chaudhary laments his naming difficulties: '[I]t was surprising how many names were already in use. In the changing landscape of London dark dots were multiplying and spreading into smudges abounding in Taj Mahals, Moti Mahals, Stars & Moons of India and Pakistan' (59). As amusingly evidenced, Hosain advances serious observations about the rise of South Asians' cuisine and their increasingly factional politics in Britain. The more Chaudhary continues to change the restaurant's name, the more ersatz its food becomes. Over time, it comes to cater to British tastes, rather than those of the South Asians who were its original clients.

Hosain accurately suggests that, at this time, Indian restaurants with names like the 'Taj Mahal' were proliferating throughout Britain. Figure 3, a photograph of a curry restaurant in Bristol, is just one real-world example. The late owner's daughter, Monira Ahmed Chowdhury, explains that the photograph depicts her father, Feroze Ahmed, in front of the first restaurant he opened—the Taj Mahal in Bristol. From Bengali Muslim stock, Feroze was a pioneer of Indian restaurants in the southwest of England. Shortly before his death in 2000, he wrote a short essay (F. Ahmed) in a collection of Bristolian migrants' personal reflections. In it, he described moving from Oxford in 1959 to open Bristol's first 'Indian' restaurant. He also opened his second (named Koh-i-Noor) and third restaurants in Bristol, as well as the inaugural Indian restaurant in Bath, thereby revolutionizing West Country cuisine.

Figure 3: Taj Mahal curry restaurant, Bristol, c. 1970.
Credit and permission: Monira Ahmed Chowdhury and Hasan Ahmed.

In her lively history, *Curry in the Crown*, Shrabani Basu affectionately parodies the typical names of the British–Asian curry house. She does this in a similar manner to Hosain, listing: 'The Jewel in the Crown, or The Gurkha Tandoori [*sic*], or the Taj Mahal, or Maharajah' (xxxi). Basu's book discusses what she terms the 'Bangladeshi curry crusaders' (xxxii). In the previous chapter, I discussed Sylheti migration to Britain in the twentieth century. Some Sylhetis established restaurants when they immigrated, as it seemed a natural progression from their previous occupations as lascars working as crew members on ships, where they had learnt to cook. However, it would be wrong to stress the East Bengali/Sylheti/Bangladeshi origins of these pre- and post-Second World War restaurateurs. Basu shows that on a single road—Drummond Street, near London's Euston Station—a sweet shop's owners were from Pakistan, a *chaat* (snack) shop proprietor hailed from Bombay, and the Patak (né Pathak) pickle makers were Kenyan Indians.

The transition to British life, customs, and culture is made smoother when migrants embrace their previous lives and cultures by starting their own cafes or restaurants. By shopping and eating together, the eighteen migrants who share a house in Urdu author Abdullah Hussein's novella 'The Journey Back' begin to form their own clan or *biradari*. In this novella, Hussein depicts the 'white flight' that often accompanied the arrival of South Asians and black people in the early days of mass migration. The whites' vacancies were taken by new arrivals from India and Pakistan, who set up their own eateries. From the 1950s to the 1980s, white people often explained their dislike of living near Asians through allusions to the smell of curry (a thinly disguised racial taunt). In 'The Journey Back', Hussein charts the way in which this attitude of disgust gradually metamorphoses into an appetite for 'hot, spicy curry' (131). He depicts a number of South Asians who turned their homes into small cafés, which became cultural hubs in the early days of migration. There, 'the customs and bureaucratic procedures of the country were explained to the newcomers. Records were played all day long' (131).

In some of the British scenes in one of his books, Salman Rushdie joins the ranks of the chapaterati with his depictions of the Shaandaar ('outstanding, brilliant, delicious') café. This restaurant is situated in London's 'Brickhall' (the name amalgamates Indian Southall and Bangladeshi Brick Lane), a district where Polish Jewish migrants have made way for South Asians. The restaurant is run by the pluralist Bangladeshi Muslim Sufyan and his gargantuan, misogynistically portrayed wife, Hind. Inspired by her open-minded husband, Hind creates delectable pan-Indian food, but the café ultimately appears to be a cultural dead end for these characters. Here, 'for all his education', Sufyan is compelled to 'behave like a servant' towards the restaurant's clientele (248). And although Hind should feel triumphant at her culinary and entrepreneurial success in this female-headed business, all she experiences is a sense of alienation in this foreign land, this *vilayet*.

The spectre of racism stalks the streets, 'but when you turned in the direction of the words you saw only empty air and smiling faces' (250). Hind consoles herself with copies of Bengali and Hindi films, which seem more like the 'real world' than the 'pastiche' of London (264, 261). In time, a rival café, the Pagal Khana ['Crazy Food' or 'Madhouse' (341)], overtakes the Shaandaar, attracting a cult following among on-trend British–Asians as well as celebrities such as Pavarotti, James Mason, and Amitabh Bachchan. This reflects the phenomenon, described in Shrabani Basu's *Curry in the Crown*, in which certain London-based Indian restaurants became gentrified and celebrified, especially from the 1980s onwards.

Zahid Hussain's novel, *The Curry Mile* (2006), is set in Manchester, and describes the intergenerational rivalry between Sorayah and her father, Ajmal, as they compete for a National Curry Award in the close-knit Rusholme restaurant trade. Religious studies scholar Philip Lewis observes that '[o]ne of the strengths of Hussain's novel [...] is Ajmal's dawning realization that discrete Pakistani and English social and cultural worlds—"ours" (*apne*) and "theirs" (*goray*)—no longer exist for their children' (149). *The Curry Mile* explores Sorayah's high wire act of trying to maintain a loving relationship with her father and follow him into the restaurant trade. Eventually, she becomes a success in the business world, as her father hoped for at least one of his children. She does this without breaking up the family and notwithstanding her gender, which Ajmal considers a handicap.

One of Rushdie's novels' characters holds that 'food passes across any boundary you care to mention' (246). As we have seen, since the early nineteenth century, Indian food has transformed British restaurant culture. In the process, it has been hybridized, as today many Indian dishes contain traditionally British (or at least Western) ingredients, such as Worcestershire sauce, cream, and tinned tomatoes. Writers working in Urdu, English, and

Bengali have evoked both South Asians living in Britain and the restaurant fare they produce. British Muslims are now routinely portrayed in tabloid newspapers as an unfamiliar post-war influx. The chapaterati show that their presence has much deeper roots, influenced royalty, and added literary and gastronomic value to Britain. Seek out and savour their fiction's masala blend.

29

Boris Johnson Lights Out for Virgin Territory

MUCH HAS BEEN WRITTEN ABOUT BORIS JOHNSON as a politician since the Brexit vote. In addition to being an inept Foreign Secretary, Johnson is also an author of fiction, verse, and journalism. As such, another way of understanding the man's worldview is to scrutinize his imaginative work. In this chapter, I examine Johnson's little-known comic novel, *Seventy-Two Virgins* (2005), which centres on the attempt by an Islamist cell to attack Westminster Hall[1] during a visit from an unnamed American president. I want to consider the book's unshakeable and inescapable Islamophobia, and the light this perspective sheds on Johnson, figurehead of the Brexit campaign. Such Islamophobia is particularly concerning in the context of the post-referendum British upsurge in xenophobia, racism, and religious hatred (see Parveen and Sherwood np.).

Seventy-Two Virgins is an unpleasant and unfunny book which presents a problematic usage of similes and relies heavily on stereotypes. Johnson's similes are usually clunky and sometimes offensive. Early on in the novel, he describes West London as being 'spread out [...] in the morning sun, like a beautiful woman surprised in bed without her make-up' (37). Not only does this reveal Johnson's patronizing view of women, but the image's derivation— unwitting or otherwise—from T. S. Eliot's superior lines, 'the evening is spread out against the sky. | Like a patient etherized upon a table' (11), does neither text any favours. Much later, clapping from an audience in Westminster Palace is compared to 'the spastic batting of a butterfly's wings as it dies against a window' (223). Here, Johnson's verbiage and the imprecision of his image flutter against his outdated and ableist use of the word 'spastic'.

Received ideas about marginalized groups are repeatedly reinforced in this novel, while stereotypes of the dominant race, class, and gender are gently unsettled. Our protagonist is Roger Barlow, a well-connected MP and cycling enthusiast with a chaotic home life. He seems to be a philanderer, with little time or interest for constituency matters, but ultimately turns out to be a good egg. Bromley's beautiful, buxom parliamentary researcher, who has the curious name of Cameron, is portrayed as smart and independent, but deep down she longs for the love of a strong man. This leads her to procure press passes for her opinionated left wing boyfriend, disastrously enabling his Islamist contacts to enter the historic chamber. Cameron acts uncharacteristically because she is fuelled by an 'endocrinal choir of happiness within' (93), caused by chemicals associated with sexual love: phenylethylamine, norepinephrine, adrenalin, serotonin, and dopamine. Women and their hormones, eh? The Nigerian parking attendant, William Eric Kinloch Onyeama, is portrayed in stereotypical manner as well—implausibly using the obsolete public school adjective 'wizard', despite being a scarified member of the Hausa 'tribe' (10, 12). Another character at the whim of Johnson's stereotyping is Dragan Panic, the nominatively deterministic Serbian tow truck driver. During the Kosovo War, Dragan set fire to a Muslim hayrick in Pristina, and he now channels his hatred into clamping cars. Ordinary people and their opinions are derided as 'cretinous' and 'moronic' (153, 273, 306), asylum seekers are 'Martians' or from 'Pluto' (25, 51)—enemy aliens, do you get it?—while racist epithets like 'wogs', 'towelheads', and 'niggers' (99, 270, 303, 11) repeatedly rear their ugly heads. Admittedly, the racial slurs are carefully framed as being communicated by various characters, but the lack of a positive ethnic minority character does little to counterbalance them. It seems that Johnson wishes to pour poison on the powerless, rather than taking up satire's usual aim of speaking truth to power.

When it comes to violent Muslim extremists, the portrayal becomes even sketchier. The cell is first introduced as 'four dark customers' (14), who enter a greasy spoon café. The group comprises its leader, who goes by the alias of Jones, and his associates, Haroun, Habib, and Dean. Strangely, we are told that Jones's father is a gynaecologist who works in Karachi, but Jones swears in Arabic and is described as looking like 'an Arab-type thing' (19). As the haziness of his national identity suggests, the character known as 'Jones the Bomb' (106) is barely present in this novel, despite his centrality to the plot. Jones, who is depicted as sexually puritanical and well-versed in the Qur'an, inexplicably eats a full English breakfast in the greasy spoon. Although pork products are carefully not mentioned, it seems highly unlikely that this meal would be halal. It emerges that Jones picked up his false name from time spent at the fictional Welsh institution of Llangollen University, which construction allows Johnson to shoehorn in some hackneyed jokes about the intellectual laxity of former polytechnics and the alleged uselessness of degrees in media studies. Little explanation is given as to what has driven this former hairdressing student to become a murderous extremist. A seemingly baffled Johnson resorts to the erotic rationalization also exploited by other Islamophobic writers such as Martin Amis: 'Because if Palestine was the cause for sickos like [the terrorists], it was only at best the proximate cause. There is one really psychologically satisfying explanation for the suicidal behaviour of young men, and it is something to do with sex, or at least with self-esteem' (131). Certainly Haroun and Habib, unequivocally Arab and almost interchangeable stock characters, are fuelled by sexual frustration and lust. They are caricatured as wily Arab Muslims with hooked noses and 'almost Disney-ish features' (67). In Disney cartoons and films such as *Aladdin* (Clements and Musker), the Arab is likewise illustrated with an aquiline proboscis and a demeanour that is blood-thirsty and barbaric. To adapt Hari Kunzru's phrasing, *Seventy-Two Virgins'* physical distortion of Arabs creates a 'Weimar feeling' (np.).

Reviewing *Seventy-Two Virgins* in the *Observer*, David Smith charitably asserts (np.) that one of the novel's strongest suits is the insight it provides into the mindset of the final terrorist, Dean, and what causes this 'young boy from Wolverhampton' to turn to extremism. I respectfully disagree. A forensic level of detail is provided regarding Dean's adoptive white parents, Dennis and Vie, and their convoluted feud with a neighbour over his home cheese-making. Despite having some potential as a character, however, the mixed-race Dean comes across simplistically as a benefits scrounger and opportunist. Indeed, he is unfailingly depicted as possessing racial self-hatred: 'The interesting thing about his half-caste looks, he decided, was that he didn't look Negroid' (101). Given his indeterminate looks, Dean decides to pass as Arab to impress a girl. Johnson predictably homes in on cultural confusion and the split self of his novel's lone biracial character, taking pains to articulate significant levels of pessimism concerning hybrid identities. Dean's biological father, we discover, was a Midlands businessman who went cruising for 'a bit of black' (70) and impregnated a non-white woman of unspecified identity. Adopted by an ageing couple, the boy is a mediocrity at school. As a teenager, he sets fire to the neighbour's partition hedge after ill-advisedly stepping in to help in the family dispute. When he is arrested for this vandalism, his adoptive father calls him a 'coon' (79) and thus sets off the boy's descent into petty crime and radicalization.

To be clear, I am not arguing that it is illegitimate for a non-Muslim author to write either about Muslims or violent extremism in the name of Islam. This is not some plea for 'authenticity'. However, artists have to do their homework. Chris Morris spent years researching and talking to people in preparation for the production of *Four Lions*, and this attention to detail is evident in the film and its warm reception from many young Muslims. By contrast, when undertaking his 'research' for *Seventy-Two Virgins*, it seems as though Johnson has simply worked from information provided on a couple of potentially unreliable websites, if that. He makes some basic mistakes; for example, he twice refers to 'a haram', which he glosses as 'a disgrace' (271, 291). However, 'haram' is an adjective rather than a noun and it means 'forbidden'—perhaps he is thinking of 'sharam', which translates as shame or disgrace? He also construes the word 'ummah' as meaning 'the diaspora of aggrieved Islamic youth' (130), when it actually denotes the global Muslim community. These kinds of error further invalidate his plot, and indicate a laziness of thinking similar to the one which got us into the current political imbroglio.

Johnson's contempt for his characters—except a certain buffoonish politician with a classical education—is barely concealed. There is little to admire in this novel: one laugh-out-loud moment when a panicky security officer speculates on whether a living terrorist can be said to have a history of suicide bombing, and a few nuggets of information about Ancient Greece and Rome. Other than that, he takes pops at all the usual right wing targets: the Labour Party, anti-Iraq War protesters, the BBC, academics. Increasingly, Johnson's narrative voice does not even pretend to stay neutral, so that we are given heavy-handed steers about how to judge 'the pathetic Islamofascistic male' or his 'perverted Wahhabi mixture of lust, terror and disgust' (246). As Britain heads further into the virgin territory of Brexit, it is worth remembering this slight and nasty little book. Let this, not his deceptively affable appearances on satirical news show *Have I Got News For You*, stand as Boris Johnson's epitaph as a cultural producer. As Jonathan Freedland warns in his article about Johnson's machinations for Brexit, 'we won't forget what you did' (np.)—or wrote.

NOTE

1. 'Predictable though it was, the plot line proved somewhat prophetic, given the attack that was perpetrated on Westminster by a lone actor in March 2017, killing four (see MacAskill).'

30

Fight the Bannonality of Evil

IN HER 1963 BOOK, *EICHMANN IN JERUSALEM*, Hannah Arendt argues that there is nothing in evil that is radical or lucid. Instead, she claims, even the most extreme evil is senseless and banal. Amos Elon summarized Arendt's argument in terms that cannot but resonate with the current political circumstances in the United States: 'Evil […] need not be committed only by demonic monsters, but—with disastrous effect—by morons and imbeciles as well' (18). As Arendt wrote about Adolf Eichmann, one of the Holocaust's prime orchestrators: '[He] was not Iago and not Macbeth […]. Except for an extraordinary diligence in looking out for his personal advancement, he had no motives at all' (307).

The world's new Orange Overlord—45th President of the United States, Donald J. Trump—has over the last year gifted us too many irrational, muddled, and downright idiotic statements and actions for enumeration. To take just one example, on the first day of Black History Month in 2017, Trump seemed to be under the misapprehension that Frederick Douglass, the nineteenth-century author of *Narrative of the Life of Frederick Douglass an American Slave*, was still alive. According to Trump, Douglass was 'an example of somebody who is doing an amazing job, who is being recognized more and more, I notice' (qtd. in PapoNika np.).

Arendt was right to observe that the slide from thoughtlessness to evil is both easy and smooth. A week before his Douglass gaffe, on Holocaust Remembrance Day 2017, Trump issued his executive order suspending all refugee resettlement for 120 days, as well as indefinitely banning the resettlement of refugees from Syria. Additionally, citizens from seven Muslim-majority countries (Syria, Iraq, Iran, Yemen, Libya, Sudan, and Somalia) were blocked from entering the United States for ninety days. What a way to commemorate the premeditated and industrial-style extermination of 6 million Jews and 200,000 Roma by singling out refugees and a specific religious group for exclusion, thus wilfully violating the First Amendment's Establishment Clause. Thankfully, Trump soon found himself struggling with implacable opposition from the US legal system and, at least at the time of writing, has been unable to execute his order.

Moreover, there was no mention of the Jewish population or anti-Semitism on Holocaust Remembrance Day. Trump's maladroit Press Secretary at the time, Sean Spicer, defensively railed against the public uproar that this glaring omission caused, stating that the White House's intention was to 'acknowledg[e] all of the people' who suffered in the Holocaust (qtd. in Bradner and Scott np.). Prince Charles appeared to respond to the incompleteness of the White House's official statement by warning that the lessons and horror of the Holocaust were in danger of being forgotten (Sherwood: np.). These lessons are, in fact, being wilfully erased by Trump and his presidential entourage.

Central to that team is the anti-Semitic, Islamophobic, far right Chief Strategist for the United States, Steve Bannon. Writing in *Foreign Policy*, Kate Brannen makes clear the former *Breitbart News* chief's significance: 'If there was any question about who is largely in charge of national security behind the scenes at the White House, the answer is becoming increasingly clear: Steve Bannon' (np.). Bannon is interpreted by many observers as the shadowy power behind the gaudy Trump Tower throne. However, a glimpse at Bannon's messy private life points to the conclusion that this is a man of staggering banality. It must be acknowledged that he is not as disorderly in his speech and manner as Trump and has a solid, if unpleasantly ruthless, political agenda that he has been steadily carving out for an extended period, reaching as far back as his early *Breitbart* days. Yet in his quotidian life, rumours of alcoholism surround Bannon, who has been divorced three times. His second wife, Mary Louise Piccard, alleges that he physically and verbally abused her, was an absent and neglectful father to their twin daughters, and told her that he 'didn't want the girls going to school with Jews' (qtd. in Singal np.).

If Indian author Hari Kunzru was right to say that there was a 'Weimar feeling' (np.) to 2016's rise of populism, then in 2017 the Muslim ban may be aimed at provoking a new Reichstag fire. While British Prime Minister Theresa May's Home Secretary, Amber Rudd, belatedly worried that the US travel ban might provoke more people into joining Daesh, she overlooked the very real possibility that this attempt at provocation could be both intentional and purposeful. When a Muslim extremist executes an act of terror on American soil, it may be just the excuse needed for the 'Bannonality of Evil' to erode democracy further and institute emergency powers.

We must remember how short society's memory can be—at least, when amnesia suits the dominant societal narrative. It is amazing how quickly people forget that there has already been a terror attack in North America since the ban (see Freeman, Bever, and Hawkins). I would argue that this amnesia arises because it was committed by a French Canadian Nazi on Muslim mosque attendees in Quebec. It seems as though more such atrocities are inevitable and will continue to be forgotten or misreported as being perpetrated by Muslims.

But I am straying far from my usual literary brief. The rise of neo-fascism in Euro-America today prompted me to consider how

Nazism has been represented in South Asian Muslim literature. Taking Anna Guttman's fine book *Writing Indians and Jews: Metaphorics of Jewishness in South Asian Literature* as a starting point, this chapter concentrates on one particular Muslim woman who fought against intolerance and persecution in the form of Nazism during the Second World War, Noor Inayat Khan, and her representations in fiction and film.

Noor-un-Nisa Inayat Khan was born in Moscow in 1914. Her father was the Sufi philosopher and musician Hazrat Inayat Khan, who was a descendant of Tipu Sultan. Inayat Khan met Noor's mother, Ora Ray Baker, in San Francisco when he was on tour, travelling throughout the United States and playing his music at concerts. Ora's family were interested in the East and were devotees of yoga, but they nonetheless opposed her marriage to this itinerant Indian. Despite their tolerant strand of Sufi Islam, Hazrat Inayat Khan's relatives also disapproved of the match. In the face of disownment, the young couple married, and Ora took the Muslim name Ameena Begum. Inayat Khan and Ameena travelled to England and France, before their first child, Noor, was born in Moscow. In Suresnes on the outskirts of Paris they established their family home, which was renamed Fazal Manzil or the House of Blessing. Large numbers of disciples from all different nationalities would flock to Fazal Manzil to listen to Inayat Khan's devotional music and seek guidance from the mystical patriarch. It can easily be imagined that, with her Indian and American parents, birth in Russia, French upbringing, and work in England during the Second World War, Noor was a multilingual and open-minded woman. In *Spy Princess: The Life of Noor Inayat Khan*, popular historian Shrabani Basu writes: 'Noor was an international person: Indian, French and British at the same time' (11).

Another formative influence on Noor was the untimely death of her father when he fell ill on a solo trip to India. At the age of just twelve years old, this gentle, imaginative girl had to take on a maternal role for her younger brothers, Vilayat and Hidayat, and only sister, Khair-un-Nisa (known as Claire). Her mother sank into a deep depression, which did not lift for a decade. The stories Noor told her siblings to get them through this dark time shaped her budding career as a children's writer.

In 1939, Noor published an illustrated volume of ancient Buddhist stories that she retold in *Twenty Jātaka Tales*. Her father's pluralist interpretation of Islam meant that she was well acquainted with, and could breathe new life into, the tales and traditions of other religions. She gave the stories a distinctive Sufi slant, emphasizing the values of truth, activism, self-sacrifice, and justice. For instance, in 'The Guilty Dogs', hounds from the royal household mischievously bite through some valuable leather leashes. The king imposes severe punishment on all the kingdom's dogs, but the chief dog is ready with a courteous rejoinder:

'O King,' said the chief in a gentle voice, 'is your command just? Why should the dogs of the palace be innocent and the dogs of the city be judged guilty? The ones you favour are saved and the ones you know not are to be killed. O just King, where is your justice?' (25–6)

In her biography of Noor aimed at children and young adults, Gaby Halberstam entirely erases the words 'Islam' and 'Muslim' from the life story, only mentioning, on one occasion, Noor's religion as Sufism and referencing the Hindu *Bhagavad Gita* as an important influence on her (15, 55). Omitting Noor's Muslim heritage and beliefs does her a disservice, because, as the quote suggests, the core Islamic principles of justice and equality are at the heart of much of her writing and political activity. And in today's Islamophobic political climate, it is of consequence to highlight that Muslims like

Noor have lived, worked, and given a great deal back to Western societies for centuries.

In 1939, war broke out, and Noor and her family were among the hundreds of thousands of people who had to flee Paris in scenes of chaotic desperation. Despite her tolerant Sufi background and mixed heritage, it had always been assumed that Noor would agree to an arranged marriage to a distant cousin in India. Instead, Noor, who was an accomplished musician herself, had fallen in love with a student attending Paris's École Normale de Musique. Some surviving family members told Shrabani Basu (263, en. 26) that they only remembered his surname, Goldberg, so strongly did they disapprove of him. However, according to Khair/Claire's son, Noor's nephew David Ray Harper, her fiancé's first name was Azeem, and he was of Turkish Jewish descent (xii). Noor's six-year engagement to Goldberg, despite her family's implacable and possibly anti-Semitic opposition, likely contributed to her fierce resistance to the Nazis. However, it also seems probable that her passion dwindled over time. For whatever reason, she broke off the engagement in 1940.

In her 2004 novel *The Tiger Claw*, Indian–Canadian author Shauna Singh Baldwin turns Noor's singular biography into historical fiction that has strong resonances for the post-9/11 era. She embellishes the relationship with Goldberg, who is renamed Armand, and imagines that the couple had an informal marriage which was quickly consummated. Noor became pregnant, but when her Jewish lover was deported from France she arranged for an abortion. Sometimes written in epistolary form, *The Tiger Claw* is partly composed of letters from Noor to the terminated child. Noor maintains hope that this baby girl will be reborn when she is reunited with the imprisoned Armand and their marriage can be legalized. Singh Baldwin presents readers with a fugue on Noor's impassioned realization that, notwithstanding her conservative uncle's principles and later her armed guard's unwanted advances, *'my life is my own, my soul and my body my own'* (116; emphasis in original). This chimes with the trope of the struggle for control over women's bodies common to much diasporic South Asian women's writing. Shompa Lahiri similarly 'map[s] Khan's shifting embodied representations' in an article in which she 'highlight[s] the performative aspects of embodiment, or the roles the body plays' (305).

Nowhere does this emphasis on Noor's bodily autonomy and physical shapeshifting take on more importance than in her activity during the Second World War. Exiled in England after the family's expulsion from Paris, Noor contributed to the British war effort. Her flawless French eventually led to her becoming one of just thirty women recruited by Selwyn Jepson to become a Special Operations Executive (SOE) operative:

> Noor Inayat Khan joined SOE, F section on 8 February 1943 and was seconded to FANY (Women's Transport Service First Aid Nursing Yeomanry) as a cover story for family and friends. There she trained in the use of firearms. On 16/17 June, after 4 months of training, she was flown to France under the code name 'Madeleine' and her cover name Jeanne-Marie Renier, one of the first female wireless operators to be infiltrated into France (Making Britain np.).

SOE operatives were saboteurs and guerrillas rather than spies. Noor, with her Indian aristocratic background, petite beauty, and pacifist views, made an unlikely operative, and her credentials were thus frequently questioned by her superiors. The wireless operator role that Noor accepted was the most dangerous designation. After deployment, these agents notoriously had an average life expectancy of just six weeks. In the documentary film *Enemy of the Reich*, however, Hanna Diamond observes that those few women operatives who worked for SOE had the advantage of going unnoticed by the Germans for much of the war. Noor had several narrow escapes from the Gestapo, using disingenuousness, quick thinking, and flirtation in these encounters to avoid trouble and potential risk.

Following these brushes with danger and the arrests of many members of her network, Noor was offered the chance to return home to her family in England. She turned this down, choosing instead to stay on and try to rebuild her SOE network, known as Prosper. Small wonder that she would posthumously receive Britain's George Cross and France's Croix de Guerre. Soon after, in autumn 1943, she was captured. At the Gestapo headquarters on Paris's Avenue Foch, she was held in isolation and treated as a *Nacht und Nebel* prisoner destined to disappear into figurative night and fog. Both on her own and with fellow prisoners, she made several unsuccessful attempts at a getaway. She was treated more harshly than others incarcerated by the Nazis, because of her intransigence and because her olive skin led officers to believe she was a Creole. Eventually, she was moved to Dachau concentration camp, where, after a night of torture and perhaps rape, she was shot. Legend has it that the last word she passionately uttered was '*Liberté!*'

According to several accounts, Noor was in favour of Indian Independence and had no sympathy with what Saikat Majumdar has called, with a nod to Arendt, the 'banality of empire'. But as a non-white French refugee, resisting fascism had to take priority over her nationalist politics. Indeed, in *Enemy of the Reich*, Pir Zia Inayat-Khan discussed his Aunt Noor's unwavering moral take on the Second World War: 'I believe if one studies history, this is one of the very few global situations in which there was such a clear contrast of values and such a clear moral imperative [...]. I think she [Noor] felt that moral imperative very viscerally' (qtd. in Gardner np.).

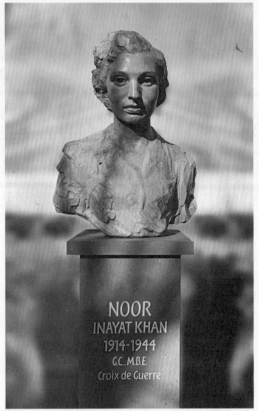

Figure 4: Statue of Noor-un-Nisa Inayat Khan,
Gordon Square, Bloomsbury, London, February 2017.
Source and copyright: Claire Chambers, with thanks
to her son Joash Webster for post-production work.

Returning to Trump, Bannon, and their henchmen's attempts to
implement rampant anti-immigration sentiment and a Muslim-
majority country travel ban, recovering Noor as a writer and a role
model is both opportune and significant. If Noor had not had the
misfortune of living during such a period of upheaval, she might
have become a major author. I feel this loss keenly, as someone
who has long been researching 'British Muslim fictions'. Moreover,

as Vrinda Grover argues, she was wise enough to know what was the right path and how best to resist (np.). Indeed, Singh Baldwin paints Noor explaining her act of resistance to her unborn child:

> *With other followers of Sufism, I performed namaaz and zikr, meditating to heal the planet. We prayed for the miraculous enlightenment of Fascists everywhere—German and French, Hindu and Muslim. […] But where did conciliation and appeasement lead? First to losing you, ma petite, then to losing the one man worth calling husband.*
>
> *And so, my first night back in Paris, I swore to Allah: I resist all tyranny* (111; emphasis in original).

Refusing to let non-violence become appeasement or spirituality become quietism, Noor-un-Nisa Inayat Khan did justice to the meaning of her first name, 'the light of womanhood'.

V

EDUCATION, THEORY, AND THE CREATIVE INDUSTRIES

31

A Fanonian Summer

THE SUMMER OF 2016 was an appropriate season and, indeed, year in which to reread Fanon and to devour for the first time David Macey's *Frantz Fanon: A Biography* (2000) and Jean Khalifa and Robert Young's new edition of Fanon's essays, *Écrits sur l'aliénation et la liberté* (Writings on Alienation and Freedom). Globally, society appeared to be descending into what Fanon, in 1952, called 'manicheism delirium' (183). Repeated terrorist attacks took place in France during 2015 and 2016. The French government responded by declaring a draconian and paranoid state of emergency, which encompassed the French Caribbean territories including Fanon's homeland of Martinique.

Fanon was born in Martinique—one of France's oldest colonies—in 1925. He was from a middle-class family living on an island struggling to deal with the residues of slavery. At this time, most of these colonies, like Quebec and parts of India such as Pondicherry, had become independent. Those that remained, such as the five '*départements*' of Mayotte, Guadeloupe, French Guiana, Réunion, and Martinique, were deemed fully French, even appearing in insets on maps of France. However, when Martinicans like Fanon travelled to Europe, their French citizenship seemed less secure. In *Black Skin, White Masks*, Fanon describes being pointed at by a young Parisian child, who exclaimed, 'Mama, see the Negro! I'm frightened' (112).

As a young man, Fanon fought for Free France in the Second

World War and was decorated for bravery. During his service, he briefly stopped in Algeria—the nation he was later to make his own. Despite becoming increasingly disillusioned with France and its second-class treatment of non-white soliders, after the war ended Fanon enrolled to study medicine in Lyon. In this deeply conservative city, he witnessed the poor treatment of Algerian immigrants at the hands of the French. For example, French-Algerians were often interrogated by the police for very little reason, who addressed them as '*tu*', rather than the polite second-person pronoun '*vous*'. Despite this troublingly unequal society, it was here that Fanon formed significant relationships with two French women. The first, Michelle, he soon abandoned, leaving her with a daughter. He married the second, Josie, with whom he would have a son. It was also in Lyon that he developed his specialism in psychiatry—a branch of medicine that enabled him to pursue his interests in philosophy, politics, and psychoanalysis.

Throughout his career, Fanon's writing exposed black people's psychological trauma and the inferiority complex imposed by colonialism. His career is bookended by his two most influential works, *Black Skin, White Masks* (1952) and *The Wretched of the Earth* (1961). In contrasting ways, these volumes aver that colonialism not only ravaged countries' economies and political structures, but also desolated the minds of colonized peoples. In order to challenge imperialism, Fanon argued, formerly colonized countries and immigrants on the receiving end of racism would have to rebuild their own psychologies. These 'wretched' peoples needed to become the subject, rather than the object, of their history.

Black Skin, White Masks is characterized by its eclectic but sharply focused reading and quotations, its neologisms and Creole inflections, and its anger. Crucially, it details the collective mental illness imposed by racism. Fanon flays European psychoanalysis's obsession with the Oedipus complex. He observes that for non-white subjects, trauma does not usually occur in early childhood within the family setting. Instead, it is experienced outside the home and at a later age. At school, colonized children are educated in contempt for their language and culture; likewise, on the street, adults are confronted with the white gaze of misrecognition (see Thompson and Yar).

His book scarcely making a ripple in the French intellectual scene, Fanon accepted a position as a psychiatrist in Algeria. He did not anticipate the War of Independence that was imminent, and nor did he have much knowledge of the country, its language, or that the French colonial regime was harsh in its treatment of Algeria (including its refusal to accord all of the nation's inhabitants French citizenship). In Algeria, he worked at the Bilda-Joinville Hospital, which was a remarkably progressive environment compared to dominant societal beliefs surrounding the mentally ill and their needs. Bilda-Joinville emphasized the need to build a community in the carceral space of the psychiatric hospital. The ill were encouraged to live as outpatients rather than inhabiting the clinic full-time. Occupational therapy was the order of the day, and Fanon wanted to tailor the chosen activities to reflect the tastes of the specific Muslim North African context in which he found himself. Nonetheless, he was still a clinician who believed in the use and effectiveness of drugs and, more controversially, in narcotherapy (induced sleep through the use of sedatives) as well as electro-convulsive shock therapy or ECT. Once war broke out, Dr Fanon treated a curious mix of French–Algerian women with mild neuroses and male Arab fighters suffering from post-traumatic mental collapse. He became increasingly involved with the National Liberation Front or FLN. His essays for their magazine, *El Moudjahid*, were posthumously compiled in *Toward the African Revolution*, and he acted as the party's ambassador in other French colonies, such as Mali. Although he was never admitted to the FLN's innermost circle, while he was recovering from a car accident at an Italian hospital he was nearly assassinated by French agents for his involvement in the Front.

In 1959, Fanon published *A Dying Colonialism*, his angrily utopian book about the Algerian War. He took a non-essentialist stance on national identity, believing that anyone could become Algerian if they embedded themselves in the country's culture and supported its struggle. In his complete immersion in Algerian culture, Fanon almost proved his own point about the fluidity of national identity, but was never fully accepted as a citizen by Algerians themselves. In *A Dying Colonialism*, he appealed to Algerian Jews to trouble the rigid racial and religious divide between *pied-noirs* (white settlers) and Arabs or Berbers. As a doctor, he excoriated the colonial medicine that was practised in 1950s Algeria, whereby French–Algerian doctors also acted as torturers. He called for the people to wrest medicine from the hands of the oppressors. The book also contains his urgent, if rather masculinist, essay 'Algeria Unveiled' which tackles the issue of modest Muslim dress and resistance. Deborah Wyrick recommends viewing Fanon as a man of his time, but also comments that his ideas about women 'can range from the dismissive to the peculiar' (24). In *Black Skin, White Masks*, for instance, Fanon attacked Mayotte Capecia's novel about a Martinican trying to make her fortune by marrying a white man; however, he didn't submit her male counterparts to similar treatment when examining their fiction. Almost a decade later, in the essay 'Algeria Unveiled', he depicted the first female Algerian freedom fighters disguising themselves in Western dress—French occupiers assuming that the wearing of Parisian fashions signalled a lack of sympathy with the FLN. As the colonizers became conscious of this ruse, the women changed tactics. Veils created a cloak of invisibility under which bombs and grenades could be secreted. Fanon speculated that Western men abhorred the veil because it disrupted their gaze on the imagined beauty of the Other women, and that the desire to unveil constituted rape fantasy.

Fanon contracted leukaemia in his mid-thirties. With the knowledge that he was dying, he wrote *The Wretched of the Earth*, dictating it, as usual, to his white wife, Josie. His final book's advocacy of violence continues to cause controversy. He writes that '[t]he colonized man finds his freedom in and through violence' and that this violence functions as a 'cleansing force' (68, 74). However, Fanon was primarily identifying the violence in the colonial system. Thus, according to him, the only way to combat this deeply racist and sadistic system was through counter-violence. Fanon was, of course, not just theorizing, but actually fought for his beliefs. Moreover, his espousal of violence has to be understood in relation to its Algerian context of torture, mass murder, and the trauma this engendered. Such trauma was exemplified when Fanon's cancer compelled him to seek treatment in the US. There, his 5-year-old son, Olivier, saw his father's intravenous blood bag and thought he had been murdered. Following this horrific discovery, the boy briefly went missing, only to be found defiantly waving an Algerian flag outside the hospital. We should remember that for many years, the French government refused to use the term 'war' when referring to the conflict in Algeria that spanned the years from 1954 to 1962. Moreover, in 1961 the River Seine ran red with the blood of hundreds of Algerian immigrants cut down by security forces at a peaceful anti-war protest. As Fanon so powerfully demonstrated, the colonizer is 'the bringer of violence into the home and into the mind of the native' (29).

The Wretched of the Earth is also about the perils of decolonization. Fanon's use of the phrase 'national bourgeoisie' (120–43) signalled that many of the nationalist leaders who replaced the British colonizers were remarkably similar to those they unseated, barring the difference in race. Fanon was scathing about the national bourgeoisie's opportunism and willingness to replicate the colonizers' divisive systems of control. He maintained that postcolonial nations should reconstruct or abandon the racially segregated cities that were a legacy of colonial rule. Instead, the countryside and the peasant were Fanon's hope for the future. With these ideas at least, he echoed Gandhi, even if the two men's attitudes towards violence were completely opposed. In *Hind Swaraj*, Gandhi asserted: 'If India copies England, it is my firm conviction that she will be ruined' (33). The Congress leader likewise believed that India's beating heart could be found in her villages.

In the summer of 2016, the Panama Papers unmasked state corruption around an Algerian petroleum industry deal (Fitzgibbon np.); a remake of *Tarzan* recalled *Black Skin, White Masks'* description of young Afro-Caribbean boys who identified with the original film's white Tarzan; and a video emerged exposing French police forcing a burkini-clad woman to strip on a beach in Cannes. In these contexts, the relevance of Fanon's work can hardly be overstated.

32

Edward Said's *Orientalism*: Its Influence and Legacy

EW TWENTIETH-CENTURY BOOKS have witnessed Silver Jubilee
celebrations, but twenty-five years after the 1978 publication
of Edward Said's *Orientalism*, it was commemorated by his faculty
at Columbia University. Months later, Said died of cancer at 67,
but the book continues to be hailed as extraordinarily innovative,
riding high in lists of the most influential academic works and
continuing to dominate the discipline of postcolonial studies
that it kick-started. *Orientalism*'s groundbreaking import lies in
the connections it makes between culture and empire-building.
Drawing on Michel Foucault's theories about the intertwining of
power and knowledge, as well as Antonio Gramsci's insistence on
the centrality of culture in securing the consent of the dominated,
Said argues that colonization was not merely about territorial
expansion, but inculcating in the minds of both rulers and the
ruled that colonization was to universal advantage.

Said claims that Western scholarship—and even that supposed
bastion of cultural transcendence, art—produces an image of the
'Orient' as the Other. Ideas about non-Western peoples are a
fantasy created by centuries of 'Orientalism', which term denotes
both scholarly and popular representations of the East. This
discourse legitimates Europe's colonial expansion into non-Western
countries. Said holds that Orientalist texts defined the Orient
through binary oppositions. If the East is always stereotyped as

the inferior partner—irrational, primitive, and despotic—it enables the West's self-definition as rational, modern, and democratic. The Other that Said examines is largely Muslim and Arab, although he does pay attention to other Others—notably, Indians, as depicted by Orientalists such as William Jones. Said was an outspoken proponent of the Palestinian cause and was often mistakenly believed to possess Islamic heritage; however, he was, in fact, '[a] Christian who is culturally a Muslim' (Majid 28).

Criticisms have been levelled at *Orientalism* for a possible gender-blindness (Abu-Lughod 'Feminist': 101); inattention to the specificities of history, 'the West', and its individual scholars (Porter; Irwin); neglect of indigenous counter-representations or resistance (A. Ahmad); and philosophical inconsistencies (Varisco). Some of these criticisms were addressed in Said's later essays (see, for example, 'Reconsidered'). However, *Orientalism* is arguably more relevant than ever in our Manichean post-9/11 political climate. Scholars of Muslim history, politics, and culture are again turning to *Orientalism* for its discussion of stereotypes and the culturally imperialist construction of a bifurcated 'West' versus the 'Muslim world'. For instance, Joseph Massad, now also a professor at Columbia, to some extent continued Said's legacy in *Desiring Arabs* and *The Persistence of the Palestinian Question*. Simultaneously, however, many rightwingers and Zionists remain hostile to Said's memory, and academics regarded as 'Saideans' were pressurized by organizations such as Campus Watch during the George W. Bush administration. Nor did much change under Barack Obama. For example, in 2014, Steven Salaita, now Edward W. Said Chair of American Studies at the American University of Beirut, received an offer for a position at the University of Illinois which was then withdrawn due to a handful of Tweets in which he openly criticized Israel (Guarino np.).

Were it not for Said, I would not be researching postcolonial literature, and *Orientalism* still informs and nourishes my teaching. Along with Frantz Fanon, Said was the first theorist I truly engaged with, not least for his emphasis on material exploitation, as well as representations. The two other members of postcolonial theory's 'Holy Trinity' (Young *Colonial Desire*: 154)—Homi Bhabha and Gayatri Spivak—also scrutinize exploitation, but their work seems abstract and abstruse when measured against Said's fearless and unerringly humane call for non-coercive knowledge of other peoples.

33

The Barbarians Are at the Gate: On Self-Construction and the 'Other'

IN *WAITING FOR THE BARBARIANS*, J. M. Coetzee's haunting novel about colonization, corporeality, and betrayal, the 'civilized' protagonist thinks about a 'barbarian' ex-lover. 'The body of the other one', muses the Magistrate, 'seems beyond comprehension. [...] I cannot imagine what ever drew me to that alien body' (42). This reflection pithily conveys several truths about what is often termed the 'Other'. Imperialists—including those operating in what British geographer Derek Gregory calls the 'colonial present' of Af-Pak and the Middle East—construct an Other who is different from the Self. Colonizers simultaneously feel desire and repulsion for this figure of their own creation. The Magistrate was once drawn to the dark, imperturbable body of the barbarian girl, and tenderly washed her feet and torture wounds. Now, locked in the saccharine embrace of a prostitute from his own racial background, he rejects his former lover as alien and unknowable.

Similarly, in his book *Colonial Desire*, Robert Young argues that although on paper racists want to keep different cultures apart, their hatred is often transposed into the new key of desire. These apparent 'purists' are surreptitiously obsessed with 'transgressive, inter-racial sex, hybridity, and miscegenation' (Young *Colonial Desire*: ix). The notion of the Other originated in psychoanalysis, was developed by existentialists and feminists, and has found particular traction in the field of postcolonial studies. Psychoanalysts utilize the term to describe how we become conscious of our identities. In Jacques Lacan's work on the mirror stage, for example, he analyses how a child peers into a looking glass, sees itself in its mother's arms, and becomes aware that it is a separate being. The Other—in this case, the mother—is indispensable in delimiting the child's sense of self.

Existentialist philosophers such as Jean-Paul Sartre understood and used the term in a different way—to illustrate how individuals fashion their lives and identities through their actions towards, and relationships with, others. Influenced by existentialism, Sartre's partner, Simone de Beauvoir, distilled the significance of this idea for women. In her feminist classic *The Second Sex*, she asserts that man 'is the Subject, he is the Absolute', while woman 'is the Other'. Another notable philosopher, Emmanuel Levinas, emphasized that the Self should be held accountable for the Other. In *Otherwise Than Being*, Levinas refers to 'my responsibility for the faults or the misfortune of others [...] my responsibility that answers for the freedom of another' (10).

Finally, postcolonialism has again redefined this noun. Published in 1961, Frantz Fanon's *The Wretched of the Earth* was prefaced by Sartre's fiery, if somewhat simplistic, foreword. In the book itself, Fanon—the Martinican psychiatrist turned Algerian revolutionary—pluralizes the term, examining how 'other[s]' turn to violence, 'sharpen[ing] their weapons' as they reject 'the governing race's' construction of them as animalistic (33, 31). In *Orientalism* (1978), Edward Said insists that non-Western peoples—Arabs, Asians, and Africans—have been treated as Other for centuries. Racial Others are usually painted in disparaging, unfamiliar hues. Their consciousness is wired differently, and they are somehow violent and threatening, weak and contemptible, at one and the same time. In colonial discourse, even apparent admiration for the Other functions to mask exoticization and structural inequality.

Said observes that imperialists apply binary oppositions in depicting Self and the Other, reinforcing the Self's sense of superiority. Non-Western people are seen as being instinctive, while Europeans are rational; 'the Rest' are portrayed as 'barbaric', while 'the West' is civilized. From their different disciplinary and political vantage points, these pioneering theorists show that we achieve selfhood by calibrating ourselves against what we are not, amid unequal power relations. As Gregory succinctly explains: 'Modernity produces its other, verso to recto, as a way of at once producing and privileging itself' (4). Simply put, it is easier to view yourself as an individual if there is someone present who shares some traits with you, but is different enough that you can feel superior.

Gayatri Spivak's essay 'Terror: A Speech After 9-11' concerns the 'War on Terror' and its ethical consequences. Writing in 2004, she outlined the already existing responses to the World Trade Centre attacks and their aftermath, mulling over what an ideal reaction would look like 'in the face of the impossibility of response' (81). As well as dealing with the Self versus the Other, she also employs plural pronouns to challenge George W. Bush and others, whom she characterizes as constantly 'us-and-them-ing' (87). Spivak maintains that we need humanities training in imagining Others' point of view. She advocates the difficult but crucial task of 'listen[ing] to the other as if it were a self, neither to punish nor to acquit' (83). This Other includes the suicide bomber, whose motivations she controversially explores, but does not endorse. Spivak claims that without at least attempting to understand the Other's rationale for his actions, all our juridical and political work will prove futile and impermanent.

A few years later, Gregory wrote *The Colonial Present* to evaluate what happens to notions of Self and Other, us and them, in times of war. He zeroes in on the three neocolonial contexts of Iraq, Palestine, and Afghanistan. By dehumanizing the populations of these nations, modern-day colonizers are able to detonate remote missiles without guilt, resulting in devastation for 'them' and impunity for 'us': 'American bombs and missiles rained down on K-A-B-U-L, not on the eviscerated city of Kabul; Israeli troops turned their guns on Palestinian "targets" not on Palestinian men, women, and children; American firepower destroyed Baghdad buildings and degraded the Iraqi military machine but never killed Iraqis' (9). This exemplifies what Gregory calls 'connective dissonance' (248–56). Through abstractions, such as the employment of the word 'targets', an imagined geography of 'us' and 'them' is created, in which some connections between peoples are exaggerated, while others are 'disavowed' (249). Instead of finding alternatives to this dissonance, groups like al-Qaida and Daesh simply flip the hate-filled binaries of 'us' and 'them' on their head. The calamitous consequences of this dehumanization of the Other have been seen many times over in recent attacks, such as those in Paris, Beirut, Brussels, Orlando, Berlin, Istanbul, and Manchester.

French–Bulgarian structuralist, Tzvetan Todorov, abjures pronouns altogether in order to explore another duality, between 'civilized people' and 'barbarians'. That barbarians are said to be 'at the gate' is really a way of demarcating the Self and its boundaries. Todorov does not doubt that civilization and barbarism exist. Yet he rejects the way that, from the Ancient Greeks until the present day, these terms have been formulated to cast 'us' in a positive light and denigrate those who live differently. Instead, he provides a powerfully simple definition of barbarians as 'those who deny the full humanity of others' (16). Todorov tries to penetrate the psychology of the barbarian who behaves as though others were not fully human and is thus able to torture them. Throughout *The Fear of Barbarians*, he demonstrates that pitting Manichean violence against Manichean violence can never succeed. Todorov resonantly explains: 'The fear of barbarians is what risks making us barbarian' (6).

Accused by his own people of 'treasonously consorting with the enemy', Coetzee's Magistrate protests that they are supposed to be at peace and have no enemies. At this moment in *Waiting for the Barbarians* the Self and Other binary breaks down, as the Magistrate, in a moment of illumination, ponders: 'Unless we are the enemy' (77). Perhaps the Other, which the Self fashions into a monstrous 'barbarian', is actually a glimpse of one's own face in the mirror.

34

Who's Saving Whom?: Postcolonialism and Feminism

INTERNATIONAL WOMEN'S DAY takes place annually on 8 March. Rarely did the day seem more necessary to observe than it did in 2015, as debate raged about the ethics and timing of the BBC documentary on the Delhi rape case, *India's Daughter*. In this film, Mukesh Singh, one of the accused rapists, inadvertently implicated himself in the crime by saying that women are more responsible for rape than their male rapists, and that 'a decent girl won't roam around at 9 o'clock at night' (Udwin np.). Troublingly, his interview was broadcast before the case went to appeal. Lest *India's Daughter* tempts us to think that violence and sexual abuse against women is a South Asian problem, a campaign was launched by the Salvation Army, capitalizing on the optical illusion dress that went viral on social media. The campaign featured a badly bruised white woman wearing the dress in white and gold (the colour combination that many of us saw in the badly lit original photograph), with the caption: 'Why is it so hard to see black and blue?' (Salvation Army: np.). This South Africa-based campaign indicates that violence against women cuts across all cultures. Here, I examine some of the key feminist essays of the last four decades in order to explore the productive overlap that exists between postcolonial studies and feminism.

Julia Kristeva's *About Chinese Women* (1977) was, in some ways, an example of a Western feminist making universalizing, even racist assumptions. In 1974, the psychoanalytic critic had spent three weeks in China with associates of the *Tel Quel* avant-garde literary journal, including her husband Philippe Sollers and philosopher Roland Barthes. Kristeva wrote her book in the context of leftist politics in France, wherein China was held up as a model society; indeed, in 1971 *Tel Quel* had proclaimed its support for Maoism. However, the critical work suffered when it was digested by an audience outside France, many members of which felt Kristeva was homogenizing the Chinese women under study. After the late 1970s, *About Chinese Women* fell out of favour with most feminist activists and academics. Kristeva seemed progressive on difference, warning against looking for answers in Chinese society to solve Western problems. She showed awareness of the symbiotic relationship between knowledge and power, claiming that she wanted to create 'open-ended' research (75). This is praiseworthy, but in a sense she was guilty of both acts she warns against—imposing a knowledge system on others and positioning Chinese culture as a blank screen on which to project and devise solutions for Western women's dilemmas. She idealized male–female relations in China, associating the Chinese woman stereotypically with 'an inexhaustible yin essence' and portraying the Chinese man as 'the delicate artisan' of the woman's *jouissance*, or sexual pleasure (80). Readers may wonder how Kristeva could have known this from a short visit and without knowledge of either Mandarin or Cantonese to communicate.

Kristeva's position was just one example of Western feminist theory—and a particularly French and psychoanalytic one at that. However, postcolonial feminism helped to identify and correct what it saw as the blind spots of Western feminist theory. According to Chandra Talpade Mohanty in her seminal essay from 1984 'Under Western Eyes: Feminist Scholarship and Colonial Discourses', this theory often produced a singular 'Third World Woman' (333). This monolith of the Third World woman was unthinkingly taken as a symbol of 'underdevelopment, oppressive traditions, high illiteracy, rural and urban poverty, religious fanaticism and overpopulation' ('Cartographies of Struggle': 5-6). Mohanty argued that such negative assumptions about the Third World woman did not capture the complexity and fluidity of the lives of these *women*, plural. A 'Third World Woman' wasn't automatically oppressed. If she was from a powerful class or family, she might have had more power and agency than a working-class woman or even man in the First World. Mohanty contended that Western feminists 'homogeniz[ed] and systematiz[ed]' Third World women ('Western Eyes': 335), painting a monochrome picture. It was problematic to use the term 'Third World' and yet not pay attention to its variegation and plurality. According to Mohanty, collapsing differences and making the Third World into a homogeneous category on the basis of apparently underdeveloped lives compared to the automatically privileged women of the First World amounted to 'discursive [...] coloniz[ation]' ('Western Eyes': 334).

Mohanty's critique of (Western) feminism might itself be criticized. She made pertinent corrections to the unwitting shortsightedness of five feminist scholars, including Fran Hosken, who worked on female genital mutilation in North Africa, and Patricia Jeffery (who happens to be my father's first cousin!), the author of *Frogs in a Well: Indian Women in Purdah*. Mohanty did provide one positive example of Western feminist scholarship, Maria Mies' work on lacemakers in Andhra Pradesh, India ('Western Eyes': 344-6). Yet, notwithstanding some disclaimers to the contrary, Mohanty to some extent simply slotted 'Western feminism' into the box of 'imperialism'. 'Under Western Eyes' was an urgent and necessary essay in the mid-1980s, and it made feminists like my father's cousin reflect on and modify their research practice. However, as Susan Watkins and I have argued elsewhere, Mohanty's essay was equally open to charges of universalization:

[T]he term 'feminism' is itself treated as a stable, transhistorical critical and political position. […] [T]he slippage in the title of the essay, which moves the term 'Western' to the main title and leaves the term 'feminism' unqualified in the subtitle, does make a series of substitutions which imply first, that all feminism is Western feminism; second, that all feminist scholarship is Western feminist scholarship; and third, that all Western feminist scholarship is the same. […] Nor does [the] essay admit the diversity and range of feminist work outside and also within the 'Western' context (Chambers and Watkins 'Postcolonial Feminism?': 298).

Shortly after Mohanty's critique, in their 1986 book *A Double Colonization*, Kirsten Holst Petersen and Anna Rutherford tried to unite postcolonialism and feminism through recognition of the overlap between colonialism and patriarchy. However, there were two problems with the 'double colonization' approach. First, it suggested that racism and sexism function in the same way; and, second, it only highlighted two possible forms of oppression.

Gayatri Spivak extended double colonization through her feminist (re-)interpretation of subalternity. She borrowed the word 'subaltern' from the prison writings of Marxist philosopher, Antonio Gramsci. Its literal meaning was a rank-and-file, lowly member of the army. Gramsci used the term to stand in for any member of an oppressed class, with his emphasis firmly on the working man. The Subaltern Studies Group in early 1980s India then resorted to the word 'subaltern' in their attempt to create new history from below of those—such as peasants, workers' unions, and the lower middle class—who did not belong to the colonial or nationalist elite (see Guha). Spivak worked with the Subaltern Studies historians and applauded their project for giving voice to people denied a place in history's annals by their lack of literacy and their powerless position. However, she wrote her important

1988 essay 'Can the Subaltern Speak?' in order to point out a few problems within Subaltern Studies.

Spivak highlighted that the (mostly male) Subaltern Studies historians often failed to recognize the 'double colonization' experienced by women in the colonial context. To take one example of this double colonization, Spivak noted that colonial and nationalist discourse on the practice of sati (or widow self-immolation) claimed to 'liberate' Indian women from their heavy responsibility to die alongside their husbands or from the oppressive cultural suppression of the British. However, amidst these sonorous cries of liberation, 'the free will of the constituted sexed subject as female was successfully effaced' ('Subaltern': 302). In other words, women did not have the option to choose whether or not they wanted to carry out sati, and thus had no agency in deciding their future. Spivak examined the difficulty of having one's voice heard (and in an undistorted way), particularly for non-elite people, such as tribals, peasants, women, low castes, and the working class: 'Clearly, if you are poor, black, and female you get it in three ways. [...] As a product of these considerations I have put together the sentence "White men are saving brown women from brown men"' (296). Here Spivak, whose writing can be impenetrable, furnished future critics with two richly suggestive phrases. First, the statement that poor, black women 'get it in three ways' has sexual connotations, which are particularly relevant in view of my opening discussion of the Delhi rape case. Spivak also testified that a person can experience more than singular or double oppressions. This anticipated the theory of intersectionality, which has gained in popularity from the 1990s until now, and to which I will return later in this chapter. Second, the now famous slogan '[w]hite men are saving brown women from brown men' was heavily ironic and foreshadowed 2000s thinking about saviours, rescue, and assumptions of superiority.

Lila Abu-Lughod wrote her influential essay 'Do Muslim Women Really Need Saving?' in 2002 against the backdrop of the initial phase of the War in Afghanistan. She took as her point of departure the toxic but hilarious George W. Bushism 'women of cover', which conflated the politically nuanced American term 'women of colour' with the issues surrounding Muslim dress and its supposed subjugation of women (783). In this essay, Abu-Lughod provided a fine-grained reading of the veiling debate. Rather than the universal symbol of oppression that many Americans assume it to be, the burqa is a Pashtun garment that can provide empowerment to the wearer—indeed, one anthropologist describes it as 'portable seclusion' (Papanek, qtd. in Abu-Lughod 785). Abu-Lughod disagrees with any enforcement of the wearing of burqas, but observed that many women wear these garments voluntarily and have no wish to discard them.

Abu-Lughod next challenged George W. Bush's wife, Laura Bush's November 2001 speech, in which she implicitly assumed that Afghan women would automatically be delighted to be rescued by American troops:

> It is deeply problematic to construct the Afghan woman as someone in need of saving. When you save someone, you imply that you are saving her from something. You are also saving her to something. What violences are entailed in this transformation, and what presumptions are being made about the superiority of that to which you are saving her? (788-9)

Abu-Lughod encouraged readers to think about women who may or may not want or need saving, but who, more importantly, demand social justice. Finally, she championed respect for difference, while not sanctioning cultural relativism—the idea that everything can be understood and justified in the context of its culture. She demonstrated that it is no self-contradiction to dislike the Taliban, while simultaneously rejecting crude online petitions that claim to act against 'Muslim men oppressing Muslim women' (787). What we should say is: a plague on both their houses.

Whereas Rutherford and Petersen spoke of 'double colonization', Spivak turned this into a triumvirate: if you are *poor*, *black*, and *female*, you get it in three ways. From a postsecular perspective, Abu-Lughod and the Turkish–American scholar Esra Mirze Santesso show that if you are poor, black, *Muslim*, and female, 'you get it in four ways' (Santesso 5). The progression from single issue feminism or postcolonialism to double, triple, and quadruple approaches demonstrates the need for a theory which takes into account multiple oppressions.

Coming out of her African American feminist legal work, Kimberlé Crenshaw's 1989 concept of intersectionality filled this gap. From a postcolonial studies outlook its most suggestive further development came from Avtar Brah (10–16) in a South Asian diasporic context and from Anjali Arondekar in relation to what she calls 'queer postcolonialities' (236). Intersectionality is a theoretical approach that recognizes multiple identity components and grounds for oppression at once. As well as race and gender, there is class (and caste), religious background, age, disability, sexual orientation, and so on. As Mohanty delineated in the 1980s, it is important not to see the woman as an ahistoric, monolithic subject. Rather, it is necessary to consider women in all their multiplicity and within their particular contexts. Intersectionality assumes that sexism and racism, rather than being separate and aberrant phenomena, actually inform and support each other.

Pnina Werbner is suspicious of intersectionality, which she calls 'a negative politics of hidden multiple inequalities' (403). Like me, Werbner identifies 'double or even triple' (but not quadruple or more; 409) social classifications that hold many women back. She follows

Nira Yuval-Davis in viewing gender or race as not functioning as 'identities' in precisely the same manner. Furthermore, as Werbner observes: 'the categories themselves disguise divisions within them; treating them as homogeneous risks naturalising or essentialising them' (409). She therefore asserts that intersectionality is a damaging theory for fixing identities and obsessing over discrimination. To counter this 'negative politics', Werbner provides fascinating but perhaps overly optimistic discussion of everyday multiculturalism and conviviality amongst British Muslim communities—even as she recognizes that these happy interactions usually take place in gender-segregated private spaces (405). Her references to displays of 'interethnic amity' (402) at the 2012 London Olympics and the mostly warm British reception of then-emerging Muslim athlete Mo Farah (name variously spelt in her article) are complicated by her own recognition that no British Asians won medals at those Games and that the *Daily Mail* unpleasantly questioned Farah and other British medal-holders born outside the UK as 'plastic Brits' (413). Furthermore, Mo Farah subsequently came under suspicion (never proven) of doping, and as a Somalia-born Briton, was affected by Donald Trump's putative travel ban. Just as her sanguinity rings hollow in a Trumpian age, so too does her criticism of intersectionality's apparent gainsaying seem premature when American women's hard-won reproductive rights are being stripped away under this new, misogynist administration.

In *Terrorist Assemblages: Homonationalism in Queer Times* (2007), Jasbir K. Puar adapts Gilles Deleuze and Félix Guattari's theorization of the assemblage as an alternative to intersectionality, and as a space where multiple ideas 'converge, diverge, and merge' (xxii). Like Werbner, Puar finds intersectionality problematic because it fixes and calcifies various identity components, even though she admires Crenshaw as an activist and scholar of integrity. Puar criticizes intersectionality's bias towards heteronormativity, and suggests that the assemblage may be a more appropriate image for defining LBTQ+ identities-in-flux. The assemblage, she suggests, is better understood as an event or a set of relationships than as a subject (indeed, Puar problematizes subjectivity). She argues that the event is subliminally present in intersectionality theory from the outset, given that Crenshaw's original idea concerned a road traffic intersection and an accident that occurred there. Puar claims that the assemblage has several advantages over intersectionality. Assemblage theory doesn't automatically assume that the body is a unitary, separate entity; nor does it assume a split between human, animal, and matter. Contra Derrida, language isn't the only thing that counts in the assemblage; and finally, the theory allows for the inclusion of technology alongside the body, rather than being limited to human identities. Puar praises assemblages' hybridity and perpetual motion, showing that different groups can be brought together in an assemblage before being reconstellated: 'The assemblage, as a series of dispersed but mutually implicated and messy networks, draws together enunciation and dissolution, causality and effect, organic and nonorganic forces' (211). She also recognizes the existence of oppressive groups—'surveillance assemblages' (175)—that try to subjugate emergent and resistant assemblages. In practice, intersectionality presumes different yet immutable identities, which come together but can be separated. By contrast, assemblage theory assumes that these identities are closely knitted together; despite this, they are contingent, in motion, and connected with affect or emotion.

Notwithstanding the limitations highlighted by Werbner and Puar, I think that intersectionality theories, when supplemented with the idea of the assemblage, provide effective psychological scaffolding for global twenty-first century feminist activists. Assemblages may provide sophisticated refinement of our understanding of identity and resistance to oppression, but it is the word 'intersectionality' that has entered common parlance to serve as a salutary corrective to single-issue feminism. As Emily Grabham detects, intersectionality has a reciprocal relationship with anti-essentialist activism 'around race, gender, disability and poverty' (183) as well as same-sex love and desire (184). At a historical moment when hatred and truculence once again appear resurgent, what intersectionality and assemblage theories teach us is the need to think about, and resist, different oppressions together, without reducing differences between them or decanting one into the other.

35

Festal or Fecal?: The Global
Literary Festival

WHEN I THINK ABOUT FESTIVALS, my first associations are enforcement and subsequent (often reactionary) dissent. At the previous university I worked at, where I was mostly very happy, the vice-chancellor rather too enthusiastically decreed the creation of (and attendance at) a staff development festival to be held annually each September. This sounds admirable, until you realize that this equated to two weeks during the school holidays when employees were not allowed to take leave. We were instead compelled to look keen during sessions on topics as eclectic as 'developing a research career', feng shui, and DJing. This Kafkaesque staff development festival therefore caused much discontent and was scrapped soon after the departure of the Vice-Chancellor whose brainchild it was. You can't coerce people into feeling festive, and a compulsory festival is surely a contradiction in terms.

Witnessing several long faces and bitter sniping when attending certain panels at 2014's Karachi Literature Festival (KLF) intimated that these participants had been similarly forced into fêting, corralled into celebrating with each other. And yet, other panels, such as the Urdu reading given by Amjad Islam Amjad which I attended, had a truly festive atmosphere, with people packed into the room, raptly listening, and one woman even wiping away tears at the end of the recital. The launch of policeman-cum-writer Omar Shahid Hamid's engrossing English-language thriller, *The*

Prisoner, was equally acclamatory, and it was interesting to see many of Hamid's police colleagues proudly occupying several seats in support of a co-worker who had written a novel showcasing their everyday lives.

The KLF of 2014 was held against the backdrop of a broader Sindh cultural festival set up by Bilawal Bhutto Zardari. The Pakistan Peoples Party leader argued that his festival would help in the publicization and restoration of Pakistan's cultural heritage, including Mohenjo-Daro—the world's oldest surviving city, which is part of the rich pre-Hindu Indus Valley civilization. Yet the Sindh Festival caused widespread controversy because many experts and conservationists felt that its inaugural concert—which included a light show and performances by famous Pakistani musicians (although this concert was notably restricted to invite-only guests, thus lending it an aura of prestige)—would harm the ruins of Mohenjo-Daro, which is supposed to be under UNESCO protection (Mahmood np.). It seems to me indisputable that Bhutto Zardari's opening ceremony was a physically destructive and strategically ruinous decision, doing untold damage to an already crumbling historical site. However, forming an opinion on Pakistan's literature festivals is not so clear-cut. Reading media reports before, during, and after the KLF and Lahore Literature Festival demonstrates a clear divide between those who view cultural festivals as festal, humanist celebrations, and others who view them as fecal, elitist commodifications of art.

In his influential book about cultural prizes, *The Economy of Prestige*, James F. English writes:

> Modern cultural prizes cannot fulfil their social functions unless authoritative people—people whose cultural authority is secured in part through those very prizes—are thundering against them. The

vast literature of mockery and derision with respect to prizes must,
in my view, be seen as an integral part of the prize frenzy itself (25).

This is also true of the literary festival: the nay-sayers are only
the other side of the coin to the yay-sayers. The 'elitist' argument
about KLF and Lahore Literature Festival is mostly formulated
by members of the elite themselves. Rather than participating
in either festival-extolling or -bashing, it may be more useful to
carve out a middle ground. A realization that those who trash
festivals are themselves central players in those festivals' acts of
myth-making might allow us to stand back and assess festivals
for both their positive and negative attributes. They *are* about big
business, corporate sponsorship, and the new phenomenon of live-
Tweeting—and, in many ways, all of these considerations do seem
antithetical to 'true art'. But such book events can also encourage
literacy, champion marginalized groups, and promote peace.

Festivals perhaps make more sense for films than they do for
books, because events like Cannes are opportunities for screenings
and film-watching marathons. Amitav Ghosh makes the point
that, by contrast, reading and writing are solitary activities that
attract mostly introverted people, because they 'provide an island
of quiet within the din of tamasha-stan' ('Festivals': np.). Ironically,
one never has much time for reading or calm contemplation amidst
the frenetic socializing of the book festival. But perhaps that's not
the point? As the saying goes: it's the economy, stupid. Festivals
are all about book sales and marketing. For example, the winners
of literary prizes are often announced at festivals, creating new
readerships and bringing maximum publicity. Think of the winner
of the DSC Prize for South Asian Literature, which is revealed
yearly at Jaipur, or the announcement of the Commonwealth Book
and Short Story Prizes at Hay-on-Wye. Sometimes a literary award
becomes the excuse for the staging of a festival or vice versa, with a

symbiotic relationship existing between prizes and festivals. At KLF 2014, three major prizes were announced: the Embassy of France Prize, which Uzma Aslam Khan claimed for *Thinner Than Skin*; the KLF Coca-Cola Prize for best non-fiction, given to Osama Siddique's book *Pakistan's Experience with Formal Law*; and a Peace Prize with German Consulate backing, won by Akbar S. Ahmad for his book *The Thistle and the Drone*.

There can also be a humanitarian aspect to festivals, as the above Peace Prize example suggests. Indeed, in 2014, the Indo–Pak peace vein ran prominently throughout the festival. One keynote address was given by the Mahatma's grandson, Rajmohun Gandhi, who elegantly spoke of South Asia as a house in which the occupants don't yet know each other properly. He claimed that this house, together with the house of Middle East, needs to be sustained and developed for the benefit of humanity. As well as encompassing the broad issues of humanitarianism and peace-building, festivals 'create a forum for displays of pride, solidarity, and celebration on the part of various cultural communities' (English 25). This is certainly the case in Pakistan, where the very existence of festivals is considered by outsiders, in particular, as an affirmation of liberal values. For example, writing in the *New York Review of Books*, Hugh Eakin senses the 'urgency' of the Lahore Literature Festival's aim to 'defend the written word' (np.). But it is also true in Britain, where two literary friends, Irna Qureshi and Syima Aslam, have done a tremendous job of establishing a new Bradford Literature Festival (J. Harris np.). This festival aims to promote literacy and literature in a city that is too often criticized, equally from within and without, and whose residents' aspirations are consequently failing to thrive. It is dramatized in an even more political way in Palestine, where Cairo-born London-resident writer Ahdaf Soueif founded PalFest in 2008 to 'use [...] the power of culture against the culture of power' (Engaged Events np.). Soueif continues to invite writers to Occupied Palestinian Territory, despite ongoing opposition from Israeli authorities.

Despite all these positive aspects to the dazzling rise of the cultural festival over the last two decades, I am reminded of my initial response, involving thoughts about coercion and enforced jollity. On the whole, festivals have not emerged organically out of grassroots movements, but they are increasingly becoming one of the only shows in town for literature, particularly during the global economic downturn which led to stringent cuts in arts funding. Cultural festivals can't be forcibly imposed from the top down, but if they work in partnership with readers and authors to champion literature and humanitarian or pressing political concerns, then this writer, at least, will feel genuinely festive.

36

The State We're In: Global Higher Education

IN A RECENT CO-AUTHORED ARTICLE, Rachael Gilmour and I discussed movements originating in South African higher education, #RhodesMustFall and #FeesMustFall (Chambers and Gilmour 3–4). Similarly, in the United States and beyond, Black Lives Matter is gathering momentum. Emerging in response to judicial indifference over the 2012 murder of Trayvon Martin, the movement works toward combatting systematic racism and discrimination, as well as police brutality against and killing of black people. There has been a vicious backlash against the group with the creation of the controversial slogan 'All Lives Matter', which response attempts to depict those who are part of the Black Lives Matter movement as violent Marxists. In July 2016, Patricia Leary, a professor at Whittier Law School, wrote a searing comeback to a student letter criticizing her decision to wear a Black Lives Matter T-shirt on campus (Jaschik np.). Leary unpicks several premises inherent in the students' political attack on her sartorial choice. Perhaps her most searing rebuttal addresses their implicit assumption that the slogan 'Black Lives Matter' is preceded by a silent 'only':

> There *are* some implicit words that precede 'Black Lives Matter', and they go something like this:

> Because of the brutalizing and killing of black people at the
> hands of the police and the indifference of society in general
> and the criminal justice system in particular, it is important
> that we say that…

This is, of course, far too long to fit on a shirt (Leary np.; emphasis
in original).

Amidst this transition from discussion of the decolonization of
higher education (particularly as regards the curriculum), which is
central to the South African protests, through to the deployment
of the Black Lives Matter movement in universities across the US,
there is a pressing need to consider, more broadly, the university as
a site of struggle. In India, Narendra Modi's Hindutva (or Hindu
Right) Bharatiya Janata Party (BJP) government has taken an
increasingly vicious stance towards artists, intellectuals, dissenters,
and minorities.[1] The murders of activists and intellectuals Govind
Pansare and Professor M. M. Kalburgi in 2015 led to almost three
dozen authors returning government-supported literary awards in
protest at the lack of investigation into these assassinations. There
was a rally in New Delhi on 20 July 2016 as part of a campaign
for an enquiry into the killings, as well as that of writer Narendra
Dabholkar in 2013. The impact of the BJP's stance in education
and the arts has been catastrophic. At the Indian Institute of
Technology in Chennai, a Dalit group—the Ambedkar Periyar
Study Circle—was banned in May 2015. Soon afterwards, the
Film and TV Institute of India had its governing council stuffed
with what Salman Rushdie calls 'Modi's Toadies' (np.). At the
University of Hyderabad in January 2016, a Dalit PhD student,
Rohith Vemula, took his life. Vemula had been stripped of his
stipend as punishment for showing a subversive documentary
and demonstrating against governmental reprisals for the 1993

Mumbai bombings. In his eloquent suicide note, this persecuted man lamented that '[n]ever was a man treated as a mind' (Vajpeyi np.). Facing international outrage, the BJP took pains to avouch that Vemula was no Dalit, and thus his death was not a 'caste issue' but a personal tragedy.

Finally, the BJP targeted Jawaharlal Nehru University (JNU), with its proud tradition of both radical and liberal scholarship. The Toadies first claimed that this university's research and focus amounted to Naxalite communism. Following this initial response, it proceeded to discuss JNU's scholarship as anti-national or even terrorist writing. In February 2016, some JNU students held a meeting to mark the third anniversary of the death penalty meted out to Mohammad Afzal Guru, one of three Kashmiris accused of the 2001 Indian Parliament attacks. For doing so, several of them, including Student Union President Kanhaiya Kumar, were arrested and, in an extraordinary incident, beaten by men dressed as lawyers outside the courtrooms. Priyamvada Gopal and Romila Thapar, inter alia, compare the current situation to Mrs Gandhi's dictatorial mid-1970s Emergency (Gopal; Thapar). Arundhati Roy writes of the BJP's 'instinctive hostility towards intellectual activity' ('Seditious': np.). This anti-intellectualism bears comparison with Donald Trump's idiocies in the United States, and Brexiteer Michael Gove's declaration that British people 'have had enough of experts' (qtd. in Deacon np.). Gopal, Thapar, and Roy are alert to the BJP's habit of flinging around the terms 'anti-national' and 'sedition' to stifle debate. This use of the anti-India charge is reminiscent of 1950s McCarthyism, or the way the Blasphemy Laws are misused to settle vendettas in present-day Pakistan. At the time of writing, crackdowns are continuing on the campuses of JNU and the University of Hyderabad.

This time of tension and uncertainty for universities seems an appropriate moment to reflect on global higher education.

In July 2016, a group of scholars did exactly that in a Northern Postcolonial Network meeting at Leeds Beckett University. There, I was one of the participants in an academic roundtable, alongside co-organizer Emily Marshall (Leeds Beckett), as well as Sarah Lawson Welsh (York St John) and Kate Houlden (Anglia Ruskin). In my presentation, I argued that education needs to decolonize, rather than just diversify. Taking our cue from critical race theory and critical race feminism (Delgado and Stefancic; Bell; Crenshaw; Essed), we need to recognize that racism is not an aberration, but pervades every aspect of society. We are all implicated in it and should be critically self-reflexive, looking to challenge systematic inequality, rather than individualistically seeking to prove that our teaching is somehow 'colour-blind'.

It is imperative to reflect on a discomforting question raised by Lucinda Newns among others—namely, 'why isn't my professor black?' In her article, 'Speaking for Others: Tensions in Post-colonial Studies', Newns claims that English is one of the most 'whitewashed' disciplines in higher education ('Speaking': np.), and that postcolonial literary studies has not accommodated non-white academics in the same way that African American literature has made great strides for US academe. Lamentable statistics have demonstrated the low proportion of Black and Minority Ethnic (BME) academics in British higher education; this was estimated at less than 2 per cent in 2011 to 2012, according to Deborah Gabriel. These statistics hint that the five-decade long rise of, first, Commonwealth literature and then postcolonial studies has done little to alter the ethnic make-up of university research and teaching staff.

In relation to university recruitment, racism and unconscious bias clearly comes into play (Sullivan; Stainback), with many positions being filled by 'people like us'. Relatedly, Frank Tuitt and Fred A. Bonner II argue that even when black scholars make it through the door of universities in the United States, 'an unwelcoming and potentially hostile campus environment awaits those who choose to teach in predominantly white institutions' (1). Nor is the student body much more diverse than the professoriate. In 2007, the Runnymede Trust found that there were more students of Caribbean origin at London Met, where Newns completed her doctoral thesis (*Home*: np.), than in the whole of the Russell Group put together. In 2012, the Runnymede Trust found that Black and Minority Ethnic students comprised 23 per cent of the UK university population in 2008 to 2009, a rise of 10 per cent over fourteen years. Despite this welcome rise, a substantially higher proportion of these BME undergraduates attended less prestigious, financially hard-pressed post-1992 universities than the white population.

In terms of my own approach to convening and teaching postcolonial literature modules (which I was asked to speak about at Leeds Beckett), what informs my decision to choose specific texts and contexts is, first, author diversity: I look for a mix of genders, sexuality, region, religion, ethnic backgrounds, age, and so forth. Second, two key priorities are ensuring coverage of the novel, short story, narrative non-fiction, theatre, poetry, and film, as well as including a range of genres within these categories. There is also a strong element of pragmatism: texts have to be in print and affordable for students from different backgrounds. In relation to knowledge, I would be chary about teaching a text or context I was unfamiliar with or wasn't prepared to research thoroughly in advance.

I also look for treatment of particular topics. To take a single case study, one of the issues I choose to discuss with students is how writing in the digital environment encourages new attitudes to authorship. Nigerian author Chimamanda Ngozi Adichie, for instance, began blogging as the character Ifemelu from her last novel, *Americanah*. In the novel, Ifemelu first joins online chat forums celebrating natural hair, and goes on to write a blog entitled *'Raceteenth or Various Observations About American Blacks (Those Formerly Known as Negroes) by a Non-American Black'* (4; emphasis in original). As her blog becomes increasingly successful, she is invited to participate in 'diversity workshops, or multicultural talks' in the United States (305), where she is expected to shear her cyberspace writing of its radical anti-racist political content. Alongside this fiction, Adichie's blog, *The Small Redemptions of Lagos* (np.), allows her to furnish readers with vignettes about Ifemelu's and Obinze's relationship after they reignite the love affair with which *Americanah* closes. She also discusses topical news items concerning Nigeria, such as the abduction of school girls that led to the #BringBackOurGirls campaign. Read alongside each other, the novel and blog work together to teach students, in a media-rich fashion, about the postcolonial digital humanities (see, for example, Philip, Irani, and Dourish; Risam), and about how cyberspace troubles boundaries between nations, genders, various ethnic groups, and fixed authorial identities (see Chambers and Watkins 'Writing Now': 262).

I feel strongly that postcolonial perspectives should form a central part of degree courses, instead of being taught as a separate literary silo. Mutual, rather than unidirectional, transformation should come out of postcolonial, world, or global literatures. Postcolonial and mainstream literature shouldn't just cosily coexist alongside each other, sharing common themes. Put simply, a sense of change and development to the core of English literature, and not just its 'margins', is paramount.

Gender is also an area of inequality in higher education, particularly when it comes to the sexual harassment of young female students by older male academics. In Britain last June, British–Pakistani feminist theorist Sara Ahmed resigned her professorship at Goldsmiths, University of London, over this thorny issue. Rather than seeing her move as passivity—resigning and therefore being resigned to the status quo—she urged people to view it as 'an act of feminist protest and an act of feminist self-care'. Ahmed claims that sexual misconduct is 'normalized and generalized' (np.), when it is a remarkably widespread and disturbing institutional problem. She inveighs against the silence that envelops sexual harassment in higher education, especially as most cases end with confidentiality clauses. Yet Ahmed argues that speaking out against the issue and building up an archive of evidence are of the utmost importance. Ahmed's position that sexual violence is endemic in academia was fortified by the case of media studies lecturer Lee Salter. He was convicted of beating, stamping on, and throwing salt at his student girlfriend, Allison Smith (Pells np.). Despite this criminal behaviour, his employer, the University of Sussex, did not see fit to suspend him from work until the media storm apparently forced the institution's hand (Le Duc np.).

Over the last year, Turkey has proven to be a flashpoint nation where tensions between government and higher education have erupted. Following a failed coup attempt against President Tayyip Erdoğan in July 2016 (*Telegraph* np.), Turkey entered a three-month state of emergency. In fact, the country is now nearing the end of its third three-month state of emergency. This climate has had a drastic impact on academia. Lecturers and researchers were 'temporar[ily]' prohibited from leaving the country and their annual leave was cancelled (Cockburn np.). Over a thousand university staff members were compelled to resign in the president's initial purge, more were forced out over the ensuing months, and in October 2016, Erdoğan gave himself the power to appoint all of the universities' senior managers (Akyol np.). Many Turks hope that this will be a temporary measure because once the state of emergency period is over, all the decree laws including the one about the appointment of rectors should be null and void. Then again, since Erdoğan (just) managed to get the result he wanted out of the referendum on 16 April 2017, he will be able to issue decree laws all by himself, and that may well mean that this practice will continue.

In 2014, Mushtaq Bilal, author of *Writing Pakistan*, wrote an article for *Dawn* entitled 'Of Doctors and Quacks'. In it, he lambasted Pakistani universities' postgraduate provision, lack of critical thinking, and paucity of genuine research. Fearing reprisals from his university, he published the piece under a pseudonym. Bilal's broader point was that in Pakistani scholarship (and society at large), there is little freedom of expression or thought. Protests such as those described earlier do not even get off the ground in Pakistan. Thinking back to Professor Leary's Black Lives Matter T-shirt controversy, many universities in Pakistan control what is worn by students through dress codes. At Bahria University, for example, male students are prohibited from wearing sandals, and shalwar kameez can be worn only in exceptional circumstances, while women must wear scarves, but only 'light' make-up (Bahria University np.). These rules are not always enforced at Bahria, but there was outcry a few years ago when security staff at the National University of Modern Languages in Islamabad turned away students dressed in chappals and sportswear (Junaidi np.). So much for freedom of expression.

Moving on to discuss freedom of thought and its place in the university environment, as discussed in Chapter 6, 'The Baloch Who Is Missing', a seminar entitled 'Unsilencing Balochistan' was to take place at the Lahore University of Management Sciences (LUMS) in April 2015 (Dawn Staff Reporter np.). According to a senior official, the university was told to cancel the event 'on the orders of the government' (A. Ahmed np.). LUMS complied, and the rearranged seminar took place at Karachi's T2F. Venue owner Sabeen Mahmud was killed soon after this seminar (Shamsie

'Murdered': np.). Relatedly, US-based security studies expert C. Christine Fair writes of a 'nasty war' being waged against herself and other American academics who interrogate Pakistan's army and intelligence agencies ('War': np.). As the author of *Fighting to the End: The Pakistan Army's Way of War*, Fair was attacked by online trolls and smeared in fallacious articles, suffering frightening, graphic threats.

In April 2016, a few, mostly female students at Beaconhouse National University, Lahore, displayed sanitary napkins on walls (Naveed np.). They were inspired to stage this protest by a similar stand taken at Delhi's Jamia Millia Islamia University in 2015 (Jain np.). Seeking, albeit crudely, to challenge the stigma around menstruation, these students faced a social media backlash so vituperative that they were forced offline.

All this is not to suggest that no critical thinking happens on Pakistani university campuses. On the contrary, there are many terrific scholars throughout the country, pockets of research excellence still exist, and Pakistani universities once boasted a strong leftist tradition. However, since Zia ul-Haq's regime, Pakistani higher education institutions, particularly their arts departments, have faced restrictions and a lack of funding, both of which have sadly limited research. In the climate of fear that has worsened in recent years, universities have been 'cleansed' more than ever. As I have discussed in this chapter, the influence of social media as both a positive and negative force in contemporary protests cannot be emphasized enough. Additionally, there is a pressing need to divest universities of racism, casteism, classism, sexism, and other oppressive forces. Education is part of the problem, but it can also spearhead the solution. As Kenyan author Ngũgĩ wa Thiong'o argues, we need to decolonize our minds.

NOTE

1. I would like to thank Tabish Khair, J. Devika, and Githa Hariharan for their suggestions that helped me sharpen this discussion of the current situation in Indian academe.

Bibliography

Abbas, Syed Sammer. 'FO Reveals Details of Eight Indian "Undercover Agents"'. *Dawn.* 3 November 2016. Online. Available at: http://www.dawn.com/news/1294023 (Accessed: 21 December 2016). Web.

Abbas, Tahir. '"Last of the Dinosaurs": *Citizen Khan* as Institutionalisation of Pakistani Stereotypes in British Television Comedy'. *South Asian Popular Culture* 11.1 (2013): 85–90. Print.

Abdelaziz, Sameh. *Sarkhet Namla* (Ant Scream). Perf. Amr Abdel Gelil, Farida Elgready, Rania Youssef. Cairo: Misr Cinema, 2011. Film.

Abdullah, Shaila. *Beyond the Cayenne Wall.* Austin, TX: iUniverse, 2005. Kindle.

Aboulela, Leila. *The Translator.* Oxford: Heinemann Educational, 2001 [1999]. Print.

──────. *Minaret.* London: Bloomsbury, 2005. Print.

Abu-Lughod, Lila. '*Orientalism* and Middle East Feminist Studies'. *Feminist Studies* 27.1 (Spring 2001): 101–13. Print.

──────. 'Do Muslim Women Really Need Saving?: Anthropological Reflections on Cultural Relativism and Its Others'. *American Anthropologist* 104.3 (2002): 783–90. Print.

──────. *Do Muslim Women Need Saving?* Cambridge, MA: Harvard University Press, 2013. Print.

Achebe, Chinua. *There Was a Country: A Personal History of Biafra.* London: Allen Lane, 2012. Print.

Adib-Moghaddam, Arshin. *On the Arab Revolts and the Iranian Revolution: Power and Resistance Today.* London: Bloomsbury, 2013. Print.

Adichie, Chimamanda Ngozi. *Americanah.* London: Fourth Estate, 2013. Print.

————. *The Small Redemptions of Lagos*. Online. Available at: http://americanahblog.com/ (Accessed: 13 July 2016). Web.

Adiga, Aravind. *The White Tiger*. London: Atlantic, 2008. Print.

Afzal-Khan, Fawzia. *A Critical Stage: The Role of Secular Alternative Theatre in Pakistan*. Calcutta: Seagull, 2005. Print.

Ahmad, Aijaz. *In Theory: Classes, Nations, Literatures*. London: Verso, 1992. Print.

Ahmad, Akbar S. *The Thistle and the Drone: How America's War on Terror Became a Global War on Tribal Islam*. Washington, DC: Brookings Institution Press, 2013. Print.

Ahmad, Imran. *Unimagined: A Muslim Boy Meets the West*. London: Aurum, 2007. Print.

Ahmad, Jamil. *The Wandering Falcon*. London: Hamish Hamilton, 2011. Print.

Ahmad, Rukhsana. Ed. and Trans. *We Sinful Women: Contemporary Urdu Feminist Poetry*. London: Women's Press, 1991. Print.

Ahmed, Adeel. 'Outcry on Social Media as LUMS Cancels Talk Featuring Mama Qadeer'. *Dawn*. 9 April 2015. Online. Available at: http://www.dawn.com/news/1174886 (Accessed: 12 January 2017). Web.

Ahmed, Feroze. 'Opening Soon'. In: Ed. Geraldine Edwards. *Origins: Personal Stories of Crossing the Seas to Settle in Britain*. Bristol: Origins, 1998. 104–6. Print.

Ahmed, Sara. 'Speaking Out'. *Feminist Killjoys Blog*. 2 June 2016. Online. Available at: https://feministkilljoys.com/2016/06/02/speaking-out/ (Accessed: 12 January 2017). Web.

Ahmed, Sufiya. *Zahra's First Term at the Khadija Academy*. London: Bibi Publishing, 2007. Print.

————. *Secrets of the Henna Girl*. London: Puffin, 2012. Print.

Akyol, Mustafa. 'Turkish Universities Latest Domino in Erdogan's Path'. *Al-Monitor*. 7 November 2016. Online. Available at: http://www.al-monitor.com/pulse/originals/2016/11/turkey-erdogan-took-full-control-of-universities.html#ixzz4bx5gGna2. Web.

Alam, M. Y. *Annie Potts Is Dead*. Castleford: Springboard, 1998. Print.

————. *Kilo*. Glasshoughton: Route, 2002. Print.

————. *Red Laal*. Pontefract: Route, 2012. Print.

Al-Aswany, Alaa. *The Yacoubian Building*. Trans. H. Davis. London: HarperCollins, 2002. Print.

———. *Chicago*. Trans. Farouk Abdel Wahab. London: Fourth Estate, 2008 [2007]. Print.

———. *On the State of Egypt: What Caused the Revolution*. Trans. Jonathan Wright. Edinburgh: Canongate, 2011. Print.

Al Hasan, Hasan Tariq. '"Arabs Are Not Ready for Democracy": The Orientalist Cravings of Arab Ruling Elites'. *Open Democracy*. 7 May 2012. Online. Available at: https://www.opendemocracy.net/hasan-tariq-al-hasan/%E2%80%98arabs-are-not-ready-for-democracy%E2%80%99-orientalist-cravings-of-arab-ruling-elites. (Accessed: 7 January 2017). Web.

Ali, Agha Shahid. *The Country Without a Post Office*. New York, NY: Norton, 1998 [1997]. Print.

Ali, Ayaan Hirsi. *The Caged Virgin: A Muslim Woman's Cry for Reason*. London: Free Press, 2006. Print.

Ali, Monica. *Brick Lane*. London: Black Swan, 2004 [2003]. Print.

Ali, Tariq. *Night of the Golden Butterfly*. London: Verson, 2010. Print.

———. 'The Story of Kashmir'. In: Tariq Ali, Hilal Bhatt, Angana P. Chatterji, Habbah Khatun, Pankaj Mishra, and Arundhati Roy. *Kashmir: The Case for Freedom*. London: Verso, 2011. 7–56. Print.

Allen, Chris. *Islamophobia*. Farnham: Ashgate, 2010. Print.

Almond, Ian. 'Mullahs, Mystics, Moderates and Moghuls: The Many Islams of Salman Rushdie'. *ELH* 70.4 (2003): 1137–51. Print.

Al-Shami, Leila and Yassin-Kassab, Robin. *Burning Country: Syrians in Revolution and War*. London: Pluto, 2016. Print.

Amis, Martin. *The Second Plane*. London: Jonathan Cape, 2008. Print.

Anam, Tahmima. *A Golden Age*. London: John Murray, 2007. Print.

———. 'Thank You, Mum and Dad. If It Hadn't Been for You, I Might Have Become a Banker'. *Guardian*. 9 October 2008. Online. Available at: https://www.theguardian.com/commentisfree/2008/oct/09/features.comment (Accessed: 5 March 2017). Web.

———. *The Good Muslim*. Edinburgh: Canongate, 2011. Print.

———. *The Bones of Grace*. Edinburgh: Canongate, 2016. Print.

Anand, Mulk Raj. 'Manifesto of the Indian Progressive Writers

Association, London'. In: Sajjad Zaheer. *A Night in London*. Trans. Bilal Hashmi. Noida: Harper Perennial, 2011 [1938]. Print.

Anderson, Benedict. *Imagined Communities: Reflections on the Origin and Spread of Nationalism*. London: Verso, 1983. Print.

Anjaria, J. S. and McFarlane, C. Eds. *Urban Navigations: Politics, Space and the City in South Asia*. Delhi: Routledge, 2011. Print.

Anon Beauty (with Brian Arthur Levine). *Not Easily Washed Away: Memoirs of a Muslim's Daughter*. London: Gully Gods, 2011. Print.

Ansari, Sarah. *Life After Partition: Migration, Community and Strife in Sindh, 1947–1962*. Karachi: Oxford University Press, 2005. Print.

Anwar, Muhammad. *The Myth of Return: Pakistanis in Britain*. London: Heinemann Educational, 1979. Print.

Arabic News Digest. 'Arabs Not Yet Ready for Democracy'. *Arabic News Digest*. 17 April 2013. Online. Available at: http://www.thenational.ae/thenationalconversation/comment/arabs-not-yet-ready-for-democracy (Accessed: 8 June 2015). Web.

Ardeshir, Cowasjee. 'Tigers of Balochistan and Elsewhere – II'. *Dawn*. 6 February 2005. Online. Available at: http://www.dawn.com/news/1072975 (Accessed: 8 June 2015). Web.

Arendt, Hannah. *Eichmann in Jerusalem: A Report on the Banality of Evil*. Intro. Elon, Amos. New York, NY: Penguin Classics, 2006 [1963]. Print.

Arondekar, Anjali. 'Border/Line Sex: Queer Postcolonialities, or How Race Matters Outside the United States'. *Interventions* 7.2 (2005): 236–50. Print.

Ashcroft, Bill, Griffiths, Gareth, and Tiffin, Helen. Eds. *The Empire Writes Back*. 2nd edn. London: Routledge, 2002. Print.

Ashraf, Saad. *The Postmaster*. Delhi: Penguin, 2004. Print.

Asian Human Rights Commission. 'The State of Human Rights in Pakistan in 2010'. Online. Available at: http://idsn.org/wp-content/uploads/user_folder/pdf/New_files/Pakistan/AHRC-Pakistan_HR_2010_Report.pdf (Accessed: 8 January 2017). Web.

Aslam, Nadeem. *Maps for Lost Lovers*. London: Faber and Faber, 2004. Print.

Associated Press. 'India, Pakistan Agree: Emotional Google Ad a Hit,

Strikes a Cultural Chord'. *The Hindu*. 15 November 2013. Online. Available at: http://www.hindustantimes.com/technology/socialmedia-updates/india-pakistan-agree-emotional-google-ad-a-hit-strikes-a-cultural-chord/article1-1151767.aspx (Accessed: 17 November 2013). Web.

Attwell, David. *J. M. Coetzee and the Life of Writing: Face to Face with Time*. Oxford: Oxford University Press, 2015. Print.

Avikunthak, Ashish. *Brihnlala ki Khelkali* or *Dancing Othello*. English language. 18.00. 16 mm. 2002. Film.

Ayaz, Babar. *What's Wrong with Pakistan?* Delhi: Hay House, 2013. Print.

Bachelard, Gaston. *The Poetics of Space*. Trans. Maria Jolas. Foreword by John R. Stilgoe. Boston: Beacon, 1994 [1964].

Bahria University. 'Dress Code'. 24 August 2015. Online. Available at: https://www.bahria.edu.pk/dress-code-for-students/ (Accessed: 12 January 2017). Web.

Baldwin, Shauna Singh. *The Tiger Claw*. Toronto: Vintage Canada, 2005 [2004]. Print.

Bannon, Colin. *The Hindostanee Coffee House (Sake Dean Mahomet Investigates Book 1)*. Uckfield: Silk Press, 2012. Print.

Bano, Sabiha. 'Challawa'. In: Ed. Faiza S. Khan. Trans. Mohammed Hanif. *The Life's Too Short Literary Review: The Magazine of New Writing from Pakistan: 01*. Lahore: Aysha Raja, 2010. 28–32. Print.

Barker, Clare. *Postcolonial Fiction and Disability: Exceptional Children, Metaphor and Materiality*. Basingstoke: Palgrave Macmillan, 2011. Print.

Baruah, Amit. *Dateline Islamabad*. Delhi. Penguin, 2007. Print.

Basu, Shrabani. *Curry in the Crown: The Story of the Nation's Favourite Dish*. Delhi: HarperCollins, 1999. Print.

———. *Spy Princess: The Life of Noor Inayat Khan*. Stroud: History Press, 2008 [2006]. Print.

Baudrillard, Jean. 'Simulacra and Simulations'. Trans. Paul Foss, Paul Patton, and Philip Beitchman. In: Mark Poster. *Jean Baudrillard: Selected Writings*. Cambridge: Polity, 1988. 166–84. Print.

BBC. 'Al-Madinah Free School in Derby to Stop Secondary Education'. *BBC News*. 7 February 2014. Online. Available at: http://www.bbc.

co.uk/news/uk-england-26083099 (Accessed: 12 September 2016). Web.

———. 'Acid Attack Victim Andreas Christopheros Tells of "Very Dark Pain"'. *BBC News*. 1 February 2016. Online. Available at: http://www. bbc.co.uk/news/uk-england-cornwall-35457800 (Accessed: 8 January 2017). Web.

Beaumont, Justin and Baker, Christopher. Eds. *Postsecular Cities: Space, Theory and Practice*. London: Continuum, 2011. Print.

Becker, Wolfgang. *Good Bye Lenin!* Perf. Daniel Brühl, Katrin Saß, Chulpan Khamatova. Berlin: X-Filme Creative Pool, 2003. Film.

Begg, Moazzam and Brittain, Victoria. *Enemy Combatant: The Terrifying True Story of a Briton in Guantánamo*. London: Pocket Books, 2007 [2006].

Bell, Derrick. *Faces at the Bottom of the Well: The Permanence of Racism*. New York, NY: Basic Books, 1992. Print.

Benn, Hilary. 'Hilary Benn Speech in Full: "We Must Now Confront this Evil"'. *Guardian*. 3 December 2015. Online. Available at: https://www. theguardian.com/politics/video/2015/dec/03/hilary-benn-airstrikes-vote-speech-full-must-confront-isis-evil-video (Accessed: 7 January 2017). Web.

Ben-Yishai, Ayelet. 'The Dialectic of Shame: Representation in the MetaNarrative of Salman Rushdie's *Shame*'. *MFS: Modern Fiction Studies* 48.1 (Spring 2002): 194–215. Print.

Bhabha, Homi K. *The Location of Culture*. London: Routledge, 2004 [1994].

Bhagat, Chetan. *One Night @ the Call Centre*. New Delhi: Rupa, 2005. Print.

Bhardwaj, Vishal. Dir. *Maqbool*. Perf. Naseeruddin Shah, Irrfan Khan, Tabu, Pankaj Kapur. Raleigh, NC: Eagle Video, 2003. Film.

———. *Omkara*. Perf. Ajay Devgn, Kareena Kapoor, Saif Ali Khan. London: Eros International, 2006. Film.

———. Dir. *Haider*. Screenplay Basharat Peer. Perf. Shahid Kapoor, Tabu, Shraddha Kapoor. Mumbai: Reliance Big Entertainment, 2014. Film.

Bhatti, Gurpreet Kaur. *Behzti*. London: Oberon, 2012. Print.

Bhutto, Fatima. *Songs of Blood and Sword*. London: Vintage, 2011. Print.

Bilal, Mushtaq. 'Of Doctors and Quacks: Getting a PhD in Pakistan'. [Published under the pseudonym Taimoor B. Khan.] *Dawn.* 21 November 2014. Online. Available at: http://www.dawn.com/ news/1145987 (Accessed: 12 January 2017). Web.

_____. *Writing Pakistan: Conversations on Identity, Nationhood and Fiction.* Noida: HarperCollins, 2016. Print.

Blaise, Clark. "'The Literary Map of India Is About to Be Redrawn ... *Midnight's Children* Sounds Like a Continent Finding its Voice. An Author to Welcome to World Company". *New York Times'.* In: Salman Rushdie, *Midnight's Children.* London: Picador, 1982 [1981]. Blurb.

Blasim, Hassan. *The Madman of Freedom Square.* Trans. Jonathan Wright. Manchester: Comma, 2009. Print.

Boal, Augusto. *Theatre of the Oppressed.* Trans. Charles A. McBride, Maria-Odilia Leal McBride, and Emily Fryer. London: Pluto, 2000 [1974]. Print.

Bostom, Andrew G. 'Is Freedom Perfect Slavery?' *Front Page Magazine.* 3 March 2006. Online. Available at: http://www.frontpagemag.com/ Articles/ReadArticle.asp?ID=21473 (Accessed: 9 January 2017). Web.

Bradley, A. C. *Shakespearean Tragedy: Lectures on Hamlet, Othello, King Lear, Macbeth.* 2nd edn. London: Macmillan, 1905. Print.

Bradley, Arthur and Tate, Andrew. *The New Atheist Novel.* London: Continuum, 2010. Print.

Bradner, Eric and Scott, Eugene. 'Sean Spicer Slams "Nitpicking" of Holocaust Statement'. *CNN Politics.* 31 January 2017. Online. Available at: http://edition.cnn.com/2017/01/30/politics/sean-spicer-holocaust-statement/ (Accessed: 23 February 2017). Web.

Brah, Avtar. *Cartographies of Diaspora: Contesting Identities.* London: Routledge, 1996. Print.

Brannen, Kate. 'Steve Bannon Is Making Sure There's No White House Paper Trail, Says Intel Source'. *Foreign Policy.* 31 January 2017. Online. Available at: http://foreignpolicy.com/2017/01/30/steve-bannon-is-making-sure-theres-no-white-house-paper-trail-trump-president/ (Accessed: 23 February 2017). Web.

Breton, Raymond. 'Institutional Completeness of Ethnic Communities and the Personal Relations of Immigrants'. *American Journal of Sociology* 70.2 (1964): 193–205. Print.

Brittain, Victoria and Slovo, Gillian. *Guantanamo: 'Honor Bound to Defend Freedom'*. London: Oberon, 2004. Print.

Brogan, Benedict. 'Corruption Rife in the Pakistani Community, Says Minister'. *Telegraph*. 22 November 2013. Online. Available at: http:// www.telegraph.co.uk/news/politics/10469448/Corruption-rife-in-the-Pakistani-community-says-minister.html (Accessed: 10 January 2017). Web.

Brooks, David. 'Defending the Coup'. *New York Times*. 4 July 2013. Online. Available at: http://www.nytimes.com/2013/07/05/opinion/brooks-defending-the-coup.html (Accessed: 9 January 2017). Web.

Brotton, Jerry. *This Orient Isle: Elizabethan England and the Islamic World*. London: Allen Lane, 2016. Print.

Brown, Dan. *The Da Vinci Code*. London: Corgi, 2009 [2003]. Print.

Brown, Louise. *The Dancing Girls of Lahore: Selling Love and Saving Dreams in Pakistan's Pleasure District*. New York, NY: Harper Perennial, 2006 [2005]. Print.

Burns, Christine. 'Equality, Diversity and Plain Good Sense for the 21st Century: A Brief History of Equalities Law in the UK'. *Just Plain Sense*. 2 February 2009. Online. Available at: http://blog.plain-sense.co.uk/2009/02/brief-history-of-equalities-law-in-uk.html (Accessed: 9 January 2017). Web.

Bury, Liz. 'Joyce Carol Oates Sparks Twitter Storm Over Egypt Remarks'. *Guardian*. 8 July 2013. Online. Available at: https://www.theguardian.com/books/2013/jul/08/joyce-carol-oates-twitter-egypt-islam (Accessed: 9 January 2017). Web.

Bush, George W. 'President Bush Addresses the Nation'. *Washington Post*. 20 September 2001. Online. Available at: http://www.washingtonpost.com/wp-srv/nation/specials/attacked/transcripts/bushaddress_092001.html (Accessed: 15 April 2014). Web.

Butler, Judith. *Bodies that Matter: On the Discursive Limits of 'Sex'*. New York, NY: Routledge, 1993. Print.

Byman, Daniel L. 'After the Hope of the Arab Spring, the Chill of an Arab Winter'. *Brookings Institution*. 4 December 2011. Online. Available at: https://www.brookings.edu/opinions/after-the-hope-of-the-arab-spring-the-chill-of-an-arab-winter/ (Accessed: 7 January 2017). Web.

Calbi, Maurizio. '*Othello*'s Ghostly Reminders: Trauma and (Post)colonial "Dis-ease": Tayeb Salih's *Season of Migration to the North*'. In: Eds. Richard Fotheringham, Christa Jansohn, and R. S. White. *Shakespeare's World/World Shakespeares: The Selected Proceedings of the International Shakespeare Association World Congress, Brisbane 2006*. Newark, DE: University of Delaware Press, 2008. 342–57. Print.

Carney, Joe Eldridge. '"Being Born a Girl": Toni Morrison's *Desdemona*'. *Borrowers and Lenders: The Journal of Shakespeare and Appropriation* 9.1 (Spring/Summer 2014). Online. Available at: http://www.borrowers.uga.edu/1217/show (Accessed: 14 March 2016). Web.

Cassar, Jon. Dir. *24*. Perf. Kiefer Sutherland, Mary Lynn Rajskub, Carlos Bernard. London: 20th Century Fox Home Entertainment, 2014. TV.

Chadda, Sarwat. *Devil's Kiss*. London: Puffin, 2009. Print.

———. *Dark Goddess*. London: Puffin, 2010. Print.

Chakraborty, Madhurima and al-Wazedi, Umme. Eds. *Postcolonial Urban Outcasts: City Margins in South Asian Literature*. New York, NY: Routledge, 2017. Print.

Chambers, Claire. *British Muslim Fictions: Interviews with Contemporary Writers*. Basingstoke: Palgrave Macmillan, 2011. Print.

———. 'Recent Literary Representations of British Muslims'. In: Eds. Michael Bailey and Guy Redden. *Mediating Faiths: Religion and Socio-Cultural Change in the 21st Century*. Farnham: Ashgate, 2011. 175–88. Print.

———. *Britain Through Muslim Eyes: Literary Representations, 1780–1988*. Basingstoke: Palgrave Macmillan, 2015. Print.

Chambers, Claire and Gilmour, Rachael. 'Editorial'. *Journal of Commonwealth Literature* 51.1 (2016): 3–8. Print.

Chambers, Claire and Huggan, Graham. 'Re-evaluating the Postcolonial City: Production, Reconstruction, Representation. Foreword'. *Interventions* 17.6 (2015): 783–8. Print.

Chambers, Claire and Watkins, Susan. 'Postcolonial Feminism?' *Journal of Commonwealth Literature* 47.3 (2012): 297–301. Print.

———. 'Writing Now'. In: Eds. Mary Eagleton and Emma Parker.

The History of British Women's Writing, Volume 10: 1970–Present.
Basingstoke: Palgrave Macmillan, 2015. 245–65. Print.

Chandra, Vikram. *Sacred Games.* London: Faber and Faber, 2006. Print.

Channel 4 News. "'Acid Attack Was a Hate Crime": London Victim
Speaks Out'. Online. Available at: https://www.youtube.com/
watch?v=9_X6WlSthsY (Accessed: 10 July 2017). Web.

Chatterjee, Upamanyu. 'Othello Sucks'. In: Ed. Ian Jack. *Granta 130:
India: New Stories, Mainly True.* London: Granta, 2015. 169-81. Print.

Chaudhuri, Amit. 'When Krishna Becomes Song'. *Caravan.* 1 October
2011. Online. Available at: http://www.caravanmagazine.in/reviews-
essays/when-krishna-becomes-song?page=0%2C2 (Accessed: 12
September 2016). Web.

———. *Odysseus Abroad.* London: Oneworld, 2015 [2014]. Print.

Chaudhuri, Sukanta. Ed. *Calcutta: The Living City: Volumes 1 and 2.* Delhi:
Oxford University Press, 1990. Print.

Chelkowski, Peter. 'Islam in Modern Drama and Theatre'. *Die Welt des
Islams* 23/24 (1984): 45–69. Print.

Chulov, Martin. 'Isis: The Inside Story'. *Guardian.* 11 December 2014.
Online. Available at: https://www.theguardian.com/world/2014/
dec/11/-sp-isis-the-inside-story (Accessed: 7 January 2017). Web.

Cilano, Cara. *National Identities in Pakistan: The 1971 War in Contemporary
Pakistani Fiction.* London: Routledge, 2011. Print.

———. "Saving Pakistan from Brown Men: Benazir Bhutto as Pakistan's
Last Best Hope for Democracy." In: Eds. Claire Chambers and
Caroline Herbert. *Imagining Muslims in South Asia and the Diaspora:
Secularism, Religion, Representations.* Abingdon: Routledge, 2015.
157–71. Print.

Cixous, Hélène. *White Ink: Interviews on Sex, Text and Politics.* Ed. Susan
Sellers. Stocksfield: Acumen, 2008. Print.

Clements, Ron and Musker, John. *Aladdin.* Perf. Scott Weinger, Robin
Williams, Linda Larkin. Burbank, CA: Disney, 1992. Film.

———. *The Princess and the Frog.* Perf. Anika Noni Rose, Keith David,
Oprah Winfrey. Burbank, CA: Disney, 2009. Film.

Cockburn, Harry. 'Turkey Coup: Erdogan Bans All Academics from
Leaving Country as Government Crackdown Intensifies'. *Independent.*

20 July 2016. Online. Available at: http://www.independent.co.uk/news/world/europe/turkey-coup-erdogan-academics-ban-leaving-country-government-crackdown-latest-a7146591.html (Accessed: 12 January 2017). Web.

Coetzee, J. M. *Waiting for the Barbarians*. New York, NY: Penguin, 1980 [1978]. Print.

——. *Slow Man*. London: Vintage 2006 [2005]. Print.

——. *Diary of a Bad Year*. London: Harvill Secker, 2007. Print.

—— and Attwell, David. *Doubling the Point: Essays and Interviews*. Cambridge, MA: Harvard University Press, 1992. Print.

Cole, Shahin and Cole, Juan. 'Tomgram: Shahin and Juan Cole, The Women's Movement in the Middle East'. *Tomdispatch*. 26 April 2011. Online. Available at: http://www.tomdispatch.com/blog/175384/tomgram%3A_shahin_and_juan_cole,_the_women's_movement_in_the_middle_east_/ (Accessed: 22 December 2016). Web.

Coleridge, Samuel Taylor. *Lectures 1808–1819. Volume 2: On Literature*. Ed. R. A. Foakes. Princeton, NJ: Princeton University Press, 1987. Print.

Conrad, Joseph. *Heart of Darkness*. Ed. and Intro. Owen Knowles. London: Penguin, 2007 [1899]. Print.

Constanzo, Mark A. and Gerrity, Ellen. 'The Effects and Effectiveness of Using Torture as an Interrogation Device: Using Research to Inform the Policy Debate'. *Social Issues and Policy Review* 3.1 (2009): 179–210. Print.

Cook, Robin. 'Robin Cook's Chicken Tikka Masala Speech'. *Guardian*. 19 April 2001. Online. Available at: https://www.theguardian.com/world/2001/apr/19/race.britishidentity (Accessed: 6 March 2017). Web.

Cornershop. 'Hanif Kureishi Scene'. *Elvis Sex-Change*. London: Wiiija, 1993. CD.

Crenshaw, Kimberlé. 'Demarginalizing the Intersection of Race and Sex: A Black Feminist Critique of Antidiscrimination Doctrine, Feminist Theory and Antiracist Politics'. *University of Chicago Legal Forum*. 140 (1989): 139–67. Print.

——. '*Mapping the Margins: Intersectionality*, Identity Politics, and

Violence Against Women of Color'. *Stanford Law Review* 43.6 (1993): 1241–99. Print.

Czernik, Ann. 'York Mosque Counters EDL Protest with Tea, Biscuits and Football'. *Guardian*. 27 May 2013. Online. Available at: http://www.theguardian.com/uk/2013/may/27/york-mosque-protest-tea-biscuits (Accessed: 29 August 2013). Web.

Dabashi, Hamid. *The Arab Spring: The End of Postcolonialism*. London: Zed, 2012. Print.

Daechsel, Markus. *Islamabad and the Politics of International Development in Pakistan*. Cambridge: Cambridge University Press, 2015. Print.

Dahya, Badr. 'The Nature of Pakistani Ethnicity in Industrial Cities in Britain'. In: Ed. Abner Cohen. *Urban Ethnicity*. London: Tavistock, 1974. 77–118. Print.

Dalrymple, William. *City of Djinns: A Year in Delhi*. London: Flamingo, 1994. Print.

Dashti, Naseer. *The Baloch and Balochistan*. Bloomington, IN: Trafford, 2012. Print.

Dathan, Matt. 'Aylan Kurdi: David Cameron Says he Felt "Deeply Moved" by Images of Dead Syrian Boy But Gives No Details of Plans to Take in More Refugees'. *Independent*. 3 September 2015. Online. Available at: http://www.independent.co.uk/news/uk/politics/aylan-kurdi-david-cameron-says-he-felt-deeply-moved-by-images-of-dead-syrian-boy-but-gives-no-10484641.html (Accessed: 12 January 2017). Web.

Dawn. 'CAA Releases Airblue Crash Report'. *Dawn*. 25 April 2012. Online. Available at: http://www.dawn.com/news/713312 (Accessed: 22 December 2016). Web.

Dawn Staff Reporter. 'Lums Students Protest "Academic Censorship"'. *Dawn*. 12 April 2015. Online. Available at: http://www.dawn.com/news/1175025 (Accessed: 12 January 2017). Web.

De Beauvoir, Simone. *The Second Sex*. London: Vintage, 1997 [1949]. Print.

De Certeau, Michel. *The Practice of Everyday Life*. Trans. S. Rendell. Berkeley, CA: University of California Press, 2011 [1980]. Print.

De Windt, Harry. *A Ride to India Across Persia and Baluchistàn*. London: Chapman and Hall, 1891. Print.

Deacon, Michael. 'Michael Gove's Guide to Britain's Greatest Enemy…
The Experts'. *Telegraph*. 10 June 2016. Online. Available at: http://
www.telegraph.co.uk/news/2016/06/10/michael-goves-guide-to-
britains-greatest-enemy-the-experts/ (Accessed: 15 July 2016). Web.

Deb, Siddhartha. *The Beautiful and the Damned: Life in the New India*.
Delhi: Viking, 2011. Print.

Delgado, Richard and Stefancic, Jean. *Critical Race Theory: An Introduction*.
New York, NY: New York University Press, 2001. Print.

Dench, Geoff, Gavron, Kate and Young, Michael. *The New East End:
Kinship, Race and Conflict*. London: Profile, 2006. Print.

Desai, Anita. 'Passion in Lahore'. *New York Review of Books*. 21 December
2000. Online. Available at: http://www.nybooks.com/articles/
archives/2000/dec/21/passion-in-lahore/ (Accessed: 17 November
2013). Web.

Desai, Kiran. *The Inheritance of Loss*. New York, NY: Grove, 2006. Print.

Dirlik, Arif. 'The Postcolonial Aura: Third World Criticism in the Age of
Global Capitalism'. *Critical Inquiry* 20. 2 (Winter 1994): 328–56. Print.

Douglass, Frederick. *Narrative of the Life of Frederick Douglass, an American
Slave*. New York, NY: Dover, 1995 [1845]. Print.

Doyle, Arthur Conan, Sir. *The Hound of the Baskervilles: Another Adventure
of Sherlock Holmes; with, The Adventure of the Speckled Band*. Ed. Francis
O'Gorman. Peterborough: Broadview, 2006. Print.

Dryland, Estelle. 'Faiz Ahmed Faiz and the Rawalpindi Conspiracy Case'.
Journal of South Asian Literature 27.2 (Summer 1992): 175–85. Online.
Available at: http://munirsaami.ca/wp-content/uploads/2014/12/
FAIZ-AHMED-FAIZ-AND-THE-RAWALPINDI
CONSPIRACY-CASE.pdf (Accessed: 28 March 2017). Web.

Dudai, Ron. 'Advocacy with Footnotes: The Human Rights Report as a
Literary Genre'. *Human Rights Quarterly* 28.3 (2006): 783–95. Print.

Dunne, Justin S. *Crisis in Baluchistan: A Historical Analysis of the Baluch
Nationalist Movement in Pakistan*. Monterey, CA: Naval Postgraduate
School Thesis. Kindle.

Dutta, Krishna. *Calcutta: A Cultural and Literary History*. Intro. Anita
Desai. Oxford: Signal, 2008. Print.

Eakin, Hugh. 'A Different Pakistan'. *New York Review of Books*. 12

March 2014. Online. Available at: http://www.nybooks.com/daily/2014/03/12/different-pakistan/ (Accessed: 11 January 2017). Web.

Edwards, David. 'Colbert Warns of Muslim Vampire "Sleeper-in-Coffin Cells"'. *Raw Story*. 29 September 2010. Online. Available at: http://www.rawstory.com/rs/2010/09/29/colbert-warns-muslim-vampires-keep-fear-alive/ (Accessed: 9 January 2017). Web.

Eliot, T. S. 'The Love Song of J. Alfred Prufrock'. In: *Selected Poems*. New York, NY: Houghton Mifflin, 1967 [1930]. 11–16. Print.

Elizabeth I. 'England's Deportation of Africans'. *Afrikan Perspective*. 6 July 2013. Online. Available at: http://afroscar.blogspot.co.uk/2013/07/englands-deportation-of-africans-by.html1 (Accessed: 12 January 2017). Web.

Elkin, Lauren. *Flaneuse: Women Walk the City in Paris, New York, Tokyo, Venice and London*. London: Chatto and Windus, 2016. Print.

Ellick, Adam B. 'No Survivors Reported in Pakistan Plane Crash'. *New York Times*. 28 July 2010. Online. Available at: http://www.nytimes.com/2010/07/29/world/asia/29pstan.html (Accessed: 22 December 2016). Web.

Elon, Amos. 'Introduction: The Excommunication of Hannah Arendt'. In Arendt, Hannah. *Eichmann in Jerusalem: A Report on the Banality of Evil*. New York, NY: Penguin Classics, 2006 [1963]. 13–18. Print.

Emerson, Blake. 'Dialectic of Color-Blindness'. *Philosophy and Social Criticism* 39.7 (2013): 693–716. Print.

Engaged Events. 'Mission Statement'. 2010. Online. Available at: http://new.thebiggive.org.uk/charity/view/6862?search=8a439092-afa1-493b-bd7f-40024b1c78ff (Accessed: 17 February 2012). Web.

English, James F. *The Economy of Prestige: Prizes, Awards, and the Circulation of Cultural Value*. Cambridge, MA: Harvard University Press, 2005. Print.

Erickson, Peter. '"Late' has no Meaning Here": Imagining a Second Chance in Toni Morrison's *Desdemona*'. *Borrowers and Lenders: The Journal of Shakespeare and Appropriation* 8.1 (Spring/Summer 2013). Online. Available at: http://www.borrowers.uga.edu/710/show (Accessed: 14 March 2016). Web.

Erlanger, Steven. 'Marriage by Force Is Addressed in Britain'. *New York Times*. 16 June 2014. Online. Available at: https://www.nytimes.com/2014/06/17/world/europe/britain-forced-marriage-is-now-illegal-in-england-wales-new-law.html?_r=0 (Accessed: 22 December 2016). Web.

Essed, Philomena. *Understanding Everyday Racism: An Interdisciplinary Theory*. London: SAGE, 1991. Print.

Fair, C. Christine. *Fighting to the End: The Pakistan Army's Way of War*. New York, NY: Oxford University Press, 2014. Print.

―――. 'Pakistan's War on Scholars'. *Huffington Post*. 24 February 2016. Online. Available at: http://www.huffingtonpost.com/c-christine-fair/pakistans-war-on-scholars_b_9286542.html (Accessed: 12 January 2017). Web.

Faiz, Faiz Ahmed. *O City of Lights: Faiz Ahmed Faiz, Selected Poetry and Biographical Note*. Ed. Khalid Hasan. Trans. Daud Kamal and Khalid Hasan. Karachi: Oxford University Press, 2006. Print.

Fanon, Frantz. *Black Skin, White Masks*. Trans. Charles Lam Markmann. Foreword Homi Bhabha. London: Pluto, 1986 [1952]. Print.

―――. *A Dying Colonialism*. Trans. Haakon Chevalier. Intro. Adolfo Gilly. New York, NY: Grove, 1965 [1959]. Print.

―――. *Toward the African Revolution: Political Essays*. Trans. Haakon Chevalier. New York, NY: Grove, 1967. Print.

―――. *The Wretched of the Earth*. Trans. Constance Farrington. Preface Jean-Paul Sartre. London: Penguin, 2001 [1961]. Print.

Faqir, Fadia. *Pillars of Salt*. London: Quartet Books, 1996. Print.

―――. *My Name Is Salma*. London: Doubleday, 2007. Print.

Farid, T. 'Wheelchair Users Deprived of Right to Free Movement'. *Daily Times*. 14 January 2012. Online. Available at: http://www.dailytimes.com.pk/default.asp?page=2012\01\14\story_14-1-2012_pg13_3 (Accessed: 17 November 2013). Web.

Farrier, David. *Postcolonial Asylum: Seeking Sanctuary Before the Law*. Liverpool: Liverpool University Press, 2011. Print.

Finn, Peter. 'Detainee Who Gave False Iraq Data Dies in Prison in Libya'. *Washington Post*. 12 May 2009. Online. Available at: http://

www.washingtonpost.com/wp-dyn/content/article/2009/05/11/ AR2009051103412.html (Accessed: 6 January 2017). Web.

Fisher, Michael H. *The First Indian Author in English: Dean Mahomed (1759–1851) in India, Ireland, and England.* Delhi: Oxford University Press, 1996. Print.

Fitzgibbon, Will. 'Algerian Gas Deals Linked to Massive Bribery'. *Panama Papers: How The Elite Hide Their Wealth.* 2016. Online. https:// panamapapers.investigativecenters.org/algeria/. Web.

Flood, Alison. 'Calls for Chinua Achebe Nobel Prize "Obscene", says Wole Soyinka'. *Guardian.* 20 May 2013. Online. Available at: https:// www.theguardian.com/books/2013/may/20/chinua-achebe-nobel- prize-wole-soyinka (Accessed: 10 January 2017). Web.

———. 'Diversity in Children's Books: Colouring in Required'. *Guardian.* 20 March 2014. Online. Available at: https://www.theguardian.com/ books/2014/mar/20/diversity-children-books-colour-young-people (Accessed: 6 January 2017). Web.

Foreign and Commonwealth Office (FCO). 'Foreign Travel Advice: Pakistan'. Online. Available at: https://www.gov.uk/foreign-travel- advice/pakistan (Accessed: 6 January 2017). Web.

Foucault, Michel. *Power/Knowledge: Selected Interviews and Other Writings, 1972–1977.* Ed. Colin Gordon. Trans. Colin Gordon, Leo Marshall, John Mepham, and Kate Soper. Hemel Hempstead: Harvester Wheatsheaf, 1980. Print.

Freedland, Jonathan. 'A Warning to Gove and Johnson: We Won't Forget What You Did'. *Guardian.* 1 July 2016. Online. Available at: https:// www.theguardian.com/commentisfree/2016/jul/01/boris-johnson- and-michael-gove-betrayed-britain-over-brexit (Accessed: 6 March 2016). Web.

Freeman, Alan, Bever, Lindsey, and Hawkins, Derek. 'Suspect in Deadly Canadian Mosque Shooting Charged with Six Counts of Murder'. *Washington Post.* 29 January 2017. Online. Available at: https://www. washingtonpost.com/news/morning-mix/wp/2017/01/29/multiple- people-reported-shot-by-gunmen-at-quebec-city-mosque/?utm_ term=.63314a3c319c (Accessed: 11 April 2017). Web.

Freeman, John. Ed. *Granta 123: Best of Young British Novelists 4*. London: Granta, 2013. Print.

French, Patrick. *The World Is What It Is: The Authorized Biography of V.S. Naipaul*. London: Picador, 2008. Print.

———. 'Last Word: Arab Spring to Islamist Winter'. *The Week*. 20 September 2015. Online. Available at: http://www.theweek.in/columns/Patrick-French/arab-spring-to-islamist-winter.html (Accessed: 10 January 2017). Web.

Gabriel, Deborah. 'Race Equality in Academia: Time to Establish Black Studies in the UK?' *Guardian*. 25 July 2013. Online. Available at: https://www.theguardian.com/higher-education-network/blog/2013/jul/25/race-equality-academia-curriculum (Accessed: 26 July 2016). Web.

Galbraith, Robert. *The Cuckoo's Calling*. London: Sphere, 2013. Print.

Gandhi, M. K. *Hind Swaraj*. Ed. Anthony J. Parents. Cambridge: Cambridge University Press, 1997 [1909]. Print.

Gardner, Robert H. Dir. *Enemy of the Reich: The Noor Inayat Khan Story*. Perf. Helen Mirren, Grace Srinivasan, Joe Isenberg. Arlington, VA: PBS, 2014. Film.

Gatrell, Peter. *Russia's First World War*. Harlow: Pearson, 2005. Print.

Gauhar, Feryal Ali. *No Space for Further Burials*. Delhi: Kali for Women, 2007. Print.

Ghai, Anita. 'Disability and the Millennium Development Goals'. *Journal of Health Management* 11.2 (2009): 279–95. Print.

Ghose, Zulfikar. *Shakespeare's Mortal Knowledge: A Reading of the Tragedies*. Houndsmills: Macmillan, 1993. Print.

Ghosh, Amitav. *The Shadow Lines*. Delhi: Oxford University Press, 1995 [1988]. Print.

———. *In an Antique Land*. London: Granta, 1992. Print.

———. *River of Smoke*. London: John Murray, 2011. Print.

———. 'Festivals and Freedom'. *Amitav Ghosh: Official Website*. 6 February 2012. Online. Available at: http://amitavghosh.com/blog/?p=2361 (Accessed: 11 January 2017). Web.

Gilman, Sander L. *Multiculturalism and the Jews*. New York, NY: Routledge, 2006. 1–22. Print.

Gilmour, Rachael. 'Living Between Languages: The Politics of Translation in Leila Aboulela's Minaret and Xiaolu Guo's A Concise Chinese–English Dictionary for Lovers'. *Journal of Commonwealth Literature* 47.2 (2012): 207–27. Print.

Gilroy, Paul. *After Empire: Melancholia or Convivial Culture*. London: Routledge, 2004. Print.

———. *Race and the Right to Be Human*. Utrecht: Utrecht University, 2009 [Inaugural Lecture]. Online. Available at: https://www.uu.nl/file/25347/download?token=5wgZe-lV (Accessed: 8 January 2017). Web.

Glover, William J. *Making Lahore Modern: Constructing and Imagining a Colonial City*. Karachi: Oxford University Press, 2011 [2007]. Print.

Goodison, Lorna. *From Harvey River: A Memoir of My Mother and Her Island*. New York, NY: Amistad, 2009 [2007]. Print.

Google India. 'The Reunion'. 15 November 2013. Online. Available at: http://www.youtube.com/watch?v=gHGDN9-oFJE (Accessed: 27 November 2013). Web.

Gopal, Priyamvada. 'This Is a Watershed Moment for India. It Must Choose Freedom Over Intolerance'. *Guardian*. 17 February 2016. Online. Available at: https://www.theguardian.com/commentisfree/2016/feb/17/india-kanhaiya-kumar-watershed-freedom-intolerance-bjp-hindu (Accessed: 15 July 2016). Web.

Grabham, Emily. 'Intersectionality: Traumatic Impressions'. In Grabham, Emily, Cooper, Davina, Krishnadas, Jane, and Herman, Didi. Eds. *Intersectionality and Beyond: Law, Power and the Politics of Location*. Abingdon: Routledge–Cavendish, 2009. 183–201. Print.

Gramsci, Antonio. *Selections from the Prison Notebooks*. Ed. and Trans. Quintin Hoare and Geoffrey Nowell-Smith. London: Lawrence and Wishart, 1971. Print.

Green, Andrew. 'Why Western Democracy Can Never Work in the Middle East'. *Telegraph*. 16 August 2014. Online. Available at: http://www.telegraph.co.uk/news/worldnews/middleeast/11037173/Why-Western-democracy-can-never-work-in-the-Middle-East.html (Accessed: 7 January 2017). Web.

Green, Nile. 'The Madrasas of Oxford: Iranian Interactions with the

English Universities in the Early Nineteenth Century'. *Iranian Studies* 44: 6 (2011): 807–29. Print.

Gregory, Derek. *The Colonial Present*. Oxford: Blackwell, 2004. Print.

Grice, Andrew and Morris, Nigel. 'Nigel Farage Sparks Race Row by Insisting Discrimination in the Workplace Should Be Legalised'. *Independent*. 12 March 2015. Online. Available at: http://www. independent.co.uk/news/uk/politics/nigel-farage-sparks-another-race-row-by-calling-for-end-to-out-of-date-legislation-on-discrimination-10102133.html (Accessed: 7 January 2017). Web.

Grover, Vrinda. 'Noor Inayat Khan Memorial Annual Lecture: The Liberté Series. The Struggle for Human Rights in India'. 7 February 2017. London: School of Oriental and African Studies (SOAS). Lecture.

Guarino, Mark. 'Professor Fired for Israel Criticism Urges University of Illinois to Reinstate Him'. *Guardian*. 9 September 2014. Online. Available at: https://www.theguardian.com/education/2014/sep/09/professor-israel-criticism-twitter-university-illinois (Accessed: 10 January 2017). Web.

Guha, Ranajit. 'Preface'. In Guha, Ranajit. Ed. *Subaltern Studies I: Writings on South Asian History and Society*. Delhi: Oxford University Press, 1982: vii–viii. Print.

Gupta, Anil, Pinto, Richard, Ray, Adil, Cary, James, and Isaac, David. *Citizen Khan*. Perf. Adil Ray, Bhavna Limbachia, Abdullah Afzal. London: BBC, 2012. TV.

Gupta, Nilanjana, Mukherjee, Sipra, and Banerjee, Himadri. Eds. *Calcutta Mosaic: Essays and Interviews on the Minority Communities of Calcutta*. Delhi: Anthem, 2009. Print.

Gupta, Sunetra. *Memories of Rain*. London: Phoenix, 1995 [1992]. Print.

Gurnah, Abdulrazak. *By the Sea*. London: Bloomsbury, 2001. Print.

———. *The Last Gift*. London: Bloomsbury, 2011. Print.

Guttman, Anna. *Writing Indians and Jews: Metaphorics of Jewishness in South Asian Literature*. New York, NY: Palgrave Macmillan, 2013. Print.

Habibullah, Shama. 'Foreword'. In: Ed. and Afterword. Aamer Hussein. *Distant Traveller: New and Selected Fiction*. Delhi: Kali/Women Unlimited. 1–17. Print.

Haddad, Bassam, Mikdashi, Maya, Salamy, Susan, Salamy, Suzy, and Shapiro, Adam. Dirs. *About Baghdad*. Perf. Sinan Antoon. New York, NY: InCounter Productions, 2004. Film.

Haddad, Yvonne Yazbeck and Smith, Jane I. Eds. *Muslim Minorities in the West: Visible and Invisible*. Walnut Creek, CA: Altamira, 2002. Print.

Hai, Yasmin. *The Making of Mr Hai's Daughter: Becoming British*. London: Virago, 2008. Print.

Hakim, Abderrezak. 'Burning the Sea: Clandestine Migration Across the Strait of Gibraltar in Francophone Moroccan "Illiterature"'. *Contemporary French and Francophone Studies* 13.4 (2009): 461–9. Print.

Halberstam, Gaby. *Real Lives: Noor Inayat Khan*. London: A. & C. Black, 2013. Print.

Hamid, Mohsin. *Moth Smoke*. London: Granta, 2000. Print.

———. *The Reluctant Fundamentalist*. London: Hamish Hamilton, 2007. Print.

———. *How to Get Filthy Rich in Rising Asia*. New York, NY: Riverhead, 2014 [2013]. Print.

Hamid, Omar Shahid. *The Prisoner*. Delhi: Pan, 2013. Print.

Hanif, Mohammed. *A Case of Exploding Mangoes*. London: Vintage, 2008. Print.

———. 'Pakistan Flood Victims "Have No Concept of Terrorism"'. *BBC Online*. 21 August 2010. Online. Available at: http://news.bbc.co.uk/1/hi/programmes/from_our_own_correspondent/8931886.stm. (Accessed: 23 February 2017). Web.

———. *Our Lady of Alice Bhatti*. London: Jonathan Cape, 2011. Print.

———. *The Baloch Who Is Not Missing and Others Who Are*. Lahore: Human Rights Commission of Pakistan, 2013. Online. Available at: http://www.scribd.com/doc/127280475/The-Baloch-Who-is-Not-Missing-Others-Who-Are-By-Mohammed-Hanif#scribd (Accessed: 7 January 2016). Web.

Hansen, Thomas Blom. *Wages of Violence: Naming and Identity in Postcolonial Bombay*. Princeton, NJ: Princeton University Press, 2001. Print.

Haq, Kaiser. 'Jumping Ship: Three Bangladeshi Diaspora Novels in English'. *Daily Star* (Dhaka). 5 February 2005. Online. Available at: http://archive.thedailystar.net/2005/02/05/d502052102119.htm (Accessed: 17 October 2015). Web.

Harlow, Barbara. 'Sentimental Orientalism: *Season of Migration to the North* and *Othello*'. In: Ed. Mona Takieddine Amyuni. *Tayeb Salih's Season of Migration to the North: A Casebook*. Beirut: American University of Beirut, 1985. 75–9. Print.

———. *Resistance Literature*. New York, NY: Methuen, 1987. Print.

Harper, David Ray. 'Introduction'. In: Noor Inayat Khan. *King Akbar's Daughter: Stories for Everyone*. New Lebanon, NY: Sulūk Press, 2012. xi–xiii. Print.

Harris, Bernard. 'A Portrait of a Moor'. In: Eds. Catherine M. S. Alexander and Stanley Wells. *Shakespeare and Race*. Cambridge: Cambridge University Press, 2000. 23–36. Print.

Harris, John. 'Can a New Bradford Emerge From a Hole in the Ground?' *Guardian*. 2 November 2015. Online. Available at: https://www.theguardian.com/cities/2015/nov/02/can-a-new-bradford-emerge-from-hole-in-the-ground-westfield (Accessed: 11 January 2017). Web.

Hart, Matthew. 'Fatwa: A Love Story'. *Public Books*. 14 February 2013. Online. Available at: http://www.publicbooks.org/briefs/fatwa-a-love-story (Accessed: 9 January 2017). Print.

Hashmi, Shadab Zeest. 'Passing Through Peshawar'. *Kohl and Chalk: Poems*. Madera, CA: Poetic Matrix Press, 2013. 36. Print.

Hassan, Waïl S. *Tayeb Salih: Ideology and the Craft of Fiction*. Syracuse, NY: Syracuse University Press, 2003. Print.

Hauthal, Janine. 'Writing Back or Writing Off?: Europe as "Tribe" and "Traumascape" in Works by Caryl Phillips and Christos Tsiolkas'. *Journal of Postcolonial Writing* 51.2 (2015): 208–19. Print.

Herding, Maruta. *Inventing the Muslim Cool: Islamic Youth Culture in Western Europe*. Bielefeld: Transcript Verlag, 2013. Print.

Highmore, Ben. 'The Taj Mahal in the High Street: The Indian Restaurant as Diasporic Popular Culture in Britain'. *Food, Culture and Society* 12.2 (2009): 173–90. Print.

Hill, Mike. 'The Empire Writes Back...Back: Postcolonial Studies in an Age of Autogenic War'. *Culture, Theory and Critique* 53.1 (2012): 59–82. Print.

Hobbes, Thomas. *The Leviathan*. Ed. Richard Tuck. Cambridge: Cambridge University Press, 1991 [1651]. Print.

Hosagrahar, Jyoti. *Indigenous Modernities: Negotiating Architecture, Urbanism, and Colonialism in Delhi*. Abingdon: Routledge, 2005. Print.

Hosain, Attia. *Phoenix Fled: And Other Stories*. Intro. Anita Desai. London: Virago, 1988 [1953]. Print.

———. *Sunlight on a Broken Column*. London: Chatto and Windus, 1961. Print.

———. 'No New Lands, No New Seas'. In: Ed. and Afterword. Aamer Hussein. *Distant Traveller: New and Selected Fiction*. Delhi: Kali/Women Unlimited. 28–71. Print.

Huggan, Graham. *The Postcolonial Exotic: Marketing the Margins*. London: Routledge, 2001. Print.

Husain, Ed. *The Islamist: Why I Joined Radical Islam in Britain, What I Saw Inside and Why I Left*. London: Penguin, 2007. Print.

Human Rights Watch. 'We Can Torture, Kill, Or Keep You for Years: Enforced Disappearances by Pakistani Security Forces in Balochistan'. 28 July 2011. Online. Available at: http://www.hrw.org/reports/2011/07/25/we-can-torture-kill-or-keep-you-years (Accessed: 8 January 2017). Web.

Huntington, Samuel P. 'The Clash of Civilizations'. *Foreign Affairs* 72.3 (1993): 22–49. Print.

———. *The Clash of Civilizations: And the Remaking of World Order*. London: Free Press, 2002 [1996]. Print.

Huq, Rupa, Abbas, Tahir, and Dudrah, Rajinder. '*Citizen Khan* or Citizen Can't? Dossier on Popular Culture: Introduction'. *South Asian Popular Culture* 11.1 (2013): 75–6. Print.

Husain, Intizar. *Basti*. Trans. Frances W. Pritchett. Intro. Asif Farrukhi. New York, NY: New York Review Books, 2013 [1979]. Print.

Hussain, Zahid. *The Curry Mile*. Manchester: Suitcase, 2006. Print.

Hussein, Aamer. 'Your Children'. In: *Mirror to the Sun*. London: Mantra, 1993. 38–60. Print.

———. 'The Book of Maryam'. In: *Insomnia*. London: Saqi, 2007. 73–9. Print.

Hussein, Abdullah. 'The Journey Back'. In: Ed. and Trans. Muhammad

Umar Memon. *Downfall by Degrees: And Other Stories*. Toronto: Tsar, 1987 [1981]. 128–96. Print.

Hutchings, Mark. Ed. 'Shakespeare and Islam'. *Shakespeare* 4.2 (2008) (Special Issue): 102–80. Print.

Hyder, Qurratulain. *Aag ka darya*. Delhi: Educational Publishing House, 2003 [1959]. Print.

———. *River of Fire*. Delhi: Kali for Women, 1998. Print.

Imtiaz, Saba. *Karachi, You're Killing Me!* London: Vintage, 2014. Print.

Irwin, Robert. *For Lust of Knowing: The Orientalists and their Enemies*. London: Allen Lane, 2006. Print.

Islam, Manzu. *The Mapmakers of Spitalfields*. Leeds: Peepal Tree, 2003 [1997]. Print.

———. *Burrow*. Leeds: Peepal Tree, 2004. Print.

———. *Song of Our Swampland*. Leeds: Peepal Tree, 2010. Print.

I'tesamuddin, Mirza Sheikh. *The Wonders of Vilayet: Being the Memoir, Originally in Persian, of a Visit to France and Britain in 1765*. Trans. Kaiser Haq. Leeds: Peepal Tree, 2001 [1780]. Print.

Jabbar, Naheem. 'Symbology and Subaltern Resistance in Hīra Mandi *Mohalla*'. *Interventions* 13.1 (2011): 95–119. Print.

Jacobs, Jane M. *Edge of Empire: Postcolonialism and the City*. London: Routledge, 1996. Print.

Jahan, Rashid. 'Behind the Veil'. In: Ed. Eunice de Souza. *Purdah: An Anthology*. Delhi: Oxford University Press, 2004 [1932]. 462–74. Print.

Jahangir, Rumeana. 'How Britain got the Hots for Curry'. *BBC Magazine*. 26 November 2009. Online. Available at: http://news.bbc.co.uk/1/hi/magazine/8370054.stm (Accessed: 16 February 2015). Web.

Jain, Mayank. 'Why Are Sanitary Pads with Little Notes Stuck on Trees and Walls of Delhi Colleges?' *Scroll*. 14 March 2015. Online. Available at: http://scroll.in/a/713498 (Accessed: 12 January 2017). Web.

Jalal, Ayesha. *The Struggle for Pakistan: A Muslim Homeland and Global Politics*. Cambridge, MA: Belknap Press of Harvard University Press, 2014. Print.

Jameel, Nabila. 'Peshawar'. In: Ed. Farhana Shaikh. *Happy Birthday to Me: A Collection of Contemporary Asian Writing*. Leicester: Dahlia, 2010. 115. Print.

Jameson, Fredric. 'Postmodernism, Or, the Cultural Logic of Late Capitalism'. *New Left Review* 146 (July–August 1984): 52–92. Print.

————. 'Cognitive Mapping'. In: Eds. Cary Nelson and Lawrence Grossberg. *Marxism and the Interpretation of Culture.* Basingstoke: Macmillan Education, 1988. 347–57. Print.

Janmohamed, Shelina Zahra. *Love in a Headscarf: Muslim Woman Seeks the One.* London: Aurum, 2009. Print.

————. *Generation M: Young Muslims Changing the World.* London: I. B. Tauris, 2016. Print.

Jaschik, Scott. 'The Law Professor who Answered Back'. *Inside Higher Ed.* 12 July 2016. Online. Available at: https://www.insidehighered.com/news/2016/07/12/law-professor-responds-students-who-complained-about-her-black-lives-matter-shirt (Accessed: 12 July 2016). Web.

Jeffery, Patricia. *Frogs in a Well: Indian Women in Purdah.* London: Zed, 1979. Print.

Jinnah, Muhammad Ali. 'An Extract from the Presidential Address of M.A. Jinnah: Lahore, March 1940'. In: Ed. Mushirul Hasan. *India's Partition: Process, Strategy and Mobilization.* Delhi: Oxford University Press, 2001 [1993]. 44–58. Print.

Johnson, Boris. *Seventy-Two Virgins.* London: HarperCollins, 2005. Print.

Johnston, Ian. 'Richard Dawkins on Fairy Tales: "I Think it's Rather Pernicious to Inculcate Into a Child a View of the World which Includes Supernaturalism"'. *Independent.* 5 June 2014. Online. Available at: http://www.independent.co.uk/news/people/professor-richard-dawkins-claims-fairy-tales-are-harmful-to-children-9489287.html (Accessed: 12 September 2016). Web.

Jones, Philip. 'Dawkins New Book Looks at Fairytales'. *Bookseller.* 27 October 2008. Online. Available at: http://www.thebookseller.com/news/dawkins-new-book-looks-fairytales (Accessed: 12 September 2016). Web.

Junaidi, Ikram. 'Formal Dress Code Enforced in Numl'. *Dawn.* 2 October 2012. Online. Available at: http://www.dawn.com/news/753717/formal-dress-code-enforced-in-numl (Accessed: 12 January 2017). Web.

Kar, Ajoy. Dir. *Saptapadi*. Perf. Suchitra Sen, Uttam Kumar, Khitish Acharya. Mumbai: Reliance Big Entertainment, 1961. Film.

Kaul, H. K. Ed. *Historic Delhi: An Anthology*. Delhi: Oxford University Press, 1997. Print.

Kennedy, Dominic. 'Most Common Last Name for Doctors Is Khan'. *Times*. 1 September 2014. Online. Available at: http://www.thetimes. co.uk/tto/health/news/article4192648.ece (Accessed: 16 September 2014). Web.

Kershner, Irvin. Dir. *The Empire Strikes Back*. Perf. Mark Hamill, Harrison Ford, Carrie Fisher. London: 20th Century Fox Home Entertainment, 1980. Film.

Khalifa, Jean and Young, Robert. Eds. Écrits *sur l'aliénation et la liberté: Textes inédits réunis, introduits et présentés par Jean Khalfa et Robert J. C. Young*. Paris: La Découverte, 2016. Print.

Khan, Adib. *Seasonal Adjustments*. St Leonards, NSW: Allen & Unwin, 1994. Print.

Khan, Faraz. 'Two Years on, Still No Justice for Sabeen Mahmud'. *Express Tribune*. 25 April 2017. Online. Available at: https://tribune.com.pk/ story/1392504/two-years-still-no-justice-sabeen-mahmud/ (Accessed: 10 July 2017). Web.

Khan, Hammad. (@HammadKhanFilm) 'Cool Analysis of Islamabad as Seen in Film & Lit. (City was True Protagonist of @SlackistanMovie.) The Novels Sound Brill - esp City of Spies'. 2 January 2017, 07:25. Tweet.

———. Dir. *Slackistan*. Perf. Shahbaz Shigri, Aisha Linnea Akthar, Ali Rehman Khan. New York, NY: FilmBuff, 2010. Film.

Khan, Noor Inayat. *Twenty Jātaka Tales*. Illus. H. Willebeek Le Mair. The Hague: East-West, 1975 [1939]. Print.

Khan, Omar Ali. *Zibakhana* (Hell's Ground). Perf. Kunwar Ali Roshan, Rooshanie Ejaz, Rubya Chaudhry. Islamabad: Bubonic Films, 2007. Film.

Khan, Sophia. *Dear Yasmeen*. London: Periscope, 2016. Kindle.

Khan, Sorayya. *Noor*. Wilmington, NC: Publishing Laboratory, University of North Carolina, 2006 [2004]. Print.

———. *Five Queen's Road*. Delhi: Penguin, 2009. Print.

_____. *City of Spies*. Delhi: Aleph, 2015. Print.

Khan, Uzma Aslam. *Trespassing*. London: Harper Perennial, 2003. Print.

_____. *Thinner Than Skin*. Northampton, MA: Clockroot, 2012. Print.

Khan-Din, Ayub. *East Is East*. London: Royal Court Theatre, 1997. Print.

King, John. 'Rawalpindi & Islamabad'. In: Eds. John King and David St Vincent. *Pakistan: A Travel Survival Kit*. Hawthorn: Lonely Planet, 1993. 215–29. Print.

Kipling, Rudyard. 'The Story of Uriah'. *The Collected Poems of Rudyard Kipling*. Ware: Wordsworth Editions, 1994 [1886]. 10. Print.

_____. 'If –'. *The Collected Poems of Rudyard Kipling*. Ware: Wordsworth Editions, 1994 [1886]. 605. Print.

_____. *Kim*. London: Pan Macmillan, 2016 [1901]. Print.

_____. 'The City of Evil Countenances'. In: Neil Moran. *Kipling and Afghanistan: A Study of the Young Author as Journalist Writing on the Afghan Border Crisis of 1884–1885*. Jefferson, NC: McFarland, 2005. 134–8. Print.

Knott, Kim. 'Cutting Through the Postsecular City: A Spatial Interrogation'. In: Eds. Arie L. Molendijk, Justin Beaumont, and Christoph Jedan. *Exploring the Postsecular: The Religious, the Political and the Urban*. Leiden: Brill, 2010. 19–38. Print.

_____. 'Religion, Space and Place: The Spatial Turn in Research on Religion'. In: Eds. Simon Coleman and Ramon Sarro. *Religion and Society: Advances in Research 1*. New York, NY: Berghahn, 2010. 29–43. Print.

Koul, Sudha. *The Tiger Ladies*. Boston, MA: Beacon, 2002 [2000]. Print.

Kraidy, Marwan M. *The Naked Blogger of Cairo: Creative Insurgency in the Arab World*. Cambridge, MA: Harvard University Press, 2016. Print.

Kristeva, Julia. 'About Chinese Women'. In: Ed. Mary Eagleton. *Feminist Literary Criticism*. London: Routledge, 1991 [1977]. 70–83. Print.

Kunzru, Hari. 'I Run Home with Trump on my Heels and Farage has Moved In'. *Guardian*. 26 June 2016. Online. Available at: https://www.theguardian.com/commentisfree/2016/jun/26/hari-kunzru-eu-referendum-nigel-farage. (Accessed: 10 January 2017). Web.

Kureishi, Hanif. *The Buddha of Suburbia*. London: Faber and Faber, 1990. Print.

————. *The Black Album*. London: Faber and Faber, 1995. Print.

————. *Intimacy*. London: Faber and Faber, 1998. Print.

————. *Collected Screenplays Volume 1: 'My Beautiful Laundrette', 'Sammy and Rosie Get Laid', 'London Kills Me', 'My Son the Fanatic'*. London: Faber and Faber, 2002. Print.

————. *My Ear at His Heart: Reading My Father*. London: Faber and Faber, 2004. Print.

————. *Something to Tell You*. London: Faber and Faber, 2008. Print.

————. 'Mad Old Men: The Writing of *Venus*'. In: *Collected Essays*. London: Faber and Faber, 2011. 259–70. Print.

————. *The Last Word*. London: Faber and Faber, 2014. Print.

Lacan, Jacques. *The Four Fundamental Concepts of Psycho-analysis: The Seminar of Jacques Lacan: Book XI*. Ed. Jacques-Alain Miller. Trans. Alan Sheridan. New York, NY: Norton, 1998 [1981].

Lahiri, Shompa. 'Clandestine Mobilities and Shifting Embodiments: Noor-un-nisa Inayat Khan and the Special Operations Executive, 1940–44'. *Gender & History* 19.2 (August 2007): 305–23. Print.

Lal, P. *Transcreation: Two Essays*. Calcutta: Writer's Workshop, 1972. Print.

————. *Transcreation: Seven Essays on the Art of Transcreation*. Calcutta: Writer's Workshop, 1996. Print.

Lalami, Laila. (@LailaLalami) '@JoyceCarolOates Sexual Assaults and Rape Are Epidemic in the U.S. Military. What Is the Predominant Religion There?' 5 July 2013, 12:12. Tweet.

Lambert-Hurley, Siobhan and Sharma, Sunil. *Atiya's Journeys: A Muslim Woman from Colonial Bombay to Edwardian Britain*. Delhi: Oxford University Press, 2010. Print.

Le Duc, Frank. 'University Lecturer from Brighton Suspended After Being Sentenced for Attacking Student Lover'. *Brighton and Hove News*. 12 August 2016. Online. Available at: http://www.brightonandhovenews. org/2016/08/12/university-lecturer-from-brighton-suspended-after-being-sentenced-for-attacking-student-lover/ (Accessed: 12 January 2017). Web.

Le Tourneur d'Ison, Claudine. *Hira Mandi: A Sensitive Portrayal of Life in Lahore's Notorious Centre of Prostitution*. Trans. P. Jhijaria. Delhi: Roli, 2012. Print.

Leary, Patricia. 'Law Professor's Response to Student Offended by Her Shirt'. *Imgur*. 8 July 2016. Online. Available at: http://imgur.com/user/revcleo (Accessed: 12 July 2016). Web.

Lefebvre, Henri. *The Production of Space*. Trans. D. Nicholson-Smith. Oxford: Blackwell, 1991 [1974]. Print.

Lentin, Alana and Titley, Gavan. *The Crises of Multiculturalism*. London: Zed, 2011. Print.

Lesser, Ian. 'Transatlantic Stakes in Europe's Migration Crisis'. In: Eds. Ian Lesser and Astrid Ziebarth. *The Refugee Crisis: Perspectives from Across Europe and the Atlantic*. Washington, DC: German Marshall Fund of the United States (Foreign and Security Policy Briefs), 2015. 1–2. Print.

Lessing, Doris. *Under My Skin: Volume One of My Autobiography, to 1949*. London: Flamingo, 1995. Print.

———. *Alfred and Emily*. London: Fourth Estate, 2008. Print.

Levinas, Emmanuel. *Otherwise Than Being: Or, Beyond Essence*. Trans. Alphonso Lingis. Pittsburgh, PA: Duquesne University Press, 2006 [1981]. Print.

Lewis, Philip. *Young, British and Muslim*. Foreword Jon Snow. London: Continuum, 2007. Print.

Lieven, Anatol. *Pakistan: A Hard Country*. London: Allen Lane, 2011. Print.

Light, Alison. *Mrs Woolf and the Servants: The Hidden Heart of Domestic Service*. London: Penguin, 2007. Print.

Linklater, Richard. Dir. *Slacker*. Perf. Richard Linklater, Rudy Basquez, Jean Caffeine. Ringwood: In2Film, 2008 [1991]. Film.

Lo, Malinda. 'Perceptions of Diversity in Book Reviews'. *Book Reviews*. 19 February 2015. Online. Available at: http://www.malindalo.com/2015/02/perceptions-of-diversity-in-book-reviews/ (Accessed: 9 January 2017). Web.

Loomba, Ania. *Shakespeare, Race, and Colonialism*. Oxford: Oxford University Press, 2002. Print.

———. 'Local Manufacture Made-in-India Othello Fellows: Issues of Race, Hybridity and Location in Postcolonial Shakespeares'. Eds

Ania Loomba and Martin Orkin. *Postcolonial Shakespeares*. London: Routledge, 1998. 142–63. Print.

Loshitzky, Yosefa. *Screening Strangers: Migration and Diaspora in Contemporary European Cinema*. Bloomington, IN: Indiana University Press, 2010. Print.

MacAskill, Ewen. 'Obama Releases Bush Torture Memos'. *Guardian*. 16 April 2009. Online. Available at: https://www.theguardian.com/world/2009/apr/16/torture-memos-bush-administration (Accessed: 7 January 2017). Web.Macey, David. *Frantz Fanon: A Biography*. London: Verso, 2012. Print.

————. 'Westminster Attacker Acted Alone and Motive May Never Be Known, Say Police'. *Guardian*. 25 March 2017. Online. Available at: http://https://www.theguardian.com/uk-news/2017/mar/25/westminster-attack-khalid-masoon-acted-alone (Accessed: 29 July 2017). Web.

MacMunn, George (Sir). *The Martial Races Of India*. London: Sampson Low, Marston, 1933. Print.

Mahfouz, Sabrina. Ed. *The Things I Would Tell You: British Muslim Women Write*. London: Saqi, 2017. Print.

Mahmood, Asif. 'Sindh Cultural Festival Kicks Off at Moenjodaro'. *Dawn*. 1 February 2014. Online. Available at: http://www.dawn.com/news/1084251 (Accessed: 10 January 2017). Web.

Mahomed, Dean. *Shampooing, Or, The Benefits Resulting from the Use of the Indian Medicated Vapour Bath*. Brighton: William Fleet, 1838 [1822].

Majid, Anouar. *Unveiling Traditions: Postcolonial Islam in a Polycentric World*. Durham, NC: Duke University Press, 2000. Print.

Majumdar, Saikat. *Prose of the World: Modernism and the Banality of Empire*. New York, NY: Columbia University Press, 2013. Print.

Making Britain. 'Noor-un-Nisa Inayat Khan'. *Making Britain Database*. n.d. Online. Available at: http://www.open.ac.uk/researchprojects/makingbritain/content/noor-un-nisa-inayat-khan (Accessed: 23 February 2017). Web.

Malak, Amin. *Muslim Narratives and the Discourse of English*. Albany, NY: State University of New York Press, 2005. Print.

Malgonkar, Manohar. *A Bend in the Ganges*. Delhi: Orient, 1964. Print.

Malik, Ayisha. *Sofia Khan Is Not Obliged*. London: Twenty7, 2016. Print.

Malik, Iftikhar H. *Islam, Nationalism and the West: Issues of Identity in Pakistan*. Basingstoke: Palgrave Macmillan, 1999. Print.

Malkani, Gautam. *Londonstani*. London: Fourth Estate, 2006. Print.

Malnick, Edward. 'Minister Apologises for Pakistani "Corruption" Remarks'. *Telegraph*. 23 November 2013. Online. Available at: http://www.telegraph.co.uk/news/politics/10470450/Minister-apologises-for-Pakistani-corruption-remarks.html (Accessed: 10 January 2017). Web.

Manzoor, Sarfraz. *Greetings from Bury Park: Race, Religion, Rock 'n' Roll*. London: Bloomsbury, 2007. Print.

Markandaya, Kamala. 'One Pair of Eyes: Some Random Reflections'. In: Ed. Alastair Niven. *The Commonwealth Writer Overseas: Themes of Exile and Expatriation*. Brussels: M. Didier, 1976. 23–32. Print.

———. *Pleasure City*. London: Chatto and Windus, 1982. Print.

Marsh, Sarah. 'Surge in Acid Attacks in England Leads to Calls to Restrict Sales'. *Guardian*. 7 July 2017. Online. Available at: https://www.theguardian.com/uk-news/2017/jul/07/surge-in-acid-attacks-in-england-leads-to-calls-to-restrict-sales (Accessed: 10 July 2017). Web.

Mason, Rowena. 'Farage: NHS Should Not Hire Doctors Who "Don't Speak Very Good English"'. *Guardian*. 4 January 2015. Online. Available at: https://www.theguardian.com/politics/2015/jan/04/nigel-farage-nhs-doctors-poor-english (Accessed: 8 January 2017). Web.

Massad, Joseph A. *The Persistence of the Palestinian Question: Essays on Zionism and the Palestinians*. Abingdon: Routledge, 2006. Print.

———. *Desiring Arabs*. Chicago, IL: Chicago University Press, 2007. Print.

Master, Irfan. *A Beautiful Lie*. London: Bloomsbury, 2011. Print.

Matar, Hisham. *In the Country of Men*. New York, NY: Dial Press, 2008 [2006]. Print.

———. *Anatomy of a Disappearance*. London: Viking, 2011. Print.

———. *The Return: Fathers, Sons and the Land In Between*. London: Viking, 2016. Print.

———. Speaking on Riz Khan. 'The Political Power of Literature'. *Al-Jazeera*. 23 February 2011. Online. Available at: http://english.

aljazeera.net/programmes/rizkhan/2011/02/201122374815992508.
html (Accessed: 9 March 2011). Web.

Matthews, David J., Shackle, Christopher, and Husain, Shahrukh. *Urdu Literature*. Islamabad: Alhamra, 2003. Print.

Mayer, Ann Elizabeth. *Islam and Human Rights: Tradition and Politics*. Boulder, CO: Westview, 1995 [1991].

Mbembe, Achille. 'Necropolitics'. Trans. Libby Meintjes. *Public Culture*. 15.1 (2003): 11–40. Print.

McEwan, Ian. *Saturday*. London: Jonathan Cape, 2005. Print.

Meer, Nasar and Modood, Tariq. 'The Racialisation of Muslims'. In: Eds. S. Sayyid and Abdoolkarim Vakil. *Thinking Through Islamophobia: Global Perspectives*. London: Hurst, 2011. 69–84. Print.

Meerza, Najaf Koolee. *Journal of a Residence in England and of a Journey From and to Syria By Their Royal Highnesses Reeza Koolee Meerza, Nejaf Koolee Meerza and Taymoor Meerza: Volume 1*. Trans. Assad Y. Kayat. Farnborough: Gregg International, 1971 [n.d.]. Print.

————. *Journal of a Residence in England and of a Journey From and to Syria By Their Royal Highnesses Reeza Koolee Meerza, Nejaf Koolee Meerza and Taymoor Meerza: Volume 2*. Trans. Assad Y. Kayat. Farnborough: Gregg International, [n.d.]. Print.

Mehmood, Tariq. *You're Not Proper*. London: Hope Road, 2015. Print.

————. *Song of Gulzarina*. Montreal: Daraja, 2016. Print.

Mehta, Suketu. *Maximum City: Bombay Lost and Found*. London: Headline Review, 2005. Print.

Milton, John. 'Theorising *Omkara*'. In: Ed. Katja Krebs. *Translation and Adaptation in Theatre and Film*. Abingdon: Routledge, 2004. 83–98. Print.

Mirza, Faiza. 'Acid-Attack Survivor Sues Sharmeen Obaid, Filmmaker Refutes Claims'. *Dawn*. 28 June 2012. Online. Available at: http://www.dawn.com/news/730208. (Accessed: 8 January 2017). Web.

Mirza, Maryam. *Intimate Class Acts: Friendship and Desire in Indian and Pakistani Women's Fiction*. New Delhi: Oxford University Press, 2016. Print.

Mishra, Pankaj. *Age of Anger: A History of the Present*. London: Allen Lane, 2017. Print.

Mitford, Bertram. *The Ruby Sword: A Romance of Baluchistan*. London: F. V. White, 1899. Print.

Mohanty, Chandra Talpade. 'Under Western Eyes: Feminist Scholarship and Colonial Discourses'. *boundary 2* 12/13 (1984): 333–58. Print.

———. 'Cartographies of Struggle: Third World Women and the Politics of Feminism'. In: Eds. Chandra Talpade Mohanty, Ann Russo, and Lourdes Torres. *Third World Women and the Politics of Feminism*. Bloomington, IN: Indiana University Press, 1991. 1-47. Print.

Mohsin, Moni. *The End of Innocence*. London: Penguin, 2007. Print.

———. *Duty Free*. London: Vintage, 2012. Print.

Moore-Gilbert, Bart. *Hanif Kureishi*. Manchester: Manchester University Press, 2001. Print.

Moran, Neil K. *Kipling and Afghanistan: A Study of the Young Author as Journalist Writing on the Afghan Border Crisis of 1884–1885*. Jefferson, NC: McFarland, 2005. Print.

Morris, Chris. Dir. *Four Lions*. Perf. Will Adamsdale, Riz Ahmed, Adeel Akhtar. Sheffield: Warp, 2010. Film.

Morris, Chris, Armstrong, Jesse, and Bain, Sam. *Four Lions: Script*. Online. Available at: https://eoicinecadiz2011.wikispaces.com/file/view/Four+Lionsscript.pdf (Accessed: 10 January 2017). Web.

Morrison, Toni. *Playing in the Dark: Whiteness and the Literary Imagination*. Cambridge, MA: Harvard University Press, 1992. Print.

———. *Sula*. London: Chatto and Windus, 1993. Print.

———. *Desdemona*. Lyrics Rokia Traoré. Foreword Peter Sellars. London: Oberon Modern Plays, 2012. Print.

Moseley, Paul. Dir. *Asian Kool*. Perf. Chris Bisson. Seattle, WA: Reel World, 2000. Print.

Mueenuddin, Daniyal. *In Other Rooms, Other Wonders*. London: Bloomsbury, 2010 [2009]. Print.

Mukherjee, Bharati. *The Tiger's Daughter*. London: Chatto and Windus, 1973 [1971]. Print.

Mukherjee, Neel. *A Life Apart*. London: Constable and Robinson, 2010 [2008]. Print.

———. *The Lives of Others*. London: Vintage, 2015 [2014]. Print.

———. '*Odysseus Abroad* by Amit Chaudhuri Review'. *Guardian*.

7 February 2015. Online. Available at: http://www.theguardian. com/books/2015/feb/07/odysseus-abroad-amit-chaudhuri-review-audaciously-redraws-modernist-map (Accessed: 17 October 2015). Web.

Mumtaz, Hajrah. 'Theatre for Change'. *Dawn*. 26 July 2009. Online. Available at: http://www.dawn.com/news/923580 (Accessed: 19 November 2016). Web.

Munro, Alice. *The View From Castle Rock*. London: Vintage, 2007 [2006]. Print.

Murad, Abdal Hakim. 'British Muslim Heritage. Marmaduke Pickthall: A Brief Biography'. n.d. Online. Available at: www.masud.co.uk/ISLAM/ bmh/BMM-AHM-pickthall_bio.htm (Accessed: 4 November 2014). Web.

N.A. 'Oona King Denounces Intimidation'. *BBC News Channel*. 11 May 2005. Online. Available at: http://news.bbc.co.uk/1/hi/uk_politics/4535885.stm (Accessed: 17 October 2015). Web.

Nadeem, Shahid. '*Dukhini*/Woman of Sorrow'. In: *Selected Plays*. Trans. Tahira Naqvi, Khalid Hasan, Shahid Nadeem, and Naila Azad. Intro. Shaista Sonnu Sirajuddin. Karachi: Oxford University Press, 2008. 188–223. Print.

Naipaul, V. S. *A House for Mr Biswas*. London: Deutsch, 1967. Print.

———. *The Mimic Men*. London: Deutsch, 1967. Print.

———. *The Enigma of Arrival*. London: Picador, 2011 [1987]. Print.

Nair, Jayaraaj Rajasekharan. Dir. *Kaliyattam*. Perf. Suresh Gopi, Lal, Manju Warrier. Delhi: Moser Baer, 1997. Film.

Nakoula, Nakoula Basseley. *The Innocence of Muslims*. 2012. Available at: https://www.youtube.com/watch?v=nGsFHAO0pMA&bpc tr=1483900295 (Accessed: 6 February 2017). YouTube.

Naqvi, H. M. *Home Boy*. New York, NY: Crown, 2010. Print.

Naveed, Babar. 'Here's Why Students at Lahore's BNU Covered Campus Walls with Sanitary Pads'. *Express Tribune*. 12 April 2016. Online. Available at: http://tribune.com.pk/story/1083272/heres-why-students-at-lahores-bnu-covered-campus-walls-with-sanitary-pads/ (Accessed: 12 January 2017). Web.

Netton, Ian Richard. *Seek Knowledge: Thought and Travel in the House of Islam*. Abingdon: RoutledgeCurzon, 1996. Print.

Newns, Lucinda. *At Home in the Metropole: Gender and Domesticity in Contemporary Migration Fiction*. London: London Metropolitan University Doctoral Thesis, 2014. Online. Available at: http://repository.londonmet.ac.uk/698/1/Lucinda%20Newns%20-%20Thesis.pdf (Accessed: 12 July 2016). Web.

———. 'Speaking for Others: Tensions in Post-colonial Studies'. *Times Higher Education*. July 2014. Online. Available at: https://www.timeshighereducation.com/comment/opinion/speaking-for-others-tensions-in-post-colonial-studies/2014501.article (Accessed: 12 July 2016). Web.

Ngũgĩ wa Thiong'o. *Decolonising the Mind: The Politics of Language in African Literature*. London: James Currey, 1986. Print.

Niven, Alistair and Lisa Appignanesi. 'Full Text of the Authors' Letter'. *Guardian*. 13 January 2005. Online. Available at: https://www.theguardian.com/politics/2005/jan/13/immigrationpolicy.politicsandthearts (Accessed: 8 January 2017). Web.

Obaid-Chinoy, Sharmeen and Junge, Daniel. Dirs. *Saving Face*. Perf. Mohammad Jawad. New York, NY: HBO, 2012. Film.

O'Donnell, Damien. Dir. *East Is East*. Perf. Om Puri, Linda Bassett, Jordan Routledge. London: FilmFour, 1999. Film.

Office for National Statistics. '2011 Census: Aggregate Data (England and Wales)' [computer file]. UK Data Service Census Support. 2011. Online. Available at: http://infuse.mimas.ac.uk (Accessed: 9 January 2017). Web.

Olivier, Laurence. *Confessions of an Actor: An Autobiography*. New York, NY: Penguin, 1982. Print.

Omaar, Rageh. *Only Half of Me: British and Muslim: The Conflict Within*. London: Penguin, 2007 [2006]. Print.

Ondaatje, Michael. *Anil's Ghost*. London: Bloomsbury, 2000. Print.

Orton, Peter. Dir. *Jerry Springer: The Opera*. Perf. David Soul, David Bedella, Leon Craig. London: Avalon, 2005. TV.

Orwell, George. *Nineteen Eighty-Four*. Intro. Thomas Pynchon. London: Penguin, 2003 [1948]. Print.

Owens, Eric. 'British Taxpayer-Funded Muslim School Bans Fairy Tales, Requires Hijabs for Females'. *Daily Caller*. 23 September 2013. Online. Available at: http://dailycaller.com/2013/09/23/british-taxpayer-funded-muslim-school-bans-fairy-tales-requires-hijabs-for-females/ (Accessed: 12 September 2016). Web.

Pamment, Claire. *Comic Performance in Pakistan: The Bhānd*. London: Palgrave Macmillan, 2017. Print.

Pamuk, Orhan. 'Nobel Lecture: My Father's Suitcase'. 7 December 2006. Online. Available at: https://www.nobelprize.org/nobel_prizes/literature/laureates/2006/pamuk-lecture_en.html (Accessed: 20 March 2017). Web.

Pandey, Gyanendra. *Remembering Partition: Violence, Nationalism, and History in India*. Cambridge: Cambridge University Press, 2001. Print.

PapoNika. 'FULL: President Donald Trump Black History Month Meeting 02-01-2017'. 1 February 2017. Online. Available at: https://www.youtube.com/watch?v=TSf_k2FmMUI (Accessed: 23 February 2017). Web.

Parveen, Nazia and Sherwood, Harriet. 'Police Report Fivefold Increase in Race-Hate Complaints Since Brexit Result'. *Guardian*. 30 June 2016. Online. Available at: https://www.theguardian.com/world/2016/jun/30/police-report-fivefold-increase-race-hate-crimes-since-brexit-result (Accessed: 11 April 2017). Web.

Pasha, Lakht, and the Punjab Lok Rehas Collective. *Saar*. n.d. Unpublished play script. Theatre.

Patel, Sujata and Thorner, Alice. Eds. *Bombay: Mosaic of Modern Culture*. Bombay: Oxford University Press, 1995. Print.

Peck, Tom. 'Arab Spring Refugees Not Welcome Here, Says William Hague'. *Independent*. 22 May 2011. Online. Available at: http://www.independent.co.uk/news/uk/politics/arab-spring-refugees-not-welcome-here-says-william-hague-2287795.html (Accessed: 12 January 2017). Web.

Peek, Sitala. 'Brick Lane: Gentrification Threat to Spitalfields Bangladeshi Community'. *BBC News*. 24 May 2015. Online. Available at: http://www.bbc.co.uk/news/uk-england-london-32707564 (Accessed: 17 October 2015). Web.

Peer, Basharat. *Curfewed Night: A Frontline Memoir of Life, Love and War in Kashmir*. London: Harper, 2010. Print.

_____. 'Kashmir's Forever War'. In: Ed. John Freeman. *Granta 112: Pakistan*. London: Granta, 2010. 69–87. Print.

_____. 'The Wandering Falcon by Jamil Ahmad: Review'. *Guardian*. 25 June 2011. Online. Available at: https://www.theguardian.com/books/2011/jun/25/wandering-falcon-jamil-ahmad-review (Accessed: 25 January 2017). Web.

Pells, Rachel. 'Sussex University Let Senior Lecturer Continue Teaching After he Beat Up Student Girlfriend'. *Independent*. 12 August 2016. Online. Available at: http://www.independent.co.uk/news/uk/home-news/sussex-university-lecturer-student-girlfriend-criminal-conviction-beat-up-assault-lee-salter-a7183391.html (Accessed: 12 January 2017). Web.

Petersen, Kirsten Holst and Rutherford, Anna. *A Double Colonization: Colonial and Post-colonial Women's Writing*. Sydney: Dangaroo, 1986. Print.

Philip, Kavita, Irani, Lilly, and Dourish, Paul. 'Postcolonial Computing: A Tactical Survey'. *Science, Technology, Human Values* 37.1 (2012): 3–29. Print.

Phillips, Maha Khan. *Beautiful from this Angle*. Delhi: Penguin, 2010. Print.

_____. 'La Femme Pakistanaise Victime de l'Islam, un Discours qui se Vend Bien'. *Libération*. 13 September 2012. Online. Available at: http://www.liberation.fr/planete/2012/09/13/la-femme-pakistanaise-victime-de-l-islam-un-discours-qui-se-vend-bien_846137 (Accessed: 8 January 2017). Web.

Phillips, Trevor. *Things We Won't Say About Race That Are True*. London: Channel 4, 19 March 2015. Online. Available at: http://www.channel4.com/programmes/things-we-wont-say-about-race-that-are-true (Accessed: 9 January 2017). Web.

Phillips, Trevor and Phillips, Mike. *Windrush: The Irresistible Rise of Multi-Racial Britain*. London: HarperCollins, 1998. Print.

Pickthall, (Muhammad) Marmaduke. *All Fools*. London: Forgotten Books, 2013 [1900]. Print.

————. *Saïd the Fisherman*. Intro. Peter Clark. London: Quartet, 1986 [1903]. Print.

————. 'Karàkter'. In: *Pot Au Feu*. London: John Murray, 1911. 289–304. Print.

————. 'Between Ourselves'. In: *As Others See Us*. London: W. Collins, 1922. 49–70. Print.

————. *The Meaning of the Glorious Qur'an: An Explanatory Translation*. Birmingham: Islamic Dawah Centre International, 2004 [1930]. Print.

Piper, Katie. *Beautiful Ever After*. London: Quercus, 2014. Print.

Pirandello, Luigi. *Six Characters in Search of an Author*. Trans. Frederick May. London: Heinemann, 1954. Print.

Plum, Hilary. 'Interview with Sinan Antoon: Literature and Uprising'. *Kenyon Review*. 24 May 2011. Online. Available at: http://www.kenyonreview.org/2011/05/interview-with-sinan-antoon-literature-and-uprising/ (Accessed: 7 January 2017). Web.

Pope, Alexander. *The Rape of the Lock*. Ed. Geoffrey Tillotson. London: Routledge, 1989 [1712]. Print.

Porter, Dennis. '*Orientalism* and its Problems'. In: Eds. Francis Barker, Peter Hulme, Margaret Iversen, and Diana Loxley. *The Politics of Theory*. Colchester: University of Essex, 1983. 179–93. Print.

Powell, Enoch. 'Enoch Powell's "Rivers of Blood" Speech'. *Telegraph*. 6 November 2007 [1968]. Online. Available at: http://www.telegraph.co.uk/comment/3643823/Enoch-Powells-Rivers-of-Blood-speech.html (Accessed: 21 March 2017). Web.

Prakash, Gyan. Ed. *Noir Urbanisms: Dystopic Images of the Modern City*. Princeton, NJ: Princeton University Press, 2010. Print.

Prakash, Vikramaditya. *Chandigarh's Le Corbusier: The Struggle for Modernity in Postcolonial India*. Seattle, WA: University of Washington Press, 2002. Print.

Puar, Jasbir K. *Terrorist Assemblages: Homonationalism in Queer Times*. Durham, NC: Duke University Press, 2007. Print.

Rae, Paul. *Theatre and Human Rights*. Foreword Rabih Mroué. Basingstoke: Palgrave Macmillan, 2009. Print.

Rahim, Masuma. 'Acid Attacks Aren't Just a "Minority" Story. The Media Must Reflect Us All' *Guardian*. 4 July 20157. Online. Available at:

https://www.theguardian.com/commentisfree/2017/jul/04/acid-attacks-minority-media-east-london (Accessed: 10 July 2017). Web.

Rahman, Zia Haider. *In the Light of What We Know*. London: Picador, 2014. Print.

Raina, Arjun. *The Magic Hour*. Delhi: Black Bakkhai Collective, 2000. Film.

Raju, Saraswati. Ed. *Gendered Geographies: Space and Place in South Asia*. Delhi: Oxford University Press, 2011. Print.

Razzaque, Russell. *Human Being to Human Bomb: Inside the Mind of a Terrorist*. Cambridge: Icon, 2008. Print.

Rennam, Srinathreddy. 'What Do the Lyrics of this Indian Song Mean?' *Quora*. 16 May 2016. Online. Available at: https://www.quora.com/What-do-the-lyrics-of-this-Indian-song-mean (Accessed: 3 March 2016). Web.

Reuters. 'Pakistan Lifts Ban on YouTube After Launch of Local Version'. *Reuters News Agency*. 19 January 2016. Online. Available at: http://www.reuters.com/article/us-pakistan-youtube-idUSKCN0UW1ER (Accessed: 8 January 2017). Web.

Riaz, Fahmida. 'The Daughters of Aai'. In: Ed. Muneeza Shamsie. *And the World Changed: Contemporary Stories by Pakistani Women*. Delhi: Kali for Women. 32–8. Print.

Risam, Roopika. 'Beyond the Margins: Intersectionality and the Digital Humanities'. *Digital Humanities Quarterly* 9.2 (2015): np. Online. Available at: http://www.digitalhumanities.org/dhq/vol/9/2/000208/000208.html (Accessed: 13 July 2016). Web.

Rowling, J. K. *Harry Potter and the Philosopher's Stone*. London: Bloomsbury, 1997. Print.

Roy, Arundhati. *The God of Small Things*. London: Flamingo, 1997. Print.

———. *Capitalism: A Ghost Story*. Chicago, IL: Haymarket, 2014. Print.

———. 'My Seditious Heart: An Unfinished Diary of Nowadays'. *Caravan*. 1 May 2016. Online. Available at: http://www.caravanmagazine.in/essay/seditious-heart-arundhati-roy (Accessed: 15 July 2016). Web.Rumi, Raza. *Delhi by Heart: Impressions of a Pakistani Traveller*. Delhi: HarperCollins, 2013. Print.

Runnymede Trust. *Islamophobia: A Challenge for Us All*. London: Runnymede, 1997. Print.

————. *Not Enough Understanding: Student Experiences of Diversity in UK Universities*. London: Runnymede Trust, 2007. Online. Available at: http://www.runnymedetrust.org/uploads/publications/pdfs/ NotEnoughUnderstanding-2007.pdf (Accessed: 12 July 2016). Web.

————. *Briefing on Ethnicity and Educational Attainment*. London: Runnymede Trust, 2012. Online. Available at: http://www. runnymedetrust.org/uploads/Parliamentary%20briefings/ EducationWHdebateJune2012.pdf (Accessed: 12 July 2016). Web.

Rushdie, Salman. *Midnight's Children*. London: Picador, 1982 [1981]. Print.

————. 'The Prophet's Hair'. In: *East, West*. London: Vintage, 1995 [1981]. 33–58. Print.

————. 'The Empire Writes Back With a Vengeance'. *Times*. 3 July 1982. 8. Print.

————. *Shame*. London: Picador, 1983. Print.

————. *The Satanic Verses*. London: Viking, 1988. Print.

————. 'V. S. Naipaul'. In: *Imaginary Homelands: Essays and Criticism, 1981–1991*. London: Granta, 1991. 148–51. Print.

————. 'The Attacks on America'. In: *Step Across This Line*. London: Vintage, 2003 [2002]. 391–3. Print.

————. *Shalimar the Clown*. London: Vintage, 2006. Print.

————. *Joseph Anton: A Memoir*. London: Jonathan Cape, 2012. Print.

————. On 'Modi's Toadies'. *Outlook India*. 6 May 2014. Online. Available at: http://www.outlookindia.com/blog/story/salman-rushdie-on-modis-toadies/3262 (Accessed: 15 July 2016). Web.

Rushe, Dominic, MacAskill, Ewen, Cobain, Ian, Yuhas, Alan, and Laughland, Oliver. 'Rectal Rehydration and Waterboarding: The CIA Torture Report's Grisliest Findings'. *Guardian*. 11 December 2014. Online. Available at: https://www.theguardian.com/us-news/2014/ dec/09/cia-torture-report-worst-findings-waterboard-rectal (Accessed 28 March 2017). Web.

Sachedina, Abdulaziz. *Islam and the Challenge of Human Rights*. Oxford: Oxford University Press, 2009. Print.

Saeed, Fouzia. *Taboo!: The Hidden Culture of a Red Light Area*. Foreword I. A. Rahman. Karachi: Oxford University Press, 2002. Print.

Sahota, Sunjeev. *Ours Are The Streets*. London: Picador, 2011. Print.

Said, Edward W. *Orientalism: Western Conceptions of the Orient*. Harmondsworth: Penguin, 1995 [1978]. Print.

———. *Covering Islam: How the Media and the Experts Determine How We See the Rest of the World*. London: Vintage, 1997 [1981]. Print.

———. *The World, The Text, and the Critic*. London: Faber and Faber, 1984 [1983]. Print.

———. 'Orientalism Reconsidered'. *Race and Class* 27 (October 1985): 1–15. Print.

Salih, Tayeb. *Season of Migration to the North*. Trans. Denys Johnson-Davies. 3rd edn. Oxford: Heinemann Educational, 1991. Print.

Salvation Army. 'South African Salvation Army Advertising Campaign Becomes Worldwide Phenomenon'. 6 March 2015. Online. Available at: http://www.salvationarmy.org/ihq/news/inf060315 (Accessed: 10 July 2017). Web.

Salvatori-Sinz, Axel. Dir. *Shebabs of Yarmouk*. Lussas: Adalios, 2013. Film.

Sánchez-Arce, Ana Maria. 'Performing Innocence: Violence and the Nation in Ian McEwan's *Saturday* and Sunjeev Sahota's *Ours Are the Streets'*. *Journal of Commonwealth Literature* 53.2 (June 2018). Forthcoming.

Sandhu, Sukhdev. 'Come Hungry, Leave Edgy'. *London Review of Books* 25.19 (9 October 2003): 10–13. Online. Available at: https://www.lrb.co.uk/v25/n19/sukhdev-sandhu/come-hungry-leave-edgy (Accessed: 28 March 2017). Web.

———. *London Calling: How Black and Asian Writers Imagined a City*. London: HarperCollins, 2003. Print.

Santesso, Esra Mirze. *Disorientation: Muslim Identity in Contemporary Anglophone Literature*. Basingstoke: Palgrave Macmillan, 2013. Print.

Sardar, Ziauddin. '*Welcome to Postnormal Times'*. *Futures* 42.5 (2010): 435–44. Print.

Sartre, Jean-Paul. *Being and Nothingness: An Essay on Phenomenological Ontology*. Trans. Hazel E. Barnes. Intro. Mary Warnock. Preface Richard Eyre. London: Routledge, 2003. Print.

Sarwar, Kabori. Dir. *Ayna* ('The Mirror'). Perf. Jahanara Akter, Shahinoor Akter, Rana Akter Ruma. Dhaka: Acid Survivors Foundation, 2015. Online. Available at: https://www.youtube.com/watch?v=lE-K1Zyon10&t=338s (Accessed: 8 January 2017). Web.

Scarry, Elaine. *The Body in Pain: The Making and Unmaking of the World.* Oxford: Oxford University Press, 1987 [1985]. Print.

Schwartz, Alexandra. 'On Doris Lessing and Not Saying Thank You'. *New Yorker.* 20 November 2013. Online. Available at: http://www. newyorker.com/books/page-turner/on-doris-lessing-and-not-saying-thank-you (Accessed: 10 January 2017). Web.

Scott, James C. *Weapons of the Weak: Everyday Forms of Peasant Resistance.* New Haven, CT: Yale University Press, 1985. Print.

Sellars, Peter. 'Foreword'. In: Toni Morrison. *Desdemona.* London: Oberon Modern Plays, 2015. 7–11. Print.

Selvadurai, Shyam. *Funny Boy.* London: Vintage, 1995. Print.

Sengupta, Mitu. 'Anna Hazare's Anti-Corruption Movement and the Limits of Mass Mobilization in India'. *Social Movement Studies* 13.3 (2014): 406–13. Print.

Serwer, Adam. 'Can Trump Bring Back Torture?' *Atlantic.* 26 January 2017. Online. Available at: https://www.theatlantic.com/politics/archive/2017/01/trump-torture/514463/ (Accessed: 4 April 2017). Web.

Sethi, Ali. *The Wish Maker.* London: Hamish Hamilton, 2009. Print.

Sethi, Mira. 'Age of Innocence'. *Friday Times.* 9 May 2014. Online. Available at: http://www.thefridaytimes.com/tft/age-of-innocence/ (Accessed: 14 September 2016). Web.

Sexton, Anne. 'The Frog Prince'. In: Ed. and Intro. Diane Wood Middlebrook and Diana Hume George. *The Selected Poems of Anne Sexton.* New York, NY: Mariner, 2000 [1988]. 164–8. Print.

Sexton, David. 'Word Games: Why Hanif Kureishi's New Novel Is the Talk of the Town'. *Evening Standard.* 21 January 2014. Online. Available at: http://www.standard.co.uk/lifestyle/london-life/word-games-why-hanif-kureishi-s-new-novel-is-the-talk-of-the-town-9074670.html (Accessed: 10 January 2017). Web.

Shafak, Elif. *Black Milk: On Motherhood and Writing*. London: Penguin, 2011 [2007]. Print.

Shah, Aga Khan III, Sir Sultan Muhammed. *The Memoirs of Aga Khan: World Enough and Time*. Foreword by W. Somerset Maugham. London: Cassell, 1954. Print.

Shah, Bina. 'Ayaan Hirsi Ali and the Big Bad Wolf'. *Chowk: Identity, Politics, Culture, and Religion of India and Pakistan*. 1 July 2006. Online. Available at: http://www.chowk.com/Views/Society/Ayaan-Ali-Hirsi-and-the-Big-Bad-Wolf (Accessed: 14 June 2012). Web.

_____. *Slum Child*. Delhi: Tranquebar, 2010. Print.

_____. *A Season for Martyrs*. Harrison, NY: Delphinium, 2014. Print.

Shahraz, Qaisra. *The Holy Woman*. London: BlackAmber, 2001. Print.

Shaikh, Farzana. *Making Sense of Pakistan*. London: Hurst, 2009. Print.

Shakespeare, William. *Othello*. Ed. Norman Sanders. 14th edn. Cambridge: Cambridge University Press, 2003. Print.

Shakespeare, William. *The Merchant of Venice*. Ed. M. M. Mahood. 2nd edn. Cambridge: Cambridge University Press, 2003. Print.

Shamsie, Kamila. *Kartography*. London: Bloomsbury, 2002. Print.

_____. *Broken Verses*. London: Bloomsbury, 2005. Print.

_____. *Burnt Shadows*. London: Bloomsbury, 2009. Print.

_____. *Offence: The Muslim Case*. Kolkata: Seagull Books, 2009. Print.

_____. *A God in Every Stone*. London: Bloomsbury, 2014. Print.

_____. 'Murdered on the Streets of Karachi: My Friend who Dared to Believe in Free Speech'. *Guardian*. 27 April 2015. Online. Available at: https://www.theguardian.com/commentisfree/2015/apr/27/murdered-karachi-free-speech-sabeen-mahmud (Accessed: 12 January 2017). Web.

Sheikh Bake. 'Somewhere in America #MIPSTERZ'. *YouTube*. 20 November 2013. Online. Available at: https://www.youtube.com/watch?v=68sMkDKMias&feature=youtu.be (Accessed: 1 July 2016). Web.

Sheikh, Bilquis. *I Dared to Call Him Father: The Miraculous Story of a Muslim Woman's Encounter with God*. Grand Rapids, MI: Chosen Books, 2003. Print.

Sherwin, Adam. 'BBC Receives Hundreds of Complaints and Is Accused of Insulting Muslims with New "Racist" Sitcom Citizen Khan'.

Independent. 29 August 2012. Online. Available at: http://www.independent.co.uk/news/media/tv-radio/bbc-receives-hundreds-of-complaints-and-is-accused-of-insulting-muslims-with-new-racist-sitcom-8092543.html (Accessed: 10 January 2017). Web.

Sherwood, Harriet. 'Lessons of Holocaust Being Forgotten, Says Prince Charles'. *Guardian.* 31 January 2017. Online. Available at: https://www.theguardian.com/world/2017/jan/31/lessons-holocaust-being-forgotten-prince-charles-world-jewish-relief (Accessed: 23 February 2017). Web.

Shingavi, Snehal. *Angaaray.* Delhi: Penguin, 2014. Kindle.

Siddiqa, Ayesha. 'Who has Sin'd?' *Express Tribune.* 25 June 2015. Online. Available at: http://tribune.com.pk/story/909114/who-has-sind/ (Accessed: 13 November 2016). Web.

Siddique, Osama. *Pakistan's Experience with Formal Law: An Alien Justice.* New York, NY: Cambridge University Press, 2013. Print.

Sidhwa, Bapsi. *The Crow Eaters.* Glasgow: Fontana/Collins, 1982 [1980]. Print.

———. *The Pakistani Bride.* Minnesota, MN: Milkweed, 2008 [1983]. Print.

———. *Cracking India.* Minnesota, MN: Milkweed, 1991 [1988]. Print.

———. *An American Brat.* Minnesota, MN: Milkweed, 1995 [1993]. Print.

———. Ed. *City of Sin and Splendour: Writings on Lahore.* Delhi: Penguin, 2005. Print.

Singal, Jesse. 'Yes, Steve Bannon Asked Why a School Had So Many Hanukkah Books'. *New York Magazine.* 15 November 2016. Online. Available at: http://nymag.com/daily/intelligencer/2016/11/yes-steve-bannon-asked-why-a-school-had-many-hanukkah-books.html (Accessed: 23 February 2017). Web.

Singh, Gurharpal. 'British Multiculturalism and Sikhs'. *Sikh Formations* 1.2 (2005): 157–73. Print.

Singh, Sujala. 'Postcolonial Children: Representing the Nation in Arundhati Roy, Bapsi Sidhwa and Shyam Selvadurai'. *Wasafiri* 19.41 (2004): 13–18. Print.

Sizemore, Christine Wick. *A Female Vision of the City: London in the Novels of Five British Women*. Knoxville, TN: University of Tennessee Press, 1989. Print.

Smith, David. 'Drats. MP Falls Foul of Facts'. *Observer*. 3 October 2004. Online. Available at: https://www.theguardian.com/books/2004/oct/03/fiction.features1 (Accessed: 10 January 2017). Web.

Smith, Ian. 'Othello's Black Handkerchief'. *Shakespeare Quarterly* 64.1 (Spring 2013): 1–25. Print.

Smith, Michelle. 'The Royal Wedding and the Lure of the Princess Myth'. *The Conversation*. 28 April 2011. Online. Available at: https://theconversation.com/the-royal-wedding-and-the-lure-of-the-princess-myth-939 (Accessed: 12 September 2016). Web.

Smith, Zadie. *White Teeth*. London: Penguin, 2001 [2000] Print.

Soja, Edward W. *Postmodern Geographies: The Reassertion of Space in Critical Social Theory*. London: Verso, 1989. Print.

———. *Postmetropolis: Critical Studies of Cities and Regions*. Oxford: Blackwell, 2000. Print.

Soueif, Ahdaf. *In the Eye of the Sun*. London: Bloomsbury, 1999 [1992]. Print.

———. 'Protesters Reclaim the Spirit of Egypt'. *BBC News*. 13 February 2011. Online. Available at: http://www.bbc.co.uk/news/world-middle-east-12393795 (Accessed: 12 February 2017). Web.

———. Speaking on Riz Khan. 'The Political Power of Literature'. *Al-Jazeera*. 23 February 2011. Online. Available at: http://english.aljazeera.net/programmes/rizkhan/2011/02/201122374815992508.html (Accessed: 9 March 2011). Web.

———. *Cairo: My City, Our Revolution*. London: Bloomsbury, 2012. Print.

———. 'On Liberty: Edward Snowden and Top Writers on What Freedom Means to Them'. *Guardian*. 21 February 2014. Online. Available at: https://www.theguardian.com/books/2014/feb/21/on-liberty-edward-snowden-freedom (Accessed: 8 January 2017). Web.

Soyinka, Wole. *You Must Set Forth at Dawn*. New York, NY: Random House, 2007 [2006]. Print.

Spivak, Gayatri Chakravorty. 'Can the Subaltern Speak?' In: Eds. Cary

Nelson and Lawrence Grossberg. *Marxism and the Interpretation of Culture*. Basingstoke: Macmillan Education, 1988. 271–313. Print.

————. 'Terror: A Speech After 9-11'. *boundary 2* 31.2 (Summer 2004): 81–111. Print.

————. 'Translating Into English'. *Nation, Language, and the Ethics of Translation*. Eds Sandra Bermann and Michael Wood. Princeton, NJ: Princeton University Press, 2005. 93–110. Print.

Stainback, Kevin. 'Social Contacts and Race/Ethnic Job Matching'. *Social Forces* 87.2 (2009): 857–86. Print.

Stockett, Kathryn. *The Help*. London: Penguin, 2010. Print.

Stott, Andrew. *Comedy: The New Critical Idiom*. London: Routledge, 2005. Print.

Stourton, Edward. 'William Hague's "Hand of Friendship" for Arab World'. *BBC News*. 23 June 2011. Online. Available at: http://www.bbc.co.uk/news/world-middle-east-13857046 (Accessed: 12 January 2017). Web.

Strandberg, Lotta. 'Images of Gender and the Negotiation of Agency in Salman Rushdie's *Shame*'. *NORA: Nordic Journal of Feminist and Gender Research* 12.3 (2004): 143–52. Print.

Suhrke, Astri. 'Refugees and Asylum in the Muslim World'. In: Ed. Robin Cohen. *The Cambridge Survey of World Migration*. Cambridge: Cambridge University Press, 1995. 457–60. Print.

Suleri, Sara. *Meatless Days*. London: University of Chicago Press, 1989. Print.

Sullivan, Shannon. *Revealing Whiteness: The Unconscious Habits of Racial Privilege*. Bloomington, IN: Indiana University Press, 2006. Print.

Sultan, Shahbano Begum Maimoona. *A Trip to Europe*. Trans. G. B. Baksh. Calcutta: Thacker, Spink, 1914. Print.

Suvorova, Anna. *Lahore: Tophophilia of Space and Place*. Karachi: Oxford University Press, 2012. Print.

Swanson, Jordan. 'Acid Attacks: Bangladesh's Efforts to Stop the Violence'. *International Health* 3.1 (Spring 2002). Online. Available at: http://www.hcs.harvard.edu/~epihc/currentissue/spring2002/swanson.php (Accessed: 8 January 2017). Web.

Syal, Meera. *Anita And Me*. London: Harper Perennial, 2004 [1996]. Print.

Tagore, Rabindranath. *The Home and the World*. Trans. Sreejata Guha. Intro. Swagato Ganguly. Delhi: Penguin, 2005 [1916]. Print.

Talbot, Ian. *Punjab and the Raj, 1849–1947*. Riverdale, MD: Riverdale Company, 1988. Print.

Tarantino, Quentin. Dir. *Pulp Fiction*. Perf. Samuel L. Jackson, John Travolta, Uma Thurman. London: Lionsgate, 2004 [1994]. Film.

Tarlo, Emma. *Visibly Muslim: Fashion, Politics, Faith*. Oxford: Berg, 2010. Print.

Tate, Claudia. 'Toni Morrison'. In: Ed. Danille Kathleen Taylor-Guthrie. *Conversations with Toni Morrison*. Jackson, MS: University Press of Mississippi, 1994. 156–70. Print.

Tehrik-i-Niswan and Sheema Kirmani. 'I am a Woman'. Online. Available at: https://www.youtube.com/watch?v=m8E9hxs_4TM (Accessed: 8 January 2017). YouTube.

Telegraph. 'Turkey Coup Against President Erdogan: Everything we Know on Monday'. *Telegraph*. 18 July 2016. Online. Available at: http://www. telegraph.co.uk/news/2016/07/15/turkey-coup-against-president-erdogan-everything-we-know-on-satu/ (Accessed: 12 January 2017). Web.

Teverson, Andrew and Upstone, Sara. Eds. *Postcolonial Spaces: The Politics of Place in Contemporary Culture*. Basingstoke: Palgrave, 2011. Print.

Thapar, Romila. '"What Has Been Happening in Recent Times Could Well Develop Into Fascism": An Interview with Romila Thapar'. *Caravan*. 1 May 2016. Online. Available at: http://www. caravanmagazine.in/vantage/notes-nationalism-interview-romila-thapar (Accessed: 18 July 2016). Web.

Thompson, Simon and Yar, Majid. Eds. *The Politics of Misrecognition*. Farnham: Ashgate, 2011. Print.

Todorov, Tzvetan. *The Fear of Barbarians: Beyond the Clash of Civilizations*. Trans. Andrew Brown. London: Polity, 2010 [2008]. Print.

Toor, Saadia. 'Moral Regulation in a Postcolonial Nation-State: Gender and the Politics of Islamization in Pakistan'. *Interventions* 9.2 (2007): 255–75. Print.

Transparency International. 'Corruption and Governance Indicators in Selected Asian Countries'. 23 February 2016. Online. Available at:

http://www.transparency.org/files/content/corruptionqas/Corruption_trends_in_Asia_Pacific_region.pdf (Accessed: 10 January 2017). Web.

Travis, Alan. 'Theresa May Is Ahead of Trump in Undermining the Refugee System'. *Guardian*. 30 January 2017. Online. Available at: https://www.theguardian.com/politics/2017/jan/30/us-travel-ban-may-is-ahead-of-trump-in-undermining-refugee-protection-system (Accessed: 9 April 2017). Web.

Trivedi, Poonam. '"Filmi" Shakespeare'. *Literature/Film Quarterly* 35.2 (April 2007): 148–58. Print.

Tryhorn, Chris. 'Springer Opera Not Blasphemous, Court Rules'. *Guardian*. 5 December 2007. Online. Available at: https://www.theguardian.com/media/2007/dec/05/independentproductioncompanies.bbc (Accessed: 10 January 2017). Web.

Tuan, Yi-Fu. *Space and Place: The Perspective of Experience*. London: Arnold, 1977. Print.

Tuitt, Frank and Bonner II, Fred A. 'Introduction'. In: Eds. Fred A. Bonner II, aretha faye marbley, Frank Tuitt, Petra A. Robinson, Rosa M. Banda, and Robin L. Hughes. *Black Faculty in the Academy: Narratives for Negotiating Identity and Achieving Career Success*. New York, NY: Routledge, 2015. 1–12. Print.

Tunio, Hafeez. 'Arrested Safoora Attack Mastermind Behind Sabeen's Murder: Sindh CM'. *The Express Tribune*. 20 May 2015. Online. Available at: http://tribune.com.pk/story/889452/arrested-safoora-attack-mastermind-confesses-to-sabeen-mahmuds-murder/ (Accessed: 21 May 2015). Web.

Tunku, Abdul Rahman Putra al-Haj. *Looking Back. Monday Musings and Memories*. Kuala Lumpar: Pustaka Antara, 1977. Print.

———. *Viewpoints*. Kuala Lumpur: Heinemann Educational Books Asia, 1978. Print.

———. *Political Awakening*. Subang Jaya: Pelanduk, 1986. Print.

Udwin, Leslee. Dir. *India's Daughter*. Perf. Asha Devi, Badri Singh, Satendra. London: BBC, 2015. TV.

Ungerer, Gustav. 'Portia and the Prince of Morocco'. *Shakespeare Studies* 31 (2003): 89–126. Print.

United Nations (UN). 'Universal Declaration of Human Rights'. Online.

Available at: http://www.un.org/en/universal-declaration-human-rights/index.html (Accessed: 21 May 2015). Web.

United Nations Educational, Scientific and Cultural Organization (UNESCO). 'Pakistan: Statistics'. Updated 27 December 2013. Online. Available at: http://www.unicef.org/infobycountry/pakistan_pakistan_statistics.html (Accessed: 28 July 2014). Web.

United Nations High Commissioner for Refugees (UNHCR). 'Refugee Protection in Countries Affected by Recent Events in the Arab World'. 2011. Online. Available at: http://www.unhcr.org/4e0334de9.pdf (Accessed: 12 January 2017). Web.

————. 'Lebanon Crisis Response Plan 2015–16'. Online. Available at: data.unhcr.org/syrianrefugees/download.php?id=7723 (Accessed: 12 January 2017). Web.

United Nations Human Rights Council. 'Out of Sight, Out of Mind: Deaths in Detention in the Syrian Arab Republic'. 3 February 2016. Online. Available at: http://www.ohchr.org/Documents/HRBodies/HRCouncil/CoISyria/A-HRC-31-CRP1_en.pdf (Accessed 17 February 2016). Web.

Updike, John. *Terrorist*. London: Hamish Hamilton, 2006. Print.

Urry, John. *The Tourist Gaze*. London: SAGE, 2001. Print.

Vajpeyi, Ananya. 'The Enduring Curse of Caste'. *New York Times*. 9 March 2016. Online. Available at: http://www.nytimes.com/2016/03/10/opinion/the-enduring-curse-of-caste.html?_r=0 (Accessed: 15 July 2016). Web.

Van Nieuwkerk, Karin. 'Creating an Islamic Cultural Sphere: Contested Notions of Art, Leisure and Entertainment: An Introduction'. *Contemporary Islam* 2.3 (2008): 169–76. Print.

Varisco, Daniel Martin. *Reading Orientalism: Said and the Unsaid*. Seattle, WA: University of Washington Press, 2007. Print.

Visram, Rozina. *Ayahs, Lascars and Princes: Indians in Britain, 1700–1947*. London: Pluto, 1986. Print.

Viswanathan, Gauri. *Masks of Conquest: Literary Study and British Rule in India*. New York. NY: Columbia University Press, 1989. Print.

Vogel, Saskia. 'Tahmima Anam: The Granta Podcast, Episode 76'. *Granta Online*. 3 June 2013. Online. Available at: https://granta.com/

Tahmima-Anam-The-Granta-Podcast-Ep-76/ (Accessed: 5 March 2017). Web.

Wadud, Amina. *Inside The Gender Jihad: Women's Reform of Islam*. Oxford: Oneworld, 2006. Print.

Waheed, Mirza. *The Collaborator*. London: Viking, 2011. Print.

Walcott, Derek. 'The Schooner *Flight*'. In: *Collected Poems: 1948–1984*. London: Faber and Faber, 1990 [1979]. 345–61. Print.

Walsh, Declan. 'Pakistan Attack Kills Punjab Governor'. *Guardian*. 4 January 2011. Online. Available at: https://www.theguardian.com/world/2011/jan/04/pakistan-attack-kills-punjab-governor (Accessed: 22 December 2016). Web.

Weaver, Matthew. 'You Can Call Me a Big Bad Wolf But Not a Bore, Says Richard Dawkins'. *Guardian*. 5 June 2014. Online. Available at: https://www.theguardian.com/books/2014/jun/05/richard-dawkins-fairytales-not-harmful (Accessed: 12 September 2016). Web.

Werbner, Pnina. 'Everyday Multiculturalism: Theorising the Difference Between "Intersectionality" and "Multiple Identities'. *Ethnicities* 13.4 (2013): 401–19. Print.

Whedon, Joss. Dir. *Buffy the Vampire Slayer*. Perf. Sarah Michelle Gellar, Nicholas Brendon, Alyson Hannigan. London: 20th Century Fox, 1997. TV.

Whitlock, Gillian. 'Branding: The Veiled Best-seller'. In: *Soft Weapons: Autobiography in Transit*. Chicago, IL: Chicago University Press, 2007. 87–105. Print.

Wood, James. 'The World As We Know It: Zia Haider Rahman's Dazzling Début'. *New Yorker*. 19 May 2014. Online. Available at: http://www.newyorker.com/magazine/2014/05/19/the-world-as-we-know-it (Accessed: 17 October 2015). Web.

Woolley, Agnes. 'Questioning Narrative Authenticity in Kay Adshead's *The Bogus Woman*'. *Moving Worlds: Asylum Accounts* 12.2 (2012): 30–43. Print.

Wyrick, Deborah. *Fanon*. Danbury, CT: For Beginners, 1998. Print.

Yassin-Kassab, Robin. *The Road from Damascus*. London: Hamish Hamilton, 2008. Print.

———. 'The Gulf Between Us'. *Qunfuz Blog*. 21 March 2009. Online.

Available at: http://qunfuz.com/2009/03/21/the-gulf-between-us/#more-111 (Accessed: 7 January 2017). Web.

———. 'Tahrir Square'. *Critical Muslim 1: The Arabs Are Alive* (January–March 2012): 19–46. Print.

———. 'Nobody Is Free of Religious Thinking'. *Dawn*. 16 June 2012. Online. Available at: http://www.dawn.com/news/727038 (Accessed: 7 January 2017). Web.

Yeats, W. B. 'Easter, 1916'. In: *Selected Poems*. London: Penguin, 2000 [1916]. Print.

Yeoh, Brenda, Hickey, Maureen, Lu, Melody Chia-Wen. Convenors. *Crossing Borders, Traversing Boundaries: Bridging the Gap Between International and Internal Migration Research and Theory*. 13–14 October. Online. Singapore: Asia Research Institute, National University of Singapore, 2011. Available at: https://ari.nus.edu.sg/Event/Detail/1159 (Accessed: 28 March 2017). Web.

Young, Robert J. C. *White Mythologies: Writing History and the West*. London: Routledge, 1990. Print.

———. *Colonial Desire: Hybridity in Theory, Culture and Race*. London: Routledge, 1995. Print.

Younger, Neil. 'The Practice and Politics of Troop-Raising: Robert Devereux, Second Earl of Essex, and the Elizabethan Regime'. *English Historical Review* CXXVII.526 (2012): 566–91. Print.

Yousaf, Farhan Navid and Purkayastha, Bandana. 'Beyond Saving Faces: Survivors of Acid Attacks in Pakistan'. *Women's Studies International Forum* 54 (January–February 2016): 11–19. Print.

Yuval-Davis, Nira. 'Intersectionality and Feminist Politics'. *European Journal of Women's Studies* 13.3 (2006): 193–210. Print.

Zakaria, Rafia. *The Upstairs Wife: An Intimate History of Pakistan*. Boston, MA: Beacon, 2015. Print.

Index

1968 revolutions xxii

7/7 London attacks 159, 168, 194, 201, 218

9/11 World Trade Centre attacks 82, 85, 104, 108, 124–6, 139, 159–60, 166, 168, 201, 206–7, 213, 217, 239, 275, 290

A

abaya 132

Abdullah, Shaila 60–2

Aboulela, Leila 6, 161, 211–13

Abu Taleb Khan, Mirza 182, 234

Abu-Lughod, Lila 207–8, 210, 212–13, 221, 251, 290, 302–3

Achebe, Chinua 8, 10

acid attacks xx, 143, 152–7, 221

academia 315, 318, 321

activism 132, 135, 149, 154, 205, 274, 306

Adichie, Chimamanda Ngozi 316–17

Adiga, Aravind xvii

Advani, Lal Krishna 59

Afghanistan (*also* Afghan; *see* Taliban (Afghani)) 46, 49, 53, 68, 87, 103–4, 111, 114, 124–6, 148, 156, 162, 164, 167, 185, 206–7, 213, 220, 230, 294, 302

    Afghan War 104, 114, 162

Africa (*also* African) 6, 8, 10, 16–20, 31–2, 139, 147, 149, 161, 164, 166, 196, 204, 215–16, 219, 231, 285, 293, 299, 303, 312–13, 315

    East 6;

    North 132, 139, 196, 299;

    South 56, 147, 297

    apartheid 147

Afzal-Khan, Fawzia 150

Ahmad, Aijaz 17, 290

Ahmad, Imran 217

Ahmad, Jamil 48–9, 56, 144

Ahmad, Rukhsana 144

Ahmed, Feroze 259

Ahmed, Sara 317–18

Ahmed, Sufiya 220–1

Ajoka (Pakistani theatre company) 150–1

Alam, M. Y. xvii

al-Aswany, Alaa 133, 135

al-Qaida 39, 122, 201, 295

al-Shami, Leila 134–5, 163

Algeria (*also* Algerian) 284–8, 293

    Algerian War of Independence 286

Ali, Agha Shahid 95

Ali, Ayaan Hirsi 215–16, 218

Ali, Monica 149, 155, 233, 236, 244, 249–50, 254–5

Ali, Tariq 6, 60, 94

Amis, Martin 35, 239, 266

373

Anam, Tahmima 6, 244, 249, 254–5
Anand, Mulk Raj 144
Anderson, Benedict 167
Angaaray (short story collection, 1933) 144
anti-Semitism 37, 182, 199, 271, 275
anti-religious discourse 145, 160, 199, 221
Antoon, Sinan 135
Anwar, Muhammad 195, 244
Arab (*see* Bedouin, Middle East) 38, 128, 130–1, 139, 190, 211, 213, 215, 267, 285–6, 290, 293
    Arab Spring xx, 85, 128–31, 138–40, 164;
    culture 191;
    identity 130–1, 170–1, 266;
    migration 163, 165, 192, 196;
    nationalism (Arabism) 134, 193;
    women 131–2;
    world 6, 131–2, 134, 139, 189, 192, 212, 216;
    writers 6, 17, 131, 134, 139, 165, 196
Arabian Nights, The 212, 216
Arabic (language) 16–17, 189, 192, 196, 211, 223–4, 247, 266
Arendt, Hannah 123, 270, 277
Ashraf, Saad 110, 112, 115
Aslam, Nadeem 3, 6–7, 11, 181
asylum 161–9, 171–2, 174, 215
    seekers 138, 159–60, 164–8, 170, 173–5, 265
atheism 35, 173
Attwell, David 10–11
Australia (*also* Australian) 17, 204
authenticity (concept) 268
autobiography 10–11, 30, 59, 125, 138, 214–15, 217–18

biography (*also* biographers) 4, 8–11, 214, 216, 252, 274–5, 283;
    life writing 86, 214, 216–18;
    memoir xxii, 8, 10–11, 38, 50, 96–7, 108, 114, 136, 153, 180, 194–5, 198, 215, 217–18
Avikunthak, Ashish 24
awards 8, 132, 220–1, 309, 313
    Man Booker Prize 241, 249;
    Muslim Writers Award 221;
    Nobel Prize for Literature 8
Ayodhya 59

B

Bachelard, Gaston 99
Bahrain 130–1
Baldwin, Shauna Singh 275, 279
Balochistan (*also* Baloch) xx, 43–54, 56–8, 60, 145
    Balochistan National Party (BNP) 61;
    poetry 53;
    struggle 47, 53;
    topography 48;
    uprising 47, 54
Balochi (language) 53, 57
Bangladesh (*also* East Bengal, Bangladeshi, East Bengali, East Pakistani; *see* Bengal) 5, 47, 65, 93, 105–6, 150, 154–5, 157, 207, 217, 232, 236, 238, 240, 243–6, 249–50, 252–5, 257, 260–1
    1971 War of Liberation xvii, 47, 57, 65, 105, 229, 254
Banglaphone fiction 232, 244, 254–5
Bannon, Steve 271–2, 278
Barthes, Roland 298
Basu, Shrabani 260, 262, 273, 275

beards 126, 166, 201

Bedouin 165, 172

Begg, Moazzam 125–6, 147, 217

Beirut 219, 290, 295

belief (*see* faith, religion) 13, 34–5, 49, 122, 142, 160, 168, 188, 199, 248, 274

Bengal (*also* Bengali) 23, 47, 52–3, 106, 180, 232–3, 235–8, 241–2, 249, 251–4, 257, 259–60, 262–3

Benn, Hilary 127

Berlin 131, 159, 221, 295

Bhabha, Homi K. (*see* hybridity) 52, 223, 291

Bhagat, Chetan xix

Bhardwaj, Vishal 16, 24, 27–9, 32, 96

Bhatti, Gurpreet Kaur 149

Bhutto, Benazir 40, 61, 104

Bhutto, Fatima 38, 47

Bhutto, Zulfikar Ali 39, 47, 50, 52, 101, 103, 141

Bible (*see* Christian, Catholic) 247

Bilal, Mushtaq 56, 319

Bildungsroman 49

bin Laden, Osama 37

binary opposition 5, 208, 289, 294

biradari 261

Black Britain (*also* Black British) 16, 203

Blasim, Hassan 164–5, 171, 173–4

blasphemy 105, 156, 228, 314

blog (*also* blogging) 316–17

Boal, Augusto 148

body 15, 30, 119–20, 122, 125–6, 212, 224, 276, 292

Bombay (*also* Mumbai) 67, 109, 184–5, 260

borders 3, 5–6, 53, 63, 68, 83, 85, 160, 162–3, 172

Bosnia (*also* Bosnian) 125, 159, 164

Bowie, David 209

Bradford, West Yorkshire 114, 219

Bradley, A. C. 30, 35

Brah, Avtar 303

Brahmin (*also* Brahminical) 23–4, 95, 252

Breton, Raymond 258

Brexit 264, 268–9

Brighton 234, 256

Britain (*also* British) xvi, xix, xxi–xxii, 3–4, 6–7, 16, 23, 31, 44–6, 48, 65, 76, 81, 87, 90–2, 96, 110–11, 127, 131, 136–7, 139–40, 149, 153–4, 157, 165–6, 168–9, 179–82, 184, 186, 189–97, 199–200, 201–5, 209, 216–17, 219–20, 223, 225–35, 237, 239, 241–6, 248–9, 252, 254–60, 262–4, 268, 272–3, 276–7, 287, 292, 301, 304, 310, 314–15, 317

British Broadcasting Corporation (BBC) 34, 145, 157, 230, 268, 297;

British Muslims (*see* identity, media, migration)

    category of 168, 190, 304;

    education 185, 188, 245;

    representations of 189, 191, 211, 243, 263;

    writing by xvi, xix, 5–6, 139, 179–80, 184, 194–5, 201–2, 209, 211, 220, 222, 235, 254, 278

British National Party (BNP) 237;

class 182;

East End 232–3, 248;

history 179, 195, 203, 232, 244;

immigration 179, 184, 193–7, 203–05, 232, 236, 244, 260;

religion 179, 189, 211;

royalty
King George III 181;
King George IV 234;
King George V 185;
King William IV 234;
Prince Charles 271;
Queen Elizabeth I 13–14;
Queen Victoria 79–80, 185, 257–8
topography 182
British Empire (*see* colonialism) 131, 147, 179
Brittain, Victoria 125, 147–8
Brotton, Jerry 13–14, 32
Brussels 159, 295
bureaucracy 55
burqa 202, 209, 302
Bush, George W. 124, 206, 290, 294, 302
Bush, Laura 302
business 13, 137, 197, 236, 238, 243, 246, 261–2, 309
Butler, Judith 165–6

C

Cairo 85, 133, 136, 187
Calcutta (*also* Kolkata) 67, 93, 181, 235, 240–1, 251–3, 255
Cameron, David 140
Canada (*also* Canadian) 8, 204, 258, 272, 275
capitalism 47, 85, 232
Caribbean 3, 204, 283, 316
cartography 80
cartoons
Danish controversy 228;
Disney 267
Ferzat, Ali 133

caste xviii, 16, 23–5, 28, 157, 303, 314
Catholic 13–14
celebrity 9, 12, 198
censorship 38, 40, 56, 68, 144, 149
Central Asia 6
Central Intelligence Agency (CIA) 103, 124
Chadda, Sarwat 222–6
Chandigarh 98
Chandra, Vikram xvi–xvii
Chatterjee, Upamanyu 16, 29–32
Chaudhuri, Amit 35, 239–40, 243–4, 248–9
Chechnya 125
children's fiction xix, 4, 33–4, 219, 222
China (*also* Chinese) 100, 105, 188, 298
Christian (*also* Christianity) 23, 66, 101, 108, 126, 141, 143, 156, 159, 182, 187, 199, 213, 217, 220, 223, 228, 246–7, 249, 290
Christie, Agatha xv
Cilano, Cara 57, 107, 221
Citizen Khan 230–1
citizenship 283, 285
city, urban 64, 67–9, 71–2, 78, 80, 84–5, 89–91, 98–9, 103, 110, 112, 232
poor 66–7;
postcolonial 66, 225
Cixous, Hélène xxii
'clash of civilizations' 130
class 62, 69–70, 83, 182
Clive, Robert 180
Coetzee, J. M. 10–11, 119–20, 292, 296
Coleridge, Samuel Taylor 25
colonialism 5, 31, 243, 284, 286, 300
comedy 190, 228–30
Conrad, Joseph 170, 191
consumerism 38
cosmopolitanism 58, 101, 247

Cook, Robin 256
Cornershop 229
corruption 24, 49, 61, 106, 131, 145, 190, 222, 227, 288
countryside (*see* pastoral, rural) 9, 71, 74, 82, 288
Crenshaw, Kimberlé Williams 205, 303–5, 315
critical race feminism 315
critical race theory 205, 315
cultural
    production 64, 132, 141, 152, 180, 255;
    heritage 47, 308
curry (*also* curry houses) xxi, 87, 232–3, 256–62

D

Dabashi, Hamid 17, 130
Daechsel, Markus 98, 101
Dahya, Badr 244
Dalrymple, William 67–8
Damascus 85, 139
Darwish, Mahmoud 134
Dawkins, Richard xix, 33–5
Dawn 58, 105, 145, 319
de Beauvoir, Simone 293
de Certeau, Michel 67, 82–4, 86
de Windt, Harry 48
Deb, Siddhartha xviii
decolonize (*also* decolonization) 32, 131, 287, 313, 315, 320
Delhi 29–30, 36, 59, 63, 67, 95, 113, 297, 301, 313, 320
democracy 123, 130, 133, 142, 272
Derrida, Jacques 165, 305
Desai, Anita 70
Desai, Kiran xvii

Devi, Mahasweta 165
Dhaka 93, 156, 237–8, 245, 251, 255
diaspora (*also* diasporic) 16, 85, 161, 172, 179, 231, 243–4, 255, 268
    writing xix, xxi, 179
digital humanities 317
disability 25, 59, 84, 105–6
    mental health 164–6, 171–3, 250
discrimination 196, 203–5
    anti-discrimination 203
diversity 219
double colonization 300–1, 303
Douglass, Frederick 270
Doxiadis, Constantinos A. 98, 101
Doyle, Arthur Conan, Sir 222
dress (*also* clothing) 15, 167–8, 172, 186, 202, 212, 220, 228, 230, 232, 286, 297, 302, 319
    cosmetic 31
drugs 66, 169, 213, 285
Dubai 255
Dudai, Ron 142–3, 146

E

East India Company (EIC) 180
education 23, 29, 88, 185, 188, 242, 245, 248, 250
    higher education xxi, 68, 245, 312–15, 317–18, 320;
    university 217, 241, 243, 245, 248, 313–20;
    anti-intellectualism 313–14
Egypt (*also* Egyptian) 128, 130–4, 136–8, 190, 192–3, 200, 213
    Egyptian revolution 135
Eid 248
Eliot, T. S. 245, 264
empires 76

England (*also* English) 8–9, 13–15, 88, 114, 149, 154–5, 170, 180–2, 184, 186, 190–3, 195, 216, 220, 223, 242–3, 245, 247–8, 250–3, 259, 262, 266, 273, 276–7, 288
   culture 229;
   northern 181–2, 220;
   returned 194–6, 244, 249, 251
English Defence League (EDL) 200, 220, 237
English, James F. 308, 310
English (language) 17, 20, 56, 66
English literature (*also* English-language fiction) xvi, 59, 233, 307
Enlightenment 35, 279
Erdoğan, Recep Tayyip 318–19
Eritrea 167
Ershad, Hussain Muhammad 254
essays 22, 24, 57, 89, 96, 113, 133, 145, 159, 190, 197, 259, 283, 285–6, 290, 294, 297–302
ethics 120, 297
Ethiopia 215
ethnic (*also* ethnicity) 5, 47, 49–50, 53, 55, 68–9, 80, 145, 161, 204–5, 219, 252, 258, 266, 315–17
   violence 69
Eurocentric 98, 147
Europe (*also* European) 5, 13, 17, 65, 90, 93, 139, 159, 162–3, 165–7, 171, 173, 180, 182, 184, 186–7, 195–6, 226, 234, 240–1, 256, 283–4, 289, 294
exile 6, 36, 192, 276
exotic 12, 18, 21, 24, 32, 242, 293
extremism 267–8

F

Fair, C. Christine 320
fairy tales xix, 33–5, 60, 88
   princess 33, 35
faith 13, 35, 75, 109, 161, 174, 187–9, 220, 224, 254
Faiz, Faiz Ahmed 113–14, 134
family
   and sexuality 108, 215;
   and women 25, 60, 108, 152–3, 210, 262, 276–7, 299
fanaticism 46, 208, 299
Fanon, Frantz 161, 283–8, 291, 293
Faqir, Fadia 6, 165, 168–70, 172, 174
fascism 277, 279
   neo-fascism 272
female genital mutilation 215, 299
feminism xxi, 132, 156, 207–8, 212, 297–300, 303, 305–6, 315, 317–18
festivals xvii, 40, 219, 307–11
feudalism 145
film 99–101, 107, 115, 141, 143, 146, 151, 162, 228–9, 297, 309
   Bollywood 24, 27–8, 96, 236;
   Lollywood 70
flânerie (*see* walking) 82
Forster, E. M. 170
Foucault, Michel 67, 77, 289
France (*also* French) 124, 162, 166, 180, 184, 196, 199, 248, 272–3, 275–7, 279, 283–6, 295, 298, 310
   colonialism (*see* Maghrib) 285;
   culture 273, 283, 285, 287–8, 298
freedom 19, 38, 147, 149, 206–13, 319
   unfreedom 208, 210, 213
      azadi (Urdu) 95, 211;
      hurriyya (Arabic) 211;
      liberty (*also* liberation) 206–13

free indirect discourse 95, 191, 211, 251
French (language) 276
French, Patrick 9–10
Frog Prince, The (fairy tale) 33–4
fundamentalism 33–4, 215, 268–9, 272
Fyzee, Atiya 184–6

G

Galbraith, Robert (*see* Rowling, J. K.) 3
Gandhi, Indira 314
Gandhi, M. K. 153, 221, 288, 310
Gauhar, Feryal Ali 156
gender 35, 69, 84, 145, 150, 207, 213, 290, 316–17
genre 5, 15, 59, 99, 143, 217–18, 223, 316
Germany (*also* German) 123, 140, 175, 197, 221, 242, 277, 279, 310
Ghai, Anita 25
ghazal (poetry) 74, 86
Ghose, Zulfikar 15–16, 39
Ghosh, Amitav 93–5, 212, 235–6, 239–40, 244, 248, 309
Gilmour, Rachael 216, 312
Gilroy, Paul 147
globalization (*also* global capitalism) xxii, 232
Goodison, Lorna 11
Google India ('The Reunion') 63
Gopal, Priyamvada 314
Gove, Michael 314
Gregory, Derek 292, 294–5
Guantánamo Bay 124–5, 147, 201, 217
Guardian, The 200, 239
Gunesekera, Romesh xvi
Gupta, Sunetra 249, 251–5
Gurnah, Abdulrazak 6, 166–7, 173–4
Guttman, Anna 273

H

hadith 220
Hague, William 139
Hai, Yasmin 217
hajj 166, 212
halal food 182, 226, 258, 266
Hamid, Mohsin 6, 39, 63, 65, 67, 69–73, 78, 80–3, 85–6, 201
Hamid, Omar Shahid 307–8
Hanif, Mohammed 37, 54, 56, 143, 145–6, 156, 164
Haq, Kaiser 245
haram 268
harem 181, 216
Hardy, Thomas xv
Harlow, Barbara 53–4
Harry Potter (*see* Rowling, J. K.) 3
Hashmi, Shadab Zeest 90
Hassan, Waïl S. 32
Hazare, Anna 25
heritage 3, 47, 60, 90, 125, 169, 207, 220, 223–4, 255, 257, 274–5, 290, 308
Heyer, Georgette xv
hijab 168, 220–1, 230
Hindoostane Coffee House 234, 248, 256
Hinduism (*also* Hindu) 59, 63, 74, 76, 79, 110, 233, 240–1, 243, 251, 253, 255
Hindu, The 98
Hobbes, Thomas 211
Hosain, Attia 209–11, 213, 258–60
Huggan, Graham 12, 24, 66, 217
humanities 67, 78, 85, 294, 317
human rights xx–xxii, 43, 54, 56, 62, 141–52, 156, 221
  abuses xx, 143, 146–7, 149, 152;

report xx, 55, 142–3, 146, 150

Huntington, Samuel P. 130

Husain, Ed 86, 102, 217

Hussain, Intizar 102

Hussain, Zahid 6, 262

Hussein, Aamer 6, 201

Hussein, Abdullah 261

hybridity (*also* hybrid) 81, 224–5, 234, 242, 267, 292, 305

Hyderabad, Sindh 59, 61, 114, 190, 313–14

Hyder, Qurratulain xxi

I

identity 4–6, 19–20, 24

imperialism 65, 96, 292, 294

Independence 58, 65, 79, 84, 277

Independent, The 55

India (*also* Indian)
   anti-corruption movement 25;
   Bharatiya Janata Party (BJP) 59, 313–14;
   present-day 4–5, 10, 16, 23–4, 26, 28–9, 31–2, 47, 50, 63–4, 66, 68–70, 85, 96–7, 134, 144, 181, 185, 204, 221, 227, 241, 300, 313–14;
   relations with Pakistan 36, 47, 58, 63, 68, 78, 83, 92–3, 102, 254;
   under British Raj (rule) 23, 44, 58–9, 65, 74, 79–81, 115, 147, 161, 180, 190, 232, 242, 258, 277, 288;
   writers 5, 9, 31, 35, 47, 93, 144, 153, 191, 226, 241, 253, 255, 272, 275

Indian subcontinent 63, 93, 134

India's Daughter 297

individualism 19

Indonesia 56

Inter-Services Intelligence (ISI) 36–7

Internally Displaced Persons (IDPs) 162–4, 175

Internet (*see* social media) 4, 132, 200, 216
   Facebook 131–2;
   Twitter (*also* tweets) 9, 36, 116, 131–2, 200, 290

intersectionality 301, 303–6

intertextuality (*also* intertextual) 18, 28

Iqbal, Muhammad (Allama) 185, 241

Iran (*also* Iranian; *see* Persia) 46, 103, 131, 173, 271
   Iranian Revolution 68

Iraq (*also* Iraqi) 38, 46, 103, 122, 124, 127, 135, 139, 162–4, 171–3, 271, 294–5
   Gulf War 38, 135, 162, 164, 201;
   Iraq War 122, 268;
   Iran-Iraq War 173

Ireland (*also* Irish) 8, 96, 107, 112, 204, 234, 236, 248, 256

Islam 13, 75, 95–6, 113, 141–2, 145, 150, 161, 166, 173–4, 189–91, 199, 201, 208, 212, 215, 217–18, 221, 225, 239, 246, 248–9, 268, 273–4
   conversion to 189–91;
   five pillars (*see* hajj, prayer);
   heterogeneity of 174;
   and human rights 142, 221;
   oppressive currents in 132, 186, 215–16, 221, 228, 302;
   representations of 13, 142, 150, 174, 191, 208, 218, 268;
   stereotypes of 130, 166, 202, 218, 227–9, 290;

Sufi (*also* Sufism) 273–5

Islam, Manzu 243–5, 248

Islamabad xx, 80, 98–108, 110–11, 115–16

Margalla Hills 98–9, 105, 107, 115
Islamic Right 254
Islamization 70, 144
Israel (*also* Israeli) 147, 162, 290, 295, 311
Istanbul 295
Italy (*also* Italian) 9, 286
I'tesamuddin, Mirza Sheikh 180–4

J

Jahan, Rashid 144
Jalal, Ayesha 114
Jameel, Nabila 90
Jameson, Fredric 67, 80
Janmohamed, Shelina Zahra 217–18
Jehan, Noor 134
Jew (*also* Jewish) 123, 159, 175, 182, 236, 261, 271–3, 275, 286
jihad 132, 160
Jinnah, Muhammad Ali (*see* Quaid-i-Azam) 69, 109
Johnson, Boris xxi, 264–9
Jones, William 181, 290
Jordan (*also* Jordanian) 162–3, 165, 172–3
journalism (*also* journalist) 8, 36–40, 54–6, 111, 114, 125, 131–2, 190, 217, 254, 264

K

Kabul 125, 207, 295
Kar, Ajoy 23
Karachi 39, 43, 58–60, 67–9, 85, 98, 143, 156, 161, 185, 201, 216, 266, 307, 319
Karim, Abdul 257–8

Kashmir (*also* Kashmiri) xx, 24, 92–7, 102, 245, 314
Dal Lake 92, 94;
independence 93;
literary representation 92–4, 96–7;
paradise 92, 94–5, 97;
sacred hair 93–4;
Srinagar 92;
topography 92, 97
Kenya (*also* Kenyan) 260, 320
Khan, Adib xviii
Khan, Ayub 98, 101
Khan, Hammad 99, 116
Khan, Liaquat Ali 113
Khan, Noor Inayat 273, 276
Khan, Noor-un-Nisa Inayat 273, 278–9
Khan, Sophia 107–8
Khan, Sorayya 101–3, 105–7
Khan, Uzma Aslam 310
Khan-Din, Ayub 229
Khyber Pakhtunkhwa (KPK) 53, 68, 87, 90, 162
literary representation 89–90;
refugees 87
Kipling, Rudyard 44, 48, 50, 56, 87, 89, 111–12, 115–16, 170
Koul, Sudha 97
Kraidy, Marwan M. 134
Kristeva, Julia 297–8
Kunzru, Hari 267, 272
Kurdi, Alan 140
Kureishi, Hanif 6, 9–12, 201–2, 214, 225, 229–30, 257

L

Lacan, Jacques 293
Lahiri, Shompa 276

Lahore (*also* Lahoris) 63–5, 67–72, 74–86, 108, 113, 141
 Heera Mandi 65–6, 73–7, 84–6, 113;
 representation of 65, 75, 83, 85–6;
 space 63–4, 66–7, 69, 72–3, 77–80, 85–6
Lalami, Laila 200
Lambert-Hurley, Siobhan 184–6
language 31, 165–6
 translation 164–5
lascars (seamen) 181, 183, 195, 232, 260
Le Corbusier 98
Le Tourneur D'ison, Claudine 66
Leary, Patricia 312–13, 319
Lebanon 162–3, 189–90
Leeds 167, 194, 205, 315–16
Lefebvre, Henri 79, 107
legislation 128, 149, 203–5, 271
 1951 Refugee Convention 139;
 First Amendment 38;
 Prevention of Anti-Women Practices Bill 2008 60;
 Race Relations Act 204;
 United Nations Security Council Resolution 47 93;
 Universal Declaration of Human Rights 123, 141, 146–7, 149
Lessing, Doris 8, 10–11
Levinas, Emmanuel 293
Lewis, Philip 161, 262
liberal(ism) 140, 310
Libya (*also* Libyan) 128, 130–1, 133, 138–9, 271, 164
Lieven, Anatol 49, 53–4, 69, 80, 85, 105, 160
literary canon 16, 32
literary form 142

Light, Alison xviii
literature festivals xxi, 40
London 13–14, 139, 144, 147, 153–4, 159, 168, 170, 181, 185–7, 189–92, 198, 201–2, 209–11, 213, 217, 219, 225, 230, 232–40, 243, 248, 250–1, 253–6, 259–62, 264, 278, 304, 310, 316–17
 7/7 London attacks 159, 168, 194, 201, 218
Lucknow 59

M

madrassah 181
Madrid 159
Maghrebi 196
magic realism xvi, xix, 70
Mahmud, Sabeen 43, 57, 319
Mahomed, Sake Dean 182, 233–5, 244, 248, 256–7
Majumdar, Saikat 277
Malak, Amin 161
Malaysia 62, 195
Malgonkar, Manohar 153
Malik, Ayisha xvii
Malkani, Gautam xvii
Man Booker Prize 241, 249
Manchester 114, 154, 262, 295
Manzoor, Sarfraz 217
Markandaya, Kamala 86, 191
marriage 25, 27, 60–1, 144, 215, 217, 220–1, 273, 275
Marxism (*also* Marxist) 47, 213, 236, 257, 300, 312
Massad, Joseph A. 290
Master, Irfan 221–2
Matar, Hisham 138, 140
May, Theresa 140, 272

McEwan, Ian 35, 239

media 36, 39–40, 61, 68, 128, 131–2, 149, 154, 158, 162, 168, 218, 266, 297, 308, 317–18, 320

Meer, Nasar 199

Meerza, Najaf Koolee 195

Meerza, Reeza Koolee 195

Meerza, Taymoor 195

Mehmood, Tariq 114–15, 219–20

memory 61, 172, 272, 290

mental illness 166, 250, 284

metafiction 241

Middle East 6, 130–1, 134, 139–40, 190, 204, 216, 223, 292, 310

migration (*also* migrants) 16–17, 32, 58–9, 63, 68, 70–1, 81, 138, 140, 159–61, 163–4, 166–75, 179, 182–4, 191, 193, 195–7, 204, 232, 235–6, 241, 244–5, 249–53, 258–61, 271–3, 283–4
   England-returned 194–6, 244, 249, 251;
   Internally Displaced Persons (IDPs) 162–4, 175;
   muhajir 160–1, 172;
   return migration 245, 249, 251

minorities 50, 141, 143, 179, 199, 202, 220, 266

Mipster (Muslim Hipster) 218

Mir, Hamid 36–7

Mirza, Maryam xviii

Mirza, Waheed 96

Mistry, Rohinton xvi

Mitford, Bertram 45–6, 48, 56

mixed-race (*also* mixed-heritage relationships/individuals, biracial) 24, 30, 107, 220, 222–5, 229, 267, 275

Modi, Narendra 313

Modood, Tariq 199

Mohanty, Chandra Talpade 298–300, 303

Mohsin, Moni 37

Morocco (*also* Moroccan) 13–15, 200

Morris, Chris 229–30, 268

Morrison, Toni 16, 19–22, 32

Morsi, Mohamed 200

mosques 64–5, 74–6, 93, 95, 103–5, 107, 173, 200, 211, 230, 236, 247, 257, 272
   Badshahi Mosque 64–5, 74–5;
   Faisal Mosque 107;
   Hazratbal Mosque 93;
   Red Mosque (*also* Lal Masjid) 105;
   Woking Mosque 257;
   York Mosque 200

movements 311–12
   Black Lives Matter 312;
   Indian anti-corruption movement 25;
   Lawyers' Movement 40

Mubarak, Hosni 128, 133, 136

Mueenuddin, Daniyal 201

Mughals 64, 74, 76, 81–2, 92

muhajirs 58, 61, 68–9, 125, 160–2, 172

mujahideen 114

Mukherjee, Bharati 251

Mukherjee, Neel 67, 239, 241–4, 248–9

mullah 156

Muller, Carl xvi

multiculturalism (*also* multicultural) 30, 76, 139, 223, 225, 304, 317

Munro, Alice 8, 10

Murad, Abdal Hakim 208–11, 258

Musharraf, Pervez 39–40, 68, 105

Muslim world 13, 32, 134, 141, 150, 159, 213, 290

Muslims (*see* Islam, migration, race)
  anti-Muslim (*see* Islamophobia) 9, 14, 59, 126, 151, 159, 168, 175, 182, 198–200, 226, 271–2, 278;
  arranged marriage 25, 144, 220–1, 275;
  biradari 261;
  chain migration 160–1, 162;
  contribution to Britain 179, 197, 225, 235, 258;
  de-Otherizing of 174;
  everyday lived Islam 166;
  immigrant communities 14, 179, 184, 194, 196, 204, 226, 244, 258, 304;
  migration history 160–1, 179;
  pilgrimage 166;
  polygamy 144;
  practice of medicine 137, 188, 234–5;
  present day 130–2, 138, 142, 159, 228–30, 263, 268, 302–3;
  purdah (*see* veil) 94, 144, 153, 185–6, 299;
  radicalization 139, 193, 217, 239, 267–7;
  stereotypes 130, 202, 266;
  students 87, 319–20;
  transcultural links 13;
  ummah (community) 6, 160, 268
myth 10, 35, 49, 60, 90, 196, 206, 227–8, 245, 251
  of the author 10;
  -making 309;
  of Return 194–6, 244–5, 249

N

Naipaul, V. S. 9–11, 193
Nair, Jayaraaj Rajasekharan 23

Naqvi, H. M. 201
nation (*also* nationality) 3, 6–7, 36, 47, 57, 65, 68–70, 75, 84–5, 98, 103–4, 109, 112, 132, 134, 138, 141–2, 147, 150, 161, 164, 180–2, 192, 203, 235, 248–9, 254, 257, 273, 284–5, 288, 295, 317–18
nationalism (*also* nationalist) 47, 54, 64, 84, 134, 192–3, 254–5, 259, 277, 287, 300–1
Nehru, Jawaharlal 97, 314
neocolonialism 98, 243, 294
Netherlands (*also* Dutch) 102, 171–2, 215
New Atheist xix, 35, 202
New Pakistani Writing xvii
New York 36, 81–2, 107, 201, 206
New York Review of Books, The 310
New York Times, The 200
Newns, Lucinda 315–16
Ngũgĩ wa Thiong'o 320
niqab 168
Nobel Prize for Literature 8
non-governmental organization (NGO) 141, 150, 154
North-West Frontier Province (NWFP) (*see* Khyber Pakhtunkhwa) 53, 89
nostalgia 37, 64–5, 85
nuclear weapons 69, 78, 86, 102

O

Obaid-Chinoy, Sharmeen 143–4, 152
Obama, Barack 124, 290
offence 156, 246
Olivier, Laurence 30–1
Omaar, Rageh 217
Ondaatje, Michael xvi

oppression 62, 215–16, 299–303, 305–6
orientalism xv, 89, 181, 187, 208, 289–91
Orwell, George 170, 198
  doublespeak 165, 199
  newspeak 198
Othello (*see* Shakespeare, William) xix, 13, 15–19, 21–6, 28–32
Oxford 3, 181, 183, 241–2, 247, 251, 259

P

Pakistan (*also* West Pakistan, Pakistani) 3–6, 36–8, 40, 43–4, 46–7, 53–6, 58, 65, 67, 69–70, 72, 75, 85, 87–8, 91, 98–100, 102, 107, 110, 125–6, 141, 143–4, 146, 150, 154, 161, 164, 185, 195, 220, 227–31, 244–5, 259, 308, 310, 317, 320
  Army (*also* military) 47, 53, 68, 98, 105, 110, 113, 115, 320;
  civil war (*see* Bangladesh, 1971 War of Liberation);
  economy 70, 244;
  floods 164;
  history of 47, 53, 67–9, 113–14;
  migration from/to 58, 63, 68, 161, 244, 261;
  minorities in 53, 66, 141;
  Pakistan Peoples Party (PPP) 61, 308;
  politics 40, 43, 47, 56, 61, 87, 105, 145, 314;
  problems in 4, 36–7, 40, 43, 47, 53, 56, 58, 60, 66–8, 87, 105, 141, 145, 147, 188, 227, 314, 319–20;
  relations with Afghanistan 49, 53, 87, 162;
  relations with India 36, 47, 58, 63, 68, 78, 83, 92–3, 102, 254;
  writers 3, 5, 15, 39, 54, 56–7, 60, 90, 108, 156, 198, 200, 202, 221, 226;
  YouTube ban 151
Palestine (*also* Palestinian) 53, 56, 86, 159, 161–2, 164, 189, 199, 266, 290, 294–5, 310–11
  Gaza 162
  West Bank 162
Palestine Festival of Literature (PalFest) 310
Pamuk, Orhan 11
Pandey, Gyanendra 64
Paris (*also* Parisian) 36, 159, 192, 273, 275–7, 279, 283, 286, 295
Parsis 75, 190
Partition 58–9, 63–5, 67–9, 76, 79, 83–4, 92–3, 97, 221–2
Pashto (language) 88, 90
Pashtun 46, 49, 53, 89–90, 92, 161, 302
pastoral (*see* countryside, rural) 71, 85, 106
patriarchy (*also* patriarchal) 62, 155, 160, 166, 300
peace 97, 309–10
Peer, Basharat 48, 93, 96–7
performance 19, 23, 121, 150, 308
performativity 165–6, 174
Persia (*also* Persian; *see* Iran) 8, 13, 45, 150, 180, 183, 185, 195–6, 234
Peshawar (*also* Peshawari) xv, xx, 49, 80, 87, 89–91, 114, 185
Petersen, Kirsten Holst 300, 303
Phillips, Maha Khan 145, 216
Phillips, Mike 204
Phillips, Trevor 203–4
Pickthall, (Muhammad) Marmaduke 189–93

Piper, Katie 153, 157
Pirandello, Luigi 46
pluralism 142
poetry (*also* poet; *see* ghazal (poetry))
 3, 8, 34, 39, 44, 50, 53, 59, 61, 74,
 89–91, 95, 108, 113–14, 134–7, 141,
 144, 159, 185, 187, 210, 241, 253–4,
 316
Pope, Alexander 108
postcolonial xix, 8, 12–13, 15–17, 19,
 24–5, 29, 31–2, 64–7, 76, 83, 86,
 130, 214, 225–6, 288–91, 293, 297–
 8, 300, 303, 315–17
 decolonization 287, 313
 feminism xxi, 297–300, 303, 306
Powell, Enoch 209, 229
Prakash, Gyan 67
prayer 64, 94, 104, 110, 166, 173, 182,
 224
Progressive Writers' Association 113,
 144
protest 62, 128–9, 131, 133, 135–7, 287,
 313, 318, 320
 Tahrir Square 128, 133–4, 136–7
publishing 5, 12
Punjab (*also* Punjabi) 29, 48, 52–4, 59,
 64–5, 67, 69–74, 76, 78, 81, 85, 88,
 103, 105

Q

Qabbani, Nizar 134
Quaid-i-Azam (*see* Jinnah, Muhammad
 Ali) 109
Quetta 44–5, 50, 57
Qur'an 49, 60, 66, 94, 173, 175, 189,
 213, 247, 266

R

race 34, 203–5, 219, 225, 287, 293,
 303–4, 306, 315
 Black Lives Matter 312
 colour blindness 203, 205
 racism xvii, xxi–xxii, 16, 18, 20, 22,
 30, 34, 46, 190–3, 196, 199, 205,
 220, 264–5, 284, 287, 297, 300, 303,
 312, 315, 320
 Blackface 30
 Xenophobia 264
Rahman, Parveen 147
Rahman, Zia Haider 207, 210, 244, 246
Raina, Arjun 24
Rawalpindi xii, xx, 98, 110–16
Ray, Adil 230
Razzaque, Russell 217
refugees xxi, 53, 87, 138–40, 159–68,
 171, 173–4, 196–7, 236, 241, 271,
 277
religion xvii–xviii, 13–14, 35, 52, 75–6,
 85–6, 142, 145, 147, 161, 167,
 173–4, 182–3, 199–201, 206, 211,
 226, 229–30, 234, 247, 249, 252,
 264, 274
 Buddhist 110, 274;
 Christianity 23, 141, 143, 156, 159,
 187, 220, 223, 246–7, 249;
 Hindu 59, 63, 74, 76, 79, 110, 233,
 240–1, 243, 251, 253, 255;
 Islam xviii, 13, 62, 75, 141–2, 145,
 150, 161, 166, 173–4, 179, 182,
 186–7, 190–91, 199, 201, 208, 212,
 215, 217–18, 228, 230, 268, 273–4,
 290
 Islamophobia xxi, 160, 175, 177,
 198–202, 224, 239, 264, 266,
 271, 274

Sufi (*also* Sufism) 273–5
resistance literature (*see* Harlow, Barbara) 53
restaurant industry 232, 234, 248, 256–63
  British curry industry (*see* curry, curry houses) xxi, 232–3, 257
revolution 130–1, 133–8
  art 132–5, 137;
  uprisings 47, 54, 130–2, 134, 138, 213
Riaz, Fahmida 59, 62, 144
romantic poetry 254
Rowling, J. K. (*see* Galbraith, Robert; *Harry Potter*) 3
Roy, Arundhati 47, 314
Rumi, Raza 36
Runnymede Trust 199, 316
rural (*see* pastoral, countryside) 18, 58, 61–2, 66–7, 70–3, 85–6, 157, 241, 299
Rutherford, Anna 300, 303

S

Sahota, Sunjeev 239
Said, Edward W. xxi, 5, 167–8, 199, 289–91, 293–4
Salih, Tayeb 16–19, 32
Salvatori-Sinz, Axel 162
Sandhu, Sukhdev 179, 236
Santesso, Esra Mirze 250, 303
Sardar, Ziauddin 129–30
Sartre, Jean-Paul 293
Scarry, Elaine 120–3, 125–6
science 35, 78, 85–6, 180, 197
Scott, James C. 62, 271
sectarianism 66, 69, 130, 135, 174, 208, 224

secularism (*also* secular) 34–5, 95, 113, 130, 132, 139, 141–2, 147, 150, 159, 161, 187, 199, 201, 211, 218, 222, 254
  postsecular 303
Sellars, Peter 19, 21
Selvadurai, Shyam 226
servants (domestic help) xviii, 101–2, 112, 211
Seth, Vikram xvi
Sethi, Ali 38
Sethi, Mira 37–8
Sexton, Anne 34
sexuality 16, 27, 34, 76, 170, 215, 219, 316
Shafak, Elif xxii
Shah, Sir Sultan Muhammed (Aga Khan III) 195
Shah, Bina 36, 39–40, 60–2, 143, 215, 226
Shahraz, Qaisra 59, 62
Shakespeare, William xix, 13, 15–19, 21–5, 27–32, 94, 242
  Macbeth 24, 270;
  Othello xix, 13, 15–19, 21–6, 28–32
Shamsie, Kamila 6–7, 37, 39, 56, 59, 89–90, 201, 319
Sharma, Sunil 184–6
Shias 53, 66, 75, 141, 173
Shibli Nomani, Maulana 185
short story form 8, 29, 39, 48–9, 55, 59–60, 94, 144, 164, 171, 173, 201, 209, 243, 245, 316
Sidhwa, Bapsi 63, 65, 67, 69–70, 73–6, 79, 81–3, 85–6, 112
Sikhs 76, 81, 149, 151, 239
silencing 20
  unsilencing 43–4

Sindh xx, 39, 58–62
  Karachi 58–60, 67–9, 85, 161;
  literary representation 58;
  protest 62;
  women's oppression 62;
  women writers 58
slavery (*also* slaves) 19–20, 147, 180, 212, 283
Slovo, Gillian 147–48
Smith, Zadie 34
social exclusion xvii
socialism (*also* socialist) 113, 238
Soja, Edward W. 67, 77–80
Somalia (*also* Somali) 53, 167, 215, 271, 304
Soueif, Ahdaf 6, 130, 134, 136–8, 140, 210, 213, 215, 310
Soyinka, Wole 8, 10
space 21, 63–4, 66–7, 69, 72–3, 77–80, 85–6, 99–101, 107, 113, 115
  cognitive mapping 80, 86;
  Gaston Bachelard 99
Spain 14
Spivak, Gayatri Chakravorty 32, 57, 164, 291, 294, 300–1, 303
stereotypes 15, 19, 25, 30, 51–2, 89, 130, 202, 227–31, 264–5, 289–90
subalternity (*also* subaltern) 57, 300–1
Sudan (*also* Sudanese) 16–18, 31, 211, 213, 271
Sufi (*also* Sufism) 273–5
Suhrke, Astri 159–60, 164, 174
Suleiman, Omar 130
Suleri, Sara 108, 215
Sunni 13, 53, 66
Sultan, Shahbano Begum Maimoona 184–5
Syal, Meera xvii

Sylhet (*also* Sylheti) 232–3, 239–41, 243, 245–6, 255, 260
syncretism (*also* syncretic) 61, 94–5, 150

T

Tablighi Jamaat 254
Tagore, Rabindranath 241
Taliban (Afghani) (*see* Tehrik-i-Taliban, Pakistan (TTP)) 162, 303
Tarantino, Quentin 100
Tarlo, Emma 168
technology 100, 131, 305, 313
  e-commerce 4;
  social media 36, 63, 131–2, 297, 320, 200, 290
Tehrik-i-Niswan (Pakistani Theatre Company) 151
Tehrik-i-Taliban, Pakistan (TTP) 87
television 36, 39–40, 63, 72, 89, 124, 131, 133, 223, 228, 230
terror 69, 103–5, 127, 141, 145, 147, 159, 162, 268, 272, 283
  war on 124, 128–9, 164, 212, 294
Teverson, Andrew 78
Thapar, Romila 314
Thatcherism 218
theatre 141, 146, 148–51, 166–7
  human rights 141;
  Theatre of the Oppressed 148
Third World 241, 298–9
thriller (*also* crime fiction) 3–4, 114, 257, 307
Todorov, Tzvetan 123–6, 295
tolerance 76
Toor, Saadia 150
torture xx, 37, 54, 119–27, 129, 139, 277, 286–7, 292, 295

translation 17, 28, 79, 145, 164–5, 184, 189, 247

travel 60, 91, 180, 184–6, 188, 192, 234, 248, 256
    ban 160, 272, 278, 304;
    writing xxi, 45, 183, 186, 189, 194, 233, 256

Trivedi, Poonam 22–3

Trump, Donald J. 124, 129, 160, 222, 270–2, 278, 304, 314

Tunisia (*also* Tunisian) 128, 130–1, 135–6

Tunku, Abdul Rahman Putra Al-Haj 195

Turkey (*also* Turkish) 13–14, 24, 46, 163, 185–8, 190, 227, 275, 303, 318

U

Uganda (*also* Ugandan) 172

ummah (community) 6, 160, 268

United Nations (UN) 93, 123, 128–9, 143, 146, 149, 162–3, 207

United States of America (USA) (*also* American) 16, 19, 31, 34, 38–9, 53, 60, 65, 68, 81–2, 90, 99–100, 102–4, 107–9, 115, 122, 124–5, 127, 131, 135, 148, 154, 160, 162, 171, 200–1, 205–8, 212, 215, 219, 225–7, 228, 251, 255, 264, 270–3, 287, 290, 295, 302–4, 312–17, 320
    anti-Americanism 104, 109

Union of Soviet Socialist Republics (USSR) (*also* Russia, Russian) 53, 68, 102–3, 113, 128–9, 162, 175, 224, 227, 273

Updike, John 239

Upstone, Sara 78

Urdu (language) 28, 88, 103, 109, 161, 211, 254;

Urdu literature 39, 59, 144, 184, 187, 261–2, 307

V

vampires 222–6

veil (*also* veiling) 83, 152, 166, 168, 186, 228, 286, 302

victim 119–20, 122–3

violence 22, 38, 48, 56, 64, 79, 92, 97, 101, 135, 146, 163, 202, 226, 266, 268, 287–8, 302
    non 279
    abduction 37, 145, 215–16, 317
    emotional 18, 21–2, 25–6, 120, 126, 153, 272, 292–3
    hate crimes 143, 154, 200, 206–8, 295
    'honour' killing 49, 59, 145, 152
    physical 26, 29, 36–7, 43, 57, 69, 78, 81, 96, 103–5, 119–26, 128–9, 141, 147, 215, 217, 272, 286, 293, 297
        acid attacks xx, 143, 152–7, 221
    sexual 16, 18, 26, 54, 59–61, 74, 86, 129, 132, 215, 217, 292, 297, 301
    torture xx, 37, 54, 119–27, 129, 139, 277, 286–7, 292, 295
        confession 121–2, 125;
        interrogation 119–21

visibility 167–8
    invisibility 25, 67, 167–8, 174

Visram, Rozina 183, 195

Viswanathan, Gauri 23, 242

voice 19, 32, 55–6, 61, 100–1, 131–2, 155, 169, 182, 202, 226, 247, 251, 255, 268, 274, 300–1

W

waderas 58, 61
Wadud, Amina 132
Waheed, Mirza 96
Walcott, Derek 3
Walsh, Declan 105
walking 82–6
    disability 84;
    gender 83–4;
    oppression 85
war
    1971 War of Liberation xvii, 47, 57, 65, 105, 229, 254;
    9/11 World Trade Centre attacks 82, 85, 104, 108, 124–6, 139, 159–60, 166, 168, 201, 206–7, 213, 217, 239, 275, 290;
    Afghan War 104, 114, 162;
    Algerian War of Independence 286;
    Cold War 68, 102, 104, 227;
    First World War 190, 193;
    Gulf War 38, 135, 162, 164, 201;
    Iraq War 122, 268;
    Iran-Iraq War 173;
    Opium Wars xxii;
    Second World War xxi, 47, 56, 93, 195–6, 248, 259–60, 273, 276–7, 283;
    Syrian War 162
weapons of the weak (*see* Scott, James C.) 62
Werbner, Pnina 303–5
Whedon, Joss 223, 225
Whitlock, Gillian (The 'Veiled Best-Seller') 216
women
    education 88, 185, 188, 317–18;
    everyday lives 83–4, 107;
    gender and racial oppression 25–8,

60, 62, 74, 84, 107, 113, 132, 143–5, 154, 157, 187, 200, 215–16, 221, 245, 228, 273, 276, 287–8, 297, 304;
    misogyny 21, 26, 156, 198–9, 261, 304;
    normative gender roles 35, 301;
    object of the male gaze 27–8, 74, 113
women writing (*also* women writers) xx, 5, 58, 62, 132, 184, 188, 209, 249, 251, 254–5, 276
Wood, James 246
Woolf, Virginia xviii
writing back xix, 16–17, 21, 23, 32
    fiction 18;
    films 16, 23–6, 28

Y

Yassin-Kassab, Robin 6, 131, 133–5, 139–40, 163, 216
Yeats, W. B. 95–6
Yemen (*also* Yemeni) 130–2, 164, 172, 271
York 11, 149, 200
Yorkshire 88, 220
young adult fiction 219, 274
Young, Robert J. C. 57, 283, 291–2
Yuval-Davis, Nira 304

Z

Zakaria, Rafia 114–15
Zanzibar (*also* Zanzibari) 160, 170
Zardari, Asif Ali 99
Zardari, Bilawal Bhutto 308
Zia ul-Haq, Muhammad 38, 50, 53, 68, 70, 87, 101, 144, 150, 320
Zibakhana (film) 100
Zoroastrianism (*see* Parsis) 75